FAULTLINES

Debating the Issues in American Politics

Second Edition

FAULTLINES

Debating the Issues in American Politics

Second Edition

David T. Canon
University of Wisconsin–Madison

John J. Coleman
University of Wisconsin–Madison

Kenneth R. Mayer
University of Wisconsin–Madison

W. W. Norton & Company
New York London

W. W. Norton & Company has been independent since its founding in 1923, when William Warder Norton and Mary D. Herter Norton first published lectures delivered at the People's Institute, the adult education division of New York City's Cooper Union. The Nortons soon expanded their program beyond the Institute, publishing books by celebrated academics from America and abroad. By mid-century, the two major pillars of Norton's publishing program—trade books and college texts—were firmly established. In the 1950s, the Norton family transferred control of the company to its employees, and today—with a staff of four hundred and a comparable number of trade, college, and professional titles published each year—W. W. Norton & Company stands as the largest and oldest publishing house owned wholly by its employees.

The text of this book is composed in Sabon with the display set in Univers.
Composition by PennSet, Inc.
Manufacturing by the Maple-Vail Book Group.
Book design by Anna Oler.
Production manager: Benjamin Reynolds.

Library of Congress Cataloging-in-Publication Data
Faultlines : debating the issues in American Politics / David T. Canon, John J. Coleman,
   and Kenneth R. Mayer. — 2nd ed.
      p. cm.
   ISBN-13: 978-0-393-93016-0 (pbk.)
   ISBN-10: 0-393-93016-5 (pbk.)
   1. United States—Politics and government. I. Canon, David T. II. Coleman,
John J., 1959– III. Mayer, Kenneth R., 1960–

JK31.F37 2007
320.973—dc22

                                                                          2006046956

W. W. Norton & Company, Inc., 500 Fifth Avenue, New York, N.Y. 10110-0017
www.wwnorton.com
W. W. Norton & Company Ltd., Castle House, 75/76 Wells Street, London W1T 3QT

1 2 3 4 5 6 7 8 9 0

Contents

FAULTLINES

Debating the Issues in American Politics

Second Edition

1

Political Culture: What Does It Mean to Be an American?

What does it mean to be an American? This question may appear to be obvious or trivial, but it turns out to be complicated. Unlike other nations, many of which are defined by a specific religious, ethnic, historical, geographic, or cultural identity, the United States appears to be united by a set of political ideals. As far back as Alexis de Tocqueville in the 1830s, scholars have tried to identify the nature of American political culture: is it a commitment to individualism? A belief in equality? A shared set of values about the appropriate role of government?

Samuel Huntington, a political scientist at Harvard University, argues that American political culture emerged from a combination of Protestantism, English as a common language, and the British traditions of limited government. From these emerged the "American Creed, with its principles of liberty, equality, human rights, representative government, and private property." Although we have always been a nation of immigrants—from the original settlers to the mass immigration of the late nineteenth and early twentieth centuries—Huntington notes that these immigrants had always assimilated into American political culture: learning English, adopting American political values, self-identifying as American, becoming absorbed into the "melting pot." This process was encouraged by a range of institutional support, from business that taught employees English to social organizations that encouraged assimilation.

Huntington sees recent immigration patterns as a threat to American political culture. To him, the recent surge in illegal immigration from Mexico and other Latin American countries, as well as that of Muslims, will undermine the values that have forged a unique American identity. Unlike earlier newcomers, these recent immigrants tend to retain their old language and national allegiances, resist assimilation, and even oppose key American political institutions and principles. They are aided by multicultural organizations that encourage them to maintain a separate identity apart from the majority culture and see themselves as victims.

The result, Huntington fears, will be a balkanized polity, cleaved by language, ethnic, and cultural differences. America could become a "country of two languages, two cultures, and two peoples." That would radically transform the country into something vastly different than the uniqueness that defines Americanism. Huntington's argument, which he has set out in articles and in a book entitled *Who Are We? The Challenges to America's National Identity*, generated substantial controversy. His harshest critics accused him of advocating a racist position that singled out Mexican immigrants for special criticism, and for promoting a form of nativism (a nationalistic and xenophobic ideology).

In a review of Huntington's book published in the *New Yorker*, writer Louis Menand critiques Huntington's view. Menand argues that Huntington has overstated the problem. Despite the influx of immigrants, Americans remain, by any standard, the "most patriotic people in the world." Huntington's real problem, according to Menand, is not deterioration of the American Creed, but rather change itself. The American Creed has never been static and has always embraced change. "Democracy is not a dogma; it is an experiment," explains Menand.

Menand claims that Huntington has mischaracterized the nature of Mexican immigration, citing survey data that show even recent illegal immigrants learn English and say they are proud of the United States. Further, he argues that fears of multicultural bifurcation are vastly overblown, and that a broader cultural heterogeneity will strengthen the United States rather than weaken it.

Samuel P. Huntington
One Nation, Out of Many

America's core culture has primarily been the culture of the seventeenth- and eighteenth-century settlers who founded our nation. The central elements of that culture are the Christian religion; Protestant values, including individualism, the work ethic, and moralism; the English language; British traditions of law, justice, and limits on government power; and a legacy of European art, literature, and philosophy. Out of this culture the early settlers formulated the American Creed, with its principles of liberty, equality, human rights, representative government, and private property. Subsequent generations of immigrants were assimilated into the culture of the founding settlers and modified it, but did not change it fundamentally. It was, after all, Anglo-Protestant culture, values, institutions, and the opportunities they created that attracted more immigrants to America than to all the rest of the world.

America was founded as a Protestant society, and for 200 years almost all Americans practiced Protestantism. With substantial Catholic immigration, first from Germany and Ireland and then Italy and Poland, the proportion of Protestants declined—to about 60 percent of the population by 2000. Protestant beliefs, values, and assumptions, however, have been the core element (along with the English language) of America's settler culture, and they continue to pervade and shape American life, society, and thought. Protestant values have shaped American attitudes toward private and public morality, economic activity, government, and public policy. They have even deeply influenced Catholicism and other religions in America.

Throughout our history, people who were not white, Anglo-Saxon Protestants have become Americans by adopting America's Anglo-Protestant culture and political values. This benefited them, and it benefited the country. Millions of immigrants and their children achieved wealth, power, and status in American society precisely because they assimilated themselves into the prevailing culture.

One has only to ask: Would America be the America it is today if in the seventeenth and eighteenth centuries it had been settled not by British Protes-

Published in *The American Enterprise*, May 2006.

tants but by French, Spanish, or Portuguese Catholics? The answer is no. It would not be America; it would be Quebec, Mexico, or Brazil.

The unfolding of British Protestant culture in America didn't just happen; it was orchestrated by our founders. As immigrants poured in during the late eighteenth century, our forefathers saw the need to "make Americans" of the new arrivals on their shores. "We must," John Jay said in 1797, "see our people more Americanized." At the peak of this effort in 1919, Justice Louis Brandeis declared that Americanization meant the immigrant "adopts the clothes, the manners, and the customs generally prevailing here . . . substitutes for his mother tongue the English language," ensures that "his interests and affections have become deeply rooted here," and comes "into complete harmony with our ideals and aspirations." When he has done all this, the new arrival will have "the national consciousness of an American." The acquisition of American citizenship, the renunciation of foreign allegiances, and the rejection of dual loyalties and nationalities are key components of this process.

During the decades before World War I, the huge wave of immigrants flooding into America generated a major social movement devoted to Americanizing these new arrivals. It involved local, state, and national governments, private organizations, and businesses. Americanization became a key element in the Progressive phase of American politics, and was promoted by Theodore Roosevelt, Woodrow Wilson, and other leaders.

Industrial corporations established schools at their factories to train immigrants in the English language and American values. In almost every city with a significant immigrant population the chamber of commerce had an Americanization program. Henry Ford was a leader in efforts to make immigrants into productive American workers. "These men of many nations must be taught American ways, the English language, and the right way to live," he stated. The Ford Motor Company instituted a six- to eight-month English language course that immigrant employees were compelled to attend, with graduates receiving diplomas qualifying them for citizenship. U.S. Steel and International Harvester sponsored similar programs, and, as one scholar has said, "a good many businessmen inaugurated factory classes, distributed civics lessons in pay envelopes, and even subsidized public evening schools."

A huge number of private nonprofit organizations also became involved in Americanization activities. The YMCA organized classes to teach immigrants English. Ethnic and religious organizations with ties to incoming immigrants actively promoted Americanization. Liberal reformers, conservative businessmen, and concerned citizens founded organizations such as the Committee on Information for Aliens, the North American Civic League for Immigrants, the Chicago League for the Protection of Immigrants, the Educational Alliance of New York City, the Baron de Hirsch Fund (aimed at Jewish immigrants), the Society for Italian Immigrants, and many similar organizations. These groups counseled newcomers, provided evening classes in the English language and American ways, and helped them find jobs and homes.

In due course, more than 30 states passed laws establishing Americanization programs. Connecticut even created a Department of Americanization. The federal government also became active, with the Bureau of Naturalization and the Bureau of Education competing vigorously to further their own assimilation efforts. By 1921 some 3,526 states, cities, towns, and communities were participating in Bureau of Naturalization programs.

The central institution for Americanization was the public school system. Indeed, public schools had been created in the nineteenth century and shaped in considerable part by the perceived need to Americanize and Protestantize immigrants. "People looked to education as the best way to transmit Anglo-American Protestant values and to prevent the collapse of republican institutions," summarizes historian Carl Kaestle. In 1921–22, as many as a thousand communities conducted "special public school programs to Americanize the foreign-born." Between 1915 and 1922, more than 1 million immigrants enrolled in such programs. School systems "saw public education as an instrument to create a unified society out of the multiplying diversity created by immigration," reports Reed Ueda.

Without these Americanizing activities starting in the early 1890s, America's dramatic 1924 reduction in immigration would in all likelihood have been imposed much earlier. Americanization made immigration acceptable to Americans. The success of the movement was manifest when the immigrants and their children rallied to the colors and marched off to fight their country's wars. In World War II in particular, racial, ethnic, and class identities were subordinated to national loyalty, and the identification of Americans with their country reached its highest point in history.

National identity then began to fade. In 1994, 19 scholars of American history and politics were asked to evaluate the level of American unity in 1930, 1950, 1970, and 1990. The year 1950, according to these experts, was the "zenith of American national integration." Since then "cultural and political fragmentation has increased" and "conflict emanating from intensified ethnic and religious consciousness poses the main current challenge to the American nation."

Fanning all of this was the new popularity among liberal elites of the doctrines of "multiculturalism" and "diversity," which elevate subnational, racial, ethnic, cultural, gender, and other identities over national identity, and encourage immigrants to maintain dual identities, loyalties, and citizenships. Multiculturalism is basically an anti-Western ideology. Multiculturalists argue that white Anglo America has suppressed other cultural alternatives, and that America in the future should not be a society with a single pervasive national culture, but instead should become a "tossed salad" of many starkly different ingredients.

In sharp contrast to their predecessors, American political leaders have recently promoted measures consciously designed to weaken America's cultural identity and strengthen racial, ethnic, and other identities. President Clinton called for a "great revolution" to liberate Americans from their dominant European culture. Vice President Gore interpreted the nation's motto, E pluribus unum (Out of many, one), to mean "out of one, many." By 1992, even some liberals like Arthur Schlesinger, Jr. were warning that the "ethnic upsurge" which had begun "as a gesture of protest against the Anglocentric culture" had become "a cult, and today it threatens to become a counter-revolution against the original theory of America as 'one people,' a common culture, a single nation."

These efforts by members of government to deconstruct the nation they led are, quite possibly, without precedent in human history. Important parts of academia, the media, business, and the professions, joined them in the effort. A study by Paul Vitz of 22 school texts published in the 1970s and 1980s for grades three and six found that only five out of 670 stories and articles in these readers had "any patriotic theme." All five dealt with the American Revolution; none had "anything to do with American history since 1780." In four of the five stories the principal person is a girl, in three the same girl, Sybil Ludington. The 22 books lack any story "featuring Nathan Hale, Patrick Henry, Daniel Boone, or Paul Revere's ride." "Patriotism," Vitz concludes, "is close to nonexistent" in these readers.

The deconstructionist coalition, however, does not include most Americans. In poll after poll, majorities of Americans reject ideas and measures that would lessen national identity and promote subnational identities. Everyday Americans remain deeply patriotic, nationalistic in their outlook, and committed to their national culture, creed, and identity. A major gap has thus developed between portions of our elite and the bulk of our populace over what America is and should be.

Popular opposition to the ideology of multiculturalism developed quickly. During the 1990s, bureaucrats and judges, including some who had earlier backed racial categorization and preferences, began to moderate and even reverse their views. New organizations of scholars and teachers grew up to counter efforts to rewrite American history and school curricula. Energetic "one America" activists and organizations forced votes to end affirmative action and bilingual education.

The American public is overwhelmingly opposed to official multilingualism. In 1986, 81 percent of the American public believed that "anyone who wants to stay in this country should have to learn English." In a 1988 poll, 76 percent of Californians rated speaking English as "very important" in making one an American, and 61 percent believed that the right to vote should be limited to English speakers. In a 1998 poll, 52 percent of Americans strongly supported, and 25 percent somewhat supported, legislation that would require all school instruction to be in English. Despite this clear consensus, legislators have been squeamish on language issues, which has forced proponents of American unity to use ballot initiatives to set the law.

From 1980 to 2000, 12 popular referenda were staged by pro-English or anti-bilingual-education groups. In all these cases political elites and establishment institutions like local newspapers and TV stations, local politicians, universities, labor unions, business federations, and religious groups overwhelmingly opposed the measures, as did heads of minority pressure groups. Yet the average vote in favor of pro-English positions was 65 percent.

In 1988, Presidential candidates George H. W. Bush and Michael Dukakis both opposed the official-English measures on the ballot in Florida, Arizona, and Colorado. In Florida the proposed constitutional amendment was also opposed by the governor, the attorney general, the secretary of state, the *Miami Herald*, the Greater Miami Chamber of Commerce, and many Hispanic organizations, yet it was approved by 86 percent of the voters and carried every county. In the bitter contest in Arizona, an official-English initiative was opposed by the governor, two former governors, both United States senators, the mayor of Phoenix, the Arizona Judges Association, the League of Arizona Cities and Towns, Jewish leaders, and the Arizona Ecumenical Council, yet it passed. In Colorado, the English measure was opposed by the governor, the lieutenant governor, the attorney general, the mayor of Denver, one United States senator, the leading Catholic bishops, the *Denver Post*, the state Democratic Party (the Republicans took no position), and Jesse Jackson. It was approved by 64 percent of Colorado's voters.

As one Stanford University professor commented, "the U.S. English leadership is probably justified in claiming that 'no one is for us but the people.' " A very similar pattern has appeared in referenda on bilingual education. Despite almost universal opposition among elites, 61 percent of California's voters (including majorities in every county except San Francisco) approved an end to bilingual education in 1998.

September 11 gave a major boost to the supporters of America as one people with a common culture. Yet the war to deconstruct our culture has not ended. It remains unresolved today whether America will be a nation of individuals with equal rights sharing a common culture, or an association of racial, ethnic, and cultural groups held together by hopes for material gains.

In this new environment, will today's immigrants assimilate as earlier waves did? Recent immigrants from India, Korea, Japan, and the Philippines—whose educational profiles more closely approximate those of American natives—have generally assimilated rapidly. Indians and Filipinos, of course, have been helped by their knowledge of English.

Latin American immigrants, particularly those from Mexico, have been slower in approximating American norms. In part this is a result of the large numbers and geographical concentration of Mexican arrivals. Also, the educational levels of Mexican immigrants and their descendants have been below that of other immigrants, and below the level of American natives. Moreover, Mexican activists have worked against assimilation.

Muslims, particularly Arab Muslims, also seem slow to assimilate compared with earlier groups. Elsewhere in the world, Muslim minorities have often proved to be "indigestible" by non-Muslim societies. A study of Los Angeles Muslims found ambivalent attitudes toward America: "A significant number of Muslims, particularly immigrant Muslims, do not have close ties or loyalty to the United States." When asked whether they had "closer ties or loyalty to Islamic countries (perhaps your country of birth) or the United States," 45 percent of the immigrants said Islamic countries, 10 percent the United States, and 32 percent "about the same." Among American-born Muslims, 19 percent chose Islamic countries, 38 percent the United States, and 28 percent about the same. Fifty-seven percent of the immigrants and 32 percent of the

American-born Muslims said that "if given the choice, [they] would leave the United States to live in an Islamic country." Fifty-two percent of the interviewees said it was very important and 24 percent said it was quite important to replace public schools with Islamic schools.

The current wave of immigration to the U.S. has increased with each decade. During the 1960s, 3 million people entered the country. During the 1980s, 7 million people did. In the 1990s it was over 9 million. The foreign-born percentage of the American population, which was a bit above 5 percent in 1960, more than doubled to close to 12 percent in 2002.

The United States thus appears to face something new in its history: persistent high levels of immigration. The two earlier waves of heavy immigration (1840s and '50s; and 1880s to 1924) subsided as a result of world events. But absent a serious war or economic collapse, over 1 million immigrants are likely to enter the United States each year for the indefinite future. This may cause assimilation to be slower and less complete than it was for past waves of immigration.

That seems to be happening with today's immigration from Latin America, especially from Mexico. Mexican immigration is leading toward a demographic "reconquista" of areas Americans took from Mexico by force in the 1830s and 1840s. Mexican immigration is very different from immigration from other sources, due to its sheer size, its illegality, and its other special qualities. [*Editor's Note:* See Mr. Huntington's earlier feature article on this subject: "The Special Case of Mexican Immigration," *The American Enterprise,* December 2000.]

One reason Mexican immigration is special is simply because there are now so very many arrivals (legal and illegal) from that one country. Thanks to heavy Mexican inflows, for the very first time in history a majority of U.S. immigrants now speak a single non-English language (Spanish). The impact of today's large flow of Mexican immigrants is reinforced by other factors: the proximity of their country of origin; their geographical concentration within the United States; the improbability of their inflow ending or being significantly reduced; the decline of the assimilation movement; and the new enthusiasm of many American elites for multiculturalism, bilingualism, affirmative action, and cultural diversity instead of cultural unity. In addition, the Mexican government now actively promotes the export of its people to the United States while encouraging them to maintain their Mexican culture, identity, and nationality. President Vicente Fox regularly refers to himself as the president of 123 million

Mexicans, 100 million in Mexico, 23 million in the United States. The net result is that Mexican immigrants and their progeny have not assimilated into American society as other immigrants did in the past, or as many other immigrants are doing now.

The lags in Mexican assimilation are clearly visible in current American social statistics. Language, education, occupation and income, citizenship, intermarriage, and identity are key criteria that can be used to gauge assimilation, and in these areas Mexicans generally lag behind other immigrants, past and present. In 2003, 89 percent of white and 80 percent of black Americans had graduated from high school, compared to 57 percent of Hispanics. In 2000, 34 percent of Mexican immigrants were high school graduates; subsequent generations of Mexican-Americans continued to lag in educational achievement. The economic position of Mexican immigrants and U.S.-born Mexicans parallels their lagging educational attainment.

The naturalization rate is one important indicator of political assimilation and is lower for Mexicans than for almost any other immigrant group. In 1990, for instance, the naturalization rate for Mexican immigrants in the country at least ten years was 32 percent, in contrast to 86 percent for immigrants from the Soviet Union, 82 percent for arrivals from Ireland, 82 percent for Poles, and 78 percent for Greek immigrants.

As for identity—the ultimate criterion of assimilation—the available evidence is limited and, in some respects, contradictory. Ron Unz states that "a quarter or more of Hispanics have shifted from their traditional Catholic faith to Protestant evangelical churches"—unquestionably a significant manifestation of assimilation. Other evidence, however, suggests a weak identification with America on the part of Mexican immigrants and their descendants. "The biggest problem we have is a cultural clash," the president of the National Council of La Raza said in 1995, "a clash between our values and the values in American society," the former being superior to the latter. One study of 1989–1990 survey data on Mexican-Americans found that "the longer the immigrants were in the United States, the less likely they were to agree that everyone should learn English," and "those more incorporated into mainstream society, the native-born Mexican-Americans, are less supportive of core American values than are the foreign-born." The growing numbers of Hispanics, according to a 1999 report, "help 'Latinize' many Hispanic people who are finding it easier to affirm their heritage . . . they find strength in numbers, as younger generations grow up with more ethnic pride and as a Latin influence starts permeating fields like entertainment, advertising, and politics."

The expansion of the Hispanic media encourages Hispanics to maintain their language and culture. The Mexican-owned Univision is the largest Spanish-language television network in the United States. Its nightly news audiences in New York, Los Angeles, and Chicago rival those of ABC, CBS, NBC, CNN, and Fox. The number of Spanish-language newspapers in the United States more than doubled from 166 in 1990 to 344 in 2003.

Problems in digesting Mexican immigrants would be less urgent if Mexicans were just one group among many. But because legal and illegal Mexicans comprise such a large proportion of our current immigrant flow, any assimilation problems arising within their ranks shape our immigrant experience. The overwhelming influence of Mexicans on America's immigration flow becomes clearly visible if one poses a thought experiment. What if Mexican immigration to the United States somehow abruptly stopped, while other immigration continued as at present? In such a case, illegal entries in particular would diminish dramatically. Agriculture and other businesses in the southwest would be disrupted, but the wages of low-income Americans would rise. Debates over the use of Spanish, and whether English should be made the official language of state and national governments, would fade away. Bilingual education and the controversies it spawns would decline. So also would controversies over welfare and other benefits for immigrants. The debate over whether immigrants are an economic burden on state and federal governments would be decisively resolved in the negative. The average education and skills of the immigrants coming to America would rise to levels unprecedented in American history. Our inflow of immigrants would again become highly diverse, which would increase incentives for all immigrants to learn English and absorb American culture. The possibility of a split between a predominantly Spanish-speaking America and English-speaking America would disappear, and with it a major potential threat to the cultural and possibly political integrity of the United States.

A glimpse of what a splintering of America into English- and Spanish-speaking camps might look like can be found in current-day Miami. Since the 1960s, first Cuban and then other Latin American immigrants have converted Miami from a fairly normal American city into a heavily Hispanic city. By 2000 Spanish was not just the language spoken in most homes in Miami, it was also the principal language of commerce, business, and politics. The local media and communications are increasingly Hispanic. In 1998, a Spanish-language television station became the number one station watched by Miamians—the first time a foreign-language station achieved that rating in a major American city.

The changing linguistic and ethnic makeup of Miami is reflected in the recent history of the *Miami Herald*, one of the most respected papers in the United States. The owners of the Herald first attempted to appeal to Hispanic readers and advertisers with a Spanish supplement, but this attempt to reach Hispanics and Anglos simultaneously, failed. Between 1960 and 1989, the percentage of Miami households reading the Herald fell from 80 percent to 40 percent. Eventually the Herald had to set up a separate Spanish paper, *El Nuevo Herald*.

Is Miami the future for Los Angeles and the southwest generally? In the end, the results could be similar: the creation of a large, distinct, Spanish-speaking community with economic and political resources sufficient to sustain its own Hispanic identity apart from the national identity of other Americans, and also sufficient to significantly influence American politics, government, and society. The process by which this might come about, however, is different. The Hispanization of Miami has been led from the top down by successful Cuban and other Central and South American immigrants. In the southwest, the overwhelming bulk of Spanish-speaking immigrants are Mexican, and have been poor, unskilled, and poorly educated. It appears that many of their offspring are likely to be similar. The pressures toward Hispanization in the southwest thus come from below, whereas those in South Florida came from above.

The persistence of Mexican immigration and the large absolute numbers of Mexicans in the southwest reduce the incentives for cultural assimilation. Mexican-Americans no longer think of themselves as members of a small minority who must accommodate the dominant group and adopt its culture. As their numbers increase, they become more committed to their own ethnic identity and culture. Sustained numerical expansion promotes cultural consolidation, and leads them not to minimize but to glory in the differences between their society and America generally.

The continuation of high levels of Mexican and Hispanic immigration and low rates of assimilation of these immigrants into American society and culture could eventually change America into a country of two languages, two cultures, and two peoples. This will not only transform America. It will also have deep consequences for Hispanics—who will be in America but not of the America that has existed for centuries.

Louis Menand

Patriot Games
The New Nativism of Samuel P. Huntington

In polls conducted during the past fifteen years, between ninety-six and ninety-eight per cent of all Americans said that they were "very" proud or "quite" proud of their country. When young Americans were asked whether they wanted to do something for their country, eighty-one per cent answered yes. Ninety-two per cent of Americans reported that they believe in God. Eighty-seven per cent said that they took "a great deal" of pride in their work, and although Americans work more hours annually than do people in other industrialized countries, ninety per cent said that they would work harder if it was necessary for the success of their organization. In all these categories, few other nations of comparable size and economic development even come close. By nearly every statistical measure, and by common consent, Americans are the most patriotic people in the world.

Is there a problem here? Samuel P. Huntington . . . believes that there is. The problem is the tiny fraction of Americans in whom national pride, patriotic loyalty, religious faith, and regard for the work ethic might possibly be less than wholehearted. He has identified these people as the heads of transnational corporations, members of the liberal élite, holders of dual citizenship, Mexican-Americans, and what he refers to as "deconstructionists." He thinks that these groups are responsible for an incipient erosion of national identity, a development that he views with an alarm that, while it is virtually unqualified, is somewhat underexplained. Although the erosion of national identity at the hands of multiculturalists and liberal élites is something that people were fretting and fighting about five or ten years ago, a lot of the conviction leaked out of the argument after the attacks of September 11th. This is partly because the public response to the attacks was spontaneously and unequivocally patriotic, suggesting that the divisions animating the so-called "culture wars" ran less deep than the cultural warriors supposed, and partly because the cultural pluralism that had once seemed threatening became, overnight, an all but official attribute of national identity. Inclusiveness turned out to be a flag around which Americans could rally. It was what most distinguished *us* from *them*. The reality, of course,

Published in *The New Yorker*, May 17, 2004.

is more complicated than the ideology, but the ideology is what Huntington is worried about, and either his book is a prescient analysis of trends obscure to the rest of us or he has missed the point.

Huntington's name for ideology is "culture." The advantage of the term is that it embraces collective beliefs and assumptions that may not be explicit most of the time; the trouble with it is that it is notoriously expansive. Culture, ultimately, is everything that is not nature. American culture includes American appetites and American dress, American work etiquette and American entertainment, American piety and American promiscuity—all the things that Americans recognize, by their absence, as American when they visit other countries. What Huntington wants to talk about is a specific cluster of American beliefs, habits, assumptions, and institutions. He calls this cluster "America's core culture." It includes, he says, "the Christian religion, Protestant values and moralism, a work ethic, the English language, British traditions of law, justice, and the limits of government power, and a legacy of European art, literature, philosophy, and music," plus "the American Creed with its principles of liberty, equality, individualism, representative government, and private property." . . . This, he maintains, is the culture of the original European settlers; it is the culture to which, until the late twentieth century, every immigrant group assimilated; and it is the culture that is now imperiled.

Huntington's core values are rather abstract. It would probably take many guesses for most of the Americans who score high in the patriotism surveys to come up with these items as the basis for their sentiments. What Americans like about their country, it seems fair to say, is the quality of life, and if the quality of life can be attributed to "a legacy of European art, literature, philosophy, and music" then Americans, even Americans who would be hard-pressed to name a single European philosopher, are in favor of those things, too.

It could be argued that Americans owe the quality of life they enjoy to America's core culture, but Huntington does not argue this. He cares about the core culture principally for its unifying effects, its usefulness as a motive for solidarity. He is, in this book, not interested in values per se; he is interested in national security and national power. He thinks that the erosion or diffusion of *any* cluster of collective ideals, whatever those ideals may be, leads to weakness and vulnerability.

Most readers who are not political scientists know Huntington from his book "The Clash of Civilizations and the Remaking of World Order," which was published in 1996, and which proposed that cultural differences would be the major cause of global tension in the future. The book was translated into thirty-three languages and inspired international conferences; its argument acquired new interest and credibility after the attacks of 2001 and the American response to them. Huntington's thesis could be taken as an answer to Francis Fukuyama's idea of "the end of history." History—that is, conflicts among groups—did not come to an end with the Cold War and the demise of liberalism's main ideological opponent, Huntington argued. The defeat of Communism did not mean that everyone had become a liberal. A civilization's belief that its values have become universal, he warned, has been, historically, the sign that it is on the brink of decline. His book therefore appealed both to people in the West who were anxious about the diversification or erosion of Western culture and to people outside the West who wanted to believe that modernization and Westernization are neither necessary nor inevitable.

The optimal course for the West in a world of potential civilizational conflict, Huntington concluded, was not to reach out to non-Western civilizations with the idea that people in those civilizations are really like us. He thinks that they are not really like us, and that it is both immoral to insist on making other countries conform to Western values (since that must involve trampling on their own values) and naïve to believe that the West speaks a universal language. If differences among civilizations are a perpetual source of rivalry and a potential source of wars, then a group of people whose loyalty to their own culture is attenuated is likely to be worse off relative to other groups. Hence his anxiety about what he thinks is a trend toward cultural diffusion in the United States.

You might think that if cultural difference is what drives people to war, then the world would be a safer place if *every* group's loyalty to its own culture were more attenuated. If you thought that, though, you would be a liberal cosmopolitan idealist, and Huntington would have no use for you. Huntington is a domestic monoculturalist and a global multiculturalist (and an enemy of domestic multiculturalism and global monoculturalism). "Civilizations are the ultimate human tribes," as he put it in "The Clash of Civilizations." The immutable psychic need people have for a shared belief system is precisely the premise of his political theory. You can't fool with immutable psychic needs.

* * *

The bad guys in Huntington's scenario can be divided into two groups. One is composed of intellectuals, people who preach dissent from the values of the "core culture."

* * *

The other group in Huntington's analysis is composed of what could be called the globalists. These are the new immigrants and the transnational businessmen. The new immigrants are people who, as Huntington describes them, "may assimilate into American society without assimilating the core American culture." Many maintain dual citizenship (Huntington calls these people "ampersands"); some do not bother to become American citizens at all, since the difference between the benefits available to citizens and those available to aliens has become smaller and smaller (a trend that originated, Huntington notes, among "unelected judges and administrators"). In a society in which multiculturalism is encouraged, the loyalty of these immigrants to the United States and its core culture is fragile. What distinguishes the new immigration from the old is the exponential increase in global mobility. As Huntington acknowledges, it has always been true that not all immigrants to the United States come to stay. A significant proportion come chiefly to earn money, and eventually they return to the countries they were born in. Transportation today is so cheap and available, though, that people can maintain lives in two nations indefinitely.

Mobility is also what distinguishes the new businessmen, the transnationals. These are, in effect, people without national loyalties at all, not even dual ones, since they identify with their corporations, and their corporations have offices, plants, workers, suppliers, and consumers all over the world. It is no longer in Ford's interest to be thought of as an American company. Ford's market is global, and it conceives of itself as a global entity. These new businessmen "have little need for national loyalty, view national boundaries as obstacles that thankfully are vanishing, and see national governments as residues from the past whose only useful function now is to facilitate the elite's global operations," Huntington says. "The distinction between America and the world is disappearing because of the triumph of America as the only global superpower." This drives him into the same perverse position he got himself into at the end of his attack on the deconstructionists: it is better to have rivals than to be dominant. It is good to compete, but it is bad to win. If we won, we would lose our national identity. The position, though, is consistent with the argument Huntington made in "The Clash of Civilizations"—the argument that nation-states ought to remain inside their own cultural boxes.

The most inflammatory section of "Who Are We?" is the chapter on Mexican immigration. Huntington reports that in 2000 the foreign-born population of the United States included almost eight million people from Mexico. The next country on the list was China, with 1.4 million. Huntington's concern is that Mexican-Americans (and, in Florida, Cuban-Americans) demonstrate less motivation to learn English and assimilate to the Anglo culture than other immigrant groups have historically, and that, thanks to the influence of bilingualism advocates, unelected judges, cosmopolites, and a compliant Congress, it has become less necessary for them to do so. They can remain, for generations, within their own cultural and linguistic enclave, and they are consequently likely to be less loyal to the United States than other hyphenated Americans are. Huntington believes that the United States "could change . . . into a culturally bifurcated Anglo-Hispanic society with two national languages." He can imagine portions of the American Southwest being ceded back to Mexico.

This part of Huntington's book was published first as an article in *Foreign Policy*, and it has already provoked responses, many in the letters column of that journal. Michael Elliott, in his column in *Time*, pointed out that in the Latino National Political Survey, conducted from 1989 to 1990, eighty-four per cent of Mexican-Americans expressed "extremely" or "very" strong love for the United States (against ninety-two per cent of Anglos). Ninety-one per cent said that they were "extremely proud" or "very proud" of the United States. As far as reluctance to learn English is concerned, Richard Alba and Victor Nee, in "Remaking the American Mainstream: Assimilation and Contemporary Immigration" report that in 1990 more than ninety-five per cent of Mexican-Americans between the ages of twenty-five and forty-four who were born in the United States could speak English well. They conclude that although Hispanic-Americans, particularly those who live close to the border, may continue to speak their original language (usually along with English) a generation longer than other groups have tended to do, "by any standard, linguistic assimilation is widespread."

Huntington's account of the nature of Mexican immigration to the United States seems deliberately alarmist. He notes, for example, that since 1975 roughly two-thirds of Mexican immigrants have entered illegally. This is the kind of statistic that is continually cited to suggest a new and dangerous demographic hemorrhaging. But, as Mae Ngai points out, in "Impossible Subjects: Illegal Aliens and the Making of Modern America," a work a hundred times more nuanced than Huntington's, the surge in illegal immigration was the predictable consequence of the reform of the immigration laws in 1965. In the name of liberalizing immigration policy, the new law imposed a uniform quota on all countries, regardless of size. Originally, Western Hemisphere countries were exempted from specific quotas, but the act was amended in 1976, and Mexico was assigned the same annual quota (twenty thousand) as, for example, Belgium. This effectively illegalized a large portion of the Mexican immigrant population. "Legal" and "illegal," as Ngai's book illustrates, are administrative constructions, always subject to change; they do not tell us anything about the desirability of the persons so constructed. (Ngai's analysis also suggests that one reason that Asian-Americans are stereotyped by other Americans as products of a culture that places a high value on education is that the 1965 immigration act gives preference to applicants with professional skills, and, in the nineteen-sixties and seventies, for reasons internal to their own countries, many Asian professionals chose to emigrate. Like professionals from any other culture, they naturally made education a priority for their children.)

Finally, some of Huntington's statistical claims are improperly derived. "Three out of ten Hispanic students drop out of school compared to one in eight blacks and one in fourteen whites," he says, and he cites other studies to argue that Hispanic-Americans are less educationally assimilated than other groups. Educational attainment is not an index of intellectual capacity, though; it is an economic trade-off. The rate of high-school graduation is in part a function of the local economy. For example, according to the Urban Institute and the Manhattan Institute for Policy Research, Florida has one of the worst high-school graduation rates in the United States. This may be because it has a service economy, in which you do not need a diploma to get reasonably steady work. To argue that Hispanic-Americans are disproportionately less likely to finish school, one would have to compare them not with non-Hispanic Americans nationally but with non-Hispanic Americans in the same region. Huntington provides no such comparisons. He is cheered, however, by Hispanic-Americans' high rate of conversion to evangelical Protestantism.

This brings us back to the weird emptiness at the heart of Huntington's analysis, according to which conversion to a fundamentalist faith is counted a good thing just because many other people already share that faith. Huntington never explains, in "Who Are We?," why Protestantism, private enterprise, and the English language are more desirable features of social life or more conducive to self-realization than, say, Judaism, kibbutzim, and Hebrew. He only fears, as an American, their transformation into something different. But how American is that? Huntington's understanding of American culture would be less rigid if he paid more attention to the actual value of his core values. One of the virtues of a liberal democracy is that it is designed to accommodate social and cultural change. Democracy is not a dogma; it is an experiment. That is what Lincoln said in the Gettysburg Address—and there is no more hallowed text in the American Creed than that.

Multiculturalism, in the form associated with people like Clinton and Gore, is part of the democratic experiment. It may have a lot of shortcomings as a political theory, but it is absurd to say that it is anti-Western. Its roots, as Charles Taylor and many other writers have shown, are in the classic texts of Western literature and philosophy. And, unless you are a monoculturalist hysteric, the differences that such multiculturalism celebrates are nearly all completely anodyne. One keeps wondering what Huntington, in his chapter on Mexican-Americans, means by "cultural bifurcation." What is this alien culture that threatens to infect Anglo-Americans? Hispanic-American culture, after all, is a culture derived largely from Spain, which, the last time anyone checked, was in Europe. Here is what we eventually learn (Huntington is quoting from a book called "The Americano Dream," by a Texas businessman named Lionel Sosa): Hispanics are different because "they still put family first, still make room in their lives for activities other than business, are more religious and more community oriented." Pull up the drawbridge!

Insofar as multiculturalism has become, in essence, an official doctrine in public education in the United States, its effects are the opposite of its rhetoric. "Diverse" is what Americans are taught to call themselves as a people, and a whole society cannot think that diversity is good and be all that diverse at the same time. The quickest and most frictionless way to nullify difference is to mainstream it. How culturally unified do Americans need to be, anyway? In an analysis like Huntington's, a nation's strength is a function of the strength of other nations. You don't need microchips if every other country on the planet is still in the Stone Age. Just a little bronze will do. But if the world is becoming more porous, more transnational, more tuned to the same economic, social, and informational frequency—if the globe is more global, which means more Americanized—then the need for national cultural homogeneity is lesser, not greater. The stronger societies will be the more cosmopolitan ones.

Perhaps this sounds like sentimental internationalism. Let's be cynical, then. The people who determine international relations are the political, business, and opinion élites, not the populace. It is overwhelmingly in the interest of those élites today to adapt to an internationalist environment, and they exert a virtually monopolistic control over information, surveillance, and the means of force. People talk about the Internet as a revolutionary populist medium, but the Internet is essentially a marketing tool. They talk about terrorist groups as representatives of a civilization opposed to the West, but most terrorists are dissidents from the civilization they pretend to be fighting for. What this kind of talk mostly reveals is the nonexistence of any genuine alternative to modernization and Westernization. During the past fifty years, the world has undergone two processes. One is de-Stalinization, and the other is decolonization. The second is proving to be much more complicated than the first, and this is because the stamp of the West is all over the rest of the world, and the rest of the world is now putting its stamp on the West. There are no aboriginal civilizations to return to. You can regret the mess, but it's too late to put the colors back in their jars.

And why isn't internationalism, as a number of writers have recently argued, a powerful resource for Americans? The United States doesn't have an exclusive interest in opposing and containing the forces of intolerance, superstition, and fanaticism; the whole world has an interest in opposing and containing those things. On September 12, 2001, the world was with us. Because of our government's mad conviction that it was *our* way of life that was under attack, not the way of life of civilized human beings everywhere, and that only *we* knew what was best to do about it, we squandered our chance to be with the world. The observation is now so obvious as to be banal. That does not make it less painful.

QUESTIONS

1. *What would you do?* Imagine you are a member of a state legislature, and are debating a bill to make English the state's official language. This would mean that all official documents, ballots, and school instruction would be in English, with no translations provided by the government (although private organizations would be free to provide translations). Should English be the "official" language of the state? What are the advantages and disadvantages in using only a single language for all government activity? Does having a common language foster assimilation and national unity? What can we learn from, say, Canada (with two official languages, English and French), or India (with two of-

ficial languages at the national level, Hindi and English, and with twenty-three more at the state level)?

2. Political scientists and historians often refer to "American Exceptionalism," or the idea that the United States is unique among industrialized democracies. Compared to other democratic countries, we place more emphasis on individual rights, have lower taxes, and have much greater decentralization of political power. Is this just a coincidence, or is there something inherent in American political culture that produces these results?

3. A visitor from another country asks you, "What does it mean to be an American?" What do you say?

2

Is Amending the Constitution Risky?

In a typical session of Congress, there are over seventy proposals to amend the United States Constitution. Some of the proposed amendments reflect efforts to overturn particularly controversial Supreme Court decisions, including amendments to prohibit abortion, make flag "desecration" a crime, and permit schools to offer voluntary prayer. Some are designed to change the government's basic structure and process: to replace the electoral college with a direct popular vote, require federal judges to be reconfirmed every ten years, limit amounts spent in election campaigns, repeal the twenty-second Amendment (which limits presidents to two terms), require a balanced budget, impose term limits on representatives and senators, repeal the Sixteenth Amendment (which permits income taxes), or allow individuals who are not natural-born citizens to be eligible for the presidency if they have been citizens for at least twenty years (labeled the Arnold Schwarzenegger amendment by some critics). Constitutional rights to affordable housing, quality health care, good education, a clean environment, or full employment would be guaranteed by other proposed amendments. An additional set includes attempts to preempt developments that proponents fear are foreshadowed by state government actions or recent Supreme Court decisions. Most notable in this category are proposals to amend the Constitution so that marriage and the legal benefits accruing to marriage would only be available to a union of one man and one woman. These proposals were designed to prevent the possibility of same-sex marriage or marriage equivalents such as "civil unions." In June 2006, proposed amendments to prohibit flag desecration and same-sex marriage failed in Congress.

Whether or not these amendments are, individually, good ideas, law professor Kathleen Sullivan is critical of efforts to alter the Constitution. The Constitution has been amended only twenty-seven times in over two hundred fifteen years, including the ten separate amendments of the Bill of Rights, which were sent to the states as a group in 1789 and ratified by them in 1791. Amendments have tended to arise during times of crisis or to redefine basic political rights. Amendments that are intended to impose a particular policy, or that arise out of short-term forces, are usually not revered in the same way as, say, the Fourteenth or Nineteenth Amendments (which, respectively, guaranteed equal protection of the laws, and gave women the right to vote). Sullivan notes that the one attempt to impose a particular policy via constitutional amendment—prohibition of alcohol, enacted in the Eighteenth Amendment and repealed in the Twenty-first—was a dismal failure. Constitutional principles should not, she concludes, be "up for grabs" or politicized, but should be slow to change; amendments should be reserved for setting out the basic structure of government and defining "a few fundamental political ideals."

Adrian Vermeule, also a law professor, disagrees with Sullivan. Disputing each of Sullivan's main points, Vermeule's central complaint is that Sullivan engages in a "nirvana fallacy." Sullivan directs searing criticism upon constitutional amendments, Vermeule argues, but she considers no alternatives or simply assumes the alternative to be better. Instead, each of the charges that Sullivan levels against constitutional amendments could just as easily be leveled against its main alternative: "The real alternative to constitutional amendment is flexible judicial interpretation that updates the Constitution over time—a practice that can also be seen as tampering with or trivializing the Constitution, that is at least as polarizing or divisive as constitutional amendment, that equally risks bad unintended consequences, and so on." Sullivan, in Vermeule's view, offers no convincing explanation of why changing the language of the Constitution is to be lamented while allowing judges to change the meaning of the Constitution through their interpretation is beneficial. As for Sullivan's concern about enacting policy into the Constitution, Vermeule argues that what one person disparages as "mere policy" that is unsuitable for the Constitution may, to another person, be a fundamental principle and value worthy of constitutional protection.

Kathleen M. Sullivan
What's Wrong with Constitutional Amendments?

Most things Congress does can be undone by the next election. Amendments to the U.S. Constitution cannot. And yet recent Congresses have been stricken with constitutional amendment fever. More constitutional amendment proposals have been taken seriously now than at any other recent time. Some have even come close to passing. An amendment calling for a balanced budget passed the House twice and came within one and then two votes of passing in the Senate. An amendment allowing punishment of flag burners easily passed the House and fell just three votes short in the Senate. These and other proposed amendments continue to circulate—including amendments that would impose term limits on members of Congress, permit subsidies for religious speech with public funds, confer procedural rights upon crime victims, denaturalize children of illegal immigrants, or require a three-fifths vote to raise taxes, to name a few.

Many of these amendments are bad ideas. But they are dangerous apart from their individual merits. The Constitution was, as Chief Justice John Marshall once wrote, "intended to endure for ages to come." Thus, it should be amended sparingly, not used as a chip in short-run political games. This was clearly the view of the framers, who made the Constitution extraordinarily difficult to amend. Amendments can pass only by the action of large supermajorities. Congress may propose amendments by a two-thirds vote of both houses. Or the legislatures of two-thirds of the states may request that Congress call a constitutional convention. Either way, a proposed amendment becomes law only when ratified by three-fourths of the states. Once an amendment clears these hurdles into the Constitution, it is equally difficult to remove.

Not surprisingly, the Constitution has been amended only twenty-seven times in our history. Half of these arose in exceptional circumstances. Ten made up the Bill of Rights, added in one fell swoop by the First Congress and ratified in 1791 as part of a bargain that induced reluctant states to accept the Constitution. And the Thirteenth, Fourteenth, and Fifteenth amendments, which abolished slavery and gave African Americans rights of equal citizenship, were passed by the Reconstruction Congress in the wake of the Civil War.

Published in *New Federalist Papers*, 1997.

The remaining amendments have tinkered little with the original constitutional design. Four extended the right to vote in federal elections to broader classes of citizens: the Fifteenth to racial minorities, the Nineteenth to women, the Twenty-fourth to voters too poor to pay a poll tax, and the Twenty-sixth to persons between the ages of eighteen and twenty-one. Only two amendments ever tried to impose a particular social policy: the Eighteenth Amendment imposed Prohibition and the Twenty-first repealed it. Only two amendments changed the original structure of the government: the Seventeenth Amendment provided for popular election of senators, and the Twenty-second imposed a two-term limit on the presidency. And only four amendments have ever been enacted to overrule decisions of the Supreme Court. The remaining handful of amendments were national housekeeping measures, the most important of which was the Twenty-fifth Amendment's establishment of procedures for presidential succession. We have never had a constitutional convention.

Our traditional reluctance to amend the Constitution stands on good reason today, the will of the framers aside. This is not because the Constitution deserves idolatry—Thomas Jefferson cautioned in 1816 that we should not treat it "like the ark of the covenant, too sacred to be touched." It is rather because maintaining stable agreement on the fundamental organizing principles of government has a number of clear political advantages over a system whose basic structure is always up for grabs. As James Madison cautioned in *The Federalist* No. 43, we ought to guard "against that extreme facility" of constitutional amendment "which would render the Constitution too mutable." What are the reasons this might be so?

First, it is a bad idea to politicize the Constitution. The very idea of a constitution turns on the separation of the legal and the political realms. The Constitution sets up the framework of government. It also sets forth a few fundamental political ideals (equality, representation, individual liberties) that place limits on how far any temporary majority may go. This is our higher law. All the rest is left to politics. Losers in the short run yield to the winners out of respect for the constitutional framework set up for the long run. This makes the peaceful conduct of ordinary politics possible. Without such respect for the constitutional framework, politics would degenerate into fractious war. But the more a constitution is politicized, the less it operates as a fundamental charter of government. The more a constitution is amended, the more it seems like ordinary legislation.

Two examples are instructive. The only modern federal constitutional amendment to impose a controversial social policy was a failure. The Eighteenth Amendment introduced Prohibition, and, fourteen years later, the Twenty-first Amendment repealed it. As Justice Oliver Wendell Holmes, Jr., once wrote, "a constitution is not meant to embody a particular economic theory," for it is "made for people of fundamentally differing views." Amendments that embody a specific and debatable social or economic policy allow one generation to tie the hands of another, entrenching approaches that ought to be revisable in the crucible of ordinary politics. Thus it is not surprising that the only amendment to the U.S. Constitution ever to impose such a policy is also the only one ever to be repealed.

Now consider the experience of the states. In contrast to the spare federal Constitution, state constitutions are typically voluminous tomes. Most state constitutions are amendable by simple majority, including by popular initiative and referendum. While the federal Constitution has been amended only twenty-seven times in more than two hundred years, the fifty state constitutions have suffered a total of nearly six thousand amendments. They have thus taken on what Marshall called in *McCulloch v. Maryland* "the prolixity of a legal code"—a vice he praised the federal Constitution for avoiding. State constitutions are loaded with particular provisions resembling ordinary legislation and embodying the outcome of special interest deals. As a result, they command far less respect than the U.S. Constitution.

A second reason to resist writing short-term policy goals into the Constitution is that they nearly always turn out to have bad and unintended structural consequences. This is in part because amendments are passed piecemeal. In contrast, the Constitution was drafted as a whole at Philadelphia. The framers had to think about how the entire thing fit together. Not so for modern amendments. Consider congressional term limits, for example. Term limits amendment advocates claim that rotating incumbents out of office would decrease institutional responsiveness to special interests and make the federal legislation more responsive to popular will. But would it? There's a better chance that term limits would shift power from Congress to the permanent civil service that staffs the executive branch and agencies, where special interest influence would remain untouched.

To take another example, advocates of the balanced budget amendment focus on claims that elimination of the deficit will help investment and growth. But they ignore the structural consequences of shifting fiscal power from Congress to the president or the courts. The power of the purse was intentionally entrusted by the framers to the most representative branch. As Madison wrote in *The Federalist* No. 58, the taxing and spending power is "the most complete and effectual weapon with which any constitution can arm the immediate representatives of the people." The balanced budget amendment, however, would tempt the president to impound funds, or at least threaten to do so in order to gain greater leverage over Congress. And it would tempt the courts to enter a judicial quagmire for which they are ill-equipped. When is the budget in balance? Whose estimates should we use? What if growth turns out faster than expected? Lawsuits over these questions could drag on for years. Such redistribution of power among the federal branches surely should not be undertaken lightly, especially not under the pressure of an election year.

A third danger lurking in constitutional amendments is that of mutiny against the authority of the Supreme Court. We have lasted two centuries with only twenty-seven amendments because the Supreme Court has been given enough interpretive latitude to adapt the basic charter to changing times. Our high court enjoys a respect and legitimacy uncommon elsewhere in the world. That legitimacy is salutary, for it enables the Court to settle or at least defuse society's most ideologically charged disputes.

Contemporary constitutional revisionists, however, suggest that if you dislike a Supreme Court decision, mobilize to overturn it. If the Court holds that free speech rights protect flag burners, just write a flag-burning exception into the First Amendment. If the Court limits student prayer in public schools, rewrite the establishment clause to replace neutrality toward religion with equal rights for religious access instead. Such amendment proposals no doubt reflect the revisionists' frustration that court packing turns out to be harder than it seems—Presidents Reagan and Bush, as it turned out, appointed more moderate than conservative justices. But undermining the authority of the institution itself is an unwise response to such disappointments.

In any event, it is illusory to think that an amendment will somehow eliminate judicial discretion. Most constitutional amendment proposals are, like the original document, written in general and open-ended terms. Thus, they necessarily defer hard questions to ultimate resolution by the courts. Does the balanced budget amendment give the president impoundment power? Congress settled this matter by statute with President Nixon, but the amendment would reopen the question. Does splattering mustard on your Fourth of July flag napkin amount to flag desecration? A committee of senators got nowhere trying to write language that would guarantee against such an absurd result. Would unisex bathrooms have been mandated if the Equal Rights Amendment had ever passed? Advocates on both sides debated the issue fiercely, but only the Supreme Court would ever have decided for sure.

For the most part we have managed to keep short-term politics out of the re-writing of the fundamental charter. Now is no time to start. Of course, on rare occasions, constitutional amendments are desirable. We have passed various structural amendments to tie our hands against short-term sentiments, for example, through the amendments expanding the right to vote. But unless the ordinary give-and-take of our politics proves incapable of solving something, the Constitution is not the place to go to fix it.

Adrian Vermeule

Constitutional Amendments and the Constitutional Common Law

Constitutions obsolesce rapidly, and must be updated over time to reflect changes in the polity's circumstances and citizens' values. What institution or process should be entrusted with the authority to do the updating? If periodic wholesale replacement of the Constitution is infeasible, the realistic choices are a constitutional amendment process involving legislatures, flexible interpretation by judges under the banner of constitutional common law, or some mix of the two.

* * *

. . . [The theses presented in this article contradict] a standard academic view that I shall call *the generic case against constitutional amendment*. On this view, there are good general reasons to reject, or to indulge a presumption against, any proposed amendment. Among these reasons are the following claims: it is bad to "tamper" with the Constitution; the Constitution should not be "cluttered up" with amendments that will "trivialize" its majesty; constitutional amendments are "divisive" or "polarizing"; constitutional amendments may have bad unanticipated consequences; and constitutional amendments diminish the coherence of the constitutional text or of judicially developed consti-

Published in *The Least Examined Branch: The Role of Legislatures in the Constitutional State*, 2006.

tutional doctrine. Something like this view has become the conventional wisdom in the legal academy, following explicit arguments by Kathleen Sullivan and others.

* * *

. . . I argue that the generic case against constitutional amendment fails. The generic case rests on a nirvana fallacy that implicitly contrasts a jaundiced view of the amendment process with a romanticized view of constitutional common law [i.e., judicial interpretation]. The real alternative to constitutional amendment is flexible judicial interpretation that updates the Constitution over time—a practice that can also be seen as tampering with or trivializing the Constitution, that is at least as polarizing or divisive as constitutional amendment, that equally risks bad unintended consequences, and so on. . . .

. . . Under what circumstances might one process or the other prove superior? What institutional considerations, or variables, determine their relative performance? I suggest that amendments show to best advantage [i.e., are preferable], relative to common-law constitutionalism, where the constitutional changes in question involve large value choices as opposed to technical improvements in the law, where constitutional change must be systemic and simultaneous rather than piecemeal, and where irreversible change is more valuable than reversible change.

* * *

The Generic Case Against Constitutional Amendment

I shall introduce the generic case against constitutional amendment with the following passage, from an essay by Kathleen Sullivan:

> [R]ecent Congresses have been stricken with amendment fever. More constitutional amendment proposals have been taken seriously now than at any other recent time. Some have even come close to passing. . . . Many of these amendment [sic] are bad ideas. *But they are dangerous apart from their individual merits.* [The Constitution] should be amended sparingly, not used as a chip in short-run political games. This was clearly the view of the framers, who made the Constitution extraordinarily difficult to amend.

* * *

This argument is the clearest statement of a view that I take to be widespread both within and without the legal academy. In the academic and popular commentaries that track Sullivan's argument, the verbal formulas vary—sometimes the injunction is against "tampering" with the Constitution, sometimes the emphasis is on the "divisiveness" of constitutional amendments, sometimes the core point is that only "structural" amendments or amendments expanding "individual rights" are permissible—but the common intellectual premise is something like Sullivan's idea: there is a generic class of reasons to believe that the amendment process is systematically or presumptively suspect.

* * *

The Generic Arguments

Here I shall list the most prominent generic arguments against constitutional amendment, and offer remarks upon each of them in turn. Each of these arguments is unsuccessful, and for similar reasons. Each of them, in different ways, rests on some version of the nirvana fallacy; each of them assumes, arbitrarily, that the objections that can be lodged against the proposed amendment do not also apply to the alternative process of common-law constitutionalism [i.e., judicial interpretation].

Amendments "Politicize the Constitution"

An initial reaction is that any slogan of this sort is puzzling in the extreme. In *any* sense that "political" might be given here, the Constitution is already political, or politicized, and it always has been. As a constitution, what else could it possibly be? Whatever else it does, the Constitution sets ground rules that govern a political association, that are politically determined, and that have political consequences.

The picture that animates this argument is a distinction between law, the sphere of constitutional rules, and politics, the sphere of action within the constitutional rules. On this picture, "[l]osers in the short run yield to the winners out of respect for the constitutional framework set up for the long run. This makes the peaceful conduct of ordinary politics possible." But this is illusory, a false alternative. The alternative to formal constitutional amendment is not the placid subconstitutional state of affairs implicitly presupposed here—perhaps the jousting of interest groups for legislative benefits. The concrete alternative to constitutional amendment is judicially developed constitutional law, which itself changes over time in response to political, social, and cultural shifts, and which itself produces *constitutional* winners and losers (not merely losers and winners of the "ordinary" sort). During the decades-long political struggle over the content of constitutional abortion law that has succeeded *Roe v. Wade,* a struggle waged simultaneously in legislatures, agencies, and courts, and at all levels of government, proposals have been advanced at various points to amend the Constitution's text to enforce one or another view of the matter. Whatever else might be said about such proposals, it is hard to see anything meaningful in the injunction not to "politicize" the Constitution by enacting them, given the background of constitutional politics—emphatically including judicial politics—against which the proposals have arisen.

Amendments "Clutter Up" the Constitution

Another idea is that amendments are objectionable because and to the extent they "clutter up" the Constitution with highly specific rules—causing the Constitution, in John Marshall's words, to "partake of the prolixity of a legal code." On this view, the Constitution's text should be limited to general or high-level principles, as opposed to detailed legal rules.

But the nirvana illusion is at work here as well. The real alternative to a prolix formal constitutional code promulgated by the amendment process is a prolix *informal* constitutional code promulgated by judges. Whatever may be said about the value of the latter, it is not "the intelligible Constitution" of general principles that the objection seems to contemplate. Shunting constitutional prolixity from the Constitution's text into the *U.S. Reports* [the publication containing federal court decisions] puts it off the textual books, but does nothing to make the overall body of constitutional law any more accessible to officials or citizens.

Consider the notoriously intricate and code-like character of judicially developed free speech law, or the tangled underbrush of Fourth Amendment search-and-seizure law. Part of the reason these bodies of law are so highly reticulated is that the underlying texts ("the freedom of speech," "unreasonable searches and seizures") are so skimpy. The judges have had to fill in their content, but would not have had to do so had those texts been more expansive and detailed, as other amendments are. A complex society will produce complex constitutional law; the only real question is whether it is good to outsource constitutional complexity from the amendment process to the adjudicative [i.e., judicial] process.

Amendments are Divisive or Polarizing

This is among the most popular of popular arguments against amendment; and it has gained new prominence in the debate over same-sex marriage. . . . [T]he claim often seems to be that the decision to formally *propose* an amendment itself has objectionable effects on public discourse or the polity at large.

Although I cannot fully defend the claim here, I believe as a general matter that injunctions not to put "polarizing" or "divisive" issues on the public agenda have repressive political and social effects. They are typically deployed by winners, or insiders, or those privileged by the status quo, to exclude from the public agenda claims of injustice on the part of the disadvantaged. This is a broad assertion, but consider that labor movements and civil rights movements and feminist movements have often been met with similar arguments. Here the injunction not to "divide" or "polarize" shades into the injunction not to "politicize." Losers or outsiders, relative to some status quo ante, want precisely to politicize, to bring political decisionmaking to bear in order to disrupt preexisting political and legal allocations that would remain entrenched absent public action, and that are (at least in the outsiders' view) unjust.

In the setting of constitutional amendments, this picture re-emphasizes the point I made above about the generic claim that amendments "politicize" the Constitution. To say that losers or outsiders in the constitutional status quo ante, meaning the status quo established by judge-made constitutional law, should not propose "divisive" or "polarizing" amendments, is to choke off one of the principal avenues of constitutional change. Formal amendment is not the only such channel, of course. Status quo losers can participate in presidential or senatorial politics, with the hope of influencing the selection of judges, in order to overturn the judge-made status quo. But that course of action will itself lead to charges of politicization, or polarization, or divisiveness. Shifting the forum in which the constitutional status quo is challenged does not eliminate the fact of the challenge itself.

So the nirvana illusion here is the same as above. . . . When judges decided that there was a constitutional right to burn the American flag, or to own slaves, the decisions sharply divided Americans who believed the courts were right from those who believed them wrong. A proposal by the latter group to amend the Constitution, over the objections of the former group, adds no additional divisiveness.

Amendments Represent a "Mutiny" against the Supreme Court

. . . [This charge] embodies the nirvana illusion that afflicts generic arguments against amendment. Here the illusion takes the form of the unjustified belief that the Court's (sociological) legitimacy is necessarily at a maximum so long as no outside agitators produce amendments that intrude upon judicially managed change. On this assumption, the Court's public standing is diminished whenever the amendment process produces outcomes that differ from those the Court would independently choose—perhaps because the amendment effects a visible public rebuke to the judiciary. Behind this assumption doubtless lurks some sort of picture in which amendments enacted to overturn particular Supreme Court decisions (such as the Eleventh and Sixteenth) reduce the Court's public standing.

There is another side to the ledger, however. . . . Overrulings, switches in time, creative and novel interpretation, all the tools that judges use to change the course of constitutional adjudication, themselves may draw down the Court's political capital by fracturing the legalistic façade of constitutional interpretation. An equally plausible causal hypothesis, then, is that increasing the rate of amendments might *increase* the Court's legitimacy by reducing the need for judicial self-correction. In particular cases, legitimacy-granting publics might react poorly to judicial flip-flops, while viewing formal amendments that overturn judicial decisions as the proper legal channel for change—the very use of which could suggest that the judges have done their job well, not poorly. This is rankly speculative, but the point is that [the charge] is rankly speculative as well. It is hard to know about any of this in the abstract; but we cannot simply assume the faith that a world without amendments is the best of all possible worlds to inhabit.

Amendments Have Bad Unintended Consequences
Amendments Undermine the Coherence of Constitutional Doctrine

I will consider these arguments jointly, for reasons that will become apparent. It is of course an admissible argument against a proposed amendment that the proposal will have some particular bad consequences. The argument from bad unintended consequences, however, is different on two counts. First, the bad consequences are precisely those *not* foreseen at the time of debating and voting on the proposal. This is the key feature that makes this a generic argument. The difference is between a caution not to cross the street lest one be hit by *that* oncoming car, and a caution not to leave the house lest something bad occur. Second, the unforeseen bad consequences are sometimes said to be "structural." As Sullivan puts it.

> A second reason to resist writing short-term policy goals into the Constitution is that they nearly always turn out to have bad and unintended structural consequences. This is in part because amendments are passed piecemeal. In contrast, the Constitution was drafted as a whole at Philadelphia. The framers had to think about how the entire thing fit together.

* * *

The comparison between the framers' globally coherent design, on the one hand, and piecemeal amendment on the other is not the right comparison to make. The principal substitute for formal amendment is . . . judicial updating of constitutional law through flexible interpretation. The question, then, is whether piecemeal amendment produces greater incoherence than piecemeal judicial updating, carried out in particular litigated cases, by judicial institutions whose agenda is partly set by outside actors.

There is little reason to believe the latter process more conducive to coherence than the former, and much evidence to suggest that judicial decisionmaking produces a great deal of doctrinal incoherence. Precisely because judicial updating requires overrulings, reinterpretations, and other breaks in the web of prior doctrine, a system that relies on judicial updating to supply constitutional change—the system that the generic case tends to produce—generates internal pressures toward incoherent doctrine. Constitutional adjudication in America, let us recall, has produced both *Plessy v. Ferguson* and *Brown v. Board*,[1] . . . and both *Bowers v. Hardwick* and *Lawrence v. Texas*.[2] Whatever else can be said about this judicial work-product, and whatever other justifications can be given for judge-made constitutional law, deep inner coherence does not seem either a plausible description of the terrain or even a plausible . . . ideal for the system.

* * *

. . . [T]he nirvana illusion . . . underestimates the capacity of specific positive enactments [i.e., constitutional amendments] to generate broader principles in the future. . . . It is easy to imagine future courts generalizing new principles from a flag desecration amendment, principles emphasizing the authority—the right, if you will—of enduring majorities to mark out as fundamental a limited class of symbols or ideals or aspirations, and to grant those symbols immunity from the ordinary hurly-burly of free speech in an open society. The precise contour of such principles is not now apparent, but that is also true whenever courts embark on the development of new lines of constitutional doctrine.

* * *

Perhaps the concern with bad unintended consequences can be justified on other grounds even if the coherence rationale fails. . . . Even if the particular concern is not that amendments will produce incoherent constitutional law, still we might hold a generic concern about the bad unforeseen . . . consequences of constitutional amendment. . . .

Yet the nirvana illusion occurs on this more general level as well. Here the illusion takes two related forms. The first is the belief that constitutional amendments represent risky action, while the steady-state of judge-made constitutional doctrine represents safe inaction. . . . Inaction may produce the worst outcome of all. . . . A persistent judicial refusal to update obsolete constitutional law can itself produce large political, social and economic harms. . . .

In a second version, the alternative to formal amendment is not judicial "inaction," but affirmative judicial action to update obsolete doctrine. Here the nirvana illusion is the failure to recognize that judicial updating, as a substitute for formal amendment, can itself produce bad and unforeseen structural consequences. . . .

I conclude that there is no way to leverage a concern for disrupting coherence, or a broader concern for unforeseen consequences more generally, into a generic caution about constitutional amendment. Anything that people or institutions do or fail to do may result in bad unforeseen consequences. Statutes may produce them, but so may the failure to enact statutory reforms; judicial decisions may produce them, but so may judicial "inaction"; and so too for constitutional amendments. The worry about perverse consequences suggests nothing in particular; it yields paralysis, not safety.

Amendments Should Not Encode "Mere Social Policies"

Usually, as in Sullivan, this argument rests on a contrast between "controversial" or "short-term" social policies, on the one hand, and "structural amendments to tie our hands against short-term sentiments," on the other. Here the stock example of constitutionalized social policy is the Eighteenth Amendment, the prohibition amendment, repealed by the Twenty-first. The prohibition amendment has often been said to result from a passing sociopolitical frenzy. . . . And the prohibition analogy has been invoked to condemn the gamut of amendment proposals, from the balanced budget and term limits amendments to flag desecration and same-sex marriage.

Here two points are important. The first is familiar: judge-made constitutional rules, no less than amendments, often represent or embody "mere social policies." What else are we to call the rule that prosecutors must hold an arraignment within 48 hours of arrest, or the rule that states may not tax interstate goods that remain in their "original packages"? . . . [T]he prohibition and flag-burning amendments both represented policy conceptions that attempted to implement larger political concepts and commitments. In the case of both amendments and judge-made law, specific legal policies can be condemned as "mere social policies" if, but only if, one detaches the policy from the underlying commitments that animate it.

Second, the idea that "social policies" should not be encoded in the Constitution, and the accompanying prohibition analogy, are in my view both vacuous at the operational level. What produces such widespread agreement on the injunction against constitutionalizing "mere" social policy is that no one ever seeks to violate it. No serious constitutional movement ever describes itself as seeking to encode a mere social policy in the Constitution, as opposed to a structural or rights-protecting or otherwise more fundamental sort of policy or legal rule. Any constitutional movement that becomes nationally prominent features at least a core of leaders and activists who describe themselves as engaged in structural or fundamental reform. . . .

* * *

It is not that anyone disputes the injunction against constitutionalizing mere social policy; it is that no one takes *their* cherished amendment to violate the principle.

The injunction against encoding social policies in the Constitution is largely vacuous, not wholly so. It might rule out a small class of low-level policies; let us have no amendments to constitutionalize the earned income tax credit! The point, however, is that there are no serious or influential constitutional movements organized for the purpose of putting policies like that in the Constitution anyway. The prohibitionists, of course, did not see themselves as advocating a constitutionalized social policy, in the disparaging sense. They saw temperance as the token of an essential moral and spiritual and socially progressive crusade. If we now see things differently, that gives us no help at all for the future, because we cannot now guess which of our own crusades that we now cherish as fundamental will be dismissed as frenzies in the hindsight of later generations. . . .

* * *

A Note on "Rights" and "Structure"

So far we have been examining strictly generic arguments, which purport to identify bad features of amendments generally. Narrower arguments, however, sometimes identify some subcategory of disfavored amendments. Usually such arguments turn on a distinction between "rights" provisions and "structure" provisions, and allow broader scope for amendments to affect structure than to affect rights. For concreteness, I will consider the following version of this view: All previous amendments can be categorized as either (1) expanding individual rights or (2) improving government structure, and amendments outside these two categories should be rejected or disfavored.

This view seems untenable, on both empirical and normative grounds. The historical premise that no amendments have limited individual rights is very dubious. . . .

But let us suppose the historical premise true, or largely so. The hard question is what normative significance this has. Why should those categories, into which previous amendments happened to fall, be taken as exclusive? Why should not other types of amendments be added as circumstances change? . . .

* * *

I conclude that the generic case against constitutional amendment fails. There is no basis for global or presumptive skepticism of the amendment process as a means of constitutional change. The standard attempts to identify deficiencies in the amendment process fail to compare the institutional alternatives: they identify features that are common to both the amendment process and the alternative institutional process of constitutional common law [i.e., judicial interpretation].

QUESTIONS

1. *What would you do?* Imagine that you are writing a memo for a member of Congress concerning two changes to the amendment process. A new proposal would allow ratification of proposed constitutional amendments to be determined by the public in a vote on a national ballot, as is now done in most states for state constitutions. A second proposal would allow the public to add proposed amendments to this national ballot by collecting the signatures of 3 percent of the voting age population (approximately 6.8 million signatures). What would you recommend to the congressperson in your memo, and why?

2. Sullivan is concerned about policy being inserted in the Constitution, while Vermeule suggests that in practice it may be difficult to determine whether something is policy or a matter of important principle. Assume that it is correct that inserting policy into the Constitution is a bad idea. Create criteria by which you could determine whether a proposed amendment falls into the category of policy.

3. Vermeule bases his argument on the premise that judicial interpretation and formal constitutional amendments are equally subject to the same problems that Sulllivan identifies with amendments. Are there important differences between the two that are overlooked by Vermeule?

3

Federalism: State Power or National Power?

From welfare reform to health care, educational funding to inner-city redevelopment, state governments have sought more control over public policy within their borders. In the 1970s and 1980s, when this devolution of power to the states was called "New Federalism," the debate was pretty simple. Republicans favored devolution because state governments were "closer to the people" and could better determine their needs. Democrats resisted the trasnfer of power from Washington, fearing that many states would not adequately care for and protect the less advantaged or protect the environment without prodding from Washington. To the extent that the courts got involved in the debate, they tended to favor the transfer of power to the states.

The debate over devolving power from the national government to the states has grown increasingly complicated in the past several years: the partisan nature of the debate shifted; the Courts have played a larger, but inconsistent role; and issues of "states' rights" increasingly tend to cut across normal ideological and partisan divisions. While Republicans continued to favor greater state control, a Democratic president, Bill Clinton, supported devolution to the states in several areas in the 1990s, especially welfare policy. Since the mid-1990s, the Supreme Court has played a central role in the shift of power to the states, but two recent cases involving medical marijuana (*Raich v. Gonzales*) and assisted suicide (*Gonzales v. Oregon*) show how the typical debate between national and state power can shift when a moral dimension is introduced.

In both cases, state voters supported liberal policies, approving medical marijuana in California and assisted suicide in Oregon. Therefore, the "states' rights" position in these cases represented the liberal perspective, rather than the conservative positions on race, labor, market regulation, welfare, and the environment that state-centered federalism is typically associated with. What's a good liberal or conservative to do? Social liberals supported the medical marijuana law (and thus the minority in *Raich*) and the assisted suicide law in Oregon (the majority in *Gonzales*). Moral conservatives were the opposite (pro-*Raich*, anti-*Gonzales*). However, on the central question of federal versus state power, which has been a central ideological divide in this nation since the Federalists and Anti-Federalists battled it out at the Constitutional Convention, liberals and conservatives would have to flip their views. A national power liberal and a moral conservative would have the same views (national power would be used to regulate medical marijuana and assisted suicide), while conservative states' rights advocates would share the views of the social liberals (because voters in California approved medical marijuana and Oregon voters supported assisted suicide).

Somewhat surprisingly, there was almost no consistency among the eight justices who voted on both cases (William Rehnquist was replaced by John Roberts between the two cases): only Justice O'Connor supported the states' rights position in both cases while Scalia voted as a moral conservative. All of the other six justices mixed their views. The Court as a whole was inconsistent on the question of federalism as well: in the medical marijuana case (*Raich v. Gonzales*), the Court upheld Congress's power to regulate the medical use of marijuana under the Controlled Substances Act. But in the assisted suicide case (*Gonzales v. Raich*), the Court said that Congress did not give the U.S. Attorney General the power under that same law to limit the drugs that doctors in Oregon could prescribe for use in an assisted suicide.

Nelson Lund is a good example of a conflicted conservative. In his article, he writes that the "people of Oregon made a terrible mistake" when they authorized doctor-assisted suicide. However, as a conservative who favors states' rights, he says that "the voters of Oregon are adults who are entitled to make their own decisions about this important policy question, even if they disagree with me." John Tabin is a moral conservative who is frustrated by the Court's inconsistency in interpreting Congress's power to regulate state behavior through the commerce clause. In his article, he reasons that if Congress has the power to regulate medical marijuana, even if it did not cross state lines (the marijuana in question was grown in a person's backyard for her own consumption for medical purposes), it should also have the power to regulate the use of lethal drugs that are used in Oregon for assisted suicides. He concludes that the Supreme Court rules in favor of state governments "when Kennedy and his liberal colleagues feel like it."

George Annas looks at the medical marijuana case (and touches on the assisted suicide case) from the perspective of doctors. Annas points out the "most interesting, and disturbing aspect of the case to physicians" is the Court's reference to "unscrupulous physicians who overprescribe when it is sufficiently profitable to do so." Annas says that such cases are rare and that the California law was narrowly written to make sure that such abuses would not occur. This article is also very useful for its excellent overview of Congress's commerce clause powers and its importance in federalism cases.

Nelson Lund
Putting Federalism to Sleep

The Bush Administration claims the authority to stop Oregon physicians from using prescription drugs to implement that state's unique program of physician-assisted suicide. But the administration's effort to use an ambiguous federal drug statute to undermine Oregon's assisted suicide law is a betrayal of conservative legal principles. *Gonzalez v. Oregon*, argued before the Supreme Court earlier this month, may give an early signal about the commitment of the emerging Roberts Court to those principles. And the Court's decision could have unexpected implications for a range of other issues, including future policies about abortion.

Like the administration, I believe that the people of Oregon made a terrible mistake when they voted in two separate popular referenda to authorize Oregon doctors to help their patients commit suicide. Physicians are uniquely empowered by their technical knowledge and the nature of their work either to heal or to kill, and their patients know it. For millennia, the chief safeguard against abuse of this power has been the Hippocratic ethic, which forbids a doctor from seeking to hasten the death of any patient. That ethic was compromised when physicians began to violate a related Hippocratic prohibition of abortion, and it has continued to crumble in the face of pressures for doctors to

Published in *The Weekly Standard*, October 2005.

make moral decisions (masquerading as medical decisions) about whose life is worth preserving. The Oregon law is a step along the path toward a world of legalized euthanasia in which seriously ill people will have good reasons to worry about what their doctors are up to.

Unlike the Bush administration, however, I believe the voters of Oregon are adults who are entitled to make their own decisions about this important policy question, even if they disagree with me. Among the signal achievements of the late Chief Justice Rehnquist was his long crusade to revive the constitutional principle of federalism. That principle demands that the people of each state be allowed to govern themselves as they see fit, so long as their decisions are not forbidden by the Constitution itself (as in certain decisions involving racial discrimination) or by federal statutes covering issues assigned by the Constitution to the jurisdiction of Congress (such as the regulation of foreign and interstate commerce).

The constitutional principle of federalism suggests that Oregon's assisted suicide law should be immune from congressional interference. Virtually all of the people affected by Oregon's law will be Oregonians, and there is nothing in Oregon's decision that will interfere with other states' ability to choose a different policy in regulating their own physicians. In any event, Congress has not clearly authorized the Bush administration to interfere with Oregon's decision. The federal statute generally requires that doctors with state licenses to prescribe drugs be given a federal license as well. Federal authorities do have a vaguely worded authorization to yank the licenses of doctors who behave irresponsibly, which was aimed at allowing federal agents to quickly shut down doctors who set up shop as drug dealers. The Bush administration is using this provision to claim a power to override any state law involving prescription drugs if the attorney general disagrees with that state's chosen policy about the proper use of such drugs.

The drug statute can easily be interpreted to leave policy decisions about medical practice to the states. The statute does not clearly grant the authority the administration is claiming, and it might be unconstitutional if it did. In any event, there was absolutely no necessity for the administration to claim this power (which reversed the Justice Department's previous position). This is a legally gratuitous departure from the principle that the states are free to manage their own internal affairs unless a valid federal law clearly constrains their discretion.

There may be further implications. If the Roberts Court eventually overrules *Roe v. Wade*, as I believe it should, the abortion issue will return to the democratic processes of each state, which is where it lay before the Supreme Court usurped state authority. We can be sure that interest groups on both sides of that issue—none of which is likely to have enough political support to obtain a clearly worded federal statute, let alone a constitutional amendment—will seek to get future administrations to attack state laws they disagree with, using maneuvers like the one the Bush administration has adopted here.

Assisted suicide is a serious issue. So is abortion. Less visibly, but no less important, this case involves the obligation of judges to be faithful to the constitutional principle of federalism. That principle should be especially significant in guiding the resolution of controversial issues, but the principle seldom has a strong political constituency. For that reason, whatever our views on assisted suicide and abortion, we should all hope that in this case the new chief justice will be true to Rehnquist's spirit rather than to the will of the president who appointed him.

John Tabin
Supreme Substances

The federal government has broad power to regulate legal and illegal drugs under the Controlled Substances Act. When must that power be curbed?

The Supreme Court has considered that question twice in the past year. Seven months ago, in *Gonzales v. Raich*, the Court ruled it constitutional for the federal government to prosecute cancer patients for using marijuana, even in a manner consistent with California's medical marijuana law, under the authority granted to Congress by the Constitution "to regulate Commerce . . . among the several States."

Justice Clarence Thomas noted in his *Raich* dissent that the respondents "use marijuana that has never been bought or sold, that has never crossed state lines, and that has had no demonstrable effect on the national market for marijuana." By counting this as interstate commerce, the Court declined to put any limit on the reach of the CSA.

But that was then. Yesterday the Court handed down its decision in *Gon-*

Published in *The American Spectator*, January 2006.

zales v. Oregon, which pitted CSA regulations against Oregon's physician-assisted suicide law, which allows doctors to prescribe lethal doses of medication. The Court sided with Oregon, and five of the six justices in the majority in *Oregon*—Stephen Breyer, Ruth Bader Ginsburg, David Souter, John Paul Stevens, and Anthony Kennedy—were also in the *Raich* majority.

This was a case of statutory rather than constitutional interpretation. But in rejecting the Justice Department's claim that suicide is not a "legitimate medical purpose," as required by federal regulation, the Court relied on the same federalist principles they rejected in *Raich*. Beyond prohibiting doctors from being drug dealers, Kennedy argued for the *Oregon* majority,

> The [CSA] manifests no intent to regulate the practice of medicine generally. The silence is understandable given the structure and limitations of federalism, which allow the States "great latitude under their police powers to legislate as to the protection of the lives, limbs, health, comfort, and quiet of all persons."

But it was the "structure and limitations of federalism" that the Court ignored in *Raich*. The majority opinion in *Raich*, written by Stevens, stated flatly that "the CSA is a comprehensive regulatory regime specifically designed to regulate which controlled substances can be utilized for medical purposes, and in what manner," and argued that this was just fine. As Thomas wrote in his *Oregon* dissent,

> While the scope of the CSA and the Attorney General's power thereunder are sweeping, and perhaps troubling, such expansive federal legislation and broad grants of authority to administrative agencies are merely the inevitable and inexorable consequence of this Court's Commerce Clause and separation-of-powers jurisprudence.

Thomas added that the "Court's reliance upon the constitutional principles that it rejected in *Raich*—albeit under the guise of statutory interpretation—is perplexing to say the least." Is it so perplexing, though? There seems to be a simple principle at work: When must CSA power be curbed? When Kennedy and his liberal colleagues feel like it.

A simple principle—just not a good one.

George J. Annas

Jumping Frogs, Endangered Toads, and California's Medical-Marijuana Law

Mark Twain wasn't thinking about federalism or the structure of American government when he wrote "The Celebrated Jumping Frog of Calaveras County."[1] Nonetheless, he would be amused to know that today, almost 150 years later, the Calaveras County Fair and Jumping Frog Jubilee not only has a jumping frog contest but also has its own Frog Welfare Policy. The policy includes a provision for the "Care of Sick or Injured Frogs" and a limitation entitled "Frogs Not Permitted to Participate," which stipulates that "under no circumstances will a frog listed on the endangered species list be permitted to participate in the Frog Jump."[2] This fair, like medical practice, is subject to both state and federal laws. Care of the sick and injured (both frogs and people) is primarily viewed as a matter of state law, whereas protection of endangered species is primarily regulated by Congress under its authority to regulate interstate commerce.

Not to carry the analogy too far, but it is worth recalling that Twain's famous frog, Dan'l Webster, lost his one and only jumping contest because his stomach had been filled with quail shot by a competitor. The loaded-down frog just couldn't jump. Until the California medical-marijuana case, it seemed to many observers that the conservative Rehnquist Court had succeeded in filling the commerce clause with quail shot—and had effectively prevented the federal government from regulating state activities. In the medical-marijuana case, however, a new majority of justices took the lead out of the commerce clause so that the federal government could legitimately claim jurisdiction over just about any activity, including the practice of medicine. The role of the commerce clause in federalism and the implications of the Court's decision in the California medical-marijuana case for physicians are the subjects I explore in this article.

Published in *The New England Journal of Medicine*, November 2005.

The Commerce Clause

The U.S. Constitution determines the areas over which the federal government has authority. All other areas remain, as they were before the adoption of the Constitution, under the authority of the individual states. Another way to say this is that the states retain all governmental authority they did not delegate to the federal government, including areas such as criminal law and family-law matters. These are part of the state's "police powers," usually defined as the state's sovereign authority to protect the health, safety, and welfare of its residents. Section 8 of Article I of the Constitution contains 18 clauses specifying delegated areas (including the military, currency, postal service, and patenting) over which "Congress shall have power," and these include the commerce clause—"to regulate commerce with foreign nations, and among the several states, and with the Indian tribes."

Until the Great Depression (and the disillusionment with unregulated markets), the Supreme Court took a narrow view of federal authority that could be derived from the commerce clause by ruling consistently that it gave Congress the authority only to regulate activities that directly involved the movement of commercial products (such as pharmaceuticals) from one state to another. Since then, and at least until 1995, the Court's interpretation seemed to be going in the opposite direction: Congress was consistently held to have authority in areas that had almost any relationship at all to commerce.

Guns in Schools and Violence Against Women

Under modern commerce clause doctrine, Congress has authority to regulate in three broad categories of activities: the use of the channels of interstate commerce (e.g., roads, air corridors, and waterways); the instrumentalities of interstate commerce (e.g., trains, trucks, and planes) and persons and things in interstate commerce; and "activities having a substantial relation to interstate commerce."[3] The first two categories are easy ones in that they involve activities that cross state lines. The third category, which does not involve crossing a state line, is the controversial one. The interpretation question involves the meaning and application of the concept of "substantially affecting" interstate commerce.

In a 1937 case that the Court characterized as a "watershed case" it concluded that the real question was one of the degree of effect. Intrastate activities that "have such a close and substantial relation to interstate commerce that their control is essential or appropriate to protect that commerce from burdens and obstructions" are within the power of Congress to regulate.[4] Later, in what has become perhaps its best-known commerce-clause case, the Court held that Congress could enforce a statute that prohibited a farmer from growing wheat on his own farm even if the wheat was never sold but was used only for the farmer's personal consumption. The Court concluded that although one farmer's personal use of homegrown wheat may be trivial (and have no effect on commerce), "taken together with that of many others similarly situated," its effect on interstate commerce (and the market price of wheat) "is far from trivial."[5]

The 1995 case that seemed to presage a states' rights revolution (often referred to as "devolution") involved the federal Gun-Free School Zones Act of 1990, which made it a federal crime "for any individual knowingly to possess a firearm at a place that the individual knows, or has reasonable cause to believe, is a school zone."[3] In a 5-to-4 opinion, written by the late Chief Justice William Rehnquist, the Court held that the statute exceeded Congress's authority under the commerce clause and only the individual states had authority to criminalize the possession of guns in school.[3]

The federal government had argued (and the four justices in the minority agreed) that the costs of violent crime are spread out over the entire population and that the presence of guns in schools threatens "national productivity" by undermining the learning environment, which in turn decreases learning and leads to a less productive citizenry and thus a less productive national economy. The majority of the Court rejected these arguments primarily because they thought that accepting this line of reasoning would make it impossible to define "any limitations on federal power, even in areas such as criminal law enforcement or education, where states historically have been sovereign."[3]

In 2000, in another 5-to-4 opinion written by Rehnquist, using the same rationale, the Court struck down a federal statute, part of the Violence against Women Act of 1994, that provided a federal civil remedy for victims of "gender-motivated violence." In the Court's words:

> Gender-motivated crimes of violence are not, in any sense of the phrase, economic activity. . . . Indeed, if Congress may regulate gender-motivated violence, it would be able to regulate murder or any other type of violence since gender-motivated violence, as a subset of all violent crime, is certain to have lesser economic impacts than the larger class of which it is a part.[6]

The Court, specifically addressing the question of federalism, concluded that "the Constitution requires a distinction between what is truly national and what is truly local. . . . Indeed, we can think of no better example of the police power, which the Founders denied to the National Government and reposed in the States, than the suppression of violent crime and vindication of its victims."[6]

Medical Marijuana in California

The next commerce-clause case involved physicians, albeit indirectly, and the role assigned to them in California in relation to the protection of patients who used physician-recommended marijuana from criminal prosecution. The question before the Supreme Court in the recent medical-marijuana case (*Gonzalez v. Raich*) was this: Does the commerce clause give Congress the authority to outlaw the local cultivation and use of marijuana for medicine if such cultivation and use complies with the provisions of California law?[7]

The California law, which is similar to laws in at least nine other states, creates an exemption from criminal prosecution for physicians, patients, and primary caregivers who possess or cultivate marijuana for medicinal purposes on the recommendation of a physician. Two patients for whom marijuana had been recommended brought suit to challenge enforcement of the federal Controlled Substances Act after federal Drug Enforcement Administration agents seized and destroyed all six marijuana plants that one of them had been growing for her own medical use in compliance with the California law. The Ninth Circuit Court of Appeals ruled in the plaintiffs' favor, finding that the California law applied to a separate and distinct category of activity, "the intrastate, noncommercial cultivation and possession of *cannabis* for personal medical purposes as recommended by a patient's physician pursuant to valid California state law," as opposed to what it saw as the federal law's purpose, which was to prevent "drug trafficking."[8] In a 6-to-3 opinion, written by Justice John Paul Stevens, with Justice Rehnquist dissenting, the Court reversed the appeals court's opinion and decided that Congress, under the commerce clause, did have authority to enforce its prohibition against marijuana—even state-approved, homegrown, noncommercial marijuana, used only for medicinal purposes on a physician's recommendation.

The majority of the Court decided that the commerce clause gave Congress the same power to regulate homegrown marijuana for personal use that it had to regulate homegrown wheat.[6] The question was whether homegrown marijuana for personal medical consumption substantially affected interstate commerce (albeit illegal commerce) when all affected patients were taken together. The Court concluded that Congress "had a rational basis for concluding that leaving home-consumed marijuana outside federal control" would affect "price and market conditions."[7] The Court also distinguished the guns-in-school and gender-violence cases on the basis that regulation of drugs is "quintessentially economic" when economics is defined as the "production, distribution, and consumption of commodities."[7]

This left only one real question open: Is the fact that marijuana is to be used only for medicinal purposes on the advice of a physician, as the Ninth Circuit Court had decided, sufficient for an exception to be carved out of otherwise legitimate federal authority to control drugs? The Court decided it was not, for several reasons. The first was that Congress itself had determined that marijuana is a Schedule I drug, which it defined as having "no acceptable medical use." The Court acknowledged that Congress might be wrong in this determination, but the issue in this case was not whether marijuana had possible legitimate medical uses but whether Congress had the authority to make the judgment that it had none and to ban all uses of the drug. The dissenting justices argued that personal cultivation and use of marijuana should be beyond the authority of the commerce clause. The Court majority disagreed, stating that if it accepted the dissenting justices' argument, personal cultivation for recreational use would also be beyond congressional authority. This conclusion, the majority argued, could not be sustained:

> One need not have a degree in economics to understand why a nationwide exemption for the vast quantity of marijuana (or other drugs) locally cultivated for personal use (which presumably would include use by friends, neighbors, and family members) may have a substantial impact on the interstate market for this extraordinarily popular substance. The congressional judgment that an exemption for such a significant segment of the total market would undermine the orderly enforcement of the entire [drug] regulatory scheme is entitled to a strong presumption of validity.[7]

The other primary limit to the effect of the California law on interstate commerce is the requirement of a physician's recommendation on the basis of a medical determination that a patient has an "illness for which marijuana provides relief." And the Court's discussion of this limit may be the most interesting, and disturbing, aspect of the case to physicians. Instead of concluding that physicians should be free to use their best medical judgment and that it was up to state medical boards to decide whether specific physicians were failing to live up to reasonable medical standards—as the Court did, for example, in its cases related to restrictive abortion laws[9]—the Court took a totally different approach. In the Court's words, the broad language of the California medical-marijuana law allows "even the most scrupulous doctor to conclude that some recreational uses would be therapeutic. And our cases have taught us that there are some unscrupulous physicians who overprescribe when it is sufficiently profitable to do so."[7]

The California law defines the category of patients who are exempt from criminal prosecution as those suffering from cancer, anorexia, AIDS, chronic pain, spasticity, glaucoma, arthritis, migraine, and "any other chronic or persistent medical symptom that substantially limits the ability of a person to conduct one or more major life activities . . . or if not alleviated may cause serious harm to the patient's safety or physical or mental health." These limits are hardly an invitation for recreational-use recommendations.[7] Regarding "unscrupulous physicians," the Court cited two cases that involve criminal prosecutions of physicians for acting like drug dealers, one from 1919 and the other from 1975, implying that because a few physicians might have been criminally inclined in the past, it was reasonable for Congress (and the Court), on the basis of no actual evidence, to assume that many physicians may be so inclined today. It was not only physicians that the Court found untrustworthy but sick patients and their caregivers as well:

> The exemption for cultivation by patients and caregivers [patients can possess up to 8 oz. of dried marijuana and cultivate up to 6 mature or 12 immature plants] can only increase the supply of marijuana in the California market. The likelihood that all such production will promptly terminate when patients recover or will precisely match the patients' medical needs during their convalescence seems remote; whereas the danger that excesses will satisfy some of the admittedly enormous demand for recreational use seems obvious.[7]

Justice Sandra Day O'Connor's dissent merits comment, because it is especially relevant to the practice of medicine. She argues that the Constitution requires the Court to protect "historic spheres of state sovereignty from excessive federal encroachment" and that one of the virtues of federalism is that it permits the individual states to serve as "laboratories," should they wish, to try "novel social and economic experiments without risk to the rest of the country." Specifically, she argues that the Court's new definition of economic activity is "breathtaking" in its scope, creating exactly what the gun case rejected—a federal police power. She also rejects reliance on the wheat case, noting that under the Agricultural Adjustment Act in question in that case, Congress had exempted the planting of less than 200 bushels (about six tons), and that when Roscoe Filburn, the farmer who challenged the federal statute, himself harvested his wheat, the statute exempted plantings of less than six acres.[5,7]

In O'Connor's words, the wheat case "did not extend Commerce Clause authority to something as modest as the home cook's herb garden."[8] O'Connor is not saying that Congress cannot regulate small quantities of a product produced for personal use, only that the wheat case "did not hold or imply that small-scale production of commodities is always economic, and automatically within Congress' reach." As to potential "exploitation [of the act] by unscrupulous physicians" and patients, O'Connor finds no factual support for this assertion and rejects the conclusion that simply by "piling assertion upon assertion" one can make a case for meeting the "substantiality test" of the guns-in-school and gender-violence cases.[7]

It is important to note that the Court was not taking a position on whether Congress was correct to place marijuana in Schedule I or a position against California's law, any more than it was taking a position in favor of guns in schools or violence against women in the earlier cases. Instead, the Court was ruling only on the question of federal authority under the commerce clause. The Court noted, for example, that California and its supporters may one day prevail by pursuing the democratic process "in the halls of Congress."[7] This seems extremely unlikely. More important is the question not addressed in this case—whether suffering patients have a substantive due-process claim to access to drugs needed to prevent suffering or a valid medical-necessity defense should they be prosecuted for using medical marijuana on a physician's recommendation.[10] Also not addressed was the question that will be decided during the coming year: whether Congress has delegated to the U.S. attorney general its authority to decide what a "legitimate medical use" of an approved drug is in the context of Oregon's law governing physician-assisted suicide.[11,12] What is obvious from this case, however, is that Congress has the authority, under the commerce clause, to regulate both legal and illegal drugs whether or not the drugs in question actually cross state lines. It would also seem reasonable to conclude that Congress has the authority to limit the uses of approved drugs.

Federalism and Endangered Species

Because *Gonzales v. Raich* is a drug case, and because it specifically involves marijuana, the Court's final word on federalism may not yet be in. Whether the "states' rights" movement has any life left after medical marijuana may be determined in the context of the Endangered Species Act. Two U.S. Circuit Courts of Appeals, for example, have recently upheld application of the federal law to protect endangered species that, unlike the descendants of Mark Twain's jumping frog, have no commercial value. Even though the Supreme Court refused to hear appeals from both of the lower courts, the cases help us understand the contemporary reach of congressional power under the commerce clause. One case involves the protection of six tiny creatures that live in caves (the "Cave Species")—three arthropods, a spider, and two beetles—from a commercial developer. The Fifth Circuit Court of Appeals noted that the Cave Species are not themselves an object of economics or commerce, saying: "There is no market for them; any future market is conjecture. If the speculative future medicinal benefits from the Cave Species makes their regulation commercial, then almost anything would be. . . . There is no historic trade in the Cave Species, nor do tourists come to Texas to view them."[13] Nonetheless, the court concluded that Congress had the authority, under the commerce clause, to view life as an "interdependent web" of all species; that destruction of endangered species can be aggregated, like homegrown wheat; and that the destruction of multiple species has a substantial effect on interstate commerce.[13]

The other case, from the District of Columbia Court of Appeals, involves the arroyo south-western toad, whose habitat was threatened by a real-estate developer. In upholding the application of the Endangered Species Act to the case, the appeals court held that the commercial activity being regulated was the housing development itself, as well as the "taking" of the road by the planned commercial development. The court noted that the "company would like us to consider its challenge to the ESA [Endangered Species Act] only as applied to the arroyo toad, which it says has no 'known commercial value'—unlike, for example, Mark Twain's celebrated jumping frogs [sic] of Calaveras County."[14] Instead, the court concluded that application of the Endangered

Species Act, far from eroding states' rights, is consistent with "the historic power of the federal government to preserve scarce resources in one locality for the future benefit of all Americans."[14]

On a request for a hearing by the entire appeals court, which was rejected, recently named Chief Justice John Roberts—who at the time was a member of the appeals court—wrote a dissent that was not unlike Justice O'Connor's dissent in the marijuana case. In it he argued that the court's conclusion seemed inconsistent with the guns-in-school and gender-violence cases and that there were real problems with using an analysis of the commerce clause to regulate "the taking of a hapless toad that, for reasons of its own, lives its entire life in California."[15] The case has since been settled. The development is going ahead in a way that protects the toad's habitat.[16]

The Future of the Commerce Clause

Twain's short story has been termed "a living American fairy tale, acted out annually in Calaveras County."[1] In what might be termed a living American government tale, nominees to the Supreme Court are routinely asked to explain their judicial philosophy of constitutional and statutory interpretation to the Senate Judiciary Committee. Asked about his "hapless toad" opinion during the Senate confirmation hearings on his nomination to replace Rehnquist as chief justice, Roberts said: "The whole point of my argument in the dissent was that there was another way to look at this [i.e., the approach taken by the Fifth Circuit Court in the Cave Species case]. . . . I did not say that even in this case that the decision was wrong. . . . I simply said, let's look at those other grounds for decision because that doesn't present this problem." These hearings provide an opportunity for all Americans to review their understanding of our constitutional government and the manner in which it allocates power between the federal government and the 50 states. To the extent that this division of power is determined by the Court's view of the commerce clause, a return to an expansive reading of this clause seems both likely and, given the interdependence of the national and global economies, proper.

Of course, the fact that Congress has authority over a particular subject—such as whether to adopt a system of national licensure for physicians—does not mean that its authority is unlimited or even that Congress will use it. Rather, as Justice Stevens noted, cases such as the California medical-marijuana case lead to other central constitutional questions, as yet unresolved. These questions include whether patients, terminally ill or not, have a constitutional right not to suffer—at least, when their physicians know how to control their pain.[12]

QUESTIONS

1. *What would you do?* If you were a state legislator or a judge, how would you decide these issues? Specifically, as a matter of policy, do you think that doctors should be able to prescribe marijuana to alleviate pain? Should they be able to prescribe lethal drugs to be used by terminally ill patients? What about as a matter of law? Do you agree with the Supreme Court's decisions on these issues?

2. Tabin argues that the Supreme Court decides to control state governments "when Kennedy and his liberal colleagues feel like it." Is this fair? Why do you think that the Supreme Court ruled in Congress's favor in the medical-marijuana case and Oregon's favor in the assisted-suicide case?

3. Do you support a state-centered or nation-centered perspective on federalism? Go back and look at your answers to the first two questions. Did you take positions that were consistent with your views on federalism or with your views on medical marijuana and assisted suicide as policies?

4. What does Mark Twain's jumping frog represent in Annas's article? Which Supreme Court case "breathed life back into the frog" and how?

4

Civil Liberties: The Tradeoff between Security and Freedom

One of the central purposes of any government is to provide security for its citizens. However, if a country places too much emphasis on security, it will have to limit freedom. Since the terrorist attacks of September 11, 2001, the United States government has been tipping the balance toward security by strengthening its police and surveillance powers. A majority of Americans (78 percent according to a poll cited in *The Progressive* article included here) support these policies and they passed by very large margins in the House and Senate. However, defenders of civil liberties and those who fear the power of government are very concerned about the recent changes.

The editorial in *The Progressive* outlines many of the concerns about the Patriot Act and other threats to civil liberties since 9/11. It lays out in very strong terms the "breathtaking assault" on our civil liberties, citing the vague language of the Patriot Act that permits the government broader access to monitor the activity of suspected terrorists in libraries and homes and on the Internet. The law also alters the attorney/client relationship to allow the government to listen in on conversations with suspected terrorists, allows the detention of designated "enemy combatants" without normal due process protections, and broadens powers for "material witness" wiretaps, warrants, and searches. John Ashcroft, who served as Attorney General from 2001–2005, is described in the article as the central threat to civil liberties as he aggressively interpreted the Patriot Act to enhance the government's police powers.

Andrew McCarthy, a former federal prosecutor, responds to complaints about one specific policy, a warrantless surveillance program that President Bush established after 9/11. Apart from the constitutional and legal issues—both decidedly in the president's favor, according to McCarthy—the program's critics have entirely missed the point about balancing civil liberties and security in wartime. The ability to conduct surveillance always comes with the risk that the power can be misused, but the need to collect intelligence information during wartime is so obvious that it makes no sense to reflexively complain about a nonexistent risk to privacy. Indeed, McCarthy argues, the program probably does not involve direct listening-in on conversations, but has more to do with analyzing network traffic patterns. There are no privacy interests at risk in this kind of program. After 9/11, the Bush Administration was criticized for failing to "connect the dots," or piecing together bits of intelligence information that could have exposed the plan. This, according to McCarthy, is precisely what the surveillance program is designed to do.

The Progressive
Casualties of War

Oh, it was too easy for a nation to turn its back on 1,200 detainees, mostly Muslim, rounded up since September 11 and held in secret. The terrorist attack was so shocking that many Americans were able to condone this violation of due process, thinking perhaps that the government would stop there. But now the government of the people has turned its attention to the rest of the people, and the war on terrorism goes from murky to muddy.

Welcome to the era of Total Information Awareness and other tomfoolery.

We're now at a time of perhaps unprecedented spying and secrecy. Richard Nixon could only dream of such powers. More than a year after the events of September 11, 2001, we are seeing the best of America—the Constitution and Bill of Rights—shredded by President George Bush and Attorney General John Ashcroft. To comprehend this breathtaking assault, we need to look back at how it all began.

The Ashcroft confirmation hearing was a bitter fight for the soul of the Jus-

Published in January 2003.

tice Department. Amidst the cantankerous rhetoric and blow-hard posturing from both sides of the narrow fence, there was some plainspoken eloquence from Senator Richard Durbin, Democrat of Illinois.

"The Attorney General, more than any other Cabinet officer, is entrusted with protecting the civil rights of Americans," Durbin said. "We know from our history that defending those rights can often be controversial and unpopular. I find no evidence in the public career or voting record of Senator Ashcroft that he has ever risked any political capital to defend the rights of those who suffer in our society from prejudice and discrimination."

How right Durbin was.

Since 9/11, our top law enforcement officer has gone to great lengths to rewrite and dismantle civil liberties in this country. For all the Attorney General's singing about patriotism and love of country, his odious record demonstrates that he does not respect the fundamental tenets of our democracy.

The opening act in this wretched tragedy started two nights after the 9/11 attack when the Senate swiftly voted, by voice, to approve an attachment to an appropriations bill that made it easier for the government to wiretap the computers of terrorism suspects without having to go through due process. That was just the beginning of what would eventually become the USA Patriot Act, an omnibus anti-terrorism law that was supposed to pacify Americans so they would return to shopping malls and sporting events.

The USA Patriot Act is full of lax language that gives the government expansive powers to peep into the lives of Americans they deem dissenters and subversives. This is the kind of law a nation gets when 78 percent of its citizens, in an NBC/Wall Street Journal poll, say they're willing to sacrifice rights to fight against extremists. It's simply one of the most regressive acts in American history.

Even the definition of a terrorist in the act is flimsy and transparent. For instance, you're a domestic terrorist if you're breaking a law at the same time that you're doing something that appears "to be intended to influence the policy of government by intimidation." Under this definition, Martin Luther King was a domestic terrorist in Birmingham.

The act lets the FBI and other law enforcement agents enter your home when you're not there, ransack your files, use your computer and search your e-mails, and place a "magic lantern" on your computer to record your every keystroke. Then they can leave without telling you they were there.

In addition, the Patriot Act lets law enforcement find out what books you're buying at stores or checking out at libraries. And it then gags the book-stores and libraries so they can't tell anyone that they've had to fork over your name.

But this lunacy goes beyond reading material. A story in the December 10 edition of *The New York Times* reports that last summer the FBI, concerned about a terrorist attack involving scuba divers, "set out to identify every person who had taken diving lessons in the previous three years."

According to the *Times*, hundreds of dive shops and organizations willingly turned over the information.

"But just as the effort was wrapping up in July, the FBI ran into a two-man revolt," the *Times* says. "The owners of the Reef Seekers Dive Company in Beverly Hills, California, balked at turning over the records of their clients . . . even when officials came back with a subpoena asking for 'any and all docu-mented and other records relating to all noncertified divers and referrals from July 1, 1999, through July 16, 2002.' "

The owners say they had several reasons to deny the FBI's request, prima-rily because terrorists would need to have far more sophisticated training than a few scuba lessons. The owners said they also worried the information would be passed on to other agencies. Some people called to say they hoped the shop would be blown up by terrorists.

"If we are going to decide as a country that because of our worry about ter-rorism that we are willing to give up our basic privacy, we need an open and full debate on whether we want to make such a fundamental change," Cindy Cohen, legal director of the Electronic Frontier Foundation, told the *Times*. The foundation represented Reef Seekers.

At about the same time Congress was ratifying the Patriot Act, Ashcroft is-sued an edict saying that prosecutors could eavesdrop on prisoner-lawyer con-versations. And he rewrote Justice Department policy to allow a return to Cointelpro.

Bush himself jumped in with his military tribunal order, which allows the Pentagon to nab any noncitizens anywhere in the world and try them in mili-tary courts with lower standards of evidence and with no appeals possible to any judge or court anywhere in the world.

Again, the Bush Administration sold this to the American people as a nec-essary protection against foreign terrorists and assured the citizenry that they would not be victimized by it.

But then came the designation of "enemy combatants" and the holding of two U.S. citizens—Jose Padilla and Yasser Hamdi—in military brigs. Neither was charged with a crime. Neither was allowed counsel.

Padilla, also known as Abdullah Al-Mujahir, an ex-Chicago gang member, is being held under suspicion of being an Al Qaeda operative who was allegedly researching how to detonate a radioactive bomb.

Hamdi was taken into custody in Afghanistan and was interrogated there by a military screening team.

Neither Padilla nor Hamdi has been allowed to meet with an attorney, much less appear before a judge to contest the detention. The administration claims it can hold both of them (and others it may deem "enemy combatants" down the road) for as long as the war on terrorism goes on.

"This seems to me the classic case for habeas corpus," said Georgetown University law professor Mark Tushnet, who was quoted in the *Los Angeles Times*. "They don't get to say, 'This is a bad guy, and we can do with him what we want.'"

Federal District Court Judge Robert G. Doumar agreed. He heard a challenge by a public defender in Hamdi's case. "This case appears to be the first in American jurisprudence where an American citizen has been held incommunicado and subjected to an indefinite detention in the continental United States without charges, without any findings by a military tribunal, and without access to a lawyer," Judge Doumar wrote. When the government tried to defend Hamdi's detention, the judge asked the Attorney General's lawyer, "So, the Constitution doesn't apply to Mr. Hamdi?"

The American Civil Liberties Union has filed suit on behalf of Padilla and Hamdi. On December 4, U.S. District Judge Michael Mukasey gave civil libertarians a respite when he ruled that alleged "dirty bomber" Jose Padilla can have his status as an "enemy combatant" reviewed in a federal court and that he must have access to counsel in the interim.

"This ruling is a crucial rejection of the Bush Administration's claim of almost unbridled power to unilaterally detain American citizens and hold them indefinitely and incommunicado," said Lucas Guttentag, director of the American Civil Liberties Union's Immigrant Rights Project, after the ruling. "The decision is a critical first step to providing a check on the government's use of the enemy combatant designation."

But not all courts have seen the light. On November 18, the Foreign Intelligence Surveillance Court of Review, established in 1978 to oversee domestic spying activities, gave the government even broader powers to snoop and sniff about the lives of ordinary Americans. What makes this new proclamation ghastly is that the court's proceedings are held in secret, its members are hand-picked by Chief Justice William Rehnquist, and the government is the only entity allowed to appear before it. Sounds like some ludicrous Stalinist-era kangaroo court, but it's right here in the good ol' U.S.A.

"The decision gives the government a green light to tear down the wall that has long existed between officials conducting surveillance on suspected foreign agents and criminal prosecutors investigating crimes," says a *New York Times* editorial from November 19. "Attorney General John Ashcroft has announced that he intends to use it to sharply increase the number of domestic wiretaps, and that he will add lawyers at the FBI and at federal prosecutors' offices around the country to hurry the process along."

The Bush Administration has constructed a repugnant parallel legal system for terrorism in which suspects, according to the *Washington Post*, could be "investigated, jailed, interrogated, tried, and punished without conventional legal protections."

The *Post* reports the new system includes indefinite detention for those— like Padilla and Hamdi—who are designated "enemy combatants." And it also includes a radically expanded use of "material witness" warrants, wiretaps, and searches.

Administration officials told the *Washington Post* that this parallel system is meant to be used selectively, "but is needed because terrorism is a form of war as well as a form of crime, and it must not only be punished after incidents occur, but also prevented and disrupted through the gathering of timely intelligence."

This is the biggest power grab since Attorney General A. Mitchell Palmer conducted his communist hunts under Woodrow Wilson!

The government wishes not to be disturbed in this war against terrorism. The government wishes not to be accountable to anyone, least of all the citizens it says it wishes to protect. Ashcroft's attitude is simple: If the government abuses some people in this fight, so be it. It's a war, and the casualties of a few are outweighed by the protection of the many.

It is this attitude that reduces the Constitution and the Bill of Rights to collateral damage.

Andrew C. McCarthy
How to "Connect the Dots"

Washington's scandal du jour involves a wartime surveillance program President Bush directed the National Security Agency to carry out after al-Qaeda killed nearly 3,000 Americans on September 11, 2001. The idea that there is anything truly scandalous about this program is absurd. But the outcry against it is valuable, highlighting as it does the mistaken assumption that criminal-justice solutions are applicable to national-security challenges.

The intelligence community has identified thousands of al-Qaeda operatives and sympathizers throughout the world. After Congress overwhelmingly authorized the use of military force immediately following the 9/11 attacks, the president, as part of the war effort, ordered the NSA to intercept the enemy's international communications, even if those communications went into and out of the United States and thus potentially involved American citizens. According to reports from the *New York Times*, which shamefully publicized leaks of the program's existence in mid-December 2005, as many as 7,000 suspected terrorists overseas are monitored at any one time, as are up to 500 suspects inside the United States.

As is typical of such wartime operations, the NSA program was classified at the highest level of secret information. It was, nevertheless, completely different from the kind of rogue intelligence operations of which the Nixon era is emblematic (though by no means the only case). The Bush administration internally vetted the program, including at the Justice Department, to confirm its legal footing. It reviewed (and continues to review) the program every 45 days. It briefed the bipartisan leadership of Congress (including the intelligence committees) at least a dozen times. It informed the chief judge of the federal Foreign Intelligence Surveillance Court (FISC), the tribunal that oversees domestic national-security wiretapping. And it modified the program in mid-2004 in reaction to concerns raised by the chief judge, national-security officials, and government lawyers.

Far from being a pretextual use of war powers to spy on political opponents and policy dissenters, the NSA program has been dedicated to national

Published in *National Review*, January 2006.

security. More to the point, it has saved lives, helping break up at least one al-Qaeda conspiracy to attack New York City and Washington, D.C., in connection with which a plotter named Iyman Fans was sentenced to 20 years' imprisonment.

As potential scandal fodder, so unremarkable did the NSA program seem that the *Times* sat on the story for a year—and a year, it is worth noting, during which it transparently and assiduously sought to exploit any opportunity to discredit the administration and cast it as a mortal threat to civil liberties. The leak was not sprung until the eleventh hour of congressional negotiations over renewal of the Patriot Act—at which point it provided ammunition to those who would gut Patriot's crucial post-9/11 domestic-surveillance powers and simultaneously served as a marketing campaign for *Times* reporter James Risen, who just happened to be on the eve of publishing a book about, among other things, Bush's domestic "spying."

In fact, so obviously appropriate was wartime surveillance of the enemy that Rep. Jane Harman, the ranking Democrat on the House Intelligence Committee, issued a statement right after the *Times* exposed the program, saying: "I have been briefed since 2003 on a highly classified NSA foreign collection program that targeted Al-Qaeda. I believe the program is essential to U.S. national security and that its disclosure has damaged critical intelligence capabilities." (With partisan "scandal" blowing in the wind, Harman changed her tune two weeks later, suddenly deciding that the "essential" program was probably illegal after all.)

A Mighty Fuss

If President Bush's reelection is any indication, what most Americans will care about is that we are monitoring the enemy. Chances are they won't be overly interested in knowing whether that monitoring is done on the president's own constitutional authority or in accordance with a statutory scheme calling for judicial imprimatur. Nevertheless, the Left is already indulging in loose talk about impeachment. Even some Republican "moderates," such as Arlen Specter, say the domestic-spying allegations are troubling enough that hearings are warranted. So it's worth asking: What is all the fuss about?

At bottom, it is about a power grab that began nearly three decades ago. Ever since it became technologically possible to intercept wire communications, presidents have done so. All of them, going back to FDR, claimed that the powers granted to the chief executive under Article II of the Constitution allowed them to conduct such wiretapping for national-security purposes. Particularly in wartime, this power might be thought indisputable. The president is the commander in chief of the armed forces, and penetrating enemy communications is as much an incident of war-fighting as bombing enemy targets is.

But surveillance power has been abused—and notoriously by President Nixon, whose eavesdropping on political opponents was the basis of a draft article of impeachment. Watergate-era domestic-spying controversies dovetailed with important developments in the law of electronic surveillance. In 1967, the Supreme Court, in *Katz v. United States*, held that Fourth Amendment protection against unreasonable searches extended to electronic surveillance—meaning that eavesdropping without a judicial warrant was now presumptively unconstitutional. Congress followed by enacting a comprehensive scheme, known as "Title III," that required law-enforcement agents to obtain a court warrant for probable cause of a crime before conducting electronic surveillance. Yet both *Katz* and Title III recognized inherent presidential authority to conduct national-security monitoring without being bound by the new warrant requirement.

The Supreme Court undertook to circumscribe this inherent authority in its 1972 *Keith* decision. It held that a judicial warrant was required for national-security surveillance if the target was a purely domestic threat—the Vietnam-era Court giving higher priority to the free-speech interests of "those suspected of unorthodoxy in their political beliefs" than to the safety of those who might be endangered by domestic terrorists. Still, the Court took pains to exempt from its ruling the "activities of foreign powers or their agents."

The true power grab occurred in 1978, when Congress enacted the Foreign Intelligence Surveillance Act. FISA attempted to do in the national-security realm what Title III had done in law enforcement: erect a thoroughgoing legal regime for domestic eavesdropping. And therein lies the heart of the current dispute. If the president has inherent authority to conduct national-security wiretapping, it is a function of his constitutional warrant. It is not a function of Congress's having failed until 1978 to flex its own muscles. A constitutional power cannot be altered or limited by statute. Period.

But limiting presidential authority is precisely what FISA purports to do. It ostensibly prohibits national-security eavesdropping (and, since 1994, physical searches) unless the executive branch can satisfy a federal judge—one of eleven who sit on a specially created Foreign Intelligence Surveillance Court—that there is probable cause that the subject it seeks to monitor is an "agent of a foreign power" (generally either a spy or a member of a foreign terrorist organization).

FISA does not aim to restrict the power to eavesdrop on all conversations. Communications that are entirely foreign—in that they involve aliens communicating overseas, for example—are exempted, as are conversations that unintentionally capture "U.S. persons" (generally, American citizens and permanent resident aliens), as long as these communications are intercepted outside the United States. But where it does apply, FISA holds that the president—the constitutional officer charged with the nation's security—is powerless to eavesdrop on an operative posing a threat to the United States unless a judge—who need not possess any national-security expertise—is persuaded that the operative is a genuine threat. One suspects that such a system would astonish the Founders.

The Bounds of FISA

Does the NSA program violate FISA? That question is difficult to answer with certainty. The program remains highly classified, and many of its details are not publicly known, nor should they be. Much has been made of the fact that FISA approval is required to intercept calls into or out of the United States if an American is intentionally being targeted. But scant attention has been given to FISA's caveat that such conversations are protected only if their participants have a reasonable expectation of privacy. It is difficult to imagine that Americans who make or receive calls to war zones in, say, Afghanistan or Iraq, or to al-Qaeda operatives anywhere, can reasonably expect that no one is listening in.

Nevertheless, it would not be surprising to learn that at least some of the NSA monitoring transgresses the bounds of FISA. For example, the statute mandates—without qualification about the reasonable expectation of privacy—that the government seek a judicial warrant before eavesdropping on any international call to or from the United States, if that call is intercepted inside our borders. A distinction based on where a call is intercepted made sense in 1978. Back then, if a conversation was intercepted inside our borders, its participants were almost certain to include at least one U.S. person. But modern technology has since blurred the distinction between foreign and domestic telephony. Packets of digital information are now routed through switches inside countries (including, predominately, the United States) where neither the sender nor the recipient of the call is located. The NSA has capitalized on this evolution, and is now able, from within the United States, to seize calls between Tikrit and Kabul, or between Peshawar and Hamburg. If done without a warrant, those intercepts present no FISA problem, because all the speakers are overseas. But it's hard to believe that the NSA is using this technology only to acquire all-foreign calls, while intercepting calls between, say, New York and Hamburg only from locations outside the United States.

Perhaps that is why the Bush administration's defense has been light on the abstruse details of FISA and heavy on the president's inherent Article II power—although carefully couched to avoid offending Congress and the FISC with suggestions that FISA is at least partly unconstitutional. Essentially, the administration argues that FISA is beneficial in ordinary times and for long-term investigations, but that it did not and cannot repeal the president's independent constitutional obligation to protect the country: an obligation that was explicitly reserved even by President Carter, who signed FISA; that has been claimed by every president since; and that is uniquely vital in a war against thousands of stateless, stealthy terrorists, in which both a "probable cause" requirement and a sclerotic bureaucracy for processing warrant applications would be dangerously impractical.

In advancing this argument, the administration finds much support in the one and only decision ever rendered by the Foreign Intelligence Court of Review—the appellate court created by FISA to review FISC decisions. That decision came in 2002, after a quarter-century of FISA experience. Tellingly, its context was a brazen effort by the FISC to reject the Patriot Act's dismantling of the "wall" that prevented intelligence agents and criminal investigators from pooling information. In overruling the FISC, the Court of Review observed that "all the other courts to have decided the issue [have] held that the President did have inherent authority to conduct warrantless searches to obtain foreign intelligence information." Notwithstanding FISA, the Court thus pronounced: "We take for granted that the President does have that authority."

The administration has also placed great stock in Congress's post-9/11 authorization of "all necessary and appropriate force" against those behind the terrorist attacks. While this resolution did not expressly mention penetrating enemy communications, neither did it explicitly include the detention of enemy combatants, which the Supreme Court, in its 2004 Hamdi decision, found implicit in the use-of-force authorization because it is a "fundamental incident of waging war." Capturing intelligence, of course, is as much a component of waging war as capturing operatives. Any other conclusion would lead to the absurdity of the president's having full discretion to kill terrorists but needing a judge's permission merely to eavesdrop on them.

FISA aside, the administration stresses that the NSA program fits comfortably within the Fourth Amendment. That Amendment proscribes *unreasonable* searches, not warrantless ones—and it is thus unsurprising that the Supreme Court has recognized numerous exceptions to the warrant requirement that are of far less moment than the imperative to protect the country from attack. Plainly, there is nothing unreasonable about intercepting potential enemy communications in wartime. Moreover, the courts have long held that searches conducted at the border are part of the sovereign right of self-protection, and thus require neither probable cause nor a warrant. Cross-border communications, which might well be triggers of terror plots, are no more deserving of constitutional protection.

Constitutional Authority

Critics have made much of a lengthy analysis published on January 6, 2006, by the Congressional Research Service that casts doubt on the administration's core contentions. Media have treated the report as bearing special weight because the CRS is a non-partisan entity. But that does not mean the CRS is objective. "The sole mission of CRS," it explains on its Web site, "is to serve the United States Congress." Yet the issue at stake is precisely a separation-of-powers dispute.

While the CRS study is an impressive compilation of the relevant law, it resorts to a fairly standard tactic for marginalizing executive power: reliance on the concurring opinion by Supreme Court Justice Robert Jackson in a 1952 case involving President Truman's failed effort to seize steel mills—a move Truman justified by referring to the exigencies of the Korean War. Jackson saw executive power as waxing or waning along a three-stage scale, depending on whether a president acted with the support, the indifference, or the opposition of Congress. On this theory, a statute like FISA could curb a president's inherent constitutional authority. The fatal problem with the Jackson construct, however, has always been that it makes Congress, not the Constitution, the master of presidential authority. It disregards the reality that the executive is a coequal branch whose powers exist whether Congress acts or not. But the CRS prefers Jackson's conveniently airy formula, which failed to command a Court majority, to relevant opinions that don't go Congress's way, such as that of the Foreign Intelligence Court of Review—which, unlike the Supreme Court, was actually considering FISA.

Frustrated by its inability to move public opinion, the Left is now emphasizing the large "volume of information harvested from telecommunication data and voice networks," as the *Times* breathlessly put it, "without court-approved warrants." But this is pure legerdemain. When we refer to "information" from "telecommunication data," we are talking about something that, legally, is worlds apart from the content of telephone calls or e-mail messages.

These data do not include the substance of what people privately say to one another in conversations, but rather comprise statistical facts about the use of telecommunications services (for example, what phone number called another number, the date and time of the call, how long it lasted, etc.). Court warrants have never been required for the acquisition of such information because, as the Supreme Court explained over a quarter-century ago in *Smith v. Maryland*, telecommunications data do not implicate the Fourth Amendment. All phone and e-mail users know this information is conveyed to and maintained by service providers, and no one expects it to be private.

Analyzing such data is clearly different from monitoring the calls and e-mails themselves. For our own protection, we should want the government to collect as many of these data as possible (since doing so affects no one's legitimate privacy interests) in order to develop investigative leads. That's how a country manages to go four years without a domestic terror attack.

Yet the Left's rage continues, despite the public's evident disinterest in the mind-numbingly technical nature of the dispute, and despite the obvious truth that the NSA program was a bona fide effort to protect the nation from harm, not to snoop on Americans—only a tiny fraction of whom were affected, and those with apparent good reason. The controversy is a disquieting barometer of elite commitment to the War on Terror. As recently as two years ago, when "connecting the dots" was all the rage, liberals ignored eight years of Clintonian nonfeasance and portrayed the Bush administration as asleep at the switch while terrorists ran amok. Now they ignore President Clinton's insistence on the very same executive surveillance power that the current administration claims and caricature Bush as the imperial president, shredding core protections of civil liberties by exaggerating the terror threat. Either way you slice it, national security becomes a game in which necessary decisions by responsible adults become political grist and if they get enough traction, phony scandals.

What remains real though, is the danger to Americans implicit in any system that can't tell a war from a crime.

QUESTIONS:

1. *What would you do?* You are a federal judge who must decide on the due process rights of suspected "enemy combatants." Should they have the same rights as all suspected criminals, or should the war on terrorism be given a different status in our legal system?

2. One of the editors of *Faultlines* was speaking to a community group shortly after the attacks of 9/11 about the tradeoff between security and freedom. After the presentation, a person in the audience made the following argument: "I have nothing to hide. I don't care if the government taps my phone or checks my e-mail. I am happy to have them do that if we can catch some terrorists. These laws only infringe on the civil liberties of the guilty, not the innocent." What do you make of this argument? Where does one draw the line between security and freedom?

3. President Bush said that the government will not torture suspected terrorists who have been arrested to find out more about their terrorist operations. Do you think the government would ever be justified in torturing a suspect? What if he or she had information about a nuclear bomb that was about to be detonated in New York City, killing millions of people? If torture would be justified in that instance, where does one draw the line on when torture should be allowed and when it should be prohibited?

5

Civil Rights: Affirmative Action in Higher Education

The Civil Rights Act of 1964 ensured, at least on paper, that all Americans would enjoy equality of opportunity. But even after the Act was passed blacks continued to lag behind whites in socio-economic status, in part because of enduring racism and inequalities in the distribution of income and the quality of education. Beginning in 1965, President Johnson tried to address these inequalities with a policy of "affirmative action." By executive order, Johnson required all federal agencies and government contractors to submit written plans to hire certain numbers of blacks, women, Asian-Americans, and Native Americans within various job categories. Throughout the 1970s and 1980s, affirmative action programs grew in the private sector and throughout higher education as well. Through such programs, employers and universities gave preferential treatment to minority and women applicants, either to make up for past patterns of discrimination or to pursue the general goals of diversity.

Affirmative action in higher education has been a hotly contested area of the law in recent years. This was not always the case. The 1978 decision in *Regents of the University of California v. Bakke* struck down racial quotas, but allowed race to be used in admissions decisions as a "plus factor" to promote diversity in the student body. This process was widely followed until 1996, when the Fifth Circuit Court of Appeals held that it was unconstitutional to consider race in law school admissions at the University of Texas. A circuit court in Washington reached the opposite conclusion and even more puzzling were two conflicting cases from the University of Michigan. A December 2000 district court case held that race-conscious undergraduate admissions was acceptable, but a decision a few months later in the same district court held that considering race in law school admissions was not constitutional. A deeply divided Supreme Court sorted out this confusion by upholding the *Bakke* principle of using race as a "plus factor" in admissions decisions (*Grutter v. Bollinger*), but rejecting the point system used by the University of Michigan in undergraduate admissions for being too rigid in the application of affirmative action (*Gratz v. Bollinger*). That system awarded every minority applicant bonus points that increased their likelihood of admission.

The crucial legal question was whether "viewpoint diversity," the idea that affirmative action brings diversity to classroom discussions, constituted a "compelling state interest" that allowed the university to make racial distinctions that would otherwise be barred by the Fourteenth Amendment's equal protection clause. There were differences of opinion on whether racial diversity produced viewpoint diversity and the validity of Michigan's argument about the "critical mass" necessary to produce viewpoint diversity. Justice Rehnquist pointed out that the necessary "critical mass" seemed to vary directly with the size of the applicant pool for a given racial group (e.g., the number of Native Americans needed to provide viewpoint diversity was much smaller than the number of African Americans), causing him to question the entire argument. Clarence Thomas's dissent in the *Grutter* case strongly rejects the viewpoint diversity argument, claiming that racial classifications of any type should not be allowed unless there is a compelling state interest, and he rejects viewpoint diversity as such an interest. Justice Thomas also decries the distinction between benign and invidious racial classifications, arguing that racial classifications of any type are bad. Much of his dissent is intensely personal; as the only African American on the Court, Justice Thomas is acutely aware that he benefitted from affirmative action himself, yet his strong objections to the practice come through loud and clear.

The Clinical Legal Education Association's brief in the *Grutter* case disagrees, saying that racial diversity is crucial to legal education because of the viewpoint diversity that it provides. While some of their arguments are specific to law school clinics, their general points about the value of racial diversity was shared by scores of other parties who filed briefs on behalf of the University of Michigan. Many Fortune 500 corporations sided with the University, saying that affirmative action was necessary to provide them with the racially diverse workforce that is necessary to compete in the multi-cultural, international business environment. The CLEA brief also addresses the legal question of a "compelling state interest" and argues that the "critical mass" necessary to provide viewpoint diversity does not constitute an arbitrary quota.

The Supreme Court has resolved the legal questions concerning affirmative action for now, but the issue remains controversial in higher education and the workplace. With Justice Sandra Day O'Connor, the pivotal vote in the decision to uphold the principle of affirmative action, having been replaced by Justice Samuel Alito in 2006, the Court may revisit this issue in the near future.

Justice Clarence Thomas
Dissent in *Barbara Grutter v. Lee Bollinger, et al.* (2003)

Justice Thomas, with whom Justice Scalia joins as to Parts I–VII, concurring in part and dissenting in part.

Frederick Douglass, speaking to a group of abolitionists almost 140 years ago, delivered a message lost on today's majority:

> In regard to the colored people, there is always more that is benevolent, I perceive, than just, manifested towards us. What I ask for the negro is not benevolence, not pity, not sympathy, but simply justice. The American people have always been anxious to know what they shall do with us. . . . I have had but one answer from the beginning. Do nothing with us! Your doing with us has already played the mischief with us. Do nothing with us! If the apples will not remain on the tree of their own strength, if they are worm-eaten at the core, if they are early ripe and disposed to fall, let them fall! . . . And if the negro cannot stand on his own legs, let him fall also. All I ask is, give him a chance to stand on his own legs! Let him alone! . . . Your interference is doing him positive injury.

Like Douglass, I believe blacks can achieve in every avenue of American life without the meddling of university administrators. Because I wish to see all students succeed whatever their color, I share, in some respect, the sympathies of those who sponsor the type of discrimination advanced by the University of Michigan Law School (the "Law School"). The Constitution does not, however, tolerate institutional devotion to the status quo in admissions policies when such devotion ripens into racial discrimination. Nor does the Constitution countenance the unprecedented deference the Court gives to the Law School, an approach inconsistent with the very concept of "strict scrutiny."

No one would argue that a university could set up a lower general admission standard and then impose heightened requirements only on black applicants. Similarly, a university may not maintain a high admission standard and grant exemptions to favored races. The Law School, of its own choosing, and for its own purposes, maintains an exclusionary admissions system that it knows produces racially disproportionate results. Racial discrimination is not a permissible solution to the self-inflicted wounds of this elitist admissions policy. . . .

[Here Thomas examines the majority opinion and the legal standard of strict scrutiny.]

The Constitution abhors classifications based on race, not only because those classifications can harm favored races or are based on illegitimate motives, but also because every time the government places citizens on racial registers and makes race relevant to the provision of burdens or benefits, it demeans us all. "Purchased at the price of immeasurable human suffering, the equal protection principle reflects our Nation's understanding that such classifications ultimately have a destructive impact on the individual and our society" [*Adarand Construction, Inc. v. Pena*, 1995].

II

Unlike the majority, I seek to define with precision the interest being asserted by the Law School before determining whether that interest is so compelling as to justify racial discrimination. The Law School maintains that it wishes to obtain "educational benefits that flow from student body diversity." This statement must be evaluated carefully, because it implies that both "diversity" and "educational benefits" are components of the Law School's compelling state interest. Additionally, the Law School's refusal to entertain certain changes in its admissions process and status indicates that the compelling state interest it seeks to validate is actually broader than might appear at first glance.

Undoubtedly there are other ways to "better" the education of law students aside from ensuring that the student body contains a "critical mass" of underrepresented minority students. Attaining "diversity," whatever it means, is the mechanism by which the Law School obtains educational benefits, not an end of itself. The Law School, however, apparently believes that only a racially mixed student body can lead to the educational benefits it seeks. How, then, is the Law School's interest in these allegedly unique educational "benefits" not simply the forbidden interest in "racial balancing," that the majority expressly rejects?

A distinction between these two ideas (unique educational benefits based on racial aesthetics and race for its own sake) is purely sophistic—so much so that the majority uses them interchangeably. . . . The Law School's argument, as facile as it is, can only be understood in one way: Classroom aesthetics yields educational benefits, racially discriminatory admissions policies are required to achieve the right racial mix, and therefore the policies are required to achieve the educational benefits. It is the educational benefits that are the end, or allegedly compelling state interest, not "diversity."

One must also consider the Law School's refusal to entertain changes to its current admissions system that might produce the same educational benefits. The Law School adamantly disclaims any race-neutral alternative that would reduce "academic selectivity," which would in turn "require the Law School to become a very different institution, and to sacrifice a core part of its educational mission." In other words, the Law School seeks to improve marginally the education it offers without sacrificing too much of its exclusivity and elite status.

The proffered interest that the majority vindicates today, then, is not simply "diversity." Instead the Court upholds the use of racial discrimination as a tool to advance the Law School's interest in offering a marginally superior education while maintaining an elite institution. Unless each constituent part of this state interest is of pressing public necessity, the Law School's use of race is unconstitutional. I find each of them to fall far short of this standard.

III

A

A close reading of the Court's opinion reveals that all of its legal work is done through one conclusory statement: The Law School has a "compelling interest in securing the educational benefits of a diverse student body." No serious effort is made to explain how these benefits fit with the state interests the Court has recognized (or rejected) as compelling, or to place any theoretical constraints on an enterprising court's desire to discover still more justifications for racial discrimination. In the absence of any explanation, one might expect the Court to fall back on the judicial policy of *stare decisis*. But the Court eschews even this weak defense of its holding, shunning an analysis of the extent to which Justice Powell's opinion in *Regents of Univ. of Cal. v. Bakke* (1978), is binding, in favor of an unfounded wholesale adoption of it.

Justice Powell's opinion in *Bakke* and the Court's decision today rest on the fundamentally flawed proposition that racial discrimination can be contextualized so that a goal, such as classroom aesthetics, can be compelling in one context but not in another. This "we know it when we see it" approach to evaluating state interests is not capable of judicial application. Today, the Court insists on radically expanding the range of permissible uses of race to something as trivial (by comparison) as the assembling of a law school class. I can only presume that the majority's failure to justify its decision by reference to any principle arises from the absence of any such principle. . . .

[Here Thomas develops the argument that Michigan does not have a "compelling state interest" in maintaining an elite public law school. He says that the Law School could simply accept "all students who meet minimum qualifications" rather than engage in racial discrimination].

A

The Court bases its unprecedented deference to the Law School—a deference antithetical to strict scrutiny—on an idea of "educational autonomy" grounded in the First Amendment. In my view, there is no basis for a right of public universities to do what would otherwise violate the Equal Protection Clause. . . .

[Here Thomas develops his argument that First Amendment protections of academic freedom do not allow universities to violate the Equal Protection Clause of the Fourteenth Amendment].

B

1

The Court's deference to the Law School's conclusion that its racial experimentation leads to educational benefits will, if adhered to, have serious collateral consequences. The Court relies heavily on social science evidence to justify its deference. The Court never acknowledges, however, the growing evidence that racial (and other sorts) of heterogeneity actually impairs learning among black students.

At oral argument in *Gratz v. Bollinger*, counsel for respondents stated that "most every single one of [the Historically Black Colleges, HBCs] do have diverse student bodies." What precisely counsel meant by "diverse" is indeterminate, but it is reported that in 2000 at Morehouse College, one of the most distinguished HBCs in the Nation, only 0.1 percent of the student body was white, and only 0.2 percent was Hispanic. And at Mississippi Valley State University, a public HBC, only 1.1 percent of the freshman class in 2001 was white. If there is a "critical mass" of whites at these institutions, then "critical mass" is indeed a very small proportion.

The majority grants deference to the Law School's "assessment that diversity will, in fact, yield educational benefits." It follows, therefore, that an HBC's assessment that racial homogeneity will yield educational benefits would similarly be given deference. An HBC's rejection of white applicants in order to maintain racial homogeneity seems permissible, therefore, under the majority's view of the Equal Protection Clause. Contained within today's majority opinion is the seed of a new constitutional justification for a concept I thought long and rightly rejected—racial segregation.

2

Moreover, one would think, in light of the Court's decision in *United States v. Virginia* (1996), that before being given license to use racial discrimination, the Law School would be required to radically reshape its admissions process, even to the point of sacrificing some elements of its character. In *Virginia*, a majority of the Court, without a word about academic freedom, accepted the all-male Virginia Military Institute's (VMI) representation that some changes in its "adversative" method of education would be required with the admission of women, but did not defer to VMI's judgment that these changes would be too great. Instead, the Court concluded that they were "manageable." That case involved sex discrimination, which is subjected to intermediate, not strict, scrutiny. So in *Virginia*, where the standard of review dictated that greater flexibility be granted to VMI's educational policies than the Law School deserves here, this Court gave no deference. Apparently where the status quo being defended is that of the elite establishment—here the Law School—rather than a less fashionable Southern military institution, the Court will defer without serious inquiry and without regard to the applicable legal standard.

C

Virginia is also notable for the fact that the Court relied on the "experience" of formerly single-sex institutions, such as the service academies, to conclude that admission of women to VMI would be "manageable." Today, however, the majority ignores the "experience" of those institutions that have been forced to abandon explicit racial discrimination in admissions.

The sky has not fallen at Boalt Hall at the University of California, Berkeley, for example. Prior to Proposition 209's adoption of Cal. Const., Art. 1, § 31(a), which bars the State from "granting preferential treatment . . . on the basis of race . . . in the operation of . . . public education," Boalt Hall enrolled 20 blacks and 28 Hispanics in its first-year class for 1996. In 2002, without deploying express racial discrimination in admissions, Boalt's entering class enrolled 14 blacks and 36 Hispanics. [University of California Law and Medical School Enrollments (available at http://www.ucop.edu/acadadv/ datamgmt/ lawmed/ law-enrolls-eth2.html.)] Total underrepresented minority student enrollment at Boalt Hall now exceeds 1996 levels. Apparently the Law School cannot be counted on to be as resourceful. The Court is willfully blind to the very real experience in California and elsewhere, which raises the inference that institutions with "reputations for excellence," rivaling the Law School's have satisfied their sense of mission without resorting to prohibited racial discrimination.

V

Putting aside the absence of any legal support for the majority's reflexive deference, there is much to be said for the view that the use of tests and other measures to "predict" academic performance is a poor substitute for a system that gives every applicant a chance to prove he can succeed in the study of law. The rallying cry that in the absence of racial discrimination in admissions there would be a true meritocracy ignores the fact that the entire process is poisoned by numerous exceptions to "merit." For example, in the national debate on racial discrimination in higher education admissions, much has been made of the fact that elite institutions utilize a so-called legacy preference to give the children of alumni an advantage in admissions. This and other exceptions to a "true" meritocracy give the lie to protestations that merit admissions are in fact the order of the day at the nation's universities. The Equal Protection Clause does not, however, prohibit the use of unseemly legacy preferences or many other kinds of arbitrary admissions procedures. What the Equal Protection Clause does prohibit are classifications made on the basis of race. So while legacy preferences can stand under the Constitution, racial discrimination cannot. I will not twist the Constitution to invalidate legacy preferences or otherwise impose my vision of higher education admissions on the nation. The majority should similarly stay its impulse to validate faddish racial discrimination the Constitution clearly forbids.

In any event, there is nothing ancient, honorable, or constitutionally protected about "selective" admissions. The University of Michigan should be well aware that alternative methods have historically been used for the admission of students, for it brought to this country the German certificate system in the late-nineteenth century. Under this system, a secondary school was certified by a university so that any graduate who completed the course offered by the school was offered admission to the university. The certification regime supplemented, and later virtually replaced (at least in the Midwest), the prior regime of rigorous subject-matter entrance examinations. The facially race-neutral "percent plans" now used in Texas, California, and Florida, are in many ways the descendents [*sic*] of the certificate system.

Certification was replaced by selective admissions in the beginning of the twentieth century, as universities sought to exercise more control over the composition of their student bodies. Since its inception, selective admissions has been the vehicle for racial, ethnic, and religious tinkering and experimentation by university administrators. The initial driving force for the relocation of the selective function from the high school to the universities was the same desire to select racial winners and losers that the Law School exhibits today. Columbia, Harvard, and others infamously determined that they had "too many" Jews, just as today the Law School argues it would have "too many" whites if it could not discriminate in its admissions process.

Columbia employed intelligence tests precisely because Jewish applicants, who were predominantly immigrants, scored worse on such tests. Thus, Columbia could claim (falsely) that " 'we have not eliminated boys because they were Jews and do not propose to do so. We have honestly attempted to eliminate the lowest grade of applicant [through the use of intelligence testing] and it turns out that a good many of the low grade men are New York City Jews.' "

Similarly, no modern law school can claim ignorance of the poor performance of blacks, relatively speaking, on the Law School Admissions Test (LSAT). Nevertheless, law schools continue to use the test and then attempt to "correct" for black underperformance by using racial discrimination in admissions so as to obtain their aesthetic student body. The Law School's continued adherence to measures it knows produce racially skewed results is not entitled to deference by this Court. The Law School itself admits that the test is imperfect, as it must, given that it regularly admits students who score at or below 150 (the national median) on the test (between 1995 and 2000, the Law School admitted 37 students—27 of whom were black; 31 of whom were "underrepresented minorities"—with LSAT scores of 150 or lower). . . .

Having decided to use the LSAT, the Law School must accept the constitutional burdens that come with this decision. The Law School may freely continue to employ the LSAT and other allegedly merit-based standards in whatever fashion it likes. What the Equal Protection Clause forbids, but the Court today allows, is the use of these standards hand in hand with racial discrimination. An infinite variety of admissions methods are available to the Law School. Considering all of the radical thinking that has historically occurred at this country's universities, the Law School's intractable approach toward admissions is striking.

The Court will not even deign to make the Law School try other methods, however, preferring instead to grant a twenty-five-year license to violate the Constitution. And the same Court that had the courage to order the desegregation of all public schools in the South now fears, on the basis of platitudes rather than principle, to force the Law School to abandon a decidedly imperfect admissions regime that provides the basis for racial discrimination.

VI

The absence of any articulated legal principle supporting the majority's principal holding suggests another rationale. I believe what lies beneath the Court's decision today are the benighted notions that one can tell when racial discrimination benefits (rather than hurts) minority groups, and that racial discrimination is necessary to remedy general societal ills. This Court's precedents supposedly settled both issues, but clearly the majority still cannot commit to the principle that racial classifications are per se harmful and that almost no amount of benefit in the eye of the beholder can justify such classifications.

Putting aside what I take to be the Court's implicit rejection of *Adarand*'s holding that beneficial and burdensome racial classifications are equally invalid, I must contest the notion that the Law School's discrimination benefits those admitted as a result of it. The Court spends considerable time discussing the impressive display of amicus support for the Law School, in this case from all corners of society. But nowhere in any of the filings in this Court is any evidence that the purported "beneficiaries" of this racial discrimination prove themselves by performing at (or even near) the same level as those students who receive no preferences.

The silence in this case is deafening to those of us who view higher education's purpose as imparting knowledge and skills to students, rather than a communal, rubber-stamp, credentialing process. The Law School is not looking for those students who, despite a lower LSAT score or undergraduate grade point average, will succeed in the study of law. The Law School seeks only a facade—it is sufficient that the class looks right, even if it does not perform right.

The Law School tantalizes unprepared students with the promise of a University of Michigan degree and all of the opportunities that it offers. These overmatched students take the bait, only to find that they cannot succeed in the cauldron of competition. And this mismatch crisis is not restricted to elite institutions. Indeed, to cover the tracks of the aestheticists, this cruel farce of racial discrimination must continue—in selection for the Michigan Law Review, and in hiring at law firms and for judicial clerkships—until the "beneficiaries" are no longer tolerated. While these students may graduate with law degrees, there is no evidence that they have received a qualitatively better legal education (or become better lawyers) than if they had gone to a less "elite" law school for which they were better prepared. And the aestheticists will never address the real problems facing "underrepresented minorities," instead continuing their social experiments on other people's children.

Beyond the harm the Law School's racial discrimination visits upon its test subjects, no social science has disproved the notion that this discrimination "engenders attitudes of superiority or, alternatively, provokes resentment among those who believe that they have been wronged by the government's use of race. These programs stamp minorities with a badge of inferiority and may cause them to develop dependencies or to adopt an attitude that they are 'entitled' to preferences" (quoted in *Adarand*).

It is uncontested that each year the Law School admits a handful of blacks who would be admitted in the absence of racial discrimination. Who can differentiate between those who belong and those who do not? The majority of blacks are admitted to the Law School because of discrimination, and because of this policy all are tarred as undeserving. This problem of stigma does not depend on determinacy as to whether those stigmatized are actually the "benefici-aries" of racial discrimination. When blacks take positions in the highest places of government, industry, or academia, it is an open question today whether their skin color played a part in their advancement. The question itself is the stigma—because either racial discrimination did play a role, in which case the person may be deemed "otherwise unqualified," or it did not, in which case asking the question itself unfairly marks those blacks who would succeed with-out discrimination. Is this what the Court means by "visibly open"?

Finally, the Court's disturbing reference to the importance of the country's law schools as training grounds meant to cultivate "a set of leaders with legiti-macy in the eyes of the citizenry" through the use of racial discrimination de-serves discussion. As noted earlier, the Court has soundly rejected the remedying of societal discrimination as a justification for governmental use of race. For those who believe that every racial disproportionality in our society is caused by some kind of racial discrimination, there can be no distinction be-tween remedying societal discrimination and erasing racial disproportionalities in the country's leadership caste. And if the lack of proportional racial repre-sentation among our leaders is not caused by societal discrimination, then "fix-ing" it is even less of a pressing public necessity. . . .

[Here Justice Thomas agrees with the majority opinion on two relatively minor points: that discrimination among preferred groups (such as Hispanics and African Americans) is unconstitutional and that after twenty-five years an ad-missions plan such as the Law School's would no longer be "narrowly tailored" (though Thomas argues that is true today as well).]

* * *

For the immediate future, however, the majority has placed its imprimatur on a practice that can only weaken the principle of equality embodied in the Declara-tion of Independence and the Equal Protection Clause. "Our Constitution is color-blind, and neither knows nor tolerates classes among citizens" (*Plessy v. Ferguson*, 1896). It has been nearly 140 years since Frederick Douglass asked the intellectual ancestors of the Law School to "do nothing with us!" and the nation adopted the Fourteenth Amendment. Now we must wait another twenty-five years to see this principle of equality vindicated. I therefore respectfully dis-sent from the remainder of the Court's opinion and the judgment.

Timothy A. Nelsen, Frances P. Kao, Eric J. Gorman, and Amy M. Gardner

Brief of the Clinical Legal Education Association as Amicus Curiae Supporting Respondents, in *Barbara Grutter v. Lee Bollinger, et al.* (2003)[1]

Interest of Amicus Curiae

The Clinical Legal Education Association (CLEA) is a nonprofit organization dedicated to expanding and improving clinical legal education; encouraging, promoting, and supporting clinical legal research and scholarship; and fostering communication among clinical law professors. CLEA works cooperatively with other organizations interested in improving clinical and legal education, as well as the legal system itself. CLEA currently counts as members more than 600 clinical law professors nationwide, who teach at approximately 180 of the 186 law schools accredited by the American Bar Association (ABA).

Personal experience, student feedback, and the academic analyses and writings of CLEA's members demonstrate that viewpoint diversity and racial diversity are critically important in training young lawyers to be effective advisors and advocates, both while studying in the legal clinics of America's law schools, and after graduation, when new lawyers enter the increasingly multicultural, multijurisdictional, and global practice of law.

CLEA believes that, should admissions practices such as the one adopted by The University of Michigan Law School (the "Law School") be forbidden, it would be extremely difficult, if not impossible, to achieve the necessary diversity in the student bodies of our law schools. As this brief explains, diverse law school student bodies aid all law students, majority and minority alike, by enhancing their exposure to people from different backgrounds and perspectives. This exposure to different backgrounds and perspectives, in turn, better equips students to render competent, ethical representation to all of their clients. . . .

Argument

To be constitutional, the Law School's consideration of race in its admissions process must (1) be a narrowly tailored measure and (2) serve a compelling governmental interest. This brief will address only the compelling state interests served by the Law School's policy as it affects law school clinics and their clients.

I. The State Has a Compelling Interest in Enrolling a Diverse Law School Student Body

A. All Law Students Benefit from Racially and Ethnically Diverse Student Bodies

All students, regardless of ethnic origin, benefit from a diverse law school student body because it provides exposure to people different from themselves. A diverse law school student body allows all students opportunities to learn to work with people of different backgrounds—a critical skill as the practice of law becomes more multicultural. Indeed, some estimates predict that the percentage of persons of color in the United States population will roughly equal the percentage of Caucasians as early as the year 2030. As a result of the demographic shift, the need for clinical educators to prepare law students to represent all clients and to understand their points of view fully will become increasingly important, "because that pluralism often introduces an extra layer of complexity to legal disputes and may create special challenges in representing diverse clients."

Further, a diverse collection of law students creates opportunities for those students, in their clinical, classroom, journal, and social interactions, to confront their own stereotypes and prejudices, and gain the ability to better critically analyze their own views. These benefits are particularly important in the clinical setting, where student-lawyers see firsthand how their own stereotypes and assumptions may impede their obligation to render ethically competent representation to, and to communicate with, clients as required by ethics rules.

B. The Focus of Clinical Legal Education Is to Prepare Student-Lawyers to Enter into a Multicultural, Global Legal Profession

In explaining why diversity is so critical to clinical legal education, there first must be an assessment of the goal for which law schools in general and clinical educators in particular are preparing students. Clearly, that goal is to become highly skilled, effective, and responsible attorneys, whether in private practice, business, government, or in some other capacity.

Since the United States is multicultural, and is becoming increasingly so, the practice of law must take this fact into account. As an objective and practical matter, the legal profession also is increasingly becoming global. Regardless of the context, lawyers are more and more faced with arrays of problems that involve multicultural considerations, from traditional constructs of contract or tort law, to providing assistance to individuals from different racial and ethnic backgrounds to enforce consumer rights or procure housing, to the criminal prosecution or defense of people of different racial backgrounds. As for private law firms, the multicultural practice is even more significant. "The question is not . . . whether or not diversity is 'good for business' but rather whether global law firms can successfully adapt to a competitive environment that will by any measure be more multicultural, multidisciplinary, and multidimensional than anything that these firms have ever faced before."

As both society and the profession become more diverse, "it will be incumbent upon lawyers to seek out and give voice to a range of viewpoints in stating legal problems and fashioning their solutions." Proper clinical education must equip students to do just this in order to practice effectively, both as student-lawyers and as future lawyers. It is from this pragmatic clinical education goal that the need for diversity arises.

* * *

[Here the brief cites the importance of clinical education, quoting Justice O'Connor.]

1. Law School Clinics Serve a Predominantly Minority Client Base   American law school clinics generally represent underprivileged clients. Depending on the law school program, student-lawyers in law clinics may be expected to defend indigent criminal defendants, or to work on cases involving child advocacy, poverty law, low-income housing, civil rights, and asylum and refugee law. The reality is that, in most instances, 60 percent or more of the underprivileged clients who use the services of law clinics consist of minorities with cultural and economic backgrounds, education levels, viewpoints, and sensibilities different from the student-lawyer. This exposure to a largely minority client base is frequently the first step in preparing young lawyers to enter the multicultural national legal market and the growing global legal profession in which they may routinely be faced with clients and problems that require a genuine ability to understand diverse cultural and racial sensibilities.

2. Student-Lawyers are Better Able to Provide Effective Client-Centered Counseling with Exposure to a Diverse Population of Law Students

(a) Client-Centered Counseling Demands Genuine Understanding of Each Client's Interests and Objectives   Over the last decade, the vast majority of law school clinical programs have concluded that the lawyer-client relationship requires a client-centered approach. A central tenet of this approach is for lawyers to communicate—and connect—with clients in a manner that elicits disclosure of complete and accurate information. Armed with this information, lawyers are better able to understand their clients' motives and best pursue their clients' true interests and objectives, not simply interests or objectives that lawyers may believe their clients have or should have.

(b) Viewpoint and Racial Diversity Are Critical to Student-Lawyers' Self-Evaluation of Biases that Might Hinder Effective Client Representation   For client-centered counseling to be successful in a law school clinic setting, student-lawyers need fully and accurately to understand their clients' viewpoints within the clients' own contextual experiences. This understanding is essential for student-lawyers to formulate case strategies designed to achieve the goals that are most important to their clients. Moreover, without such understanding, student-lawyers are unable to convey their clients' viewpoints and experiences accurately to opposing counsel and parties, as well as judges and juries.

The achievement of these objectives is almost necessarily predicated on the presence in the law school of a truly diverse student body. Student-lawyers working in the areas of, for example, poverty law, welfare law, child advocacy, immigration, and refugee law meet many clients who have backgrounds and experiences totally foreign to, and often difficult even to comprehend by, many or most law students.

With backgrounds that fall all along the spectrum of privilege, many law students may also have subconscious biases regarding race, culture, social status, wealth, and poverty. To understand and communicate effectively with clients from backgrounds vastly different from their own, student-lawyers must first be able to identify their own biases. They must then attempt to set aside their biases and to consider the actions and objectives of their clients from the perspectives of their clients and in the context of their clients' racial, cultural, and socio-economic backgrounds.

For the student-lawyer, the process of self-identification and analysis often begins and progresses through discourse with a racially, culturally, and socio-economically diverse mix of fellow student-lawyers. It is through this discourse that students test their own perceptions about race, poverty, and culture against those of their peers. This discourse enables student-lawyers to understand how race and culture can form clients' (and their own) worldviews and influence clients' (and their own) actions and objectives. Such a discourse also enables student-lawyers to understand that there is no single, uniform minority viewpoint held generally by members of a minority group, just as there is no single "white" viewpoint. In essence, having a diversity of viewpoints teaches student-lawyers to recognize personal bias, eliminate reliance on stereotypes, and undertake an unencumbered evaluation of each client's background and problems to achieve each client's unique objective.

Studies have shown that members of minority groups often view a given set of facts differently than do non-minorities. Furthermore, race can even play a role in the way employees perceive feedback from their superiors. Clinical law professors believe it imperative for this discourse and self-identification to begin early in lawyers' training. Indeed, where student-lawyers enter into attorney-client relationships without being aware of their own cultural perspectives, whatever they might be, myriads of harm can result to clients.

Additionally, early exposure to diverse viewpoints and discourse enhances the abilities of student-lawyers to consider and resolve problems and teaches students to reexamine assumed solutions and develop creative approaches to clients' unique needs. The benefits conferred by a racially diverse law student body thus far outweigh the benefits of admitting only law students who, say, scored above 172 on the Law School Admissions Test (LSAT).

The consequences of failing to provide law students with a diverse student body, from a clinical law perspective, are real and immediate. When student-lawyers represent clients of different cultural backgrounds, and make judgments based on misinformation or inability to appreciate the clients' cultural norms, they run the risk of "misjudging a client or . . . providing differential representation based on stereotype or bias."

3. Law Students Have Experienced the Benefits of Racial Diversity   The benefits of racial diversity in law schools have been recognized not only by clinical law professors and admissions deans, but by law students themselves. Law students—the intended beneficiaries of both legal education and law school diversity—report that exposure to racial diversity has enhanced their abilities to

analyze problems and find solutions to legal issues. Furthermore, law students recognize that a diverse law school student body can prepare them for the multicultural practice they will enter upon graduation. For example, in a survey of students at The University of Michigan Law School and Harvard Law School, 72 percent of students at Michigan, and 67 percent of students at Harvard, agreed that having a racially diverse law school student body had enhanced their abilities to work more effectively and get along better with individuals of other racial backgrounds.

"Confronting different opinions and taking ideas very seriously are hallmarks of a good education. This is all the more true for legal education, where students need to understand all sides of conflicts and how to argue difficult issues in contentious, high-stakes settings." Again, 68 percent of Harvard law students and 75 percent of Michigan law students believe that conflicts because of racial differences challenged them to rethink their own values. It is exactly this confrontation and reevaluation of beliefs that is so critical to properly training student-lawyers and, ultimately, enhancing their ability to promote fairness and work equity in the legal system.

D. Enrolling a Critical Mass of Minority Law Students Requires Law Schools to Consider Applicants as Complete Individuals, and to Weigh the Contributions Each Student Can Make to the Law School as a Whole

Close to two centuries of overt discrimination—including criminal sanctions for educating minorities, and enforced segregation—against disfavored minority groups in this country have resulted in an elementary and secondary educational system whose well-documented shortcomings fall disproportionately on the very minority groups the Law School's policy seeks to help admit. As petitioner's own amicus admits, there is an "enormous academic gap" between minority and majority secondary students, and "most black and Hispanic students operate at a huge academic disadvantage"—to the extent they stay in school at all.

Saddled with these obstacles, it is little wonder that applicants from disfavored minority groups often score lower on standardized tests than majority students. Consequently, an admissions system based solely on LSAT numbers and undergraduate grade-point averages (UGPA) may not yield a student body with a critical mass of minority students.

To realize the benefits of diversity, law schools must be allowed to consider applicants as complete individuals—individuals who, among other things, come from particular racial and ethnic backgrounds and experiences. Law schools must not, as petitioner urges, be restricted to considering only such limited and incomplete data as LSAT scores and UGPA. Although petitioner's argument assumes that such cramped criteria "objectively" measure so-called merit, that assumption, and the resulting argument, cannot withstand scrutiny. At best, such scores present a severely limited view of law school applicants, and the qualities each prospective student would bring to his law school studies, the student body, and the law school as a whole.

Heedless of the warnings provided by the very people who draft and administer petitioner's preferred tests, petitioner urges the Court to declare a legal rule forbidding law schools from considering applicants' racial and ethnic backgrounds. Petitioner's assumption that "merit" can be reduced to a series of numbers makes all the more ironic her effort to seize the mantle of equal protection and individual opportunity.

Petitioner assumes, without support, that barring law schools from considering individual applicants' racial and ethnic backgrounds, and the contributions such backgrounds make to legal education (especially clinical legal education), would allow for the enrollment of more qualified law students. While such a practice might result in higher average LSAT and UGPA numbers, however, higher numbers are not necessarily indicative of greater merit. Indeed, there is no suggestion, and no evidence, that minority students admitted as part of the Law School's critical mass approach are unqualified for the study or practice of law, or inadequate for admission to the Law School. On the contrary, the record below demonstrates that minority students perform well in law school, graduate, and go on to successful careers in the law.

As a result, donning the blinders demanded by petitioner would not result in the matriculation of more qualified law students. In fact, such a limited view of applicants would actually compromise the legal education applicants seek, by depriving all law students, and especially clinical law students and their clients, of the essential leavening factor of diversity.

II. The Benefits of Diversity Cannot Materialize Without a Critical Mass of Minority Students

A. Critical Mass Is Not a Quota

Petitioner and her amici strain to equate the concept of "critical mass" with a quota system. Quotas, they argue, cannot withstand constitutional scrutiny because they have the purpose and effect of directly benefitting members of a pre-ferred group at the expense of others outside the preferred group.

These arguments mischaracterize the Law School's admissions practices. Critical mass is not a quota system. As the Law School discusses in its own sub-mission, there are no seats set aside for minorities, nor was the critical mass goal designed to act as a functional equivalent of a quota.

In any event, petitioner's "quota" argument does not square with what CLEA understands and believes to be the rationale behind the Law School's ad-missions program, and is certainly inapplicable to the rationale behind CLEA's interest in significant diversity: to attain a critical mass of diverse students for purposes of clinical training.

B. A Critical Mass of Minority Students Is Necessary to Realize the Benefits of Diversity

The Law School's admissions policy was adopted to aid the school in achieving its stated goal of attaining a diverse student body, a goal whose legitimacy was explicitly approved in *Bakke*. Witnesses testified in the district court that "racial diversity is part of the diversity of perspectives needed to enhance the 'classroom dynamic.' " They testified that a "critical mass" of minority students is required to achieve this diversity of perspectives because minority students need to "feel free to express their views, rather than to state 'expected views' or 'politically correct views.' " Indeed, they testified that "when a critical mass of minority students are present, racial stereotypes are dismantled because non-minority students see that there is no 'minority viewpoint.' " Thus, based on the record below, it is apparent that the benefits to be obtained from a criti-cal mass are by no means intended by the Law School to inure wholly to mi-nority students. Rather, the concept of critical mass is designed to enhance the legal education of every student in the Law School.

From the perspective of CLEA, the benefit to minority students of having a critical mass of such students is no greater (and no less) than the benefit re-ceived by majority students. As explained above, a multiplicity of viewpoints helps each student to test his or her own viewpoints and perspectives by demonstrating both that minorities can and do have world views and experi-ences that are foreign to majority students, and vice versa, and that there is no single minority opinion or experience, just as there is no single majority view. The "robust exchange of ideas" brought about by diversity and exposure to di-versity are particularly "central to clinical legal education which focuses on lawyering in an increasingly pluralistic and multicultural society and which usually entails small classes and interactive and collaborative educational experiences."

The issue then becomes whether these benefits can exist without a critical mass of minority students. Both academic research and the experiences of clinical law professors tend to show that they cannot.

In a more formal—classroom or clinical—setting, in the absence of a critical mass of minority students, minority students often feel a lack of support in voicing an opinion and, as a result, suppress their opinions. When this self-censoring takes place, the opportunity to hear, challenge, and learn from differing perspectives is lost. The educational experiences of all students are made immeasurably poorer by such suppression of divergent opinions.

A "critical mass" of minority students is also essential in order for all students to be able to be exposed to differing perspectives in the various informal settings that are central to the educational process. A small number of minority students is simply insufficient to provide the opportunities for interaction with much larger numbers of non-minority students on a routine basis in unstructured, relaxed settings. Such settings often provide the opportunity for much more open, frank, and intense discourses and learning than does a structured classroom (or even a clinical) setting, and in the views of many represents the paradigm of the university experience.

III. Enrolling a Critical Mass of Minority Law Students Is Essential to Fostering and Maintaining Public Confidence in America's Legal System

In a legal and political system, such as ours, that depends in large part on the consent of the governed, it is critically important to foster and maintain the public's sense that the law and the legal system are impartial, fair, and legitimate. Indeed, the effectiveness of the legal system, and legal service providers, depends on the trust, confidence, respect, and cooperation of this nation's citizens. Gaining that trust, confidence, respect, and cooperation, however, depends in large measure on building a legal system that includes judges, lawyers, jury members, and other participants of all races and backgrounds.

Attaining a diverse student body in the clinics of America's law schools can make important contributions in regaining trust and respect for the legal system among minorities. . . . [L]aw school clinics tend to serve a predominantly poor and minority client base. Serving that client base effectively, with a racially and ethnically diverse group of student-lawyers who represent their clients through the client-centered approach utilized by many law school clinics, is important in rebuilding minority clients' confidence and trust in the legal system. In addition to the representation provided directly by law school clinics, the graduates of those clinics also continue to play a role in serving the legal needs of minorities and the poor. For example, Justice O'Connor has cited the experiences of her former clerks who participated in law school clinical programs. "As my former clerks describe it, once they are in private practice, they miss the feeling of personal connection they got out of their clinical work in school. They recapture that feeling by taking on a steady stream of pro bono clients, which in turn benefits all of us."

Finally, it is axiomatic that to have a racially and ethnically diverse legal system, the law schools themselves—the only source of lawyers—must also reflect that diversity. Pluralism among federal and state judges, law professors, prosecutors, public defenders, lawyers for government agencies, corporate general counsel, and attorneys in private law firms necessarily depends on true diversity being achieved in America's law schools. It is equally true that for racial and ethnic diversity to seep into the highest, most prestigious positions in our legal system, minority law students must attain a critical mass at America's elite law schools, including the University of Michigan Law School, because the graduates of such law schools disproportionately occupy these positions. For these reasons, too, enrolling a critical mass of minority law students is a compelling state interest.

Conclusion

"Although the law is a highly learned profession . . . it is an intensely practical one. The law school, the proving ground for legal learning and practice, cannot be effective in isolation from the individuals and institutions with which the law interacts." For decades, clinical educators have known that they and the student-lawyers they teach, cannot, as a practical matter, properly deliver legal services to their predominantly minority client base if student-lawyers have not learned to evaluate their own biases and engage in value-neutral communication with clients. These skills do not develop in a vacuum. Indeed, they can be instilled only when there is a genuine, critical mass of diversity in the law school class—the people with whom law students relate on a day-to-day basis.

In the interests of properly and rigorously training the next generation of lawyers, CLEA respectfully requests that the Court affirm the decision of the Court of Appeals.

QUESTIONS

1. *What would you do?* There were four clear votes in the *Grutter v. Bollinger* case to uphold affirmative action in higher education and four votes to strike it down. If you were Justice O'Connor, how would you have decided this case? To what extent should race be used as a "plus factor" to promote racial diversity and viewpoint diversity, if at all? How would you justify your decision?

2. Is viewpoint diversity an important goal? Think of your own experiences from high school and college. Has racial diversity contributed to viewpoint diversity? What else does? Should admissions procedures take these other factors into account?

3. Do you think that "reverse discrimination" (that is, discrimination against whites because of affirmative action policies) is a problem? Should today's generation help compensate for past discrimination?

4. Justices Thomas and Rehnquist both made the argument that the state of Michigan does not have a compelling interest in having an elite law school. The simple answer, they argue, is to lower their admissions standards overall, given that the school already admits students who fall below the "standards." Then slots can be allocated randomly to students who meet the lower threshold for admissions. Would this be a good approach?

5. Some states have used a "10 percent solution" to the issue of racial diversity in higher education. That is, any student who graduates in the top 10 percent of his or her high school class is admitted into the top public university in the state. What are the merits and disadvantages to this approach compared to using race as a "plus factor" in the admissions decision?

6

Public Opinion: Is a Polarized America Myth or Reality?

The idea of a "culture war" in the United States has been around for some time. In 1992, Patrick Buchanan famously stated at the Republican National Convention that the United States was in the midst of a culture war that posited traditional, conservative social values against liberal, secular values. Bill Clinton's defeat of President George H. W. Bush seemed to defuse that idea: Clinton was a southern Democrat who had pushed his party toward the ideological center and, although only garnering 43 percent of the vote, he won states in all regions of the country. His 1996 victory was broader, adding states he had lost in 1992. In the 2000 presidential election, however, a striking regional pattern emerged in the results. Al Gore, the Democratic candidate, did well on the coasts and in the upper Midwest, while George W. Bush, the Republican candidate, picked up the remaining states. Many analysts were struck by this "blue state/red state" pattern—named after the coloring of the states on post-election maps—and suggested that it told us something more fundamental about American politics. Indeed, these analysts argued, Patrick Buchanan was in large measure right: the American public was deeply divided and polarized and in many respects living in two different worlds culturally. This polarization showed up not only in voting, but in presidential approval ratings, with the partisan gap in evaluations of Bill Clinton and George W. Bush being larger than for any previous presidents.

The 2004 presidential election proved to be a near carbon copy of 2000: with a few exceptions, the red states stayed red and the blue states stayed blue. President Bush picked up the votes of 78 percent of white, born-again evangelical Christians, while John Kerry received the support of 56 percent of all other voters. Bush received 60 percent of the votes of those individuals attending religious services at least once weekly; Kerry picked up 57 percent of the votes of individuals who attended services a few times a year or not at all. Eighty-five percent of conservatives voted for Bush; the same percentage of liberals voted for Kerry. Moderates split 54–45 percent for Kerry. Among those who believe abortion should be illegal in most or all cases, Bush received 75 percent of the vote. Among those who believe abortion should be legal in most or all cases, Kerry received 66 percent.

Is America deeply polarized along partisan lines on the important issues of the day? Is there a culture war? Is the red state/blue state split real? Is there division on certain highly charged issues but not on most others? Are the political elite polarized, while the general public is relatively moderate? In this debate, political scientists James Q. Wilson and Morris Fiorina agree that the political elite—elected leaders, the media, and interest groups—are polarized, but they disagree on the answers to the rest of the questions. Wilson argues that the cultural split is deep and is reflected in party competition and the public opinion of partisans within and across the red and blue states. Fiorina counters that the idea of a cultural war is vastly exaggerated—there might be a skirmish, but there is no war.

Morris P. Fiorina
What Culture Wars? Debunking the Myth of a Polarized America

"There is a religious war going on in this country, a cultural war as critical to the kind of nation we shall be as the Cold War itself, for this war is for the soul of America."

With those ringing words insurgent candidate Pat Buchanan fired up his supporters at the 1992 Republican National Convention. To be sure, not all delegates cheered Buchanan's call to arms, which was at odds with the "kinder,

Published in *The Wall Street Journal*, 2004.

gentler" image that George H. W. Bush had attempted to project. Election analysts later included Buchanan's fiery words among the factors contributing to
the defeat of President Bush, albeit one of lesser importance than the slow economy and the repudiation of his "Read my lips, no new taxes" pledge.

In the years since Buchanan's declaration of cultural war, the idea of a clash
of cultures has become a common theme in discussions of American politics.
The culture war metaphor refers to a displacement of the classic economic conflicts that animated twentieth-century politics in the advanced democracies by
newly emergent moral and cultural ones. The literature generally attributes
Buchanan's inspiration to a 1991 book, *Culture Wars*, by sociologist James
Davison Hunter, who divided Americans into the culturally "orthodox" and
the culturally "progressive" and argued that increasing conflict was inevitable.

No one has embraced the concept of the culture war more enthusiastically
than journalists, ever alert for subjects that have "news value." Conflict is high
in news value. Disagreement, division, polarization, battles, and war make
good copy. Agreement, consensus, moderation, compromise, and peace do not.
Thus, the notion of a culture war fits well with the news sense of journalists
who cover politics. Their reports tell us that contemporary voters are sharply
divided on moral issues. As David Broder wrote in the *Washington Post* in November 2000, "The divide went deeper than politics. It reached into the nation's psyche . . . It was the moral dimension that kept Bush in the race."

Additionally, it is said that close elections do not reflect indifferent or ambivalent voters; rather, such elections reflect evenly matched blocs of deeply
committed partisans. According to a February 2002 report in *USA Today*,
"When George W. Bush took office, half the country cheered and the other half
seethed"; some months later the *Economist* wrote that "such political divisions
cannot easily be shifted by any president, let alone in two years, because they
reflect deep demographic divisions. . . . The 50-50 nation appears to be made
up of two big, separate voting blocks, with only a small number of swing voters in the middle."

The 2000 election brought us the familiar pictorial representation of the
culture war in the form of the "red" and "blue" map of the United States. Vast
areas of the heartland appeared as Republican red, while coastal and Great
Lakes states took on a Democratic blue hue. Pundits reified the colors on the
map, treating them as prima facie evidence of deep cultural divisions: Thus
"Bush knew that the landslide he had wished for in 2000 . . . had vanished into
the values chasm separating the blue states from the red ones" (John Kenneth

White, in *The Values Divide*). In the same vein, the *Boston Herald* reported Clinton adviser Paul Begala as saying, on November 18, 2000, that "tens of millions of good people in Middle America voted Republican. But if you look closely at that map you see a more complex picture. You see the state where James Byrd was lynch-dragged behind a pickup truck until his body came apart—it's red. You see the state where Matthew Shepard was crucified on a split-rail fence for the crime of being gay—it's red. You see the state where right-wing extremists blew up a federal office building and murdered scores of federal employees—it's red."

Claims of bitter national division were standard fare after the 2000 elections, and few commentators publicly challenged them. On the contrary, the belief in a fractured nation was expressed even by high-level political operatives. Republican pollster Bill McInturff commented to the *Economist* in January 2001 that "we have two massive colliding forces. One is rural, Christian, religiously conservative. [The other] is socially tolerant, pro-choice, secular, living in New England and the Pacific Coast." And Matthew Dowd, a Bush re-election strategist, explained to the *Los Angeles Times* why Bush has not tried to expand his electoral base: "You've got 80 to 90 percent of the country that look at each other like they are on separate planets."

The journalistic drumbeat continues unabated. A November 2003 report from the Pew Research Center led E. J. Dionne Jr. of the *Washington Post* to comment: "The red states get redder, the blue states get bluer, and the political map of the United States takes on the coloration of the Civil War."

And as the 2004 election approaches, commentators see a continuation, if not an intensification, of the culture war. *Newsweek*'s Howard Fineman wrote in October 2003, "The culture war between the Red and Blue Nations has erupted again—big time—and will last until Election Day next year. Front lines are all over, from the Senate to the Pentagon to Florida to the Virginia suburbs where, at the Bush-Cheney 2004 headquarters, they are blunt about the shape of the battle: 'The country's split 50–50 again,' a top aide told me, 'just as it was in 2000.' "

In sum, observers of contemporary American politics have apparently reached a new consensus around the proposition that old disagreements about economics now pale in comparison to new divisions based on sexuality, morality, and religion, divisions so deep and bitter as to justify talk of war in describing them.

Yet research indicates otherwise. Publicly available databases show that the

culture war script embraced by journalists and politicos lies somewhere be-
tween simple exaggeration and sheer nonsense. There is no culture war in the
United States; no battle for the soul of America rages, at least none that most
Americans are aware of.

Certainly, one can find a few warriors who engage in noisy skirmishes.
Many of the activists in the political parties and the various cause groups do
hate each other and regard themselves as combatants in a war. But their hatreds
and battles are not shared by the great mass of Americans—certainly nowhere
near "80–90 percent of the country"—who are for the most part moderate in
their views and tolerant in their manner. A case in point: To their embarrassment, some GOP senators recently learned that ordinary Americans view gay
marriage in somewhat less apocalyptic terms than do the activists in the Republican base.

If swing voters have disappeared, how did the six blue states in which
George Bush ran most poorly in 2000 all elect Republican governors in 2002
(and how did Arnold Schwarzenegger run away with the 2003 recall in blue
California)? . . . If voter partisanship has hardened into concrete, why do virtually identical majorities in both red and blue states favor divided control of the
presidency and Congress, rather than unified control by their party? Finally,
and ironically, if voter positions have become so uncompromising, why did a
recent CBS story titled "Polarization in America" report that 76 percent of Republicans, 87 percent of Democrats, and 86 percent of Independents would like
to see elected officials compromise more rather than stick to their principles?

Still, how does one account for reports that have almost 90 percent of Republicans planning to vote for Bush and similarly high numbers of Democrats
planning to vote for Kerry? The answer is that while voter positions have not
polarized, their choices have. There is no contradiction here; positions and
choices are not the same thing. Voter choices are functions of their positions
and the positions and actions of the candidates they choose between.

Republican and Democratic elites unquestionably have polarized. But it is a
mistake to assume that such elite polarization is equally present in the broader
public. It is not. However much they may claim that they are responding to the
public, political elites do not take extreme positions because voters make them.
Rather, by presenting them with polarizing alternatives, elites make voters
appear polarized, but the reality shows through clearly when voters have a
choice of more moderate alternatives—as with the aforementioned Republican
governors.

Republican strategists have bet the Bush presidency on a high-risk gamble. Reports and observation indicate that they are attempting to win in 2004 by getting out the votes of a few million Republican-leaning evangelicals who did not vote in 2000, rather than by attracting some modest proportion of 95 million other non-voting Americans, most of them moderates, not to mention moderate Democratic voters who could have been persuaded to back a genuinely compassionate conservative. Such a strategy leaves no cushion against a negative turn of events and renders the administration vulnerable to a credible Democratic move toward the center. Whether the Democrats can capitalize on their opportunity remains to be seen.

James Q. Wilson
How Divided Are We?

The 2004 election left our country deeply divided over whether our country is deeply divided. For some, America is indeed a polarized nation, perhaps more so today than at any time in living memory. In this view, yesterday's split over Bill Clinton has given way to today's even more acrimonious split between Americans who detest George Bush and Americans who detest John Kerry, and similar divisions will persist as long as angry liberals and angry conservatives continue to confront each other across the political abyss. Others, however, believe that most Americans are moderate centrists, who, although disagreeing over partisan issues in 2004, harbor no deep ideological hostility. I take the former view.

By polarization I do not have in mind partisan disagreements alone. These have always been with us. Since popular voting began in the 19th century, scarcely any winning candidate has received more than 60 percent of the vote, and very few losers have received less than 40 percent. Inevitably, Americans will differ over who should be in the White House. But this does not necessarily mean they are polarized.

By polarization I mean something else: an intense commitment to a candidate, a culture, or an ideology that sets people in one group definitively apart from people in another, rival group. Such a condition is revealed when a candi-

Published in *Commentary*, February 2006.

date for public office is regarded by a competitor and his supporters not simply as wrong but as corrupt or wicked; when one way of thinking about the world is assumed to be morally superior to any other way; when one set of political beliefs is considered to be entirely correct and a rival set wholly wrong. In extreme form, as defined by Richard Hofstadter in *The Paranoid Style in American Politics* (1965), polarization can entail the belief that the other side is in thrall to a secret conspiracy that is using devious means to obtain control over society. Today's versions might go like this: "Liberals employ their dominance of the media, the universities, and Hollywood to enforce a radically secular agenda"; or, "conservatives, working through the religious Right and the big corporations, conspired with their hired neocon advisers to invade Iraq for the sake of oil."

Polarization is not new to this country. It is hard to imagine a society more divided than ours was in 1800, when pro-British, pro-commerce New Englanders supported John Adams for the presidency while pro-French, pro-agriculture Southerners backed Thomas Jefferson. One sign of this hostility was the passage of the Alien and Sedition Acts in 1798; another was that in 1800, just as in 2000, an extremely close election was settled by a struggle in one state (New York in 1800, Florida in 2000).

The fierce contest between Abraham Lincoln and George McClellan in 1864 signaled another national division, this one over the conduct of the Civil War. But thereafter, until recently, the nation ceased to be polarized in that sense. Even in the half-century from 1948 to (roughly) 1996, marked as it was by sometimes strong expressions of feeling over whether the presidency should go to Harry Truman or Thomas Dewey, to Dwight Eisenhower or Adlai Stevenson, to John F. Kennedy or Richard Nixon, to Nixon or Hubert Humphrey, and so forth, opinion surveys do not indicate widespread detestation of one candidate or the other, or of the people who supported him.

Now they do. Today, many Americans and much of the press regularly speak of the President as a dimwit, a charlatan, or a knave. A former Democratic presidential candidate has asserted that Bush "betrayed" America by launching a war designed to benefit his friends and corporate backers. A senior Democratic Senator has characterized administration policy as a series of "lies, lies, and more lies" and has accused Bush of plotting a "mindless, needless, senseless, and reckless" war. From the other direction, similar expressions of popular disdain have been directed at Senator John Kerry (and before him at President Bill Clinton); if you have not heard them, that may be because (unlike many of my relatives) you do not live in Arkansas or Texas or other locales where the *New York Times* is not read. In these places, Kerry is widely spoken of as a scoundrel.

In the 2004 presidential election, over two-thirds of Kerry voters said they were motivated explicitly by the desire to defeat Bush. By early 2005, President Bush's approval rating, which stood at 94 percent among Republicans, was only 18 percent among Democrats—the largest such gap in the history of the Gallup poll. These data, moreover, were said to reflect a mutual revulsion between whole geographical sections of the country, the so-called Red (Republican) states versus the so-called Blue (Democratic) states. As summed up by the distinguished social scientist who writes humor columns under the name of Dave Barry, residents of Red states are "ignorant racist fascist knuckle-dragging NASCAR-obsessed cousin-marrying roadkill-eating tobacco-juice-dribbling gun-fondling religious fanatic rednecks," while Blue-state residents are "godless unpatriotic pierced-nose Volvo-driving France-loving leftwing Communist latte-sucking tofu-chomping holistic-wacko neurotic vegan weenie perverts."

To be sure, other scholars differ with Dr. Barry. To them, polarization, although a real enough phenomenon, is almost entirely confined to a small number of political elites and members of Congress. In *Culture War?* (2004), which bears the subtitle "The Myth of a Polarized America," Morris Fiorina of Stanford argues that policy differences between voters in Red and Blue states are really quite small, and that most are in general agreement even on issues like abortion and homosexuality.

But the extent of polarization cannot properly be measured by the voting results in Red and Blue states. Many of these states are in fact deeply divided internally between liberal and conservative areas, and gave the nod to one candidate or the other by only a narrow margin. Inferring the views of individual citizens from the gross results of presidential balloting is a questionable procedure.

Nor does Fiorina's analysis capture the very real and very deep division over an issue like abortion. Between 1973, when *Roe v. Wade* was decided, and now, he writes, there has been no change in the degree to which people will or will not accept any one of six reasons to justify an abortion: (1) the woman's health is endangered; (2) she became pregnant because of a rape; (3) there is a strong chance of a fetal defect; (4) the family has a low income; (5) the woman is not married; and (6) the woman simply wants no more children. Fiorina may be right about that. Nevertheless, only about 40 percent of all Americans will support abortion for any of the last three reasons in his series, while over 80 percent will support it for one or another of the first three.

In other words, almost all Americans are for abortion in the case of maternal emergency, but fewer than half if it is simply a matter of the mother's preference. That split—a profoundly important one—has remained in place for over three decades, and it affects how people vote. In 2000 and again in 2004, 70 percent of those who thought abortion should always be legal voted for Al Gore or John Kerry, while over 70 percent of those who thought it should always be illegal voted for George Bush.

Division is just as great over other high-profile issues. Polarization over the war in Iraq, for example, is more pronounced than any war-related controversy in at least a half-century. In the fall of 2005, according to Gallup, 81 percent of Democrats but only 20 percent of Republicans thought the war in Iraq was a mistake. During the Vietnam war, by contrast, itself a famously contentious cause, there was more unanimity across party lines, whether for or against: in late 1968 and early 1969, about equal numbers of Democrats and Republicans thought the intervention there was a mistake. Pretty much the same was true of Korea: in early 1951, 44 percent of Democrats and 61 percent of Republicans thought the war was a mistake—a partisan split, but nowhere near as large as the one over our present campaign in Iraq.

Polarization, then, is real. But what explains its growth? And has it spread beyond the political elites to influence the opinions and attitudes of ordinary Americans?

The answer to the first question, I suspect, can be found in the changing politics of Congress, the new competitiveness of the mass media, and the rise of new interest groups.

That Congress is polarized seems beyond question. When, in 1998, the House deliberated whether to impeach President Clinton, all but four Republican members voted for at least one of the impeachment articles, while only five Democrats voted for even one. In the Senate, 91 percent of Republicans voted to convict on at least one article; every single Democrat voted for acquittal.

The impeachment issue was not an isolated case. In 1993, President Clinton's budget passed both the House and the Senate without a single Republican vote in favor. The same deep partisan split occurred over taxes and supplemental appropriations. Nor was this a blip: since 1950, there has been a steady increase in the percentage of votes in Congress pitting most Democrats against most Republicans.

In the midst of the struggle to pacify Iraq, Howard Dean, the chairman of the Democratic National Committee, said the war could not be won and Nancy Pelosi, the leader of the House Democrats, endorsed the view that American forces should be brought home as soon as possible. By contrast, although there was congressional grumbling (mostly by Republicans) about Korea and complaints (mostly by Democrats) about Vietnam, and although Senator George Aiken of Vermont famously proposed that we declare victory and withdraw, I cannot remember party leaders calling for unconditional surrender.

The reasons for the widening fissures in Congress are not far to seek. Each of the political parties was once a coalition of dissimilar forces: liberal Northern Democrats and conservative Southern Democrats, liberal coastal Republicans and conservative Midwestern Republicans. No longer; the realignments of the South (now overwhelmingly Republican) and of New England (now strongly Democratic) have all but eliminated legislators who deviate from the party's leadership. Conservative Democrats and liberal Republicans are endangered species now approaching extinction. At the same time, the ideological gap between the parties is growing: if there was once a large overlap between Democrats and Republicans—remember "Tweedledum and Tweedledee"?— today that congruence has almost disappeared. By the late 1990s, virtually every Democrat was more liberal than virtually every Republican.

The result has been not only intense partisanship but a sharp rise in congressional incivility. In 1995, a Republican-controlled Senate passed a budget that President Clinton proceeded to veto; in the loggerhead that followed, many federal agencies shut down (in a move that backfired on the Republicans). Congressional debates have seen an increase not only in heated exchanges but in the number of times a representative's words are either ruled out of order or "taken down" (that is, written by the clerk and then read aloud, with the offending member being asked if he or she wishes to withdraw them).

It has been suggested that congressional polarization is exacerbated by new districting arrangements that make each House seat safe for either a Democratic or a Republican incumbent. If only these seats were truly competitive, it is said, more centrist legislators would be elected. That seems plausible, but David C. King of Harvard has shown that it is wrong: in the House, the more competitive the district, the more extreme the views of the winner. This odd finding is apparently the consequence of a nomination process dominated by party activists. In primary races, where turnout is low (and seems to be getting lower), the ideologically motivated tend to exercise a preponderance of influence.

All this suggests a situation very unlike the half-century before the 1990s, if perhaps closer to certain periods in the eighteenth and nineteenth centuries. Then, too, incivility was common in Congress, with members not only passing the most scandalous remarks about each other but on occasion striking their rivals with canes or fists. Such partisan feeling ran highest when Congress was deeply divided over slavery before the Civil War and over Reconstruction after it. Today the issues are different, but the emotions are not dissimilar.

Next, the mass media: Not only are they themselves increasingly polarized, but consumers are well aware of it and act on that awareness. Fewer people now subscribe to newspapers or watch the network evening news. Although some of this decline may be explained by a preference for entertainment over news, some undoubtedly reflects the growing conviction that the mainstream press generally does not tell the truth, or at least not the whole truth.

In part, media bias feeds into, and off, an increase in business competition. In the 1950s, television news amounted to a brief 30-minute interlude in the day's programming, and not a very profitable one at that; for the rest of the time, the three networks supplied us with westerns and situation comedies. Today, television news is a vast, growing, and very profitable venture by the many broadcast and cable outlets that supply news twenty-four hours a day, seven days a week.

The news we get is not only more omnipresent, it is also more competitive and hence often more adversarial. When there were only three television networks, and radio stations were forbidden by the fairness doctrine from broadcasting controversial views, the media gravitated toward the middle of the ideological spectrum, where the large markets could be found. But now that technology has created cable news and the Internet, and now that the fairness doctrine has by and large been repealed, many media outlets find their markets at the ideological extremes.

Here is where the sharper antagonism among political leaders and their advisers and associates comes in. As one journalist has remarked about the change in his profession, "We don't deal in facts [any longer], but in attributed opinions." Or, these days, in unattributed opinions. And those opinions are more intensely rivalrous than was once the case.

The result is that, through commercial as well as ideological self-interest, the media contribute heavily to polarization. Broadcasters are eager for stories to fill their round-the-clock schedules, and at the same time reluctant to trust the government as a source for those stories. Many media outlets are clearly liberal in their orientation; with the arrival of Fox News and the growth of talk radio, many are now just as clearly conservative.

The evidence of liberal bias in the mainstream media is very strong. The Center for Media and Public Affairs (CMPA) has been systematically studying television broadcasts for a quarter-century. In the 2004 presidential campaign, John Kerry received more favorable mentions than any presidential candidate in CMPA's history, especially during the month before election day. This is not new: since 1980 (and setting aside the recent advent of Fox News), the Democratic candidate has received more favorable mentions than the Republican candidate in every race except the 1988 contest between Michael Dukakis and George H. W. Bush. A similarly clear orientation characterizes weekly newsmagazines like *Time* and *Newsweek*.

For its part, talk radio is listened to by about one-sixth of the adult public, and that one-sixth is made up mostly of conservatives.[1] National Public Radio has an audience of about the same size; it is disproportionately liberal. The same breakdown affects cable-television news, where the rivalry is between CNN (and MSNBC) and Fox News. Those who watch CNN are more likely to be Democrats than Republicans; the reverse is emphatically true of Fox. As for news and opinion on the Internet, which has become an important source for college graduates in particular, it, too, is largely polarized along political and ideological lines, emphasized even more by the culture that has grown up around news blogs.

At one time, our culture was only weakly affected by the media because news organizations had only a few points of access to us and were largely moderate and audience-maximizing enterprises. Today the media have many lines of access, and reflect both the maximization of controversy and the cultivation of niche markets. Once the media talked to us; now they shout at us.

And then there are the interest groups. In the past, the major ones—the National Association of Manufacturers, the Chamber of Commerce, and labor organizations like the AFL-CIO—were concerned with their own material interests. They are still active, but the loudest messages today come from very different sources and have a very different cast to them. They are issued by groups concerned with social and cultural matters like civil rights, managing the environment, alternatives to the public schools, the role of women, access to firearms, and so forth, and they directly influence the way people view politics.

Interest groups preoccupied with material concerns can readily find ways to arrive at compromise solutions to their differences; interest groups divided by issues of rights or morality find compromise very difficult. The positions taken by many of these groups and their supporters, often operating within the two political parties, profoundly affect the selection of candidates for office. In brief, it is hard to imagine someone opposed to abortion receiving the Democratic nomination for President, or someone in favor of it receiving the Republican nomination.

Outside the realm of party politics, interest groups also file briefs in important court cases and can benefit from decisions that in turn help shape the political debate. Abortion became a hot controversy in the 1970s not because the American people were already polarized on the matter but because their (mainly centrist) views were not consulted; instead, national policy was determined by the Supreme Court in a decision, *Roe v. Wade*, that itself reflected a definition of "rights" vigorously promoted by certain well-defined interest groups.

Polarization not only is real and has increased, but it has also spread to rank-and-file voters through elite influence.

In *The Nature and Origins of Mass Opinion* (1992), John R. Zaller of UCLA listed a number of contemporary issues—homosexuality, a nuclear freeze, the war in Vietnam, busing for school integration, the 1990–91 war to expel Iraq from Kuwait—and measured the views held about them by politically aware citizens. (By "politically aware," Zaller meant people who did well answering neutral factual questions about politics.) His findings were illuminating.

Take the Persian Gulf war. Iraq had invaded Kuwait in August 1990. From that point through the congressional elections in November 1990, scarcely any elite voices were raised to warn against anything the United States might contemplate doing in response. Two days after the mid-term elections, however, President George H. W. Bush announced that he was sending many more troops to the Persian Gulf. This provoked strong criticism from some members of Congress, especially Democrats.

As it happens, a major public-opinion survey was under way just as these events were unfolding. Before criticism began to be voiced in Congress, both registered Democrats and registered Republicans had supported Bush's vaguely announced intention of coming to the aid of Kuwait; the more politically aware they were, the greater their support. After the onset of elite criticism, the support of Republican voters went up, but Democratic support flattened out. As Bush became more vigorous in indicating his aims, politically aware voters began to differ sharply, with Democratic support declining and Republican support increasing further.

Much the same pattern can be seen in popular attitudes toward the other issues studied by Zaller. As political awareness increases, attitudes split apart, with, for example, highly aware liberals favoring busing and job guarantees and opposing the war in Vietnam, and highly aware conservatives opposing busing and job guarantees and supporting the war in Vietnam.[2]

But why should this be surprising? To imagine that extremist politics has been confined to the chattering classes is to believe that Congress, the media, and American interest groups operate in an ideological vacuum. I find that assumption implausible.

As for the extent to which these extremist views have spread, that is probably best assessed by looking not at specific issues but at enduring political values and party preferences. In 2004, only 12 percent of Democrats approved of George Bush; at earlier periods, by contrast, three to four times as many Democrats approved of Ronald Reagan, Gerald Ford, Richard Nixon, and Dwight D. Eisenhower. Over the course of about two decades, in other words, party affiliation had come to exercise a critical influence over what people thought about a sitting President.

The same change can be seen in the public's view of military power. Since the late 1980s, Republicans have been more willing than Democrats to say that "the best way to ensure peace is through military strength." By the late 1990s and on into 2003, well over two-thirds of all Republicans agreed with this view, but far fewer than half of all Democrats did. In 2005, three-fourths of all Democrats but fewer than a third of all Republicans told pollsters that good diplomacy was the best way to ensure peace. In the same survey, two-thirds of all Republicans but only one fourth of all Democrats said they would fight for this country "whether it is right or wrong."

Unlike in earlier years, the parties are no longer seen as Tweedledum and Tweedledee. To the contrary, as they sharpen their ideological differences, attentive voters have sharpened their ideological differences. They now like either the Democrats or the Republicans more than they once did, and are less apt to feel neutral toward either one.

How deep does this polarization reach? As measured by opinion polls, the gap between Democrats and Republicans was twice as great in 2004 as in 1972. In fact, rank-and-file Americans disagree more strongly today than did politically active Americans in 1972.

To be sure, this mass polarization involves only a minority of all voters, but the minority is sizable, and a significant part of it is made up of the college-educated. As Marc Hetherington of Vanderbilt puts it: "people with the greatest ability to assimilate new information, those with more formal education, are most affected by elite polarization." And that cohort has undeniably grown.

In 1900, only 10 percent of all young Americans went to high school. My father, in common with many men his age in the early twentieth century, dropped out of school after the eighth grade. Even when I graduated from college, the first in my family to do so, fewer than one-tenth of all Americans over the age of twenty-five had gone that far. Today, 84 percent of adult Americans have graduated from high school and nearly 27 percent have graduated from college. This extraordinary growth in schooling has produced an ever larger audience for political agitation.

Ideologically, an even greater dividing line than undergraduate education is postgraduate education. People who have proceeded beyond college seem to be very different from those who stop with a high-school or college diploma. Thus, about a sixth of all voters describe themselves as liberals, but the figure for those with a postgraduate degree is well over a quarter. In mid-2004, about half of all voters trusted George Bush; less than a third of those with a postgraduate education did. In November of the same year, when over half of all college graduates voted for Bush, well over half of the smaller cohort who had done postgraduate work voted for Kerry. According to the Pew Center for Research on the People and the Press, more than half of all Democrats with a postgraduate education supported the antiwar candidacy of Howard Dean.

The effect of postgraduate education is reinforced by being in a profession. Between 1900 and 1960, write John B. Judis and Ruy Teixeira in *The Emerging Democratic Majority* (2002), professionals voted pretty much the same way as business managers; by 1988, the former began supporting Democrats while the latter supported Republicans. On the other hand, the effect of postgraduate education seems to outweigh the effect of affluence. For most voters, including college graduates, having higher incomes means becoming more conservative; not so for those with a postgraduate education, whose liberal predilections are immune to the wealth effect.

The results of this linkage between ideology, on the one hand, and congressional polarization, media influence, interest-group demands, and education on the other are easily read in the commentary surrounding the 2004 election. In their zeal to denigrate the President, liberals, pronounced one conservative pundit, had "gone quite around the twist." According to liberal spokesmen, conservatives with their "religious intolerance" and their determination to rewrite the Constitution had so befuddled their fellow Americans that a "great nation was felled by a poisonous nut."

If such wholesale slurs are not signs of polarization, then the word has no meaning. To a degree that we cannot precisely measure, and over issues that we cannot exactly list, polarization has seeped down into the public, where it has assumed the form of a culture war. The sociologist James Davison Hunter, who has written about this phenomenon in a mainly religious context, defines culture war as "political and social hostility rooted in different systems of moral understanding." Such conflicts, he writes, which can involve "fundamental ideas about who we are as Americans," are waged both across the religious/secular divide and within religions themselves, where those with an "orthodox" view of moral authority square off against those with a "progressive" view.

To some degree, this terminology is appropriate to today's political situation as well. We are indeed in a culture war in Hunter's sense, though I believe this war is itself but another component, or another symptom, of the larger ideological polarization that has us in its grip. Conservative thinking on political issues has religious roots, but it also has roots that are fully as secular as anything on the Left. By the same token, the liberal attack on conservatives derives in part from an explicitly "progressive" religious orientation—liberal Protestantism or Catholicism, or Reform Judaism—but in part from the same secular sources shared by many conservatives.

But what, one might ask, is wrong with having well-defined parties arguing vigorously about the issues that matter? Is it possible that polarized politics is a good thing, encouraging sharp debate and clear positions? Perhaps that is true on those issues where reasonable compromises can be devised. But there are two limits to such an arrangement.

First, many Americans believe that unbridgeable political differences have prevented leaders from addressing the problems they were elected to address. As a result, distrust of government mounts, leading to an alienation from politics altogether. The steep decline in popular approval of our national officials has many causes, but surely one of them is that ordinary voters agree among themselves more than political elites agree with each other—and the elites are far more numerous than they once were.

In the 1950s, a committee of the American Political Science Association (APSA) argued the case for a "responsible" two-party system. The model the APSA had in mind was the more ideological and therefore more "coherent" party system of Great Britain. At the time, scarcely anyone thought our parties could be transformed in such a supposedly salutary direction. Instead, as Governor George Wallace of Alabama put it in his failed third-party bid for the presidency, there was not a "dime's worth of difference" between Democrats and Republicans.

What Wallace forgot was that, however alike the parties were, the public liked them that way. A half-century ago, Tweedledum and Tweedledee enjoyed the support of the American people; the more different they have become, the greater has been the drop in popular confidence in both them and the federal government.

A final drawback of polarization is more profound. Sharpened debate is arguably helpful with respect to domestic issues, but not for the management of important foreign and military matters. The United States, an unrivaled superpower with unparalleled responsibilities for protecting the peace and defeating terrorists, is now forced to discharge those duties with its own political house in disarray.

We fought World War II as a united nation, even against two enemies (Germany and Italy) that had not attacked us. We began the wars in Korea and Vietnam with some degree of unity, too, although it was eventually whittled away. By the early 1990s, when we expelled Iraq from Kuwait, we had to do so over the objections of congressional critics; the first President Bush avoided putting the issue to Congress altogether. In 2003 we toppled Saddam Hussein in the face of catcalls from many domestic leaders and opinion-makers. Now, in stabilizing Iraq and helping that country create a new free government, we have proceeded despite intense and mounting criticism, much of it voiced by politicians who before the war agreed that Saddam Hussein was an evil menace in possession of weapons of mass destruction and that we had to remove him.

Denmark or Luxembourg can afford to exhibit domestic anguish and uncertainty over military policy; the United States cannot. A divided America encourages our enemies, disheartens our allies, and saps our resolve—potentially to fatal effect. What General Giap of North Vietnam once said of us is even truer today. America cannot be defeated on the battlefield, but it can be defeated at home. Polarization is a force that can defeat us.

Polarized America?

February 21, 2006
To the editor:
James Q. Wilson (February) takes issue with my demonstration in *Culture War? The Myth of a Polarized America* (with Samuel Abrams and Jeremy Pope) that the polarization evident among the members of the American political class has only a faint reflection in the American public. As a long-time admirer of Wilson's work I am naturally concerned when his take on some aspect of American politics differs from mine. But I believe that his criticisms are a result of misunderstanding. I would like to address two of them.

First, Wilson discounts our red state-blue state comparisons with the comment that "Inferring the views of individual citizens from the gross results of presidential balloting is a questionable procedure." Indeed it is, which is why we did not do that. As we wrote in the book, inferring polarization from close elections is precisely what pundits have done and why their conclusions have been wrong. In contrast, we report detailed analyses of the policy views expressed by voters in 2000 and 2004 and contrary to the claims of Garry Wills, Maureen Dowd, and other op-ed columnists, we find surprisingly small differences between the denizens of the blue states and the red states. As we show in the book and emphasize repeatedly, people's *choices* (as expressed, say, in presidential balloting) can be polarized while their *positions* are not, and the evidence strongly indicates that this is the case.

Moreover, we report that not only are red and blue state citizens surprisingly similar in their views, but other studies find little evidence of growing polarization no matter how one slices and dices the population—affluent v. poor, white v. black v. brown, old v. young, well educated v. the less educated, men v. women, and so on. Like many before him, Wilson confuses partisan *sorting* with polarization—the Democrats have largely shed their conservative southern wing while Republicans have largely shed their liberal Rockefeller wing, result-

Published in *Commentary*, May 2006.

ing in more distinct parties, even while the aggregate distribution of ideology and issue stances among the citizenry remains much the same as in the past.

Second, Wilson criticizes our analysis of Americans' views on the specific issue of abortion, contending that the small numerical differences expressed by people on a General Social Survey scale constitute a significantly larger substantive difference. Although we disagree, even if one accepted Wilson's contention, it would not apply to our supporting analysis of a differently-worded Gallup survey item that yields the same conclusions, or to numerous other survey items that clearly show that most Americans are "pro-choice, buts."

For example, Wilson notes that "70 percent of those who thought abortion should always be legal voted for Al Gore or John Kerry, while over 70 percent of those who thought it should always be illegal voted for George Bush." True enough, but he does not mention that Gallup repeatedly finds that a majority of the American people place themselves between those polar categories—they think abortion should be "legal only under certain circumstances." Even limiting the analysis to avowed partisans, in 2005 only 30 percent of Democrats thought abortion should always be legal, and fewer than 30 percent of Republicans thought it should always be illegal. One can raise questions about every survey item that has ever been asked, but the cumulative weight of the evidence on Americans' abortion views is overwhelming. Contrary to the wishes of the activists on both sides, the American people prefer a middle ground on abortion, period.

Wilson approvingly cites James Davison Hunter, whose book, *Culture War*, inspired Patrick Buchanan's 1992 speech at the Republican National Convention. In a forthcoming Brookings Institution volume, Hunter now limits his thesis to "somewhere between 10 and 15 percent who occupy these opposing moral and ideological universes." That leaves more than 80 percent of the American public not engaged in the moral and ideological battles reveled in by the political class. Note that Wilson's examples of incivil discourse reference "the press," "a former Democratic presidential candidate," "a senior Democratic Senator," "liberal spokesmen," and "one conservative pundit." Absent from this list are well-intentioned, ordinary working Americans not given to the kind of incendiary remarks that get quoted by journalists.

I share Wilson's concern with the potentially harmful consequences of polarization. But the first step in addressing those concerns is to get the facts correct. I remain convinced that we have done that. If Americans are offered competent, pragmatic candidates with a problem-solving orientation, the shallow popular roots of political polarization will be exposed for all to see.

Morris P. Fiorina
Stanford, California

QUESTIONS

1. *What would you do?* If you were an adviser for one of the two major parties, how would you advise them to address the issue of polarization or culture war? Should they emphasize issues where broader consensus might be possible? Or is it the job of political parties to emphasize precisely those issues that might be the most divisive in order to mobilize their base?

2. Do Wilson and Fiorina have the same definition of polarization? If not, how do they differ?

3. According to Wilson, what are the chief factors contributing to polarization and cultural division in the United States? What part of Wilson's argument would Fiorina agree with? Are these factors likely to change any time soon?

4. Based on the articles and other information you might have, do you think Fiorina is right that the American public is not deeply split on a range of issues and that they tend to favor more moderate solutions to problems rather than taking extreme positions? Can you think of issues, other than abortion, for which this would be true?

7

Blogs and the Mainstream Media

Major changes in communications technology have produced major changes in the practice of politics and the way people get political information. Earlier technologies do not necessarily fade away, but their role changes and their dominance diminishes. Pamphlets, then newspapers, then radio, and then television all had their eras of ascendancy and all continued to play important roles when other technologies emerged. Political talk radio in the 1980s and 1990s, for example, gave new life to radio in the age of television, creating another kind of information exchange with which politicians had to become conversant. Inevitably, these technological shifts raise concerns that the new form of information dissemination will drive out some of the positive features of the previous technology.

The rise of the Internet since the 1990s is the most recent dramatic change in communication technology. Access to information about public affairs that was unthinkable a decade ago is now commonplace, and the volume is staggering. For a decade, most of the analysis on how the Internet might change politics focused on e-mail and Web sites. Today, the focus is on a particular form of Web site, the weblog, or blog. At their simplest, blogs provide a forum for an individual to express his or her point of view on the news, link to other sites and stories of interest, and invite reader feedback. The sites are easy to create and maintain, making them accessible to most people who know the basics of computer operation. More so than any other medium, blogs allow individuals the opportunity to reach large numbers of readers at very little cost other than time. Because blogs are being added and abandoned at a rapid pace, it is virtually impossible to know with any certainty how many are in existence and updated regularly. Estimates range anywhere from 4 or 5 million to 60 million worldwide. Very few of these blogs, however, attract any appreciable readership, and even those that do have far fewer visitors than the Web sites operated by established news media companies like the *New York Times, Wall Street Journal,* Cable News Network, and Fox News. Still, that politicians need to take notice of the blogs was evident in 2006 when leading contenders for the 2008 Democratic presidential nomination spoke to attendees at a blogging convention in Las Vegas.

The explosive growth of the "blogosphere" has led to both optimistic and pessimistic interpretations of its place in politics. Supporters note that blogs provide a check on powerful individuals in government and business, by allowing ordinary citizens to express and share their views. By combining the knowledge, memory, and energy of multitudes of bloggers and their readers, blogs can reveal faulty reporting by the mainstream media. Blogging enthusiasts note that blogs were essential and leading sources of information in the aftermath of Hurricane Katrina, refuting self-serving statements by public officials at the local, state, and national level, and introducing stories later picked up by mainstream media. Critics worry that bloggers may gain increasing sway over politicians and the public, while not being held to high journalistic standards, and that they are as likely to generate misleading interpretations as uncover truth. Like mainstream journalists, bloggers want to be the first to break a story, but they are less likely to worry whether a post is true, critics say, because they believe that the nature of the blogosphere inevitably debunks stories that are false. Some observers worry that the mainstream media, not wanting to allow blogs to have a monopoly on publishing the most sensational stories, might become more bloglike themselves.

The readings in this chapter reflect both the optimistic and pessimistic assessments of the place and impact of blogs in American politics. Daniel Perlmutter and Misti McDaniel note many instances where bloggers "pushed and prodded old media to change the ways they work." They argue that blogs have a place in news delivery because of their adaptability, innovation, and expression of diverse voices, and mainstream media need to accept that. The old news media's problems, in their view, have little to do with blogs and are mostly self-inflicted. And blogs, in their view, make a strongly positive contribution to democratic politics.

Cass Sunstein and Ted Vaden offer less rosy assessments. Sunstein notes that with newspapers, magazines, and broadcasters, readers and viewers almost inevitably came into contact with diverse viewpoints and stories they would not have explicitly chosen to see. This, he argues, serves an important function in a democratic society. He worries that blogs, as well as other parts of the Internet, encourage filtering of ideas and stories we do not choose to encounter. The result is greater polarization, as blog readers gravitate to sites with strong views in the direction they already favor, which Sunstein sees as a danger for democracy. Groupthink encourages ever more extreme points of view to thrive. Vaden does not discount the contributions blogs might make, but laments that quality control and concern for careful reporting vary widely. Too many bloggers, he writes, start with their opinions and worry about facts later rather than the other way around.

David D. Perlmutter and Misti McDaniel
The Ascent of Blogging

New media are not new to those who've grown up with or use them everyday. To 18-year-olds at our journalism school at Louisiana State University, iPods, satellite-reception, Wi-Fi, laptops, cell phones, PDAs, digital photography, and the Internet are technologies as familiar as the wheel and fire. But while ancient innovations took millennia to spread, today a new gadget or idea can catch on globally within a few years.

The ascent of the Web log, Weblog (or blog) is one example. Within five years, online journals of political and personal expression and debate rose from obscurity to become ubiquitous. In examining how the mainstream press has reacted to blogs, we discern lessons about the relationship between technology and journalism:

- Events don't drive new media technology. Rather, new media technology succeeds by finding ways to exploit events.

Published in *Nieman Reports*, 2005.

- News coverage tends to focus on the sexy or "hot" aspects of new media technology, which can obscure other trends that will be potentially more influential in the long run.
- Old media portrays new media technologies as darlings, only to cynically then dethrone them.
- Traditional media's vulnerabilities to such upstarts aren't just technological but are economic and psychological. Mainstream media believe new things might destroy, result in unemployment, or make them obsolete; they don't know how to adapt.
- The best response to blogs by television, radio and print is not to ape them but to determine what blogs do and why they do it well or poorly.

Certainly blogs seem to be everywhere—some estimates put the number of blogs in the tens of millions. According to several Pew studies, of the estimated 120 million U.S. adults who use the Internet, some seven percent have created a blog while more than 30 million look at them regularly. Many blogs are basement setups—scribbled by one, read by few. In contrast, some popular blogs, like Instapundit, Power Line and Daily Kos, receive more daily traffic than many major newspapers or TV news programs.

But blogs aren't talked about just because of their numbers, rather for the news they make while critiquing journalism and tracking events, such as blogging about the rise and fall of presidential candidate Howard Dean, Dan Rather's "memogate," Trent Lott's praise of Strom Thurmond's Dixiecrat campaign, and the South Asian tsunami. In each case—and others—bloggers pushed and prodded old media to change the ways they work. In response, some journalists and news organizations have created blogs and use them for newsgathering, self-reflection, opinion-testing, and interaction with readers, listeners, and viewers.

Though blog-like sites existed during the 1990s—most notably the Drudge Report—blogs were officially born in December 1997, when Jorn Barger, editor of Robot Wisdom.com, created the term "Weblog." In the spring of 1999, Peter Merholz broke "Weblog" into the phrase "we blog" and put it on his homepage. As the term spread, in August 1999 software-maker Pyra Labs released the program Blogger, making blogs user-friendly and generally accessible.

Blogs were not an instant big story in the mainstream media. One of the first hits for "blog" in the press was in October 1999 when Great Britain's *New*

Statesman described it as "a Web page, something like a public commonplace book, which is added to each day. . . . If there is any log they resemble, it is the captain's log on a voyage of discovery." The first newspaper reference likely occurred in January 2000 when Canada's *Ottawa Citizen* quoted pop star Sarah McLachlan from her Web site. One of the first broadcast stories about blogs was in May 2000 when National Public Radio's "The Connection" interviewed several bloggers.

Overall, in tracking mainstream media's reporting on blogs between January 1998 and April 2005, we found 16,350 items mentioning the words "Web log," "Weblog," and "blog." In gauging "blog-throughs"—events commonly ascribed to have propelled blogs to media attention—we found that journalists were barely acknowledging blogs in the wake of 9/11.

Blog obscurity changed decisively in 2002, when Senate Majority Leader Trent Lott, while attending a reception for South Carolina Senator Strom Thurmond, made a racially insensitive comment. The item was first mentioned by ABC News and posted on its Web site, but bloggers drumbeat the story into widespread salience. Lott ended up resigning his leadership position under party pressure. Still, as blogs gained stature as agenda-setters, they remained relatively lightly cited by the press.

In 2003, as the presidential primary season kicked off, Howard Dean's team—led by technology-savvy Joe Trippi, Dean's campaign manager—pioneered the campaign blog for the public and the press. Users posted messages to other supporters, and this networking ability enabled them to meet for events. Supporters were encouraged to "decentralize" by starting their Dean Web sites and to raise funds through their blogs. By September 2003 Dean's blog was getting 30,000 unique visitors a day. When General Wesley Clark entered the race, he cited a "Draft Wes" Web site's popularity and supportive blog comments as one reason to get in. The political parties and many candidates also began blogging. For example, the Democratic National Committee started up "Kicking Ass: Daily Dispatches from the DNC," which promised "frank, one-on-one communication. . . . Blogs make that possible."

Blogs were now being portrayed as voices of the people, political players, and as trip-wires for breaking stories.

Blogs Arrive

2004 was the year of the blog. That word became the most searched-for definition on several online dictionaries. Indeed in our tracking, October 2004 was the time at which 50 percent of blog coverage occurred before and after: In other words there has been as much blog news in the last half-year as in the previous five. What follows are some of the more memorable news stories about blogs:

- As Howard Dean started his political slide out of the race, stories about blogs grew by 50 percent. Instead of seeking disgruntled supporters for face-to-face interviews, reporters cited Dean's bloggers as newspapers carried articles about Dean's blog and how its participants reacted to the campaign's changing fortunes.
- In July 2004 the Democratic National Convention credentialed 35 bloggers. While 15,000 journalists were issued press passes, attention focused on the "bloggeratti."
- Blogging exploded into view on September 8, 2004, when on CBS News's "60 Minutes II" Dan Rather reported a story questioning President George W. Bush's 1970s National Guard service. Offered as evidence were papers, allegedly written by Bush's then-supervisor Lieutenant Colonel Jerry Killian, stating that Bush did not fulfill his service requirements.

Pushing the Rather "memogate" story, bloggers simultaneously displayed their main virtue and vice—speedy deployment of unedited thought. One blogger on freerepublic.com posted his doubt about the memos' authenticity: "They are not in the style that we used when I came in to the USAF. They looked like the style and format we started using about 12 years ago (1992). Our signature blocks were left justified, now they are rigth [sic] of center . . . like the ones they just showed." Bloggers such as Power Line's Scott Johnson launched an investigation of the purported memos. Innovatively, the blog little green footballs posted a file that contrasted a modern Microsoft Word recreation over CBS's version of the disputed papers. The text was almost an exact match.

Within days, the story leapt from new media to the mainstream news media. For two weeks CBS News stood by its reporting, but then admitted that its document examiners could not verify the memos' authenticity. The network launched an investigation to determine how the invalidated material ended up on the air. Eventually four people at CBS were blamed for the error. Rather, who anchored the evening news for 24 years, announced his retirement in November and left his position in March 2005. Many bloggers rejoiced at their power to topple venerable institutions. Freerepublic.com blogger "Rrrod" warned, "NOTE [sic] to old media scum. . . . We are just getting warmed up!"

More big blog news was ahead, including the following incidents:

- When some bloggers heard of Sinclair Broadcasting Group's plan to air an anti-[John] Kerry documentary, they organized letter-writing campaigns and boycotts and again pushed the item until it became a major story in the mainstream media.
- On Election Day, early exit polls indicated John Kerry held a lead over George Bush in a number of key states. Some bloggers pushed a "Kerry is winning big" headline. But the flexibility of the blogosphere was shown when bloggers Hugh Hewitt and Mark Blumenthal (Mystery Pollster) pointed out that exit polls were only scientifically valid in a state until after voting had finished.
- The December tsunami in Southeast Asia contributed to a 39 percent growth in newspaper coverage of blogs. Stories of victims surfaced in blogs, and for the first time traditional media were bypassed as a source as relatives searched for information about loved ones online.

In the tsunami coverage, in particular, old media took another step toward co-opting the new. Uncensored and unedited video surfaced in video blogs (vlogs) and people relied on the Internet to watch scenes from the disaster. Free of Federal Communications Commission regulations, vlogs showed grisly and gripping footage, while TV newscasts often censored their reports to avoid upsetting the American public. WaveofDestruction.org, created by an Australian blogger, posted 25 amateur videos of the event and in five days logged nearly 700,000 visitors. Soon American TV networks vied for broadcast rights. Norwegian editor Oliver Orskaug sold his video for $20,000 to CNN and ABC News.

Even as blogs soared in attention and influence, a blowback from the mainstream media was underway.

- Blame fell on bloggers for leaking the raw exit poll results on Election Day and spreading conspiracy theories afterwards.
- Some bloggers were outed for faking data or retroactively changing posts without notation.
- Some bloggers accepted pay from political candidates or parties but did not reveal the arrangement to their readers.
- Questions arose about whether blogs were, indeed, the "voice of the people" since most domestic and foreign blog creators are white journalists, professors, lawyers or middle-class professionals.
- CNN was ridiculed for creating an "Inside the Blogs" segment that consisted of people reading blogs on air—an exercise in synergy that drew laughs even from bloggers.
- In March 2005, "The Daily Show" skewered one of the intellectual fathers of blogging, New York University's Jay Rosen, as the program's correspondent satirized the entire idea of amateurs hosting a news and commentary Web site.
- Questions are raised about whether the number of blogs is inflated by ones that are inactive or are spam.

Blogs vs. Old Media

Given what's happened with blogs and journalism, can we say that their upward trend is now in decline? Or are blogs being relegated to places where journalists troll for funny stories or human interest filler? Neither seems a likely outcome.

Blogs are likely to thrive due to their adaptability and innovation. Bloggers' personal style, their technology, the use of open-end sourcing, and their ability to get information and speculation out quickly enable this new media to go around the clunky logistical trails and leadership—bypassing what economists call the "structural rigidity" of the old. Moments after the "60 Minutes II" story aired, for example, ABC News's Peter Jennings was not going to break onto the air and proclaim, "There's something screwy about a story on CBS." And when a few bloggers had an idea about how to speed up and collate information about tsunami victims and survivors, they didn't have to wait for an OK from senior editors or management. Blog failures cost much less than do those of mainstream media, so bloggers can experiment on a whim and do so faster than giant operations.

"Old world panic" is also a problem. At some level, blogs seem a threat to almost everything in the news business. OhmyNews, for example, is a South Korean Web site where anybody can post news stories and editorials; if the content proves popular enough, the author gets paid for it. If such a model becomes dominant, it would mean the end of journalism, not to mention journalism schools. But forcing new technology into old holes doesn't work, either. Reading blogs on TV is artificial and unworkable, as is "hipping up" a newspaper column by calling it a blog or trying to feign technical innovation by telling readers that one's musings were done on a Blackberry (though suspiciously without typos).

Regular media are challenged, too, about how to cover novelties in their business. Journalists noticed blogs late, but interest intensified as bloggers showcased their potential. Now a frenzy of attention by journalists is coupled with mocking. Is this an inevitable cycle—building up what is new to unwarranted levels of praise, then despairing at its flaws, which were evident at the start?

Blogs cannot be stuffed into ill-fitting stereotypes. Blogs represent the divergent voices of millions. Though some news-related blogs have more "hits" than others, blogging lacks both defined leadership and a constituency. Post an item on a blog and comments range from complete agreement to irate dissent. It's messy, but that's what blogs are, and we hope they stay that way.

Certainly traditional journalists have a right to feel as sports stars do when they have to endure catcalls and advice shouted at them by obnoxious fans. And compared with most journalists, a lot of the bloggers have not paid their dues in education, training or experience. But the problems that mainstream journalism is experiencing today have little to do with bloggers. After all, it wasn't bloggers who slashed newsroom budgets for basic beat and investigative reporting. Nor did bloggers create a star system of astronomically paid anchors and pundits. And bloggers were not the ones who reduced coverage of political campaigns and elections to sound- and visual- bytes and horserace handicapping.

Finally, let's step back and take the longer view into this blogger/mainstream media debate. Once upon a time, as historian Gwenyth L. Jackaway documented, a new medium came along—loud, raucous, uncontrolled and full of unprofessional and discordant voices. It was called radio. The print press of the 1920s and 1930s saw radio as a danger, not only to their livelihoods but also to the future of the republic itself. The *New York Times* fumed, "If the

American people . . . were to depend upon scraps of information picked up from air reporting, the problems of a workable democracy would be multiplied incalculably." *Editor & Publisher* asserted that radio was "physically incapable of supplying more than headline material," and thus it was "inconceivable that a medium which is incapable of functioning in the public interest will be allowed to interfere with the established system of news reporting in a democracy."

Print news survived and thrives and radio did not destroy democracy. There will always be a mainstream media, though perhaps blogs will blur into it. But the point worth remembering is that the rise of new media should not make the old media panic or be dismissive or fearful. Rather what is new ought to remind us of the need to grasp ever more tightly ahold of the fundamentals of journalism as we journey forward.

Cass R. Sunstein
Democracy and Filtering

Is the Internet a wonderful development for democracy? In many ways it is. As a result of the Internet, we can learn far more than we could before, and learn it much faster. If you want to get information to a wide range of people, you can do it quickly, via e-mail and Web sites, and [this] is another sense in which the Internet is a great boon for democracy. In particular, the rise of specialized sites and blogs increases the opportunity for people to read and write on an extraordinary array of topics. If you have an opinion and want to express it in public or want to find an opinion of almost any kind, chances are you can, at trivial cost.

But in the midst of the celebration, I want to raise a note of caution. I do so by emphasizing one of the most striking benefits provided by emerging technologies: the growing power of consumers to "filter" what they see. As a result of the Internet and other technological developments, many people are increasingly engaged in the process of personalization, limiting their exposure to topics and points of view of their own choosing. They filter in, and out, with unprecedented powers of precision. These developments make life much more

Published in *Communications of the ACM*, December 2004.

convenient and in some ways much better; we all seek to reduce our exposure to uninvited noise, and many of us like to read opinions we find congenial.

But from the standpoint of democracy, filtering is a mixed blessing. Above all, I urge that in a heterogeneous society, such a system would require something other than free, or publicly unrestricted, individual choices. On the contrary, it imposes a distinctive requirement: People should be exposed to materials they would not have chosen in advance. Unanticipated encounters, involving topics and points of view we have not sought out and perhaps find irritating, are central to democracy and even to freedom itself.

Complete Individuation

To explore this issue, consider the following thought experiment. It involves an apparently utopian dream, that of complete individuation, in which consumers can entirely personalize (or customize) their own communications universe. Imagine a system of communications in which each person has unlimited power of individual design. If people want to watch news all the time, they are entirely free to do so. If they dislike news and want to watch football in the morning and situation comedies at night, that is fine, too. If they care only about America and want to avoid international issues entirely, it is simple indeed; so too if they care only about New York or Chicago or California. If they want to restrict themselves to certain points of view, say, conservative, moderate, liberal, vegetarian, or Nazi, it is entirely feasible with a simple point and click. If they want to isolate themselves and speak only with like-minded others, that is feasible, too. If they seek to read only those authors who agree with them and support the political candidates they favor, they are perfectly able to do so.

At least as a matter of technological feasibility, and with the rise of countless options, the U.S. communications market is moving quickly toward this apparently utopian picture. It is not entirely different from what has come before. People who read newspapers do not all read the same newspaper, and some people do not read any newspaper at all. But in the emerging environment, there is a difference of degree if not of kind. What is different is a dramatic increase in individual control over content, along with a corresponding decrease in the power of general-interest intermediaries, including newspapers, magazines, and broadcasters. For all their problems, and their unmistakable limitations and biases, these intermediaries have performed some important democratic functions.

People who rely on such intermediaries experience a range of chance encounters with diverse others, as well as exposure to material they did not specifically choose. You might, for example, read a city newspaper and in the process come across stories you would not have selected if you had the power to control what you see. You might watch a particular television channel, and when your favorite program ends, you might see the beginning of another show, one you would not have chosen in advance.

In fact, a risk with a system of perfect individual control is that it can reduce the importance of the "public sphere" and of common spaces in general. One of the important features of these spaces is that they tend to ensure that people will encounter materials on important issues, whether or not they have specifically chosen the encounter. And when people see material they have not chosen, their interests and even their views might change as a result. At the very least, they will know a bit more about what their fellow citizens are thinking.

We can sharpen our understanding of this problem if we attend to the phenomenon of group polarization. Found in many settings, it involves like-minded people going to extremes. More precisely, group polarization means that after deliberating with one another, people are likely to move toward a more extreme point of view in the direction to which they were already inclined. With respect to the Internet, the implication is that groups of people, especially if they are like-minded, will end up thinking the same thing they thought before—but in more extreme form, and sometimes in a much more extreme form.

Consider some examples of the basic phenomenon, as studied in more than a dozen nations. (a) After discussion, the citizens of France become more critical of the United States and its intentions with respect to economic aid. (b) After discussion, whites predisposed to show racial prejudice offer more negative responses to the question of whether white racism is responsible for certain conditions faced by African Americans. (c) After discussion, whites predisposed not to show racial prejudice offer more positive responses to the same question. (d) After discussion, a group of moderately pro-feminist women become more strongly pro-feminist. (e) Republican appointees to the federal judiciary show far more conservative voting patterns when they are sitting on a panel consisting solely of Republican appointees; and Democratic appointees show far more liberal voting patterns when they are sitting on a panel consisting solely of Democratic appointees.

It follows that, for example, after discussion with one another, those who tend to dislike President Bush and the war in Iraq will come to dislike him and the war intensely; that those inclined to favor more aggressive affirmative-action programs will become extreme on the issue; and that those who believe tax rates are too high will come to think that large, immediate tax reductions are an extremely good idea.

The phenomenon of group polarization has conspicuous importance to the U.S. communications market, where groups with distinctive identities increasingly engage in within-group discussion. Customization makes this possible; specialized Web sites and blogs compound the problem. If the public is balkanized, and if different groups design their own preferred communications packages, the consequence will be further balkanization, as group members move one another toward more extreme points of view in line with their initial tendencies. At the same time, different deliberating groups, each consisting of like-minded people, will be driven increasingly far apart, simply because most of their discussions will be with one another. Extremist groups will often become even more extreme.

We cannot say, from the mere fact of polarization, that there has been a movement in the wrong direction. Perhaps the more extreme tendency is better; indeed, group polarization is likely to have fueled many movements of great value, including, for example, the ones for civil rights, abolishing slavery, and gender equality. All were extreme in their time, and within-group discussion bred greater extremism. Still, extremism need not be a word of opprobrium. If greater communications choices produce greater extremism, society may, in many cases, be better off as a result. But when group discussion tends to lead people to more strongly held versions of the same view with which they began, and if social influences and limited argument pools are responsible, there is legitimate reason for concern about sensible self-government.

Dangers to Democracy

Emerging technologies, including the Internet, are hardly an enemy here. They hold out at least as much promise as risk, especially because they allow us all to widen our horizons. We can certainly use them to learn more, rather than to live in an echo chamber. But to the extent they weaken the power of general-interest intermediaries and increase our ability to wall ourselves off from topics and opinions we would prefer to avoid, they create serious dangers to democracy. And if we believe that a system of free expression calls for unrestricted choice by individual consumers, we will not even understand the dangers as such.

Whether such dangers materialize ultimately depends on the aspirations, for freedom and democracy alike, by whose light we evaluate our practices. What I have sought to establish here is that in a free society, citizens aspire to a system that provides a range of experience—with people, topics, and ideas— they would not have selected in advance.

Ted Vaden
Blogs Challenge Newspaper Standards

There's been a good bit of chatter about blogging on *The News & Observer* blog sites recently. The gist of the discussion: What effect does online communication have on traditional journalistic standards? . . .

What is a blog? I think of it as the online equivalent of a letter home, addressed to whoever wants to read it. A blog is often personal, written by a single individual, but blogging can come from institutions like *The N&O*, which launched several blogs over the past six months.

As they gain popularity and readership, blogs are challenging the position of "mainstream media" as sources of information on news and public policy. They also are causing newspapers, as they get into the blogging game themselves, to re-examine long-held standards of journalistic practice.

"I think the new media are going to force us to look at very closely held journalistic values and think carefully about how we apply them—keep some, change some, maybe discard some in order to succeed," Kerry Sipe, news online coordinator for the *Norfolk Virginian-Pilot,* told me. "The new media is a different game and requires a different set of values, maybe a more complex set of values."

Example: It is a generally a no-no in the newspaper business to give a news source the chance to read a story before it's published. That's to prevent compromise to the story's integrity.

But Sipe asks, "Why wouldn't you show a source a story? The fact is that the source knows more about the story than you do." Allowing pre-publication

Published in *The News & Observer*, October 2005.

review doesn't have to mean giving that person veto or editing authority over the story.

The real-time nature of blogging also means compromising the traditional newspaper editing that, we think, ensures accuracy, balance, fairness, thoroughness. In the blogosphere, the editing process is having to yield to the online demand for instant information, regularly updated. Some N&O reporters, used to almost oppressive editing, are nonplussed to find their blogs going online without being touched by an editor.

If newspapers have to adjust their standards for blogging, what kind of standards apply in that world? At their best, blogging advocates say, higher standards. John Robinson, editor of *The Greensboro News & Record,* says the best bloggers provide electronic links to their information sources, so readers can fact-check behind the blogger; update as new information becomes available; quickly correct mistakes; and are more responsive to readers. "They do a better job than journalists partly because of the difference in the online medium," said Robinson, whose newspaper has attracted national attention for its ambitious portfolio of staff-produced blogging.

But not all bloggers meet that "best" standard. One reason is that so much blogging begins with opinion, rather than fact. "There are a lot of bloggers who put opinion out there with the idea that it will lead to the truth, rather than do what reporters do, which is to start with the facts," Robinson said. "What we get with some bloggers is that there is no reporting. That's where I'm not sure that the standards of some bloggers are up to the standards of newspapers." . . .

I talked to one Raleigh blogger last week who writes critically about *The N&O* but refuses to put his name on his Web site. Asked why, he said, "I want my blog to be about the material on the blog. I don't want to be John Personality." OK, but so much for accountability.

After the Greensboro conference, I wrote a blog saying Rosen, the press critic, claimed higher standards for bloggers than journalists. In an e-mail to me, he took issue with my characterization of his remarks. He said his purpose had been not to claim a higher ethical standard but to jolt journalists out of a complacency that they have standards and bloggers do not. In the interest of equal time, I share his e-mail at length:

> "What this (complacent) view overlooks are a number of ways in which bloggers at the high end meet higher standards than journalists at the high

end," he wrote. "I mentioned the art of linking, where bloggers set the pace, speed of correction and the willingness to correct, interactivity, transparency, being in conversation with others on the Web.

"I didn't mention, but it was implicit, that in other ways professional journalists do have more stringent standards: their rules for verification, right of reply, and not engaging in speculation would be examples there. My purpose was to complicate the picture, not to raise the triumphant hand of the bloggers and call them the winner, which would be obnoxious—and untrue."

So where does all this leave us? In the area of journalistic standards, I for one am not getting too hung up on the relative merits of newspaper journalists versus bloggers. My sense is that readers will gravitate to those communicators, print or online, who over the long term demonstrate adherence to basic journalistic values of accuracy, fairness and pursuit of truth.

And we should be reminded that blogs are not a replacement for traditional journalism. For one thing, much online content is not original but feeds on the reporting done by newspapers and other media. "Most of what you know, you know because of the mainstream media," Bill Keller, executive editor of *The New York Times*, told an audience recently. "Bloggers recycle and chew on the news. That's not bad. But it's not enough."

Finally, we need to be aware that there is an important part of our population, the poor and disadvantaged, who are disproportionately left out of the public debate as it moves online. Wherever this wild ride in the blogosphere takes us, it needs to serve all of society.

QUESTIONS

1. *What would you do?* You are a blogger and you have come across some damaging information about a presidential candidate. Do you blog it? On one hand, it might not be true. On the other, if it is true, it is critical information that voters should know. Do you put the information into the blogosphere and trust it will be filtered and proven true or false by other blogs? Or do you approach it as mainstream media journalists traditionally would, requiring more corroboration—which can take time to obtain—before presenting the story to the public? Would your answer depend on how late in the campaign it is? Now imagine the same scenario, except that the office in question is an

elected position in your hometown, where people know you personally. Do you handle this differently?

2. Do you agree with Sunstein that Internet users are likely to gravitate to sites that reinforce their point of view? If not, why not? If so, do you agree that this is the problem for democracy that Sunstein suggests?

3. Based on your own experience as well as the information in the articles, what do you see as the relative strengths and weaknesses of television news programs, newspapers, news Web sites, and blogs? Should the standards for what they broadcast or publish as news be the same?

8

Ballot Initiatives: Voice of the People or the Powerful?

One of the central threads running through American political culture and political history is a fear of concentrated political power. For the Founders, this fear dictated the necessity of a federal system of checks and balances and separation of powers. For citizens, this fear has led to periodic attempts to reform the political system to "give government back to the people." The most recent of these efforts on the national scale were Ross Perot's surprisingly strong presidential candidacies in 1992 and 1996 and the rise of political movements to impose term limits on elected officials and reform campaign finance laws. Although the term llimits movement has stalled, significant campaign finance reform was passed in the form of the Bipartisan Campaign Reform Act of 2002, and a number of states have passed or are investigating so-called "clean elections" laws, in which candidates receive full public funds for their campaigns.

Early in the twentieth century, Progressive reformers introduced some of the most significant efforts to allow citizens to challenge concentrated power: the recall (allowing citizens to remove an elected official from office), the initiative (allowing citizens to put proposed legislation on the ballot), and the referendum (allowing citizens to approve or reject decisions of the legislature and executive). In 2003, Californians threw Governor Gray Davis out of office in a recall election, replacing him with Arnold Schwarzenegger. Initiatives and referendums have been used to decide questions on the use of race as a factor in college admissions, the level of state or local tax revenues, which services would be provided to immigrants, and the use of bilingual education in public schools, among many others.

David Broder argues that although the initiative might have started with the intention of preventing the concentration of political power, the reality has been quite different. To Broder, initiatives are a tool of powerful interests, not a way to challenge concentrated power. Organized interests with substantial financial resources are especially advantaged. Initiative campaigns, he writes, often mask the economic interests of those advocates on either side of the issue. Well-funded scare campaigns lead voters to support, frequent unknowingly, the position of large, wealthy, special interests. Broder is concerned that citizens so often assume legislatures, elected by the public, are corrupt, but seem to accept at face value that initiatives are a tool of the people.

Despite Broder's critique, ballot initiatives do have their defenders. Lino Graglia argues that government tends to be overwhelmingly dominated by a liberal mindset, and the initiative is one of the key tools available to conservatives to keep government in check. The effect of the initiative in recent years, he suggests, has been largely to allow the conservative views held by a majority of Americans to influence public policy directly. Listing a long string of successes in California, including the termination of school busing for racial balance, the abolishment of compulsory bilingual education, and ending the use of racial preferences in college admissions, Graglia notes that "it is hardly possible to ask more from any political device." Indeed, Graglia would like to see the ballot initiative extended to national elections.

Conservatives' success with the initiative has not gone unnoticed by liberals. While some liberals might complain about ballot initiatives, David Sarasohn reports that other liberals are determined to challenge conservatives and use the initiative to push progressive causes. He discusses the plan of the Economic Opportunity Institute in Washington state to use the initiative process in an aggressive manner to achieve liberal victories, such as mandating that the state's minimum wage be adjusted annually to compensate for rising prices. Although the two authors disagree on whether government at the time they wrote was controlled by liberals or conservatives, both Graglia and Sarasohn suggest that the initiative can be used to challenge concentrated power, just as it was intended to do.

David S. Broder
Dangerous Initiatives: A Snake in the Grass Roots

An alternative form of government—the ballot initiative—is spreading in the United States. Despite its popular appeal and reformist roots, this method of lawmaking is alien to the spirit of the Constitution and its carefully crafted set of checks and balances. Left unchecked, the initiative could challenge or even subvert the system that has served the nation so well for more than two hundred years.

Though derived from a century-old idea favored by the Populist and Progressive movements as a weapon against special-interest influence, the initiative has become a favored tool of interest groups and millionaires with their own political and personal agendas. These players—often not even residents of the states whose laws and constitutions they seek to rewrite—have learned that the initiative is a more efficient way of achieving their ends than the cumbersome and often time-consuming process of supporting candidates for public office and then lobbying them to pass legislation. In hundreds of municipalities and half the states—particularly in the West—the initiative has become a rival force to City Hall and the State House. (The District of Columbia allows voters to enact laws by initiative, but the states of Maryland and Virginia do not.) In a single year, 1998, voters across the country bypassed their elected representatives to end affirmative action, raise the minimum wage, ban billboards, permit patients to obtain prescriptions for marijuana, restrict campaign spending and contributions, expand casino gambling, outlaw many forms of hunting, prohibit some abortions and allow adopted children to obtain the names of their biological parents. Of 66 statewide initiatives that year, 39 became law. Simply put, the initiative's growing popularity has given us something that once seemed unthinkable—not a government of laws, but laws without government.

This new fondness for the initiative—at least in the portion of the country where it has become part of the political fabric—is itself evidence of the increasing alienation of Americans from our system of representative government. Americans have always had a healthy skepticism about the people in public office: The writers of the Constitution began with the assumption that

Published in *The Washington Post*, March 2000.

power is a dangerous intoxicant and that those who wield it must be checked by clear delineation of their authority.

But what we have today goes well beyond skepticism. In nearly every state I visited while researching this phenomenon, the initiative was viewed as sacrosanct, and the legislature was held in disrepute. One expression of that disdain is the term-limits movement, which swept the country in the past two decades, usually by the mechanism of initiative campaigns. It is the clearest expression of the revolt against representative government. In effect, it is a command: "Clear out of there, you bums. None of you is worth saving. We'll take over the job of writing the laws ourselves."

But who is the "we"? Based on my reporting, it is clear that the initiative process has largely discarded its grass-roots origins. It is no longer merely the province of idealistic volunteers who gather signatures to place legislation of their own devising on the ballot. Billionaire Paul Allen, co-founder of Microsoft, spent more than $8 million in support of a referendum on a new football stadium for the Seattle Seahawks. Allen, who was negotiating to buy the team, even paid the $4 million cost of running the June 1997 special election—in which Washington state voters narrowly agreed to provide public financing for part of the $425 million stadium bill.

Like so many other aspects of American politics, the initiative process has become big business. Lawyers, campaign consultants, and signature-gathering firms see each election cycle as an opportunity to make money on initiatives that, in many cases, only a handful of people are pushing. Records from the 1998 election cycle—not even one of the busiest in recent years—show that more than $250 million was raised and spent in this largely uncontrolled and unexamined arena of politics.

This is a far cry from the dream of direct democracy cherished by the nineteenth-century reformers who imported the initiative concept from Switzerland in the hope that it might cleanse the corrupt politics of their day. They would be the first to throw up their hands in disgust at what their noble experiment has produced.

The founders of the American republic were almost as distrustful of pure democracy as they were resentful of royal decrees. Direct democracy might work in a small, compact society, they argued, but it would be impractical in a nation the size of the United States. At the Constitutional Convention in 1787, no voice was raised in support of direct democracy.

A century later, with the rise of industrial America and rampant corruption in the nation's legislatures, political reformers began to question the work of the Founders. Largely rural protest groups from the Midwest, South, and West came together at the first convention of the Populist Party, in Omaha in 1892. The Populists denounced both Republicans and Democrats as corrupt accomplices of the railroad barons, the banks that set ruinous interest rates, and the industrial magnates and monopolists who profited from the labor of others while paying meager wages.

Both the Populists and Progressives—a middle-class reform movement bent on rooting out dishonesty in government—saw the initiative process as a salve for the body politic's wounds. An influential pamphlet, "Direct Legislation by the Citizenship through the Initiative and Referendum," appeared in 1893. In it, J. W. Sullivan argued that as citizens took on the responsibility of writing the laws themselves, "each would consequently acquire education in his role and develop a lively interest in the public affairs in part under his own management."

Into this feisty mix of reformers came William Simon U'Ren, a central figure in the history of the American initiative process. In the 1880s, U'Ren apprenticed himself to a lawyer in Denver and became active in politics. He later told Lincoln Steffens, the muckraking journalist, that he was appalled when the Republican bosses of Denver gave him what we would now call "street money" to buy votes.

In the 1890s, having moved to Oregon in search of a healthier climate, U'Ren helped form the Direct Legislation League. He launched a propaganda campaign, distributing almost half a million pamphlets and hundreds of copies of Sullivan's book in support of a constitutional convention that would enshrine initiative and referendum in Oregon's charter. The proposal failed narrowly in the 1895 session of the legislature, in part because the *Portland Oregonian* labeled it "one of the craziest of all the crazy fads of Populism" and "a theory of fiddlesticks borrowed from a petty foreign state."

Eventually, U'Ren lined up enough support for a constitutional amendment to pass easily in 1899. It received the required second endorsement from the legislature two years later, with only one dissenting vote. The voters overwhelmingly ratified the amendment in 1902 and it withstood a legal challenge that went all the way to the Supreme Court.

U'Ren's handiwork is evident today in his adopted state. The official voters' pamphlet for the 1996 Oregon ballot—containing explanations for sixteen citizen-sponsored initiatives and six others referred by the legislature—ran 248 pages.

It also included paid ads from supporters and opponents.

Money does not always prevail in modern-day initiative fights, but it is almost always a major—even a dominant—factor. In the fall of 1997, more than two hundred petitions were circulating for statewide initiatives that sponsors hoped to place on ballots the following year. The vast majority did not make it. The single obstacle that eliminated most of them was the ready cash needed to hire the companies that wage initiative campaigns.

In 1998, the most expensive initiative campaign was the battle over a measure legalizing casino-style gambling on Indian lands in California. The Nevada casinos, fearful of the competition, shelled out $25,756,828 trying to defeat the proposition. The tribes outdid them, spending $66,257,088 to win. The $92 million total was a new record for California.

But of all the ventures into initiative politics that year, perhaps the most successful was engineered by three wealthy men who shared the conviction that the federal "war on drugs" was a dreadful mistake. They banded together to support medical-marijuana initiatives in five Western states. The best known of them was billionaire financier George Soros of New York, who had made his fortune in currency trading. He and his political partners—Phoenix businessman John Sperling and Cleveland businessman Peter B. Lewis—personally contributed more than 75 percent of the $1.5 million spent on behalf of a successful medical-marijuana initiative in just one of the states, Arizona.

The issue isn't whether medical-marijuana laws are good or bad. As Arizona state Rep. Mike Gardner complained to me, "The initiative was part of our constitution when we became a state, because it was supposed to offer people a way of overriding special interest groups. But it's turned 180 degrees, and now the special interest groups use the initiative for their own purposes. Why should a New York millionaire be writing the laws of Arizona?"

When I relayed Gardner's question to Soros, he replied: "I live in one place, but I consider myself a citizen of the world. I have foundations in thirty countries, and I believe certain universal principles apply everywhere—including Arizona."

It won't be long before the twin forces of technology and public opinion coalesce in a political movement for a national initiative—allowing the public to substitute the simplicity of majority rule for what must seem to many Americans the arcane, out-of-date model of the Constitution. In fact, such a debate is already underway, based on what I heard at a May 1999 forum sponsored by the Initiative and Referendum Institute here in Washington.

M. Dane Waters, the institute's president, cut his political teeth on the term-limits movement, and the group's membership includes firms in the initiative industry. But Waters strove to keep the forum intellectually honest, inviting critics as well as supporters of the initiative process.

There was no doubt about the leanings of most of those in attendance. The keynote speaker was Kirk Fordice, then governor of Mississippi, who was cheered when he saluted the audience as "the greatest collection of mavericks in the world. The goal that unites us is to return a portion of the considerable power of government to individual citizens . . . and take control from the hands of professional politicians and bureaucrats."

Fordice, a Republican, noted that his state was the most recent to adopt the initiative, in 1992. Since then, he lamented, "only one initiative has made it onto the ballot," a term-limits measure that voters rejected. "Thank God for California and those raggedy-looking California kids who came in and gathered the signatures," he said. "Now the [Mississippi] legislature is trying to say we can't have them come in, and we're taking it to court."

Then came Mike Gravel, former Democratic senator from Alaska and head of an organization called Philadelphia II, which calls for essentially creating a new Constitution based on direct democracy. Gravel's plan—simplicity itself—is to take a national poll, and if 50 percent of the people want to vote on an issue, it goes on the next general election ballot. Then Congress would have to hold hearings on the issue and mark up a bill for submission to the voters. Once an issue gets on the ballot, only individuals could contribute to the campaign for passing or defeating it.

When I began researching the initiative process, I was agnostic about it. But now that I've heard the arguments and seen the initiative industry in action, the choice is easy. I would choose James Madison and the Constitution's checks and balances over the seductive simplicity of Gravel's up-or-down initiative vote. We should be able to learn from experience, and our experience with direct democracy during the last two decades is that wealthy individuals and special interests—the very targets of the Populists and Progressives a century ago—have learned all too well how to subvert the initiative process to their own purposes. Admittedly, representative government has acquired a dubious reputation today. But as citizens, the remedy isn't to avoid our elected representatives. The best weapon against the ineffective, the weak, and the corrupt is in our hands each Election Day.

Lino A. Graglia
Revitalizing Democracy

Government—organized, legitimized coercion—presents a dilemma. On the one hand, government is necessary to obtain certain benefits, such as the creation and enforcement of property rights that are essential to the efficient use of resources. On the other hand, giving some individuals organized power over others is very dangerous. Power, the ability to command and enforce obedience, is not good for the soul; it seems inevitably to lead to an exaggerated appraisal of one's wisdom and goodness as compared to those qualities in others. Power expands ego, and ego yearns for more power, with the result that government tends inexorably to grow far beyond what justifies its existence and therefore to limit human freedom unnecessarily.

Because government is dangerous, we should have no more of it than necessary and strive to make what we must have as little dangerous as possible. The only way this can be done is by making it effectively democratic, that is, subjecting it in a fairly direct and immediate way to popular control. One way in which the American system as it now operates can be made more democratic is the adoption of measures of direct democracy.

* * *

Almost half the states now provide for some form of direct democracy on important issues by allowing initiatives and referenda. It would greatly revitalize and enhance democracy in this country if such measures were adopted by all of the states, if they were made easier to implement in the states that already have them, and perhaps most important, if they were adopted by the national government.

The initiative and referendum were promoted at the turn of the century by so-called progressives who saw direct democracy as a way of overcoming the

Published in the *Harvard Journal of Law and Public Policy*, 2000.

conservative political influence of corporate and financial interests. Today, however, the dominant influences on government are not conservative, and direct democracy therefore serves primarily to protect conservative and traditional interests. Whatever may have been the case earlier, it now seems that the leaders of any political organization in the United States, from the local school board to the United States Senate, will be substantially to the left of its membership or constituents. It is apparently an inherent property of democratic government that it will inevitably fall into the hands of liberals, who are inherently distrustful of their fellow citizens, and thus become less and less democratic. Liberals are by definition (in the modern American context) unhappy the world is not better, while conservatives are grateful it is not worse. Liberals, therefore, are up and doing, seeking new ways to improve the world, which always results in more government, law, coercion, and, inevitably, more power to liberals. Conservatives, convinced that most changes would be for the worse, are largely content to leave the world alone and hope it reciprocates the favor.

The unfortunate tendency of democratic governments to fall into the hands of liberals has greatly increased in recent times as current leaders tend to be more highly educated than leaders in the past. Studies indicate that people tend to become more conservative, that is, more skeptical of innovation as they become better educated, but only through college. The over-educated, those with post-graduate degrees, tend to become more liberal. Perhaps they become disoriented from living too long in a world of words or perhaps it is only the already disoriented who stay too long in academia. The respect that was once given to business leaders for worldly success is today more typically given to our more educated leaders for their intellectual attainment. The Supreme Court Justices all have post-graduate degrees—albeit only from law schools—and usually from the most liberal of institutions. Like other government officials, they seek the commendation of academics and others of our intellectual elite, and this requires that they give evidence of their intellectual growth by moving to the left.

Whatever the reason, it seems clear that the influence of academics and other intellectuals on policymaking has greatly increased since the New Deal, which was openly founded and implemented by a "brain trust." The nightmare of the American intellectual, overwhelmingly on the far left of the American political spectrum, is that policymaking should fall into the hands of the American people. The American people, after all, favor such things as neighborhood schools, capital punishment, prayer in schools, restrictions on pornography, and the prohibition of flag burning, all anathema to the enlightened academic and certainly to the typical law professor. For them, direct democracy is a realization of their nightmare.

The effect of direct democracy in recent years has been, in almost every case, to reject liberal policy measures adopted by political leaders and substitute more conservative measures favored by a majority of the people. It is hardly too much to say that every socially beneficial policy choice in recent years to come out of California, the bellwether of the nation, has been the result of a referendum. Referenda have enabled Californians to impose limits on taxation, reinstitute capital punishment, terminate school busing for racial balance, abolish compulsory bilingual education, and prohibit the use of racial preferences in higher education, employment, and contracting. It is hardly possible to ask more from any political device. Racial preferences were also ended by referendum in the state of Washington. In Colorado, it was used to reinstitute the right of property owners to make individual choices on the basis of sexual orientation. The latter result, of course, was overturned by the Supreme Court, illustrating that the results of referenda, no less than ordinary legislation, are subject to the basic rule of our peculiar system that elections are fine as long as Supreme Court Justices get the last vote.

George Orwell is supposed to have remarked that there are some ideas so preposterous that only the highly educated can believe them. William Buckley expressed the same idea with the observation that he would rather be governed by the first 2,000 names in the Boston phone book than by the Harvard faculty. The ordinary Boston citizen is much less educated than a typical Harvard faculty member and therefore much less likely to devise a grand scheme of social improvement that would probably leave us worse off and surely make us less free. The source of many of our current problems is that we *are* to a large extent being ruled by the Harvard faculty and their academic counterparts, with the Supreme Court functioning essentially as their mirror, mouthpiece, and enacting arm. Initiatives and referenda are means of escaping or modifying this rule, of counteracting the socially destructive schemes of deep thinkers with the native realism and inherent good sense of the average citizen.

David Sarasohn
Taking (Back) the Initiative

The Economic Opportunity Institute sounds like a typical think tank—of any political persuasion. Each of the name's three interchangeable words evokes Dupont Circle, position papers, and regression analysis.

But the institute, from the small building it shares with an architect a few blocks from the University of Washington—about as far from the other Washington as you can get without the Pacific lapping over your fax machines—sees itself differently.

Progressive policy institutes, explains the group's statement of philosophy, come in three flavors. There's "think-tank hands-off research," as in universities. There's "more populist analyses that are picked up by local and national media"—still not quite the institute's style. The third category, in which policy development meets real-world advocacy, "is the niche that we want to exploit," says EOI. "Our job is to develop populist majoritarian policy and push that policy forward into the public eye." In other words: less think, more tank.

Because of that attitude, Washington is now the first state in the country with a minimum wage adjusted for inflation. From another EOI innovation, the state has a program to develop a childcare career ladder, to provide some professional respect and better pay for a generally minimum-wage work force that has major responsibilities and huge turnover and gets treated like a Play-Doh proletariat.

A bill EOI supported in the 2000 state legislative session that would use surpluses in the unemployment fund to create a paid-family-leave program—standard in Europe, unimaginable in the United States—made it through a State Senate committee, then died. Now, EOI's founder and executive director, John Burbank, is working on the idea with Washington's U.S. Senator Patty Murray, who is interested in proposing it as a federal pilot program.

And this spring, the institute announced that it would push its second statewide ballot initiative, this one allying with Washington health providers for a measure that would add a 60-cent tax to a pack of cigarettes, using the proceeds for health care for 50,000 working-poor Washingtonians. EOI

Published in *The Nation*, June 2001.

developed the measure, did preliminary polling, and helped assemble the coalition. In the campaign this fall, the institute will run statewide media tours, meet with editorial boards and reporters, develop one-page issue blurbs on different parts of the measure, and boldly go to places where progressive activists have rarely gone before—like talk radio.

Over many years as a community organizer, Democratic staff member, political director of the Washington State Labor Council and graduate student John Burbank concluded that progressive forces weren't just losing the struggle, they weren't fighting the right one. While progressives talked social theory, the right turned to the ballot box and the airwaves. And it was winning.

"The right has understood the power of the initiative, shaping debate, forcing debate onto their part of the field," says Burbank, sitting in one of Seattle's many espresso shops, as central to the local culture as Microsoft. "Some people say they're an abominable way to make law, but [initiatives] are there, and if you dismiss them, you're turning them over to the right wing." In Washington—as in many other states—there are well-funded, well-connected conservative advocacy institutes eager to seize any opportunity to set the terms of discussion.

The Economic Opportunity Institute—starting out three years ago in a few cubicles in what the *Seattle Times* calls the "funky, ultraliberal Fremont neighborhood"—wasn't born on the barricades, or out of a single inspired and overstuffed checkbook. It came out of Burbank's 1997 master's thesis at the University of Washington's school of public administration (several of his fellow students would later become EOI staff members). His thesis designed—in precise detail, including a budget and proposed board—an Economic Security Institute to take on Washington State's four conservative think tanks. Burbank also intended to challenge forces on the progressive side, which he saw as focusing too heavily on foreign policy and social issues, losing some of the bread-and-butter focus that appealed to both poorer and middle-class voters.

That's why EOI—which works on the slogan "New Tools for Building the Middle Class"—likes to focus on gritty, practical issues like health care for the working poor and childcare development. It also works to present the issues in a media-savvy way that appeals to middle-class voters: For example, treating quality child-care not as a question of equity, but as a way to promote parental employment.

"Work has an enormous resonance with the middle class," Burbank says.

"One of the sieves that we put issue development through is, 'Can it distribute benefits up and down the income ladder?' Some issues may disproportionately benefit lower-income people but resonate with middle-income people."

EOI's childcare campaign is a case in point. Not only did the institute's efforts lead Washington Governor Gary Locke to set up the childcare career ladder, but when a fiscal crunch threatened the program during the current legislative session, EOI's positioning as a public advocacy force helped produce 1,200 personal messages to the governor's office. Partly as a result, Burbank expects Locke to back not just maintaining but expanding the program.

And Burbank's playing with another idea: a city initiative in Seattle to raise $10 million a year for childcare with a tax on espresso drinks. This is a little like taxing wine in Bordeaux, and he remarks musingly, "Everybody laughs at that." But it could solidify local childcare funding and quality, would have to carry only the solidly liberal Seattle electorate and with success might spread to other cities. At least, Burbank argues, the effort would "build a database and catalyze discussion."

Burbank, a thin, intense man who tends to explain things at loving length, argues that some activists insist on portraying themselves as advocates for the poor, which leads to a double trap: They can't draw enough mainstream, middle-class support to win anything, and they "tend to isolate the lower-income constituency."

To some of those advocates, EOI's strategies seem indirect—and insufficiently relevant. "While I appreciate the work that they do, most of it doesn't really help the work that we do," says Jean Colman, director of the Welfare Rights Organizing Coalition in Seattle. "If the institute would help us do linking with middle-income folks to explain why there's a safety net and why it helps everybody, that would be a wonderful thing for them to do. I haven't seen them do that."

Still, EOI seeks to represent the interests of a diverse set of players in progressive politics. The board of EOI—in the move from thesis to practice, "Security" was replaced by "Opportunity"—reflects both Burbank's philosophy and his strategy. It includes union representatives, academics, a pollster and state legislators (including one who has since become co-speaker of the State House). A policy adviser to Governor Locke is a former board president, and still a member. They're not the figures swimming in the standard think tank; they show why Burbank prefers the term "activist public policy institute."

To Kim Cook, an EOI board member and regional director of the Service

Employees International Union, the institute reflects the kind of approach—and alliance—needed to challenge an atmosphere that's proving toxic to progressive ideas. "There's been a lot of talk on the board about broadening the public debate and [changing] the antitax attitude," says Cook. The goal is "to bring more progressive initiatives to the electorate."

EOI's successful minimum-wage campaign, launched in early 1998 as the institute was just getting off the ground, confirmed Burbank's feeling that the initiative could be an effective liberal tool. The vote gave the state not just a minimum wage among the nation's highest, but the only one in the country indexed to inflation to rise automatically. Running initiatives, admits Spokane Democratic State Senator Lisa Brown, another EOI board member and an economics professor at Eastern Washington University, "can be risky. If you run a progressive initiative and lose, it can set you back. But with the chances of something happening legislatively so low, you work on other ways."

This is, of course, what the original progressives realized at the beginning of the past century when they created the initiative, and what right-wingers understood at the end of it when they seized on the tactic. Burbank wants liberals to reclaim the initiative at the start of the new one. To him, the initiative is not only a tool but an opportunity. A campaign to collect the 225,000 signatures to put something on the state ballot, he notes, is a chance for "building a terrific database from signatures and donors." Which, at least potentially, can help in building a real grassroots movement.

To compete at the ballot box, progressive activists need tight connections to the sympathetic institutions on their side. "The right-wing institutes are powerful not just in how they define the terms of the debate, but how they're linked to their financial power," Brown points out. Practically, that means progressives need unions in the room. And, as Brown's prominence on the board suggests, it means reaching around the state, expanding progressive efforts beyond their permanent bridgehead in Seattle and Puget Sound.

From the outset, EOI has focused on the role and use of media, of making connections in a world of quick-hit consciousness. "We can pursue all the policy development we want, but if we correspond only with the policy elites, we have failed in our mission," explains an early "Tool Kit" for the group. "We must develop and implement a comprehensive media plan that brings our policy issues to the public and engages them."

It's a matter of both whom the institute wants to reach, and whom it wants to help. The poor, and people who have dropped out, aren't "easily organizable politically, but they do listen to and are influenced by the media," argues Burbank. "To me that's very important stuff, talk-radio. We shouldn't shy away from it."

So Burbank, as part of the media theme that he calls "organically part of what we do," goes on any talk-radio show that will have him, even if that means talking to lots of people complaining that Hillary Clinton keeps breaking into their houses to steal their guns. The goal is to battle on every front—including the ones that progressives have generally evacuated. And the group, in listing its accomplishments, lists its press clippings along with its policy advances.

Increasingly, the EOI is in a position to move on multiple issues at once. Its staff, which started with Burbank and a press aide, is now up to ten and growing. Its budget is rising, with 80 percent of its funding coming from foundations.

And the foundations are encouraged. "One of the exciting things about EOI," says Michael Caudell-Feagan, a board member of the Stern Family Fund, "is that it's trying to change the terms of the debate with proposals that have broad appeal but deal with economic justice." Around the country, the foundation has been trying to seed similar institutes, such as the Center for Economic Justice in Texas, Good Jobs First in Washington, D.C., and the Oregon Center for Public Policy. Caudell-Feagan thinks EOI is setting out a direction and a pattern that liberals haven't been following, but which is gaining ground politically. "Slowly but surely," he says, "a number of foundations have begun to encourage groups that deal with bread-and-butter issues."

In dealing with those issues—and in focusing on media strategies, broad alliances and the initiative process—EOI has begun to turn around a battle progressives have been losing. "They seem to be doing a better job than anyone I can think of in our region, in a way that seems to have legs, at building a program for economic security for working-class and middle-class people," says Jeff Malachowsky, founder of the Portland, Oregon-based Western States Center.

Burbank's approach may be more mundane than some progressive strategies, and his vision of the middle class as the new liberal constituency—and the media as the new barricades—may lack a certain work-shirt romance. But he insists, and he's beginning to pile up some evidence, that on issues such as minimum-wage increases, health care coverage and childcare subsidies, progressives can build successes and alliances. The first step is to retake the initiative—the one on the ballot.

QUESTIONS

1. *What would you do?* Assume that Broder's concerns about ballot initiatives are well-founded. Assume also that you work for a governor in a state where initiatives are considered an important part of the democratic process. There is no chance of eliminating ballot initiatives in this state, but your boss would like to reform the process. Describe at least two reforms that the governor could propose that address issues raised by Broder.

2. Do the articles by Graglia and Sarasohn leave you less concerned about the complaints leveled by Broder, or do they intensify your concerns? If both conservative and liberal "special interests" can use the initiative as a means to political ends, are Broder's criticisms of ballot initiatives really all that damning?

3. As the articles indicate, the initiative process exists at the state level but not the national level. Would you favor expanding the ballot initiative process to national politics? Why or why not? Would the initiative reject the governing principles favored by the Founders? If so, is that alone enough reason to reject the idea?

9

Is It Time for a New Third Party?

The American political system is dominated by the Republican and Democratic parties. Other political parties do run candidates and sometimes occasionally win, but the electoral record of "third" or "minor" parties is generally quite poor. Political scientists point to a number of behavioral and structural reasons for this pattern. As for behavior, voters are often reluctant to "waste" their vote for a candidate they believe has no chance to win, especially if they also believe that casting such a vote would increase the chances that a candidate they strongly dislike would win. Liberal Democrats faced this dilemma in 2000 when deciding whether to vote for Ralph Nader, the Green Party candidate for president, or Al Gore, the Democrat. When Gore lost by 537 votes in Florida, sealing the victory for Bush, many of the more than 97,000 Floridians who voted for Nader no doubt wondered if they had made a mistake. And as for structure, most electoral districts in the United States elect a single person to an office, so that means the candidate with the highest number of votes will win. Because of this arrangement, potential smaller parties have an incentive to join forces with one of the larger parties, and skilled candidates are more likely to want to run on the ticket of one of those larger parties. It is certainly not impossible for more than two parties to have a solid, durable presence in such a system—the British system similarly has single-member districts but has two major parties and a competitive third party—but it is difficult. The most successful third party in American history, the Republican party, was not a "third" party for long, as it quickly replaced the collapsing Whig Party.

In the 1990s, Ross Perot ran for president twice, gaining a very respectable 19 percent of the popular vote in 1992 and 8 percent in 1996 as a candidate of the Reform Party. Even though he did not win a single state, many observers credit Perot with introducing issues and perspectives into the campaign that the two major party candidates would have been less likely to discuss were he not in the race. Ralph Nader's presence in the race in 2000 may have pushed Al Gore to strike a more populist tone than he otherwise would have. Although third parties are unlikely to win, their supporters often suggest that they nonetheless can influence public debate. At certain moments, however, there is a sense among some political analysts that the time is especially ripe for possible third party electoral success. They believe this despite the obstacles mentioned above and a slew of others such as the need to raise substantial financial resources; the time and expense of getting on the ballot in all the states, which often involves lawsuits; the relative lack of attention from news media; and Americans' ingrained sense that the two-party system is what is "normal."

Peggy Noonan, a former speechwriter for President Ronald Reagan, believes that now might be the right time for a significant third party. The high decibel partisanship in Washington has worn thin the patience of the American public. The problem is not that the parties are too far apart. Rather, she says, both parties seem to be distant from the public. Neither party, she argues, is tapping into concerns "on the ground in America" on issues like government spending, immigration, and safety from terrorism. Important issues are treated as simply good ways to demonize opponents and attract supporters. To Noonan, a new party that challenges the disconnect between the bipartisan elite and the public can succeed. Ryan Lizza agrees. He argues that Howard Dean's bid for the Democratic presidential nomination in 2004 showed that the Internet could overcome many of the traditional obstacles facing third-party candidates. The net allowed Dean to manage a nationwide ballot access project quickly and efficiently. He demonstrated that a candidate with a message could reach thousands of supporters on the Internet and raise substantial amounts of campaign funds. In addition, Dean relied on a network of organizations and expertise outside the Democratic party that third-party candidates can draw on as well, especially if they are successful at fundraising. The only monopoly the major parties still have, Lizza contends, are the reputations attached to their brand names, and these are of decreasing value in a time of political alienation.

Tom DeLay and David Brooks question the need for a third party. In his 2006 farewell address to the House of Representatives, former Republican Majority Leader DeLay offered a passionate defense of the partisanship in Washington. It is, in DeLay's view, a direct result of important and principled differences about the direction public policy should take. The sparring between Democrats and Republicans is, he argues, a sign of the strength of America's democracy, not a sign of a problem: "You show me a nation without partisanship, and I'll show you a tyranny. For all its faults, it is partisanship, based on core principles, that clarifies our debates, that prevents one party from straying too far from the mainstream, and that constantly refreshes our politics with new ideas and new leaders." Compromise, to DeLay, should never be an end in and of itself.

Brooks sees signs of political change that might negate the strength of Noonan's and Lizza's call for a third party. The balance of power in the two major parties is turning more to centrists whose goals are less ideological and more about making government work well. The extreme voices of each party are increasingly being marginalized, as is their rigid stay-on-message political style. As Brooks sees it, "the smartest people in both parties have shifted attention from the past to the future, and a sense of flexibility and promise is in the air."

Peggy Noonan
Third Time

Something's happening. I have a feeling we're at some new beginning, that a big breakup's coming, and that though it isn't and will not be immediately apparent, we'll someday look back on this era as the time when a shift began.

All my adult life, people have been saying that the two-party system is ending, that the Democrats' and Republicans' control of political power in America is winding down. According to the traditional critique, the two parties no longer offer the people the choice they want and deserve. Sometimes it's said they are too much alike—Tweedledum and Tweedledee. Sometimes it's said they're too polarizing—too red and too blue for a nation in which many see things through purple glasses.

In 1992 Ross Perot looked like the breakthrough, the man who would make

Published in *The Wall Street Journal Online*, June 2006.

third parties a reality. He destabilized the Republicans and then destabilized himself. By the end of his campaign *he* seemed to be the crazy old aunt in the attic.

The Perot experience seemed to put an end to third-party fever. But I think it's coming back, I think it's going to grow, and I think the force behind it is unique in our history.

This week there was a small boomlet of talk about a new internet entity called Unity '08—a small collection of party veterans including moderate Democrats (former Carter aide Hamilton Jordan) and liberal-leaning Republicans (former Ford hand Doug Bailey) trying to join together with college students and broaden the options in the 2008 election. In terms of composition, Unity seems like the Concord Coalition, the bipartisan group (Warren Rudman, Bob Kerrey) that warns against high spending and deficits.

Unity seems to me to have America's growing desire for more political options right. But I think they've got the description of the problem wrong.

Their idea is that the two parties are too polarized to govern well. It is certainly true that the level of partisanship in Washington seems high. (Such things, admittedly, ebb, flow and are hard to judge. We look back at the post-World War II years and see a political climate of relative amity and moderation. But Alger Hiss and Dick Nixon didn't see it that way.) Nancy Pelosi seems to be pretty much in favor of anything that hurts Republicans, and Ken Mehlman is in favor of anything that works against Democrats. They both want their teams to win. Part of winning is making sure the other guy loses, and part of the fun of politics, of any contest, of life, can be the dance in the end zone.

But the dance has gotten dark.

Partisanship is fine when it's an expression of the high animal spirits produced by real political contention based on true political belief. But the current partisanship seems sour, not joyous. The partisanship has gotten deeper as *less* separates the governing parties in Washington. It is like what has been said of academic infighting: that it's so vicious because the stakes are so low.

The problem is not that the two parties are polarized. In many ways they're closer than ever. The problem is that the parties in Washington, and the people on the ground in America, are polarized. There is an increasing and profound distance between the rulers of both parties and the people—between the elites and the grunts, between those in power and those who put them there.

On the ground in America, people worry terribly—really, there are people who actually worry about it every day—about endless, weird, gushing government spending. But in Washington, those in power—Republicans and Democrats—stand arm in arm as they spend and spend. (Part of the reason is that they think they can buy off your unhappiness one way or another. After all, it's worked in the past. A hunch: It's not going to work forever or much longer. They've really run that trick into the ground.)

On the ground in America, regular people worry about the changes wrought by the biggest wave of immigration in our history, much of it illegal and therefore wholly connected to the needs of the immigrant and wholly unconnected to the agreed-upon needs of our nation. Americans worry about the myriad implications of the collapse of the American border. But Washington doesn't. Democrat Ted Kennedy and Republican George W. Bush see things pretty much eye to eye. They are going to educate the American people out of their low concerns.

There is a widespread sense in America—a conviction, actually—that we are not safe in the age of terror. That the port, the local power plant, even the local school, are not protected. Is Washington worried about this? Not so you'd notice. They're only worried about seeming unconcerned.

More to the point, people see the Republicans as incapable of managing the monster they've helped create—this big Homeland Security/Intelligence apparatus that is like some huge buffed guy at the gym who looks strong but can't even put on his T-shirt without help because he's so muscle-bound. As for the Democrats, who co-created Homeland Security, no one—no one—thinks they would be more managerially competent. Nor does anyone expect the Democrats to be more visionary as to what needs to be done. The best they can hope is the Democrats competently serve their interest groups and let the benefits trickle down.

Right now the Republicans and Democrats in Washington seem, from the outside, to be an elite colluding against the voter. They're in agreement: immigration should not be controlled but increased; spending will increase, etc.

Are there some dramatic differences? Yes. But both parties act as if they see them not as important questions (gay marriage, for instance) but as wedge issues. Which is, actually, abusive of people on both sides of the question. If it's a serious issue, face it. Don't play with it.

I don't see any potential party, or potential candidate, on the scene right now who can harness the disaffection of growing portions of the electorate. But a new group or entity that could define the problem correctly—that sees the big divide not as something between the parties but between America's ruling elite and its people—would be making long strides in putting third party ideas in play in America again.

Ryan Lizza
But Is a Third Party Possible?

The political world is rife with portents of the imminent appearance of a third party. Alienation from the two parties is peaking. Polarization has created an issues vacuum in the center. New Web-based organizational tools have made creating a party a simpler DIY [do-it-yourself] project. In fact, for a third party to spring into action, just one sign is missing: a heartbeat.

The last vestiges of the Reform Party were stamped out in 2000. Ralph Nader rode the national Green Party into the ground. Jesse Ventura has exited the political stage. All the high-profile characters who flirted publicly with a third-party run in the past decade decided against it. Colin Powell, the great hope of 1996, passed up his chance. The maverick pols who dubbed themselves the Gang of Seven, including Bill Bradley, Gary Hart, and Lowell Weicker, never moved beyond discussing a third party via speakerphone. Howard Dean decided to take over the Democratic Party rather than start his own. The final patch of dirt seemed to have been thrown on the coffin this year when John McCain, the great hope for third-party dreamers, started sucking up to Jerry Falwell.

The constellation of third-party fantasists seems depressed. I called John Anderson, the man who won 6.6 percent as an independent in 1980. Now 84, he thinks the moment is right but doesn't detect much action. "There is no clear clarion voice that I can point you to," he told me. "I think we're pretty much inured in the throes of the iron grip of the two-party system at the moment." He wondered what became of the last third-party insurgent. "I don't know what happened to Ross Perot," he asked quizzically. "He just completely went underground. He's still alive, but you don't hear anything from him."

Clay Mulford, Perot's son-in-law, longtime adviser, and 1992 campaign

Published in *New York Magazine*, April 2006.

manager, confirmed for me that Perot is indeed still alive. But Mulford sounded similarly discouraged. "What we have lost in America," he says, "is the ability for things to bubble up from the body politic and give voice to things that aren't being voiced by the major parties."

The closest thing I could find to an effort to launch a new third force was a semi-regular meeting in Washington of a few burned-out consultants from the Ford and Carter campaigns. They are led by ex-Ford adviser Doug Bailey and are trying to think through the mechanics of how a new party could be launched. Bailey declined to discuss the venture with me, but one person familiar with it says it is tentatively called the Unity Party. "It's a group of old Republican and Democratic consultants, none of whom are in the business anymore, people who are locked out or chose to opt out," says the source. "To be honest, it's like a bunch of old guys sitting around drinking beer."

But the old guys drinking beer are onto something. They understand why third parties emerge. In the nineteenth century, third parties were single-issue creatures that grew up around great causes that the major parties were ignoring. Abolition, women's suffrage, and the direct election of senators all started as third-party movements. The twentieth century was different. It has almost always taken a splashy candidate to light the fire of a third-party movement in the past hundred years—from Teddy Roosevelt in 1912 to George Wallace in 1968 to Ross Perot in 1992. But even as third parties have changed from bottom-up to top-down endeavors—tracking the same candidate-centric trend as the major parties—they have thrived most often when the two parties allowed hot issues to be exploited. Political scientists call this "major-party failure," moments in history when the Democrats and Republicans "neglect the concerns of significant blocs of voters, mismanage the economy, or nominate unqualified candidates," according to the single best study on the subject, *Third Parties in America.*

Is there any doubt we are in the midst of major-party failure today? Whether it's the once-again-relevant centrist issues championed by Perot (the exploding deficits, political reform), the great issues on the left waiting for a champion (universal health care, global warming), or the always festering anxieties of the nationalist right (immigration, isolationism), there is no shortage of ideas for a third-party candidate to seize.

But as important as issues have always been to starting a third party, there is another essential ingredient: political alienation. Americans today are as alienated from the major parties as they have ever been. Independents and third-party registrants are the fastest-growing bloc of voters. They made up 22 percent of the electorate in 2004—a new high. It seems obvious that Perot's 1992 campaign—stoked by frustration with congressional scandals and a recession—coincided with a low point in political alienation. It didn't. Political allegiance to the two parties, disaffection with Bush and Clinton, and anxiety over the economy were actually no worse in 1992 than they were in 1980 when John Anderson ran. But Perot won 19 percent of the vote, while Anderson won just 6.6 percent. What this comparison, laid out in detail by the authors of *Third Parties in America*, suggests is that, rather than a pendulum that swings back and forth, political alienation has become a permanent fixture of our politics. Third-party voters, at least the kind that Anderson and Perot stirred, exist as a lode ready to be mined.

So why hasn't there been a serious attempt to start a third party since Perot? Every big-name politician who has looked at the idea has come to the same conclusion: The institutional barriers to creating a third-party are too high. The first and most discouraging obstacle is that America's ballot laws are a mishmash of arcane procedures that were written by the two parties to keep third parties out of the system. "The biggest problem that I faced back in 1980," says Anderson, "was simply the question of ballot access. How do you get a new party on the ballot? You can't start a new party and expect it to take wing and soar if it can't even get on the ballot. I at one time had lawsuits going in about nine different federal courts. We spent somewhere between $2 million and $3 million paying lawyers to knock down restrictive ballot-access laws." Eventually, Anderson made it onto all 50 state ballots, but his campaign turned into one for ballot access rather than president.

Today's maze of ballot laws has its roots in the early thirties, when fears of communism encouraged states to make it difficult for third parties to qualify. In some states, a large percentage of registered voters must sign a party's ballot petition (in California you need 153,000 valid signatures). In some states the petition circulators must be local residents (Nader was kicked off the Ohio ballot for using out-of-staters). Some states require that petitions be circulated by congressional district. West Virginia once demanded that "magisterial districts" be used. To be safe, a campaign must collect one and a half times the number of names required. Signatures can be struck in some states if the person voted in a party primary. In other states, the circulator of the petition must be a registered voter. Until 1986, Texas required every signatory to know their voter-registration I.D. "The Republican Party was founded on July 6 of 1854," says

Richard Winger, a Californian libertarian who has made the arcana of ballot-access laws his life's work. "It went on to win a plurality in the House in that election. That couldn't happen today."

Running 50 separate ballot-access campaigns with varying deadlines and booby-trapped rules requires a great deal of money. In 2008, a third-party candidate would need some 700,000 valid signatures to qualify for the ballots in all 50 states. To be safe, he would want to collect well over a million. And that's before spending any money on ads, polling, and the rest of a campaign's costs. "You need between $70 million and $100 million," says Russell Verney, Perot's 1996 manager. "Either personal wealth or contributions."

If a third-party candidate does get on the ballot and raises enough money, one major goal remains: getting into the presidential debates. The debate commission is heavily rigged toward the Democrats and Republicans. Its main criterion for accepting a third-party candidate is evidence of widespread support reflected in polls. There is a chicken-and-egg problem to gaining this legitimacy. The most successful third-party candidates are the ones who convince voters that they have a chance of winning—in other words, the ones who successfully rebut the two major candidates' arguments that a vote for a third choice will be wasted. The debates—high-profile moments when all three candidates share the same stage—can create that credibility.

That litany of hardships was what any politician heard from advisers when contemplating a third-party run. No wonder so few of them took the plunge. But then came the Internet—and Howard Dean's campaign.

The Dean campaign proved many things, but its most enduring legacy may be that it gave us a glimpse of the beginning of the end of the two-party system. First, he showed the next budding Ross Perot how to manage a 50-state ballot-access project easily and cost-efficiently. It is not widely understood, but candidates running in the presidential primaries of the two major parties also must qualify for the ballot of every state they want to contest. Dean was the only insurgent Democratic-primary candidate in history to qualify in all 50 states, a stunning organizational achievement. Using a ballot-access function of the campaign's Website, Deaniacs in every state had downloadable petitions and details about the rules for their state. Goals were tracked in real time. "Both parties have set up nominating and ballot hurdles, so an insurgency can't happen," says Joe Trippi, Dean's first campaign manager and now an evangelist for a third party. "We blew through that in 2003."

The second hurdle—fund-raising—also has a technological solution. Dean proved a message candidate could work outside any established infrastructure and raise massive amounts of money. After Perot, the assumption was that only a self-financed candidate could mount a credible third-party challenge. Dean exploded that conventional wisdom.

Dean's campaign not only suggested that the traditional obstacles to starting a third party are surmountable, but it also raised questions about the purpose of the two parties themselves. What assets, after all, do the Democratic and Republican parties bestow on a nominee? There was once a time when the parties served a policy role for the presidential candidate. The nominating convention was a time when delegates drew up a party platform for the candidate to run on. No more. Candidates routinely ignore the platform—in 1996, Bob Dole famously said he hadn't read it—and run on their own issues.

What's left? The other assets parties offer are a fund-raising infrastructure (e-mail lists, donor databases) and an organizational infrastructure (county chairs, precinct captains, local volunteers). But the parties no longer have a monopoly on these two networks. A charismatic candidate can build his own alternative fund-raising base overnight and collect an army of volunteers in a matter of weeks. In fact, with the rise of political groups known as 527s, which raise money (often from billionaires like George Soros), run ads, and turn out voters, the parties have already gone a long way toward outsourcing their core activities. The only assets controlled by the two parties that can't be reproduced by an entrepreneurial independent are their distinctive brands, the value of which is in steep decline.

"You have these two parties where lots of people aren't happy with either one of them," says Trippi. "You've got this way for all those people to connect together behind a candidate who is third-party or an independent. I think it's inevitable that it's going to happen. There's no way we are going to be looking at a two-party system—or these two parties. My feeling is we're sort of there already and it just takes one bold candidacy. Someone bolting one of the two major parties right now could make that party go the way of the Whigs." Any takers?

Representative Tom DeLay
Farewell Address

Mr. Speaker, political careers tend to end in one of three ways: defeat, death, or retirement. And despite the fervent and mostly noble exertions of my adversaries over the years, I rise today to bid farewell to this House under the happiest of the available options. . . .

The dome above us, Mr. Speaker, is a light house, a star even, by which all of the people in the world, no matter how oppressed, how impoverished, how seemingly without hope can chart a course toward security, prosperity, and freedom.

It is worth considering, though I will admit it is considerably easier to consider after you have announced your retirement, whether the days we lead here, the debates we wage, the work we do is always worthy of the elevated ideals embodied in that dome.

I submit that we could do better, as could all people in all things at all times, but perhaps not in the way some might think. In preparing for today, I found that it is customary in speeches such as these to reminisce about the good old days of political harmony, and across-the-aisle camaraderie, and to lament the bitter divisive partisan rancor that supposedly now weakens our democracy.

Well, I cannot do that, because partisanship, Mr. Speaker, properly understood, is not a symptom of democracy's weakness, but of its health and its strength, especially from the perspective of a political conservative.

Liberalism, after all, whatever you may think of its merits, is a political philosophy and a proud one, with a great tradition in this country with a voracious appetite for growth. In any place, or any time, on any issue, what does liberalism ever seek, Mr. Speaker? More. More government. More taxation. More control over people's lives and decisions and wallets.

If conservatives do not stand up to liberalism, no one will. And for a long time around here, almost no one did. Indeed, the common lament over the recent rise in political partisanship is often nothing more than a veiled complaint instead about the recent rise of political conservatism.

I should add here that I do not begrudge liberals their nostalgia for the days

Given June 8, 2006.

of a timid, docile, and permanent Republican minority. If we Republicans had ever enjoyed that same luxury over the last twelve years, heck, I would be nostalgic too.

Had liberals not fought us tooth and nail over tax cuts and budget cuts and energy and Iraq and partial birth abortion, those of us on this side of the aisle can only imagine all of the additional things we could have accomplished.

But the fact of the matter is, Mr. Speaker, they did not agree with us. So to their credit, they stood up to us. They argued with us. And they did so honorably on behalf of more than 100 million people, just like we did against President Clinton and they did against President Reagan.

Now, it goes without saying, Mr. Speaker, that by my count, our friends on the other side of the aisle lost every one of those arguments over the last 22 years, but that is besides the point. The point is, we disagree. On first principles, Mr. Speaker, we disagree. And so we debate, often loudly and often in vain, to convince our opponents and the American people of our point of view.

We debate here on the House floor. We debate in committees. We debate on television, and on radio and on the Internet and in the newspapers; and then every two years we have a huge debate, and then in November, we see who won.

That is not rancor; that is democracy. You show me a Nation without partisanship, and I will show you a tyranny. For all its faults, it is partisanship based on core principles that clarifies our debates, that prevents one party from straying too far from the mainstream, and that constantly refreshes our politics with new ideas and new leaders.

Indeed, whatever role partisanship may have played in my own retirement today, or in the unfriendliness heaped upon other leaders in other times, Republican or Democrat, however unjust, all we can say is that partisanship is the worst means of settling fundamental political differences, except for all of the others.

Now, politics demands compromise, and, Mr. Speaker, even the most partisan among us have to understand that. But we must never forget that compromise and bipartisanship are means, not ends, and are properly employed only in the service of higher principles. It is not the principled partisan, however obnoxious he may seem to his opponents who degrade our public debate, but the preening self-styled statesman who elevates compromise to a first principle.

For the true statesmen, Mr. Speaker, are not defined by what they compromise, but what they do not. Conservatives, especially less enamored of government's lust for growth, must remember that our principles must always drive our agenda and not the other way around. . . .

The great Americans honored here in bronze and marble, the heroes of our history and the ghosts of these halls were not made great because of what they were but because of what they did. . . We honor men with monuments not because of their greatness or even simply because of their service, but because of their refusal even in the face of danger or death to ever compromise the principles they served.

Washington's obelisk still stands watch because democracy will always need a sentry. Jefferson's words will still ring because liberty will always need a voice. And Lincoln's left hand still stays clenched because tyranny will always need an enemy. And we are still here, Mr. Speaker, as a House and as a Nation because the torch of freedom cannot carry itself.

Here on this floor, I have caught and thrown spears of every sort. Over the course of 22 years, I have probably worked with and against almost everyone in this Chamber at least once. I have scraped and clawed for every vote, every amendment for every word of every bill that I believed in my heart would protect human freedom and defend human dignity. I have done so at all times honorably and honestly, Mr. Speaker, with God as my witness and history as my judge. And if given the chance to do it all again, there is only one thing I would change. I would fight even harder. . . .

David Brooks
Don't Worry, Be Happy

Can you spare a moment for the nation's sole remaining optimist?

The *Times*/CBS News Poll that was reported yesterday [May 10, 2006] revealed that Americans are more pessimistic about the country's direction than at almost any time in the past 23 years. George Bush's approval numbers are so low that he's now only five points more popular than John Kerry and three points more popular than Al Gore.

But from where I sit as president of the Prozac Would Be Redundant Society, all the negativity is a few months out of date.

Published in *The New York Times*, May 2006.

First, look at some fundamentals. The International Monetary Fund predicts that the world economy will grow at 4.9 percent, which would be the second fastest annual rate in three decades. Free institutions spread more quickly last year than in any year since 1972, when Freedom House began measuring these things. According to the Human Security Report, the number of wars with at least 1,000 deaths in battle has dropped by 80 percent since 1992. Air pollution levels are plummeting; over the last three years we've had the lowest level of ozone smog violations on record.

The reason people are down is not because their own lives are awful—it's because they're suffering a crisis of authority. They no longer have confidence in the institutions that are supposed to maintain order in their lives, whether the topic's terrorism, gas prices, or federal spending.

But even here, the latest news is good. Look around at all the green shoots of political renewal.

Not long ago, the temper-tantrum left seemed to be on the verge of capturing the Democratic Party, but now the Clintonite centrists are reasserting their intellectual, financial, and political supremacy.

Last month, Hillary Clinton gave a proto-campaign speech in Chicago, laying out an economic agenda that Kevin Hassett of the American Enterprise Institute called remarkably centrist. Clinton called for a return to "pay as you go" budget rules. Congress couldn't raise spending or cut taxes unless it filled the hole in the budget right away, the only effective way to restore fiscal balance.

Robert Rubin and others have begun the Hamilton Project, which is churning out policy ideas that defy easy categorization and serve as a blueprint for an innovative, moderate administration. The Democratic agenda will be fleshed out by the free-trade progressive Gene Sperling, and by Rahm Emanuel and Bruce Reed, whose coming book will push ideas on how to increase savings and such.

On the Republican side, meanwhile, most of the news in the next 18 months will be made by John McCain, Mitt Romney, and Rudy Giuliani. This is a party in the midst of fundamental change. Some of the professional conservative groups that claim they have veto power over who runs the party are about to be exposed.

The intra-Republican debate is less well developed than the Democratic debate because until a few months ago, conservatives passively awaited leadership from the White House. But that has changed, too, and the signs of rethinking are everywhere.

Yesterday in the House, Mark Kirk and other Republicans unveiled a "suburban agenda" to help suburban families, not K Street lobbyists. On the Cato Institute's Web site, there is a roiling debate about fundamentals led by David Frum and Bruce Bartlett. These free marketeers acknowledge that in an aging society it's going to be hard to cut the size of government, so they ask, What do we do now? In *The Weekly Standard*, Irwin Stelzer wonders if it may be time to cut the payroll tax and raise the top rates, to shift the burden away from those who bear the brunt of trade and immigration.

In short, the smartest people in both parties have shifted attention from the past to the future, and a sense of flexibility and promise is in the air.

There's been an even bigger shift in attitudes about how politics should be done. The Stalinist on-message style is passé. The rising young politicians like Barack Obama and Lindsey Graham never talk in that predictable party-hack way. Mark Warner and Romney are building their campaigns around their ability to find common ground with political opponents.

The pseudopopulist renegades who rail against the establishment are being eclipsed by the canny establishmentarians. They're the ones who know how to use the levers of government to get things done.

Remember, my downcast fellow citizens, nothing stays the same. Spring brings rebirth, and the dewy green faeries of sanity are flittering down the think tank corridors and o'er the politicians' upturned brows.

QUESTIONS

1. *What would you do?* Imagine that it is a presidential election year and you are living in a closely contested "battleground" state. Each of the major parties believes its candidate can win your state, and each will need your state in order to win a majority of the electoral college votes and the presidency. Public opinion surveys indicate the election to be essentially tied between the two major party candidates. A third party candidate that you have strongly supported throughout the election year is also running. Supporters of one of the major party candidates urge you to forget about voting for the third party candidate because he cannot win. Even worse, because you are not voting for

their candidate, you are in effect helping the other major party win, and you dislike that candidate most of all. Do you vote on election day? Do you vote for the third party or the major party candidate? Why?

2. If Brooks is right, is the need for a third party along the lines outlined by Noonan and Lizza less convincing?

3. Can a third party be successful with a pragmatic agenda ("We believe in health care for all") rather than one that has specific policy plans ("Everyone should pay a new 10 percent sales tax so we can provide some level of insurance for all Americans")? Should a party recruit candidates that agree on solutions to problems, as DeLay's vision of a political party would suggest? Or is it enough that all the candidates are committed to solving the problem?

10

The Electoral College:
Reform It or Leave It Alone?

The 2000 presidential election raised a new series of questions about the place of the Electoral College within our political system. Al Gore won the popular vote by more than a half a million votes, yet lost the presidency to George W. Bush in an Electoral College squeaker (271–267). This is the fourth time (or third, depending on how one counts the 1824 election) in which the popular vote winner did not become president. There have also been other close calls in which the shift of several thousand votes in a couple of states could have produced other popular vote losers (Woodrow Wilson, Harry Truman, John F. Kennedy, and Gerald Ford).

The authors in this chapter have a range of views about the wisdom of reforming the Electoral College. Arthur Schlesinger, the eminent historian, makes a strong argument for change. He notes that the Electoral College was a compromise that balanced regional interests against federal authority. Conventional wisdom holds that this nod to state power now serves as the largest impediment to reform: the small states that benefit from the Electoral College are unlikely to ratify any Constitutional amendment changing the system. However, Schlesinger argues that the Electoral College actually benefits the larger states. While the direct popular election of the president is appealing for its simplicity and fairness, Schlesinger recognizes the problems associated with the proposal, especially its impact on the party system. Instead, he advocates a creative solution of giving a bonus of 102 electoral votes to the popular vote winner. This would guarantee that the popular vote winner would become president, while preserving some of the virtues of the Electoral College system.

Norman Ornstein argues for preserving the Electoral College, warning that all reforms have unintended consequences. For example, if we elected presidents by popular vote, one nightmare scenario would be a national recount in which presidential candidates scrounged for every vote out of the more than 105 million cast, in half a million precincts. This would make Florida in 2000 look positively tame by comparison. Instead of reforming the Electoral College, Ornstein favors electoral reforms that would improve voting technology and smooth the registration process.

More than 1,000 proposals to change the Electoral College have been introduced in Congress in our history, including many that are less drastic than abolishing the institution and replacing it with the popular vote. Proposals include getting rid of the two-seat bonus in each state (a reform that would have given Gore the presidency in 2000), making the Electoral College automatic (to get rid of the "faithless elector" problem), or dividing the vote proportionally within each state, either by congressional district or by popular vote within the state. The congressional district plan, which is currently practiced in Maine and Nebraska, is the approach favored by the author of our last selection, James Glassman. This approach would not require a constitutional amendment and would introduce more competition into the system by getting rid of the winner-take-all characteristic of the Electoral College.

Arthur M. Schlesinger Jr.
Not the People's Choice

The true significance of the disputed 2000 election has thus far escaped public attention. This was an election that made the loser of the popular vote the president of the United States. But that astounding fact has been obscured: first by the flood of electoral complaints about deceptive ballots, hanging chads, and so on in Florida; then by the political astuteness of the court-appointed president in behaving as if he had won the White House by a landslide; and now by the

Published in *The American Prospect*, March 2002.

effect of September 11 in presidentializing George W. Bush and giving him commanding popularity in the polls.

"The fundamental maxim of republican government," observed Alexander Hamilton in the 22d *Federalist*, "requires that the sense of the majority should prevail." A reasonable deduction from Hamilton's premise is that the presidential candidate who wins the most votes in an election should also win the election. That quite the opposite can happen is surely the great anomaly in the American democratic order.

Yet the National Commission on Federal Election Reform, a body appointed in the wake of the 2000 election and co-chaired (honorarily) by former Presidents Gerald Ford and Jimmy Carter, virtually ignored it. Last August, in a report optimistically entitled *To Assure Pride and Confidence in the Electoral Process,* the commission concluded that it had satisfactorily addressed "most of the problems that came into national view" in 2000. But nothing in the ponderous eighty-page document addressed the most fundamental problem that came into national view: the constitutional anomaly that permits the people's choice to be refused the presidency.

Little consumed more time during our nation's Constitutional Convention than debate over the mode of choosing the chief executive. The Framers, determined to ensure the separation of powers, rejected the proposal that Congress elect the president. Both James Madison and James Wilson, the "fathers" of the Constitution, argued for direct election by the people, but the convention, fearing the parochialism of uninformed voters, also rejected that plan. In the end, the Framers agreed on the novel device of an electoral college. Each state would appoint electors equal in number to its representation in Congress. The electors would then vote for two persons. The one receiving a majority of electoral votes would then become president; the runner-up, vice president. And in a key sentence, the Constitution stipulated that of these two persons at least one should not be from the same state as the electors.

The convention expected the electors to be cosmopolitans who would know, or know of, eminences in other states. But this does not mean that they were created as free agents authorized to routinely ignore or invalidate the choice of the voters. The electors, said John Clopton, a Virginia congressman, are the "organs . . . acting from a certain and unquestioned knowledge of the choice of the people, by whom they themselves were appointed, and under immediate responsibility to them."

Madison summed it up when the convention finally adopted the electoral college: "The president is now to be elected by the people." The president, he assured the Virginia ratifying convention, would be "the choice of the people at large." In the First Congress, he described the president as appointed "by the suffrage of three million people."

"It was desirable," Alexander Hamilton wrote in the 68th *Federalist*, "that the sense of the people should operate in the choice of the person to whom so important a trust was to be confided." As Lucius Wilmerding Jr. concluded in his magisterial study of the electoral college: "The Electors were never meant to choose the President but only to pronounce the votes of the people."

Even with such a limited function, however, the electoral college has shaped the contours of American politics and thus captured the attention of politicians. With the ratification of the Twelfth Amendment in 1804, electors were required to vote separately for president and vice president, a change that virtually guaranteed that both would be of the same party. Though unknown to the Constitution and deplored by the Framers, political parties were remolding presidential elections. By 1836 every state except South Carolina had decided to cast its votes as a unit-winner take all, no matter how narrow the margin. This decision minimized the power of third parties and created a solid foundation for a two-party system.

"The mode of appointment of the Chief Magistrate [President] of the United States," wrote Hamilton in the 68th *Federalist*, "is almost the only part of the system, of any consequence, which has escaped without severe censure." This may have been true when Hamilton wrote in 1788; it was definitely not true thereafter. According to the Congressional Research Service, legislators since the First Congress have offered more than a thousand proposals to alter the mode of choosing presidents.

No legislator has advocated the election of the president by Congress. Some have advocated modifications in the electoral college—to change the electoral units from states to congressional districts, for example, or to require a proportional division of electoral votes. In the 1950s, the latter approach received considerable congressional favor in a plan proposed by Senator Henry Cabot Lodge Jr. and Representative Ed Gossett. The Lodge-Gossett amendment would have ended the winner-take-all electoral system and divided each state's electoral vote according to the popular vote. In 1950 the Senate endorsed the amendment, but the House turned it down. Five years later, Senator Estes Kefauver revived the Lodge-Gossett plan and won the backing of the Senate Judiciary Committee. A thoughtful debate ensued, with Senators John F. Kennedy and Paul H. Douglas leading the opposition and defeating the amendment.

Neither the district plan nor the proportionate plan would prevent a popular-vote loser from winning the White House. To correct this great anomaly of the Constitution, many have advocated the abolition of the electoral college and its replacement by direct popular elections.

The first "minority" president was John Quincy Adams. In the 1824 election, Andrew Jackson led in both popular and electoral votes; but with four candidates dividing the electoral vote, he failed to win an electoral-college majority. The Constitution provides that if no candidate has a majority, the House of Representatives must choose among the top three. Speaker of the House Henry Clay, who came in fourth, threw his support to Adams, thereby making him president. When Adams then made Clay his secretary of state, Jacksonian cries of "corrupt bargain" filled the air for the next four years and helped Jackson win the electoral majority in 1828.

"To the people belongs the right of electing their Chief Magistrate," Jackson told Congress in 1829. "The first principle of our system," he said, is "that the majority is to govern." He asked for the removal of all "intermediate" agencies preventing a "fair expression of the will of the majority." And in a tacit verdict on Adams's failed administration, Jackson added: "A President elected by a minority can not enjoy the confidence necessary to the successful discharge of his duties."

History bears out Jackson's point. The next two minority presidents—Rutherford B. Hayes in 1877 and Benjamin Harrison in 1889—had, like Adams, ineffectual administrations. All suffered setbacks in their midterm congressional elections. None won a second term in the White House.

The most recent president to propose a direct-election amendment was Jimmy Carter in 1997. The amendment, he said, would "ensure that the candidate chosen by the votes actually becomes President. Under the Electoral College, it is always possible that the winner of the popular vote will not be elected." This had already happened, Carter said, in 1824, 1876, and 1888.

Actually, Carter placed too much blame on the electoral system. Neither J. Q. Adams in 1824 nor Hayes in 1876 owed his elevation to the electoral college. The House of Representatives, as noted, elected Adams. Hayes's election was more complicated.

In 1876, Samuel J. Tilden, the Democratic candidate, won the popular vote, and it appeared that he had won the electoral vote too. But the Confederate states were still under military occupation, and electoral boards in Florida, Louisiana, and South Carolina disqualified enough Democratic ballots to give Hayes, the Republican candidate, the electoral majority.

The Republicans controlled the Senate; the Democrats, the House. Which body would count the electoral votes? To resolve the deadlock, Congress appointed an electoral commission. By an 8–7 party-line vote, the commission gave all the disputed votes to Hayes. This was a supreme election swindle. But it was the rigged electoral commission, not the electoral college, that denied the popular-vote winner the presidency.

In 1888 the electoral college did deprive the popular-vote winner, Democrat Grover Cleveland, of victory. But 1888 was a clouded election. Neither candidate received a majority, and Cleveland's margin was only 100,000 votes. Moreover, the claim was made, and was widely accepted at the time and by scholars since, that white election officials in the South banned perhaps 300,000 black Republicans from the polls. The installation of a minority president in 1889 took place without serious protest.

The Republic later went through several other elections in which a small shift of votes would have given the popular-vote loser an electoral-college victory. In 1916, if Charles Evans Hughes had gained 4,000 votes in California, he would have won the electoral-college majority, though he lost the popular vote to Woodrow Wilson by more than half a million. In 1948, a shift of fewer than 30,000 votes in three states would have given Thomas E. Dewey the electoral-college majority, though he ran more than two million votes behind Harry Truman. In 1976, a shift of 8,000 votes in two states would have kept President Gerald Ford in office, though he ran more than a million and a half votes behind Jimmy Carter.

Over the last half-century, many other eminent politicos and organizations have also advocated direct popular elections: Presidents Richard Nixon and Gerald Ford; Vice Presidents Alben Barkley and Hubert Humphrey; Senators Robert A. Taft, Mike Mansfield, Edward Kennedy, Henry Jackson, Robert Dole, Howard Baker, and Everett Dirksen; the American Bar Association, the League of Women Voters, the AFL-CIO, and the U.S. Chamber of Commerce. Polls have shown overwhelming public support for direct elections.

In the late 1960s, the drive for a direct-election amendment achieved a certain momentum. Led by Senator Birch Bayh of Indiana, an inveterate and persuasive constitutional reformer, the campaign was fueled by the fear that Governor George Wallace of Alabama might win enough electoral votes in

1968 to throw the election into the House of Representatives. In May 1968, a Gallup poll recorded 66 percent of the U.S. public in favor of direct election—and in November of that year, an astonishing 80 percent. But Wallace's 46 electoral votes in 1968 were not enough to deny Nixon a majority, and complacency soon took over. "The decline in one-party states," a Brookings Institution study concluded in 1970, "has made it far less likely today that the runner-up in popular votes will be elected President."

Because the danger of electoral-college misfire seemed academic, abolition of the electoral college again became a low-priority issue. Each state retained the constitutional right to appoint its electors "in such manner as the legislature thereof directs." And all but two states, Maine and Nebraska, kept the unit rule.

Then came the election of 2000. For the fourth time in American history, the winner of the popular vote was refused the presidency. And Albert Gore Jr. had won the popular vote not by Grover Cleveland's dubious 100,000 but by more than half a million. Another nearly three million votes had gone to the third-party candidate Ralph Nader, making the victor, George W. Bush, more than ever a minority president.

Nor was Bush's victory in the electoral college unclouded by doubt. The electoral vote turned on a single state, Florida. Five members of the Supreme Court, forsaking their usual deference to state sovereignty, stopped the Florida recount and thereby made Bush president. Critics wondered: If the facts had been the same but the candidates reversed, with Bush winning the popular vote (as indeed observers had rather expected) and Gore hoping to win the electoral vote, would the gang of five have found the same legal arguments to elect Gore that they used to elect Bush?

I expected an explosion of public outrage over the rejection of the people's choice. But there was surprisingly little in the way of outcry. It is hard to imagine such acquiescence in a popular-vote-loser presidency if the popular-vote winner had been, say, Adlai Stevenson or John F. Kennedy or Ronald Reagan. Such leaders attracted do-or-die supporters, voters who cared intensely about them and who not only would have questioned the result but would have been ardent in pursuit of fundamental reform. After a disappointing campaign, Vice President Gore simply did not excite the same impassioned commitment.

Yet surely the 2000 election put the Republic in an intolerable predicament—intolerable because the result contravened the theory of democracy. Many expected that the election would resurrect the movement for direct election of presidents. Since direct elections have obvious democratic plausibility and since few Americans understand the electoral college anyway, its abolition seems a logical remedy.

The resurrection has not taken place. Constitutional reformers seem intimidated by the argument that a direct-election amendment would antagonize small-population states and therefore could not be ratified. It would necessarily eliminate the special advantage conferred on small states by the two electoral votes handed to all states regardless of population. Small-state opposition, it is claimed, would make it impossible to collect the two-thirds of Congress and the three-fourths of the states required for ratification.

This is an odd argument, because most political analysts are convinced that the electoral college in fact benefits large states, not small ones. Far from being hurt by direct elections, small states, they say, would benefit from them. The idea that "the present electoral-college preserves the power of the small states," write Lawrence D. Longley and Alan G. Braun in *The Politics of Electoral Reform*, ". . . simply is not the case." The electoral college system "benefits large states, urban interests, white minorities, and/or black voters." So, too, a Brookings Institution report: "For several decades liberal, urban Democrats and progressive, urban-suburban Republicans have tended to dominate presidential politics; they would lose influence under the direct-vote plan."

Racial minorities holding the balance of power in large states agree. "Take away the electoral college," said Vernon Jordan as president of the Urban League, "and the importance of being black melts away. Blacks, instead of being crucial to victory in major states, simply become 10 percent of the electorate, with reduced impact."

The debate over whom direct elections would benefit has been long, wearisome, contradictory, and inconclusive. Even computer calculations are of limited use, since they assume a static political culture. They do not take into account, nor can they predict, the changes wrought in voter dynamics by candidates, issues, and events.

As Senator John Kennedy said during the Lodge-Gossett debate: "It is not only the unit vote for the Presidency we are talking about, but a whole solar system of governmental power. If it is proposed to change the balance of power of one of the elements of the solar system," Kennedy observed, "it is necessary to consider all the others. . . . What the effects of these various changes will be on the Federal system, the two-party system, the popular plurality system and the large-State–small-State checks and balances system, no one knows."

Direct elections do, however, have the merit of correcting the great anomaly of the Constitution and providing an escape from the intolerable predicament. "The electoral college method of electing a President of the United States," said the American Bar Association when an amendment was last seriously considered, "is archaic, undemocratic, complex, ambiguous, indirect, and dangerous." In contrast, as Birch Bayh put it, "direct popular election of the president is the only system that is truly democratic, truly equitable, and can truly reflect the will of the people."

The direct-election plan meets the moral criteria of a democracy. It would elect the people's choice. It would ensure equal treatment of all votes. It would reduce the power of sectionalism in politics. It would reinvigorate party competition and combat voter apathy by giving parties the incentive to get out their votes in states that they have no hope of carrying.

The arguments for abolishing the electoral college are indeed powerful. But direct elections raise troubling problems of their own—especially their impact on the two-party system and on JFK's "solar system of governmental power."

In the nineteenth century, American parties inspired visiting Europeans with awe. Alexis de Tocqueville, in the 1830s, thought politics "the only pleasure which an American knows." James Bryce, half a century later, was impressed by the "military discipline" of the parties. Voting statistics justified transatlantic admiration. In no presidential election between the Civil War and the end of the century did turnout fall below 70 percent of eligible voters.

The dutiful citizens of these high-turnout years did not rush to the polls out of uncontrollable excitement over the choices they were about to make. The dreary procession of presidential candidates moved Bryce to write his famous chapter in *The American Commonwealth* titled "Why Great Men Are Not Chosen Presidents." But the party was supremely effective as an agency of voter mobilization. Party loyalty was intense. People were as likely to switch parties as they were to switch churches. The great difference between then and now is the decay of the party as the organizing unit of American politics.

The modern history of parties has been the steady loss of the functions that gave them their classical role. Civil-service reform largely dried up the reservoir of patronage. Social legislation reduced the need for parties to succor the poor and helpless. Mass entertainment gave people more agreeable diversions than listening to political harangues. Party loyalty became tenuous; party identification, casual. Franklin D. Roosevelt observed in 1940: "The growing independence of voters, after all, has been proved by the votes in every presidential election since my childhood—and the tendency, frankly, is on the increase."

Since FDR's day, a fundamental transformation in the political environment has further undermined the shaky structure of American politics. Two electronic technologies—television and computerized polling—have had a devastating impact on the party system. The old system had three tiers: the politician at one end, the voter at the other, and the party in between. The party's function was to negotiate between the politician and the voter, interpreting each to the other and providing the links that held the political process together.

The electronic revolution has substantially abolished this mediating role. Television presents politicians directly to the voters, who judge candidates far more on what the box shows them than on what the party organization tells them. Computerized polls present voters directly to the politicians, who judge the electorate far more on what the polls show them than on what the party organization tells them. The political party is left to wither on the vine.

The last half-century has been notable for the decrease in party identification, for the increase in independent voting, and for the number of independent presidential candidacies by fugitives from the major parties: Henry Wallace and Strom Thurmond in 1948, George Wallace in 1968, Eugene McCarthy in 1976, John Anderson in 1980, Ross Perot in 1992 and 1996, and Ralph Nader and Pat Buchanan in 2000.

The two-party system has been a source of stability; FDR called it "one of the greatest methods of unification and of teaching people to think in common terms." The alternative is a slow, agonized descent into an era of what Walter Dean Burnham has termed "politics without parties." Political adventurers might roam the countryside like Chinese warlords, building personal armies equipped with electronic technologies, conducting hostilities against various rival warlords, forming alliances with others, and, if they win elections, striving to govern through ad hoc coalitions. Accountability would fade away. Without the stabilizing influences of parties, American politics would grow angrier, wilder, and more irresponsible.

There are compelling reasons to believe that the abolition of state-by-state, winner-take-all electoral votes would hasten the disintegration of the party system. Minor parties have a dim future in the electoral college. Unless third parties have a solid regional base, like the Populists of 1892 or the Dixiecrats of 1948, they cannot hope to win electoral votes. Millard Fillmore, the Know-Nothing candidate in 1856, won 21.6 percent of the popular vote and only 2 percent of the electoral vote. In 1912, when Theodore Roosevelt's candidacy turned the Republicans into a third party, William Howard Taft carried 23 percent of the popular vote and only 1.5 percent of the electoral votes.

But direct elections, by enabling minor parties to accumulate votes from state to state—impossible in the electoral-college system—would give them a new role and a new influence. Direct-election advocates recognize that the proliferation of minor candidates and parties would drain votes away from the major parties. Most direct-election amendments therefore provide that if no candidate receives 40 percent of the vote the two top candidates would fight it out in a runoff election.

This procedure would offer potent incentives for radical zealots (Ralph Nader, for example), freelance media adventurers (Pat Buchanan), eccentric billionaires (Ross Perot), and flamboyant characters (Jesse Ventura) to jump into presidential contests; incentives, too, to "green" parties, senior-citizen parties, nativist parties, right-to-life parties, pro-choice parties, anti-gun-control parties, homosexual parties, prohibition parties, and so on down the single-issue line.

Splinter parties would multiply not because they expected to win elections but because their accumulated vote would increase their bargaining power in the runoff. Their multiplication might well make runoffs the rule rather than the exception. And think of the finagling that would take place between the first and second rounds of a presidential election! Like J. Q. Adams in 1824, the victors would very likely find that they are a new target for "corrupt bargains."

Direct election would very likely bring to the White House candidates who do not get anywhere near a majority of the popular votes. The prospect would be a succession of 41 percent presidents or else a succession of double national elections. Moreover, the winner in the first round might often be beaten in the second round, depending on the deals the runoff candidates made with the splinter parties. This result would hardly strengthen the sense of legitimacy that the presidential election is supposed to provide. And I have yet to mention the problem, in close elections, of organizing a nationwide recount.

In short, direct elections promise a murky political future. They would further weaken the party system and further destabilize American politics. They would cure the intolerable predicament—but the cure might be worse than the disease.

Are we therefore stuck with the great anomaly of the Constitution? Is no remedy possible?

There is a simple and effective way to avoid the troubles promised by the direct-election plan and at the same time to prevent the popular-vote loser from being the electoral-vote winner: Keep the electoral college but award the popular-vote winner a bonus of electoral votes. This is the "national bonus" plan proposed in 1978 by the Twentieth Century Fund Task Force on Reform of the Presidential Election Process. The task force included, among others, Richard Rovere and Jeanne Kirkpatrick. (And I must declare an interest: I was a member, too, and first proposed the bonus plan in the *Wall Street Journal* in 1977.)

Under the bonus plan, a national pool of 102 new electoral votes—two for each state and the District of Columbia—would be awarded to the winner of the popular vote. This national bonus would balance the existing state bonus—the two electoral votes already conferred by the Constitution on each state regardless of population. This reform would virtually guarantee that the popular-vote winner would also be the electoral-vote winner.

At the same time, by retaining state electoral votes and the unit rule, the plan would preserve both the constitutional and the practical role of the states in presidential elections. By insulating recounts, it would simplify the consequences of close elections. By discouraging multiplication of parties and candidates, the plan would protect the two-party system. By encouraging parties to maximize their vote in states that they have no chance of winning, it would reinvigorate state parties, stimulate turnout, and enhance voter equality. The national-bonus plan combines the advantages in the historic system with the assurance that the winner of the popular vote will win the election, and it would thus contribute to the vitality of federalism.

The national-bonus plan is a basic but contained reform. It would fit comfortably into the historic structure. It would vindicate "the fundamental maxim of republican government . . . that the sense of the majority should prevail." It would make the American democracy live up to its democratic pretensions.

How many popular-vote losers will we have to send to the White House before we finally democratize American democracy?

Norman Ornstein

No Need to Repeal the Electoral College

Until this November, the Electoral College was a vague remembrance from high school civics classes, a subject to master for SATs (and then forget immediately afterward) or an occasional final *Jeopardy* category. Not anymore.

The election controversy of 2000, the first of any major magnitude since 1876, has put the Electoral College right in front of Americans' faces, on their television screens, and in daily conversations in barber shops, coffee houses, at office water coolers, and the dinner table.

Of course, if the Electoral College was civics trivia for most citizens, it has been a matter of great disagreement and concern to lawmakers and other opinion leaders since its inception. It was, after all, a compromise born of a struggle at the Constitutional Convention between small states and large states, or more accurately, between confederalists, who wanted to incorporate most of the Articles of Confederation, and those who wanted a large, national republic. As the late political theorist Martin Diamond has written, the confederalists wanted the president to be chosen directly by state legislatures. James Madison, James Wilson, and Governor Morris preferred a direct popular vote. That option was vehemently rejected by the confederalists. So Madison and his allies hit upon the Electoral College as a way to keep the states involved, but retain a role for the people. The state legislatures would choose electors, but they would be guided by the popular vote.

Their compromise did not stop the controversy. Actually, nothing has. The EC was changed early on (in 1804) via the Twelfth Amendment to the Constitution, creating separate votes by electors for president and vice president to avoid the problem of a president elected from one party and a vice president from the other. (Until then, the candidate with the most electoral votes became president and the runner up became vice president). The EC was changed again via legislation in states in the nineteenth century, as they responded to the democracy movement and went to having the electors selected via direct popular vote within the states (almost always on a winner-take-all basis).

Published in *State Legislatures*, February 2001.

1,028 Proposals to Change the System

But those adjustments have not erased the broader debate. The Congressional Research Service has uncovered 1,028 legislative proposals for changing the system since the First Congress. Between 1889 and 1946, 109 constitutional amendments to reform the Electoral College were introduced in Congress, with another 265 between 1947 and 1968. In 1967, an American Bar Association commission recommended that the Electoral College be scrapped and replaced by direct popular vote for the president, with a provision for a runoff if no candidate achieved the threshold of 40 percent of the votes. The ABA plan, introduced by Indiana Senator Birch Bayh and endorsed by the Nixon White House, passed the House 338–70, but died on a filibuster in the Senate led by North Carolina Senator Sam Ervin.

Since 1969, there have been at least 113 reform proposals introduced in Congress—with many more certain to come next year. Most of the proposals call directly for abolition of the EC, and its replacement by direct popular vote. Others call for retaining the EC, but mandating that states divide their electoral votes by congressional district (as is now done voluntarily in Nebraska and Maine), or by proportion of popular votes cast in each state. A small number calls simply for the elimination of electors—the real-live, flesh-and-blood people who go to their state capitols in mid-December to cast the electoral votes—and their replacement by an automatic system.

Why Reform?

Why the insistent calls for reform, mostly via elimination? The main reason is the broader cultural and societal impetus for more and more "democracy"—the same impetus that has extended the vote to women, minorities, and young people, and that has generated the movement to direct democracy via initiatives and referendums.

Another reason is the trend toward nationalization of politics in America—the sense that an emphasis on states is archaic for a modern national government. A third reason is the fear of an election outcome that would be viewed as illegitimate—especially one where a presidential candidate wins a majority of the national popular vote but still loses the presidency to a candidate who prevails in the Electoral College.

America has certainly had its electoral crises related to the Electoral College: in 1800, when an EC tie between Thomas Jefferson and Aaron Burr required the House to select the president, taking 36 ballots and ending up with Jefferson winning and his foe Burr serving as vice president; in 1824, when a four-way race left no candidate with a majority of electoral votes, and House maneuvering made John Quincy Adams, who led neither in popular nor electoral votes, the winner; in 1876, when disputed electoral slates in three states (including Florida) had to be sorted out by an electoral commission. In addition, in 1888, we had the dreaded result of a president (Grover Cleveland) elected without a popular vote majority or plurality (albeit with little evident national controversy or disagreement).

But three (or four) crises out of more than fifty presidential elections is remarkably small. And the drive for reform, based on the actual crises or the threat of another precipitated by the Electoral College, tends to ignore the crises that could be generated by direct national popular vote for the president.

The calls for reform accelerated with the 2000 presidential vote count, which started as a bad dream and ended up as a recurring nightmare—kind of like the movies *Groundhog Day* and *Friday the 13th* combined. The subsequent calls for repeal of the Electoral College were led by Senator-elect Hillary Rodham Clinton.

Iron Law of Unintended Consequences

It is only natural, of course, when a problem emerges, to seek a way to solve that problem. But the impulse to do so also brings with it what many have called "The Iron Law of Unintended Consequences." This election snarl provides a perfect example. As an exercise, let's look at this election through the lens of Frank Capra's *It's a Wonderful Life*: What would have happened if there were no Electoral College?

For one thing, we would have had no quick and clean resolution of the election. On the morning after the election, Al Gore led George W. Bush by around 200,000 votes, or about 0.2 percent. That on the surface might seem substantial enough. But there were approximately 3 million absentee and vote-by-mail ballots yet to be counted, including well over one million in California, and several hundred thousand each in Oregon and Washington. It took more than three full weeks for all those absentee and vote-by-mail ballots to be tallied, with doubt remaining over the final leader for nearly all that period.

The almost-final difference between the candidates was 333,576 votes, roughly 0.3 percent [*Editors' note:* The official vote tally shows Gore winning 543,895 more votes than Bush, or .516 percent; see http://www.fec.gov/ pubrec/fe2000/prespop.htm]. That is well below the number that triggers an automatic recount in Florida and many other states (some use 0.5 percent, some 0.33 percent, and so on.) Can anyone doubt that a hard-fought presidential campaign ending with a cloud over the counts in a number of counties and precincts around the country would call for a recount?

But that would not be a recount like Florida—confined to sixty-seven counties, each with its own clear-cut partisan power structure and administration. Instead we would have a nationwide recount, taking place in thousands of election units, some counties, some cities, some precincts, depending on individual states. All the ballot boxes in the country would have to be impounded. Instead of the squadron of lawyers who have descended on Florida to oversee, sue, and kibitz about the recounts, we would have armies of lawyers, exceeding the troops massed for the D-Day invasion, fanning out across the country to argue, bicker, and litigate.

This horrific nightmare would not likely be a one-time thing if the Electoral College were abolished. There has been a sharp trend in the country toward absentee ballots and vote-by-mail. The parties have encouraged it, because it is easier and cheaper to get out the vote by targeting voters and getting commitments in advance, fulfilled just by filling out a ballot and mailing it in. The states have moved in that direction because it can increase turnout and reduce their costs of keeping polling places open and filled with workers. California has up to a third of its voters going absentee, Washington about 60 percent, and Oregon went to a total vote-by-mail system this time. In 1996, the Census Bureau calculated that 20 percent of voters nationwide voted absentee; the number from this [2004] election will approach 30 percent.

Problems with Absentees

But there are huge problems with absentee voting, starting with the fact that more and more people are voting weeks before the campaign ends, before they know what happens or how the candidates react under the intense pressure of the final days of the process.

Imagine if a fifteen-round heavyweight championship fight had the judges vote on a winner after the twelfth round. The staggered voting has sharply increased the costs of campaigning, and has actually increased the amount of negative campaign advertising; instead of saving their firepower until the final two weeks, when most voters begin to pay attention, candidates and parties in heavy absentee states have been forced to advertise much sooner for the early voters, and then spend more to target the later ones.

More significant for the purposes of evaluating the Electoral College, absentee votes and vote-by-mail have other important characteristics: one, they are more laborious to count—envelopes have to be opened individually, signatures checked, ballots certified, and searches done to be sure citizens vote only once, and counts taken. Oregon's self-vaunted all vote-by-mail system was a national embarrassment; the state only included ballots that arrived by the close-of-business Election Day, but it couldn't come up with any counts for days thereafter.

Of course, in most states, a large share of the absentee ballots don't arrive by Election Day. Many states are like Florida, allowing ten days after an election for overseas and other ballots postmarked by Election Day to come in and be counted. In Washington, any ballot postmarked Election Day is counted no matter when it arrives, adding to potential delays. So brace yourselves: Eliminate the Electoral College, and it will be a rare presidential election where we know the outcome even a week after!

Proponents of the repeal of the Electoral College might argue that this scenario is not a great brief in favor of it. If both the EC and direct popular vote have even equal potential built in for nightmares, why not opt for the more directly democratic process?

The answer is that there are many other powerful arguments in favor of the Electoral College. The EC tends to produce larger and more decisive margins for wins when the popular vote is very close, leading to a more definitive judgment of victory, and giving presidents some greater sense of legitimacy and mandate—a necessity in a system of checks and balances where a president relies heavily on intangibles like credibility.

John F. Kennedy's 1960 popular-vote margin over Richard Nixon was 118,000 votes, or just over 0.1 percent, one vote per precinct. But Kennedy won 303 electoral votes, 56 percent of them, a cushion large enough to discourage a challenge from Nixon and enough to give him some running room as president.

This factor is even more important when there is a three-way race for president and the winner ends up well below 50 percent of the popular vote. In 1968, with George Wallace running as an independent, Richard Nixon received only

43.4 percent of the popular vote, a precarious margin overall and with only a slender popular advantage over Democrat Hubert Humphrey. But even though Wallace siphoned off 46 electoral votes that year, Nixon still received 301 electoral votes, 31 over the majority necessary, 120 more than Humphrey and enough to give him some sense of mandate in a difficult, divisive, and bitter year.

In 1992, with H. Ross Perot running as an independent, Bill Clinton received just over 43 percent of the popular votes—but won with a near-landslide 370 electoral votes, 69 percent of the total.

Clout for Small States

The EC was designed originally to give states both large and small some role in presidential contests. It has done just that, while also encouraging candidates to campaign in small states and sparsely populated regions and to do retail, face-to-face campaigning instead of just television air wars targeting the large cities and other populous areas.

Large states, partly because they have all retained their winner-take-all electoral vote formula, have remained important, although the importance of one-party dominant large states would clearly increase with direct popular vote (hence Senator-elect Clinton's position.) But smaller states have clearly greater importance than they would have without the EC; indeed, in most elections, small states would be largely irrelevant without their electoral votes as lures.

Because of the obvious clout the EC gives to small states, the chances of Electoral College repeal remain small. They are smaller yet because of the public reaction to the November (or should we say December) 2000 results—the clear prospect after this election that a George W. Bush presidency would come with Al Gore having won the national popular vote caused not the slightest hint of public outrage.

So what will happen—and what should happen—in the aftermath of this election? One constitutional amendment would make some sense: the elimination of electors themselves and their replacement with automatic votes. Any concept of electors as actual deliberators disappeared in the early nineteenth century. Even though real examples of "faithless" electors are rare, the prospect is always there of rogue or faithless electors changing their votes, reneging on their pledges or being swayed by inducements, and especially with a very close election.

It also makes sense to remind states that they do not need a constitutional amendment to change the distribution of their electoral votes, perhaps joining Maine and Nebraska and dividing them by congressional district. In small one-party states, especially, this can give them more clout by dangling for the opposite party the prospect of winning one or two electoral votes out of the four or five because of a congressional district or two with different political leanings than the overall state. (In large states, on the other hand, division by congressional district could dilute their power and add to the confusion and close results in a tight election.) Remember too, that if large states like California allocated their electors by congressional district, it would create opportunities for more third- and fourth-party candidates like Ralph Nader to run for president, pick off a handful of districts (and electors), and perhaps throw the election into the House of Representatives.

But there is more that should happen now than direct reform or change in the Electoral College itself. [In November 2000] Americans learned as vividly as one can imagine that in our elections, every vote counts. Unfortunately, they have also learned, just as vividly, that not every vote is counted—not even close. For all except a handful of election aficionados, the messy, sloppy, underfunded, undermanned, sometimes incompetent and occasionally corrupt administration of our elections, in a process more decentralized than any area other than garbage collection, has come as a shock.

Election Reform

It demands reform—major, swift, and comprehensive—in the way Americans run our elections. Elections are woefully underfunded, resulting in outdated equipment, misaligned machines, poorly trained and inadequate personnel, out-of-date voter registration information at the polling places, poorly designed ballots, and huge voter errors.

The first step to reform is more money. And the money—probably $250 million, a small sum in the context of a nearly $2 trillion federal budget, but huge for local officials—becomes the key to substantive reform. States should consider their own reform programs, providing grants to election districts. And Congress should pass a bill providing the money in the form of matching grants (like the Highway Trust Fund, with a 90 percent to 10 percent ratio) to localities that agree to implement the following substantive reforms:

- Uniform ballots for federal elections. No more "butterfly" ballots or other comparable monstrosities; all voters should confront the same, simple, and easy-to-use ballot, with clearly defined and directed choices.
- Uniform use of modern "touch-screen" technology. In many jurisdictions in the country, including Baltimore city for example, voting is done by touch screens similar to ATM machines that most Americans are familiar with. The capital investment in new equipment is significant, but because of the costs of printing paper ballots, maintaining the old machines, and hiring the personnel to count the paper ballots, the long-term costs of using modern technology are actually lower.
- Updating and upgrading voter registration data. Many legally registered voters went to the polls on November 7 only to be told that their names were not on the registration printout lists. Some lists had not been updated or synchronized; some had not been transferred from motor vehicle offices. It is an affront to democracy to prevent people who want to vote and have complied with the rules from doing so. Money and effort can fix the problem.
- Use of local area networks (LANs) so that voters can cast their ballots either near their homes or their workplaces. Voting by Internet would exacerbate the problems listed below with absentee balloting. But information technology can make it easier for people with difficult work schedules to vote, and have the vote count in their home precincts.
- Weekend, twenty-four-hour voting, with uniform poll-closing times. It is time to move the system from elections on the first Tuesday following the first Monday in November to elections that run from, say, 8:00 a.m. Saturday morning to 8:00 a.m. Sunday morning. Opening and closing times should be staggered across the time zones so that all the polls close at the same time. This might make election eve less dramatic for viewers and for networks, but it would enhance turnout, and make for fewer media muffs.
- Discouragement of runaway absentee voting. Absentee ballots used to be for military personnel and those unavoidably away from home. Now voting by mail has become an easy tool of convenience—convenience for election officials who can ease the burden and cost at

polls on Election Day; for parties, who can more easily target voters in their get-out-the-vote drives; and for voters who can avoid the hassle of voting at the polls. But those voters also lose the protection of privacy of the closed curtain in the polling place, and the importance of the collective act of gathering to exercise the sacred franchise. Absentee voting also raises the prospect of widespread corruption, a fact in many areas, with widespread use of absentee voting. Absentee voting should be for absentees—period. Make voting at the polls easier, but stop the trend of voting by mail.

The Electoral College will always remain controversial. The controversy may grow in the Information Age, with individual empowerment and the drive for direct democracy ascendant. But this "archaic" device is not anti-democratic—any more than a World Series that picks a winner by best-of-seven games, instead of by the overall number of runs scored, is wrong or illegitimate. As the data and arguments above suggest, the EC has legs—it continues to provide major benefits to American democracy. We need reform, and we need it now—in election administration and campaign finance. We do not need repeal of the Electoral College.

James Glassman
Reform the Electoral College, Don't Toss It

The five-week post-election contest between Al Gore and George W. Bush has utterly demystified the Electoral College in the minds of Americans. Most of them tell pollsters they want to get rid of it.

So do lots of politicians, including Hillary Rodham Clinton, the most famous Senator-elect, who announced that she would sponsor legislation "to do away with the Electoral College and move to the popular election of our Presidents." Senator Arlen Specter (R-Penn.) concurred.

Both Senators later admitted that passing a constitutional amendment to switch to a popular vote was a long shot. The reason, of course, is that the Electoral College gives disproportionate power to small states—that was one of

Published in *The American Enterprise*, March 2001.

the main reasons the Framers invented it—making those states unlikely ratifiers of any amendment.

It is true we don't elect our president by direct democracy, but that's precisely the point. The Constitution is a blueprint for protecting citizens, either as individuals or as members of minority groups, from the passions of majority rule. In fact, until 1832, electors were chosen almost exclusively by state legislators. The Framers wanted a system that preserved federalism. They considered giving each state an equal vote, then compromised. In the Electoral College, a state has an elector per congressional district plus an elector for each of its two Senators.

The Electoral College has three practical effects. First, candidates have to pay attention to smaller states, as both Gore and Bush did [in 2000], battling over the five votes of West Virginia and even Delaware's three. Second, the system usually magnifies small differences in popular votes, providing the winner with a more substantial mandate. For example, in 1960, John F. Kennedy beat Richard Nixon by just a few tenths of a percentage point in the popular vote but won, 303–219, in the Electoral College.

Third, the Electoral College nearly eliminates the power of third parties and regional candidates. In the vast majority of elections, someone wins a majority. Rarely is a second round, with corrupt deal-making (as in 1824), required in the House of Representatives.

Still, the system has drawbacks. While candidates often pay great attention to smaller states, they sometimes completely ignore larger ones. In 2000, for instance, New York was written off by the GOP from the start, as was Texas by the Democrats. In a state like Massachusetts, which almost always goes Democratic, dispirited Republicans believe their votes never count; ditto, Democrats in Wyoming. Finally, as we saw in Florida, an excruciatingly tight race within a state can hold a bundle of electoral votes in the balance.

But there is a practical way to improve the system, and it doesn't require amending the Constitution. States, which have broad powers in choosing their electors, could change their state election statutes and adopt the system used in Maine since 1972 and in Nebraska since 1992: each state gives one electoral vote to the candidate who wins the most votes within each congressional district, and the state's other two electoral votes go to the candidate with the most votes statewide.

[In 2000], both of Maine's congressional districts went to Gore, all three of

Nebraska's went to Bush. But imagine the consequences of such a system for other states. In Virginia, for example, Democrats have strength in the D.C. suburbs and in the urban areas of Norfolk and Richmond. Bush swept the state easily, winning all thirteen electoral votes, as has every Republican since 1968.

But under proportional voting, Gore would have taken three congressional districts—and thus three electoral votes. So Bush's margin (with the two Senate votes) would have been 10–3. Meanwhile, in Maryland, all of whose ten votes went to Gore this time, a proportional system would have given two votes to Bush.

Which party would gain with this reform? It's hard to say. Republicans would be able to take seats in New York and Florida, while Democrats would score in states where they are now shut out, such as Georgia and Colorado. Key industrial states, such as Illinois, Ohio, and Pennsylvania, which are usually close, would award some of their votes to each candidate, which seems more fair.

A month after the election, *USA Today* analyzed the 2000 vote as though every state were using the Maine–Nebraska system. The final margin: Bush 271, Gore 267—the exact finish under the current scheme. That's a freak; in most cases, results would differ.

Since the election, bills have been introduced in the legislatures of Texas, California, and Indiana to change to proportional voting. It's a good idea. The campaign will be broader, more voters will feel they were recognized, and the risk of dozens of electoral votes hanging on a single county will be eliminated.

The two-party system will still dominate, even though it will be slightly easier for smaller parties to win a few electoral votes by concentrating on individual districts. Federalism—at least in presidential elections—will survive, and the Electoral College will keep providing its mystical benediction on each president.

QUESTIONS

1. *What would you do?* You are a House member from a small state that voted for Al Gore. Many of your constituents are angry that he won the popular vote but lost the election, and they want you to introduce a constitutional amendment to abolish the Electoral College. *Do you?*

2. If the politics of getting approval for a proposal was not relevant, which reform from the articles would you support? Taking politics into account, how would this change your position?

3. What do you think Norman Ornstein would say about Arthur Schlesinger's proposal to reform the Electoral College? Are there any unintended consequences to this proposal? Do you think he would be more supportive of James Glassman's proposal?

4. Another recent reform proposal being considered in several states would give a state's Electoral College votes to the winner of the national popular vote, rather than to the candidate who won the most votes in the state. The law would go into effect only if states with a combined total of 270 electoral votes—the number now required to win the presidency—agreed to the same process. The California state legislature passed this proposal in 2006, but Governor Arnold Schwarzenegger vetoed the bill. What would you have done if you were the governor of California? Do you think this proposal is a good idea?

11

Interest Groups: A Force for Change or the Status Quo?

In his famous essay *Federalist* 10, future president James Madison expressed concern about the "mischief of factions." It was natural, he argued, for people to organize around a principle or interest they held in common, and the most common motivation for organizing such factions was property—those who had it versus those who did not, creditors versus lenders. The danger in such efforts, however, was that a majority faction might usurp the rights of a minority. In a small direct democracy, where a majority of the people could share a "common passion," the threat was very real. Expand the geographic size of the country, however, and replace direct democracy with a system of elected representatives, separation of powers, and checks and balances, and the threat diminished. The likelihood of any one faction appealing to a majority of citizens in a large republic governed by representatives from diverse geographic regions was remote. To Madison, factions were a natural outgrowth of the differences between people, and the only way to eliminate factions would be to eliminate liberty. Eliminating factions might not be possible or desirable, but the mischief resulting from factions could be controlled with a system of representation based upon varied constituencies that embraced multiple, diverse interests. From the competition of diverse interests would arise compromise and balanced public policy.

Madison's concerns about interests, and particularly organized interests, have resonated through American history. At various times in the United States, the public has seemed to become especially concerned with the power of interests in politics. Political scientists refer to this as the "ideals vs. institutions" gap—there are times when "what is" is so different from what Americans believe "should be," that pressure mounts to reform lobbying laws, campaign regulations, business practices, and so on. Positions on these issues do not always neatly sort out into the typical liberal and conservative categories. For example, a Democratic senator (Russ Feingold of Wisconsin) and Republican senator (John McCain of Arizona) joined forces to lead the effort for campaign finance reform in 2002, but liberal and conservative groups joined forces in 2003 to challenge the constitutionality of some of the new law's limits on interest group campaign advertising. In recent years, outrage at corporate accounting scandals at companies like Enron and Worldcom that bilked people out of their pensions, illegal favor-trading between lobbyists such as Jack Abramoff and government officials, and prodigious fundraising by candidates have once again placed the balance of ideals and institutions on the political agenda.

Was Madison right about the benefits that would emerge from the competition of interests? In the following excerpt from "The Group Basis of Politics," Earl Latham answers with an emphatic "yes!" Despite the popular criticism of "special" interests that seem to taint the political process with their dominant influence, Latham argues that such groups have been a common and inevitable feature of American government. Groups form to give individuals a means of self-expression and to help individuals find security in an uncertain world. In fact, the uncertainty of the social environment, and the resulting threat to one's interests, is a chief motivation for groups to form and "taming" this environment is a central concern for group members. Rather than leading to a system ruled by a few dominant powers, Latham suggests the reality is much more fluid. Although it is true that groups that are highly organized are likely to be more powerful, Latham argues that "organization begets counterorganization." The ascendancy of one group will prompt other groups to form to advance their cause. Defeated groups can always try again: "Today's losers may be tomorrow's winners." Groups that lose in the legislature may have more luck with a bureaucratic agency or in a courtroom. There are, in short, multiple avenues of influence and many roads to political success for organized groups, and there are no permanent winners or losers.

Jonathan Rauch disagrees. He views with pessimism the ever-expanding number of interest groups in the political process. Whether groups claim to represent narrow economic interests or a broader public interest, Rauch does not see balance and compromise as the result of their competition in the political arena. Rather, he sees a nation suffering from "hyperpluralism," or the explosion of groups making claims on government power and resources. When elected officials attempt to reduce budget deficits or to establish new priorities and refocus expenditures, they are overwhelmed by the pressures of a wide range of groups. As a result, government programs are never terminated or restructured; tough budget cuts or tax changes are rarely made; and a very rich democratic country and its government become immobile. Rather than the dynamic system of change and compromise envisioned by Latham, Rauch sees a system characterized primarily by inertia because of the power of groups to prevent government action.

Earl Latham
The Group Basis of Politics: Notes for a Theory

The chief social values cherished by individuals in modern society are realized through groups. These groupings may be simple in structure, unicellular, so to speak, like a juvenile gang. Or they may be intricate meshes of associated, federated, combined, consolidated, merged, or amalgamated units and sub-units of organization, fitted together to perform the divided and assigned parts of a common purpose to which the components are dedicated. They may operate out of the direct public gaze like religious organizations, which tend to have a low degree of visibility. Or they may, like Congress and many other official groups, occupy the front pages for weeks at a time. National organizations are usually conspicuous; indeed, so much is this so at times that they tend to divert the eye from the great number of groups which stand at the elbow of the citizen of every small town. Everywhere groups abound, and they may be examined at close range and from afar.

* * *

So far, we have been concerned with the nature of the structure of society and its principal communities, and with the composition and classification of the group forms which are basic to both. They have been held still, so to speak, while they

Published in *American Political Science Review*, June 1952.

were being viewed. But they do not in fact hold still; they are in a state of constant motion, and it is through this motion and its interactions that these groups generate the rules by which public policy is formulated and the community is to be governed. It is necessary now to consider the impulses which animate the group motion and produce these penetrating and far-reaching results.

To consider further a point which has been made, groups organize for the self-expression and security of the members which comprise them. Even when the group is a benevolent, philanthropic association devoted to the improvement of the material and spiritual fortunes of people outside its membership—a temperance or a missionary organization, for example—the work towards this goal, the activity of the organization, is a means through which the members express themselves. Satisfaction in the fulfillment of the received purposes of the group is an important element in keeping groups intact, as Barnard has shown. Indeed, if these satisfactions are not fulfilled, the group suffers loss of morale, energy, and dedication. It is for this reason that military organizations and the civil authorities to which they are responsible seek to inculcate in the soldier some sense of the general purposes for which force by arms is being employed, in an attempt to identify the soldier's personal purpose with that of the community he serves. The soldier then can fulfill his own purposes in combat, as well as those of various groups in the country whose uniform he bears.

At the same time, security is an object of every group organization if security is understood only in its elemental sense of the survival of the group itself in order to carry forward its mission. At the very least, the interest of security means the maintenance of the existence of the group. In different groups one or the other of these impulses—self-expression or security—will predominate.

Self-expression and security are sought by the group members through control of the physical and social environment which surrounds each group and in the midst of which it dwells. It is an elemental fact that environments are potentially dangerous to every group, even as homes are potentially dangerous to the members of the household, as the statistics of accidents in the home will attest. The military battalion runs the risk of being shot up. The church, new or old, runs the risk of losing its members to other and competing claims of interest and devotion. The businessman runs the risk of losing his profit or his customer to his rival. The philanthropic organization devoted to good works often regards other agencies in the same field with a venomous eye. Councils of social agencies in large cities are sometimes notorious for the rancor with which the struggle for prestige and recognition (i.e., self-expression and security) is conducted among them. Every group, large and small, must come to terms with its environment if it is to endure and to prosper.

There are three modes by which this is done. First, the environment may be made safe and predictable by putting restraints upon it. Jurisdictional fights between unions may be explained in this way. Jurisdictional fights are battles in which each claimant union seeks to make an environment for itself in the area of dispute, but to exclude its rival from this environment. On the employer side, the Mohawk Valley Formula was a pattern of actions in a planned sequence by which employers, if they followed it, could break union movements. The objective of this formula was to discredit each union and its leadership and to enlist the support of the townspeople on the side of the plant; it thus was a concerted plan to make an environment unfavorable to the success of unions. One overcomes the hostility in the environment most directly by destroying the influence which creates the hostility.

Second, the environment may be made safe and predictable by neutralizing it. In the propaganda war of giant world powers, the effort is ceaseless to neutralize the effects of propaganda with counterpropaganda so as to render the international environment favorable, or at least not hostile—that is, neutral. The Atlantic and Pacific Tea Company similarly bought a great deal of advertising space in newspapers all over the country to counteract the expectedly unfavorable impressions created by a Department of Justice action against it under the anti-trust laws. The object, among other purposes, was to make the customer-inhabited environment of the business enterprise favorable if possible, neutral at the least, concerning the merits of the charges against it.

Third, the environment may be made safe and predictable, and therefore secure, by conciliating it and making it friendly. Even where there is no manifest hostile influence, a credit of good will may be accumulated by deeds and words which reflect favorably upon the doer. It is true that concessions to a potential hostile force may work sometimes, and again they may not. In the struggle of free nations with the dictatorships, appeasement did not succeed in producing that conciliation which was hoped for it. Nonetheless, politicians are constantly at work making friends and increasing votes by performing favors of one kind or another. Friendliness towards soap [radio soap operas] is generated on the radio by endless broadcasts of simple tales of never-ending strife and frustration. And during the Second World War advertising by business enterprises was a means of cultivating and keeping goodwill for the products advertised, even though there was no market for them because of the wartime restrictions on production.

All of these are methods by which the environment in which groups dwell is made safe and predictable to them, and therefore secure. And because the relations of people are myriad and shifting, subject to cycles of deterioration and decay, because the environment itself changes with each passing hour, there is a ceaseless struggle on the part of groups to dominate, neutralize, or conciliate that part of their environment that presses in upon them most closely. In this struggle, there is an observable balance of influence in favor of organized groups in their dealings with the unorganized, and in favor of the best and most efficiently organized in their dealings with the less efficiently organized. Strong nations tend to take advantage of the weak, and imperial powers to take advantage of their colonies. Or, to put it another way, organization represents concentrated power, and concentrated power can exercise a dominating influence when it encounters power which is diffuse and not concentrated, and therefore weaker.

The classic struggle of farmers against business enterprise is a case in point, the latter at first being more efficiently organized, and able (before the farmer became "class conscious") to gain advantages which the farmers thought exorbitant, under conditions which the farmers found offensive. But organization begets counterorganization. The farmer organizes in the American Farm Bureau Federation or the National Grange, and uses his influence with the legislatures to write rules to his advantage. In some states of the Middle West, for example, legislation even prescribes the terms of contracts for the sale of farm equipment. But the organized farmer pays little attention to the tenant and the sharecropper, and they in turn experience an impulse to organize for their own advantage. The history of the development of farmers' organizations is instructive; the whole program of farm subsidies which has evolved in the last twenty years may be seen as an effort on the part of the farmer (organized for the purpose) to make himself independent of the vicissitudes of the business economy, that is, to take himself out of the environment which he can control only imperfectly, and to insulate himself against economic adversity.

In the constant struggle of groups to come to terms with their environments, one other phenomenon of group politics may be noted. Simple groups tend to become more complex. And the more complex they become, the greater is the tendency to centralize their control. The structure of the business community in 1950 is different from that of 1860 precisely in that relatively simple forms of business organization have become complex—have gone through federations, combinations, reorganizations, mergers, amalgamations, and consolidations in a growing tendency to rationalize the complexity and to integrate the elements in comprehensive structures. Monopolies, combinations, cartels, giant integrated enterprises are characteristic of a mature phase of the evolution of group forms. Furthermore, the history of federal administration amply shows that the tendency of simple forms of organization to become complex by combination and to develop centralized bureaucracies to cope with this complexity is to be observed among official groups as well as among the groups, like the CIO and the American Legion, which dwell outside the domain of public government.

* * *

The struggle of groups to survive in their environments and to carry forward the aims and interests of their members, if entirely uninhibited, would produce violence and war. Social disapproval of most of the forms of direct action, however, reduces this struggle to an effort to write the rules by which groups live with each other and according to which they compete for existence and advantage. Thus, in the development of mature institutions of collective bargaining from the raw material of unorganized workers, the time comes when violence, disorder, and force are put to one side as the normal aspect of labor relations and the conduct of negotiations occupies the energies of the leaders. In the relations of nations to each other, there has been a persistent effort to substitute diplomacy and the rule of law for war as the arbiter of the differences among national groups. As groups come to put away gross forms of coercion in their dealings with each other, by equal degree the area widens within which the behavior of each is subject to codification by rules. The struggle for advantage, for benefits to the group, for the self-expression and security of its members, tend then to concentrate upon the writing of the rules. Among the forms which the rules may take are statutes, administrative orders and decrees, rules and interpretations, and court judgments.

* * *

The legislature referees the group struggle, ratifies the victories of the successful coalitions, and records the terms of the surrenders, compromises, and conquests in the form of statutes. Every statute tends to represent compromise because the very process of accommodating conflicts of group interest is one of deliberation and consent. The legislative vote on any issue thus tends to represent the composition of strength, i.e., the balance of power among the contending groups at the moment of voting. What may be called public policy is actually the equilibrium reached in the group struggle at any given moment, and it represents a balance which the contending factions of groups constantly strive to weight in their favor. In this process, it is clear that blocks of groups can be defeated. In fact, they can be routed. Defeated groups do not possess a veto on the proposals and acts that affect them. But what they do possess is the right to make new combinations of strength if they are able to do so—combinations that will support a new effort to rewrite the rules in their favor. This process of regrouping is fully in accord with the American culture pattern, which rates high in the characteristics of optimism, risk, experimentalism, change, aggressiveness, acquisitiveness, and colossal faith in man's ability to subdue and bend nature to his desire. The entire process is dynamic, not static; fluid, not fixed. Today's losers may be tomorrow's winners.

In these adjustments of group interest, the legislature does not play the part of inert cash register, ringing up the additions and withdrawals of strength; it is not a mindless balance pointing and marking the weight and distribution of power among the contending groups. * * * Legislators have to be approached with a certain amount of deference and tact; they may be pressured, but some forms of pressure will be regarded as too gross. The Congressman, like men everywhere, comes to his position bearing in his head a cargo of ideas, principles, prejudices, programs, precepts, beliefs, slogans, and preachments. These represent his adjustment to the dominant group combination among his constituents. * * *

The function of the bureaucrat in the group struggle is somewhat different from that of the legislator. Administrative agencies of the regulatory kind are established to carry out the terms of the treaties that the legislators have negotiated and ratified. They are like armies of occupation left in the field to police the rule won by the victorious coalition. * * * The defeated coalition of groups, however, does not cease striving to wring interpretations favorable to it from the treaties that verbalize its defeats. Expensive legal talent is employed to squeeze every advantage which wit and verbal magic can twist from the cold prose of official papers; and the regulatory agencies are constantly besought and importuned to interpret their authorities in favor of the very groups for the regulation of which they were originally granted. This campaign against unfavorable rules which losing coalitions of groups address to the bureaucrats appointed to administer them is, of course, in addition to their constant effort to rewrite the rules in their favor through compliant legislators. Where the balance of power is precarious, the law will remain unsettled until the balance is made stable. * * *

* * *

Jonathan Rauch
The Hyperpluralism Trap

Anyone who believes Washington needs to get closer to the people ought to spend a little time with Senator Richard Lugar, the Indiana Republican. "Take a look at the people coming into my office on a normal Tuesday and Wednesday," Lugar said in a speech not long ago. "Almost every organization in our society has a national conference. The typical way of handling this is to come in on a Monday, rev up the troops, give them the bill number and send them up to the Hill. If they can't get in on Tuesday, strike again on Wednesday. I regularly have on Tuesday as many as fifteen constituent groups from Indiana, all of whom have been revved up by some skillful person to cite bills that they don't understand, have never heard of prior to that time, but with a score sheet to report back to headquarters whether I am for or against. It is so routine, it is so fierce, that at some point you [can't be] immune to it."

This is the reality of modern government. The rhetoric of modern politics, alas, is a little different. Take today's standard-issue political stem-winder, which goes something like this: "I think perhaps the most important thing that we understand here in the heartland . . . is the need to reform the political system, to reduce the influence of special interests and give more influence back to the kind of people that are in this crowd tonight by the tens of thousands." That stream of boilerplate is from Bill Clinton (from his election-night speech), but it could have come from almost any politician. It's pitched in a dominant key of political rhetoric today: *standard populism*—that is, someone has taken over the government and "we" must take it back, restore government to the people, etc. But who, exactly, are those thousands of citizens who troop weekly through Senator Lugar's suite, clutching briefing packets and waving score-

Published in *The New Republic*, June 1994.

cards? Standard populism says they are the "special interests," those boils on the skin of democracy, forever interposing themselves between the American people and the people's servants in Washington.

Well, fifty years ago that analysis may have been useful, but not anymore. In America today, the special interests and "the people" have become objectively indistinguishable. Groups are us. As a result, the populist impulse to blame special interests, big corporations and political careerists for our problems—once a tonic—has become Americans' leading political narcotic. Worse, it actually abets the lobbying it so righteously denounces.

Begin with one of the best-known yet most underappreciated facts of our time: over the past three or four decades we have busily organized ourselves into interest groups—lobbies, loosely speaking—at an astonishing rate. Interest groups were still fairly sparse in America until about the time of World War II. Then they started proliferating, and in the 1960s the pace of organizing picked up dramatically.

Consider, for instance, the numbers of groups listed in Gale Research's *Encyclopedia of Associations*. The listings have grown from fewer than 5,000 in 1956 to well over 20,000 today. They represent, of course, only a small fraction of America's universe of interest groups. Environmental organizations alone number an estimated 7,000, once you count local clean-up groups and the like; the Washington *Blade*'s resource directory lists more than 400 gay groups, up from 300 at the end of 1990. Between 1961 and 1982 the number of corporate offices in Washington increased tenfold. Even more dramatic was the explosion in the number of public-interest organizations and grass-roots groups. These barely existed at all before the 1960s; today they number in the tens of thousands and collect more than $4 billion per year from 40 million individuals, according to political scientist Ronald Shaiko of American University.

Well, so what? Groups do many good things—provide companionship for the like-minded, collect and disseminate information, sponsor contests, keep the catering industry solvent. Indeed, conventional political theory for much of the postwar period was dominated by a strain known as *pluralism*, which holds that more groups equals more representation equals better democracy. Yet pluralism missed something. It assumed that the group-forming process was self-balancing and stable, as opposed to self-feeding and unstable. Which is to say, it failed to grasp the danger of what American University political scientist James Thurber aptly calls *hyperpluralism*.

In economics, inflation is a gradual increase in the price level. Up to a point, if the inflation rate is stable, people can plan around it. But if the rate starts to speed up, people start expecting more inflation. They hoard goods and dump cash, driving the inflation still faster. Eventually, an invisible threshold is crossed: the inflation now feeds on its own growth and undermines the stability of the whole economic system.

What the pluralists missed is that something analogous can happen with interest groups. People see that it pays to organize into groups and angle for benefits, so they do it. But as more groups make more demands, and as even more hungry groups form to compete with all the other groups, the process begins to feed on itself and pick up momentum. At some point there might be so many groups that they choke the political system, sow contention and conflict, even erode society's governability. That's hyperpluralism. And if it is less destabilizing than hyperinflation, it may be more insidious.

The pattern is most visible in smaller social units, such as local school districts, where groups colonize the curriculum—sex education for liberals, values instruction for conservatives, recycling lessons for environmentalists, voluntary silent prayer for Christians. But even among the general population the same forces are at work. Fifty years ago the phrase "the elderly" denoted a demographic category; today, thanks largely to federal pension programs and the American Association of Retired Persons (AARP), it denotes a giant and voracious lobby. In the 1930s the government set up farm-subsidy programs, one per commodity; inevitably, lobbies sprang up to defend each program, so that today American agriculture is fundamentally a collection of interest groups. With the help of group organizers and race-based benefits, loose ethnic distinctions coalesce into hard ethnic lobbies. And so on.

Even more depressing, any attempt to fight back against the proliferating mass of subdivision is foiled by the rhetoric of standard populism and its useful stooge: the special interest. The concept of a "special interest" is at the very core of standard populism—the "them" without which there can be no "us." So widely accepted is this notion, and so useful is it in casual political speech, that most of us talk routinely about special interests without a second thought. We all feel we know a special interest when we see one, if only because it is a group of which we are not a member. Yet buried in the special interest idea is an assumption that is no longer true.

The concept of the special interest is not based on nothing. It is, rather, out of date, an increasingly empty relic of the time of machine politics and political bosses, when special interests were, quite literally, special. Simply because of who they were, they enjoyed access that was available to no one else. But the process of everyone's organizing into more and more groups can go only so far before the very idea of a special interest loses any clear meaning. At some point one must throw up one's hands and concede that the hoary dichotomy between special interests and "us" has become merely rhetoric.

According to a 1990 survey conducted for the American Society of Association Executives, seven out of ten Americans belong to at least one association, and one in four Americans belongs to four or more. Practically everyone who reads these words is a member of an interest group, probably several. Moreover, formal membership tallies omit many people whom we ordinarily think of as being represented by lobbies. For example, the powerful veterans' lobbies enroll only perhaps one-seventh of American veterans, yet the groups lobby on behalf of veterans as a class, and all 27 million veterans share in the benefits. Thus the old era of lobbying by special interests—by a well-connected, plutocratic few— is as dead now as slavery and Prohibition. We Americans have achieved the full democratization of lobbying: influence-peddling for the masses.

The appeal of standard populism today comes precisely from the phony reassurance afforded by its real message: "Other people's groups are the special interests. Less for them—more for you!" Spread that sweet manure around and the natural outgrowth is today's tendency, so evident in the Clinton style, to pander to interest groups frantically while denouncing them furiously. It is the public's style, too: sending ever more checks to the AARP and the National Rifle Association and the National Federation of Independent Business and the National Wildlife Federation and a million others, while railing against special interests. Join and join, blame and blame.

So hyperpluralism makes a hash of the usual sort of standard populist prescription, which calls for "the people" to be given more access to the system, at the expense of powerful Beltway figures who are alleged to have grown arrogant or corrupt or out of touch. Activists and reformers who think the answer to democracy's problems is more access for more of the people need to wake up. Uncontrolled access only breeds more lobbies. It is axiomatic that "the people" (whatever that now means) do not organize to seek government benefits; lobbies do. Every new door to the federal treasury is an opportunity for new groups to queue up for more goodies.

Populists resolutely refuse to confront this truth. Last year, for example, Republicans and the editors of the *Wall Street Journal* campaigned fiercely— and successfully—for new congressional rules making it easier for legislators and groups to demand that bottled-up bills be discharged from committee. The idea was to bring Congress closer to "the people" by weakening the supposedly high-handed barons who rule the Hill. But burying the Free Christmas Tree for Every American Act (or whatever) in committee—while letting members of Congress say they *would* have voted for it—was one of the few remaining ways to hold the door against hungry lobbies clamoring for gifts.

A second brand of populism, *left-populism,* is even more clueless than the standard brand, if that's possible. Many liberals believe the problem is that the wrong groups—the rich, the elites, the giant corporations, etc.—have managed to out-organize the good guys and take control of the system. One version of this model was elaborated by William Greider in his book *Who Will Tell the People.* The New Deal legacy, he writes, "rests upon an idea of interest group bargaining that has gradually been transformed into the random deal-making and permissiveness of the present. The alterations in the system are decisive and . . . the ultimate effects are anti-democratic. People with limited resources, with no real representation in the higher levels of politics, are bound to lose in this environment." So elaborate is the Washington machine of lobbyists, consultants, P.R. experts, political action committees and for-hire think tanks, says Greider, that "powerful economic interests," notably corporations and private wealth, inevitably dominate.

What's appealing about this view is the truism from which it springs: the wealthy enjoy a natural advantage in lobbying, as in almost everything else. Thus many lobbies—even liberal lobbies—are dominated by the comfortable and the wealthy. Consider the case of environmental groups. Anyone who doubts they are major players in Washington today need only look at the massive 1990 Clean Air Act, a piece of legislation that business gladly would have done without. Yet these groups are hardly battalions of the disfranchised. "Readers of *Sierra,* the magazine of the Sierra Club, have household incomes twice that of the average American," notes Senior Economists Terry L. Anderson of the Political Economy Research Center. And *The Economist* notes that "in 1993 the Nature Conservancy, with $915 million in assets, drew 73 percent of its income from rich individuals." When such groups push for emissions controls or pesticide rules, they may be reflecting the priorities of people who buy BMWs and brie more than the priorities of people who buy used Chevies and hamburger. So left-populism's claim to speak for "the people" is often suspect, to say the least.

The larger problem with left-populism, however, is its refusal to see that it is feeding the very problem it decries. Left-populism was supposed to fix the wealth-buys-power problem by organizing the politically disadvantaged into groups: unions, consumer groups, rainbow coalitions and so on. But the strategy has failed. As the left (the unions, the environmentalists) has organized ever more groups, the right (the bosses, the polluters) has followed suit. The group-forming has simply spiralled. This makes a joke of the left-populist prescription, which is to form more "citizens' groups" on the Naderite model, supposedly reinvigorating representative democracy and giving voice to the weak and the silenced. Greider proposes giving people subsidies to spend on political activism: "Giving individual citizens the capacity to deploy political money would inevitably shift power from existing structures and disperse it among the ordinary millions who now feel excluded."

Inevitably, it would do no such thing. Subsidies for activism would perforce go straight into the waiting coffers of (what else?) interest groups, new and old. That just makes matters worse, for if one side organizes more groups, the other side simply redoubles its own mobilization ad infinitum. That escalating cycle is the story of the last three decades. The only winner is the lobbying class. Curiously, then, left-populism has come to serve the very lobbying elites—the Washington lawyers and lobby shops and P.R. pros and interest group execs—whom leftists ought, by rights, to loathe.

The realization that the lobbying class is, to a large extent, both entrepreneurial and in business for itself has fed the third brand of populism, *right-populism*. In the right-populist model, self-serving political careerists have hijacked government and learned to manipulate it for profit. In refreshing contrast to the other two brands of populism, however, this one is in touch with reality. Washington *is* in business for itself, though not only for itself. Legislators and lobbies have an interest in using the tax code to please their constituents, but they also have an interest in churning the tax code to generate campaign contributions and lobbying fees. Luckily for them, those two imperatives generally coincide: the more everyone hunts for tax breaks, the more lobbying jobs there are. Right-populism has tumbled to the fact that so-called public interest and citizens' groups are no more immune to this self-serving logic of lobbying—create conflict, reap rewards—than is any other sort of professional lobby.

Yet right-populism fails to see to the bottom of the problem. It looks into the abyss but flinches. This is not to say that term limits and other procedural fine-tunes may not help; such reforms are no doubt worth trying. But even if noodling with procedures succeeded in diluting the culture of political careerism, it would help (or hurt) mainly at the margins. No, tinkering with the process isn't the answer. What we must do is go straight at the beast itself. We must attack and weaken the lobbies—that is, the *people's* lobbies.

It sounds so simple: weaken the lobbies! Shove them aside, reclaim the government! "It's just that simple," twinkles Ross Perot. But it's not that simple. Lobbies in Washington have clout because the people who scream when "special interests" are attacked are Medicare recipients defending benefits, farmers defending price supports, small businesses defending subsidized loans, racial groups defending set-asides and so on. Inherently, challenging these groups is no one's idea of fun, which is why politicians so rarely propose to do it. The solution is to strip away lobbies' protections and let competition hammer them. In practice, that means:

Balance the Federal Budget

It is a hackneyed prescription, but it is the very first thing we should do to curtail the lobbies' ability to rob the future. Deficits empower lobbies by allowing them to raid the nation's scarce reserves of investment capital. Deprived of that ability, they will be forced to compete more fiercely for money, and they'll be unable to steal from the future.

Cut the Lobbies' Lifelines

Eliminate subsidies and programs, including tax loopholes, by the hundreds. Killing a program here or there is a loser's game; it creates a political uproar without actually making a noticeable difference. The model, rather, should be the 1986 tax reform measure, which proved that a wholesale housecleaning really is possible. Back then, tax loopholes were cleared away by the truckload. The trick was—and is—to do the job with a big package of reforms that politicians can tout back home as real change. That means ditching whole Cabinet departments and abolishing virtually all industry-specific subsidies. Then go after subsidies for the non-needy—wholesale, not retail.

Promote Domestic Perestroika

Lobbies live to lock benefits in and competition out, so government restraints on competition should be removed—not indiscriminately, but determinedly.

President Carter's deregulation of transportation industries and interest rates, though imperfectly executed, were good examples. Air travel, trucking, and rail shipping are cheaper *and* safer. The affected industries have been more turbulent, but that's exactly the point. Domestic competition shakes up interest groups that settle cozily into Washington.

Encourage Foreign Competition

This is most important of all. The forces that breed interest groups never abate, and so fighting them requires a constant counterforce. Foreign competition is such a counterforce. Protection invariably benefits the industries and groups with the sharpest lobbyists and the fattest political action committees; stripping away protection forces them to focus more on modernizing and less on lobbying.

No good deed, they say, goes unpunished. We sought to solve pressing social problems, so we gave government vast power to reassign resources. We also sought to look out for ourselves and bring voices to all of our many natures and needs, so we built countless new groups to seek government's resources. What we did not create was a way to control the chain reaction we set off. Swarming interest groups excited government to perpetual activism, and government activism drew new groups to Washington by the thousands. Before we knew it, society itself was turning into a collection of ravenous lobbies.

Why was this not always a problem? Because there used to be control rods containing the chain reaction. Smoke-filled rooms, they were called. On Capitol Hill or in Tammany Hall, you needed to see one of about six people to have any hope of getting what you wanted, and those six people dispensed (and conserved) favors with parsimonious finesse. Seen from today's vantage, smoke-filled rooms and political machines did a creditable job of keeping a lid on the interest group frenzy—they just didn't do it particularly fairly. That's why we opened up access to anyone who wants to organize and lobby, and opened up power to subcommittee chairs and caucus heads and even junior legislators. In doing so, we abolished the venal gatekeepers. But that was only the good news. The bad news was that we also abolished the gate.

No, we shouldn't go back to smoke-filled rooms. But the way forward is harder than it ever was before. The maladies that now afflict government are ones in which the public is wholly, enthusiastically implicated. Still, there are sprigs and shoots of encouragement all around. There was the surprisingly strong presidential bid of former Senator Paul Tsongas, which built something of a constituency for straight talk. There's the rise of a school of Democrats in Congress—among them Senator Bob Kerrey and retiring Representative Tim Penny—who are willing to drag the White House toward sterner fiscal measures. There was the Clinton-led triumph of NAFTA in 1993. Those developments show promise of a political movement that is counter-populist yet also popular. Maybe—is it too much to hope?—they point beyond the desert of populism.

QUESTIONS

1. *What would you do?* Placing restrictions on interest group activities is difficult because of the constitutional protections afforded to these groups. The Constitution guarantees the people the right to assemble and to petition government regarding their grievances, and it also guarantees freedom of speech. All these are the essence of interest group activity. Nonetheless, many Americans are uneasy with the influence wielded by interest groups. Imagine you are a staffer for a senator elected on a platform that promised to limit the power of "special interests" in politics. The senator has asked you to draft a position paper outlining some possible restrictions on interest-group activity. Would these restrictions create constitutional difficulties?

2. Among the many forms of interest-group activity, campaign contributions seem to provoke some of the harshest criticisms. Is this reasonable? Is there any reason to be more concerned about campaign contributions than about lobbying, lawsuits, funding research, or other activities groups employ to pursue their cause?

3. Rauch complains that interest groups slow down the policy-making process. Is the interest-group system as portrayed by Rauch a danger to democracy? Is it in fact implementing the principles of the Framers that are implicit in the Constitution? And is there a problem if you have answered "yes" to both of these questions?

12

Representation in Congress: The Politics of Pork

The articles in this chapter highlight the importance legislators place on serving their constituents by delivering specific benefits, such as a new highway overpass, water treatment plant, or veterans' hospital. Although the strategy might work for re-election, it may undermine the capacity of Congress to deal effectively with national problems and priorities. The debate over "pork barrel politics" captures this institutional tension and illustrates the difficulties of defining "national" interests rather than parochial or local interests.

Examples of pork barrel spending are plentiful. The infamous "bridge to nowhere" is one of the most well-known examples of wasteful pork barrel spending. It would connect Ketchikan, Alaska, a town with 8,600 residents, with Gravina Island, which has a population of 50 and a small local airport. This bridge would be nearly as long as the Golden Gate Bridge and taller than the Brooklyn Bridge. Assuming traffic of 1,000 cars a day (which is generous), the cost per trip would be $43.15 over the life of the bridge. Currently the airport on the island is served by a ferry that charges $6 a car for the seven-minute trip. One commentator called the bridge a "national embarrassment," and said that it "has become an object of national ridicule and a symbol of fiscal irresponsibility." After the national outcry, Congress pulled the plug on the project. A recent compromise meant that Alaska would still get the money, but would use it for highway projects other than the bridge.

The bridge is unusual only in its scale rather than its kind. Congress routinely attaches pork to "must pass" emergency legislation, such as a recent supplemental appropriation to fund the war in Iraq that included amendments to fund a research station at the South Pole and repair a dam in Vermont. Editorial boards and political pundits around the country criticized members of the Senate for exploiting the war for their local economic interests.

Sean Paige and Jonathan Cohn, both writing at the end of the 1990s, view pork barrel politics from different perspectives. For Paige, the $520 billion spending bill passed in late 1998 tossed aside the "hard-won gains" of budget balancing achieved in 1997 and was "larded . . . with heapings of pork-barrel projects." Paige recognizes the difficulties of practicing fiscal discipline when every member of Congress wants and needs to provide something for their home districts. Nevertheless, he criticizes the practice of attaching last-minute pork barrel "riders" to the budget, something done even by members who built their careers on deficit reduction. The national interest in a balanced budget, according to Paige, should take priority over local projects.

Where Paige sees waste and abuse of the nation's resources, however, Cohn views pork as the "glue" of legislating. If it takes a little pork for the home district or state to get important legislation through Congress, so be it. Cohn also questions the motives of budget reform groups that call for greater fiscal discipline in Congress; most of these groups, in his view, are not truly concerned about waste, but are simply against government spending in general. The policies they identify as pork, he argues, can have important national implications: military readiness, road improvements for an Olympic host city, or the development of new agricultural and food products. In other words, "pork" is in the eye of the beholder: one person's pork is another person's essential spending. From the latter perspective, national interests can be served by allowing local interests to take a dip into the pork barrel. Finally, Cohn argues that pork, even according to the critics' own definition, constitutes less that one percent of the overall federal budget.

The typical form of pork is an "earmark" that is targeted for a specific project with funding that is not subjected to spending formulas or a competitive process. Earmarks went up by more than 10-fold over six years: the four most heavily earmarked appropriations bills contained 764 earmarks in 2000 and about 8,600 in 2005 (defense and transportation are the two areas with the most earmarks). Overall, Congress approved more than 15,000 earmarks in the 2006 fiscal year worth about $55 billion. Two members of Congress, Rep. Jeff Flake (R-AZ) and

Sen. Larry Craig (R-ID), take different perspectives on the use of earmarks. Rep. Flake links the use of earmarks to the lobbying scandal surrounding Jack Abramoff (which will end with several members either going to jail or being defeated), an increase in spending, and more difficult oversight of the bureaucracy. His call for comprehensive reform is rejected by Sen. Craig, who argues that funneling money to constituents is what elected representatives are *supposed* to do. Who would you rather have making decisions about how to spend money, he asks, "lawmakers who are accountable to you, or some nameless, faceless bureaucrat in Washington, D.C., who has never stepped foot in Idaho?"

Sean Paige
Rolling Out the Pork Barrel

The fall of 1997 was a triumphant time for deficit hawks in Congress: Step by laborious step they finally had maneuvered President Clinton into signing the first balanced-budget bill in two decades, a long-sought political grail. Yet only a year later, as Congress rushed to cram a year's worth of budget writing into the waning weeks before the midterm elections, the hard-won gains of 1997 vanished like a mirage and the madness of budget seasons past made a triumphant return.

"There's a lot of little things tucked away there that I wish weren't," the president said, talking not about the latest batch of White House interns but rather the $520 billion omnibus spending bill he was signing into law. "But on balance, it honors our values and strengthens our country and looks to the future."

Critics, however, say the values it honors most are political expediency, fiscal opportunism and the scruples of the horse trader—while the only future to which its politician authors looked was their own.

All but a few members of Congress claimed to hate the damned thing.

However, a majority in both chambers held their noses and voted for it, larded as it was with heapings of pork-barrel projects, the distribution of which remains a staple of the incumbency protection racket, and some breathtaking acts of budget wizardry. The more than $21 billion in spending that exceeded

Published in *Insight on the News*, January 1999.

budget caps set only a year earlier was declared "emergency" spending, as members continued to exploit a loophole that threatens to make the U.S. Treasury a federal disaster area. And some $9.1 billion in additional spending was "forward funded"—which means that Congress will spend it now and figure out how to pay for it later.

Criticism of the bill was rancorous and bipartisan. But even the opposition was divided: One faction hated what it saw as a retreat from fiscal restraint and responsibility; the other was appalled by the opacity of the process, in which a handful of negotiators from the White House and Congress worked out the horse trades behind closed doors. "This is a sham," cried Republican Rep. Jon Christensen of Nebraska. "This Congress ought to be ashamed of itself," scolded Wisconsin Democrat Rep. David Obey.

Retiring Speaker Newt Gingrich—who hasn't been quite the same since the federal-government brownout of 1995, a game of chicken with the White House that went badly for Republicans—found himself fending off a rearguard action from the right, of all places, and had to put the ingrates (he called them "petty dictators" and the "perfectionist caucus") in their place. "It is easy to get up and say, 'Vote No!' Then what would you do?" shrugged a world-wizened Gingrich. "Those of us who have grown up and matured . . . understand that we have to work together on the big issues."

Even the old sausage-maker himself, Democratic Sen. Robert Byrd of West Virginia, was shocked at what he saw. Renowned for his own cagey use of the budget process to bring billions of dollars in pork back to the Mountain State (and perhaps a bit peeved at finding himself excluded from all the behind-the-scenes horse trading), Byrd condemned the bill as a "gargantuan monstrosity"—a "Frankenstein monster patched together from old legislative body parts that don't quite fit."

Members of both parties chafed at having to vote on legislation crafted in such haste that few actually knew what was inside the 40-pound, 16-inch, 4,000-page end product (except, of course, for that quick peek at page 2,216, Part B, subsection 3[a], just to be sure that a wastewater-treatment facility and $4 million grant for the alma mater made it in). But by now a bit more is known about how this particular sausage was made and what ingredients went into it. The measure included funding for eight unfinished spending bills, a $21 billion emergency-spending measure and a cornucopia of legislative riders ranging from the substantial (one resulted in a major reorganization of the State Department) to the trivial (another extended duck-hunting season in Mississippi for 11 days) to the ludicrous (still another bans nude sunbathing at a beach near Cape Canaveral, Fla.).

Fiscal conservatives, led by House Budget Committee Chairman John Kasich of Ohio, had entertained the notion of dusting off the old budget battle ax. But perennial targets for their imagined whacks, such as the National Endowment for the Arts and the Tennessee Valley Authority, sailed through unscathed. Moreover, even some old budget bogeymen—such as the wool, mohair, and sugar subsidies—came roaring back from the brink of extinction.

If and when disputes arose between Democrats and Republicans, they invariably hinged not on where the ax might fall but on whom would be supping upon the larger ladle of gravy.

Clinton and the Democrats got $1.2 billion to begin hiring 30,000 of 100,000 new teachers (meaning much more money will be needed in the future); an $18 billion bailout for the International Monetary Fund; $1.7 billion in new home-health-care money for Medicare (reversing changes to the program made in 1996); and more than most Republicans wanted in farm aid (which even Senate Agriculture Committee Chairman Richard Lugar of Indiana said would "undermine" recent efforts to wean farmers off federal aid). Democrats also prevailed on a measure expanding coverage of the federal-employee health-insurance plan to include oral contraceptives; restored $35 million in food and oil shipments to North Korea; and turned back the Republican push for tax relief.

Republicans got $6.8 billion in increased military spending (some of which is classified), $1 billion for antimissile defense (although the Pentagon already is spending $3 billion annually on missile defense, with no deployment in sight) and $690 million for antidrug efforts (including the purchase of $40 million gulf-stream jets for law-enforcement agencies reportedly surprised by the windfall and $90 million for helicopters for Colombia). The GOP also was successful in its push to increase visa quotas for hightech workers and, striking a blow for peduncles everywhere, blocked a Department of Transportation move that would have mandated peanut-free zones on commercial airliners.

. . . Other interesting bill provisions, without any known partisan parentage, include: a cut in foreign aid to countries that haven't paid parking tickets in the District of Columbia; a measure allowing the Secretary of Agriculture to lend Russia money, which the Russians then can use to buy frozen chickens from Mississippi; $325 million inserted to buy enriched uranium from Russia;

and $1 billion during the next five years to help the Tennessee Valley Authority refinance its debt.

Some of the $21.4 billion in "emergency" spending extras included: $3.35 billion to tackle the Y2K computer problem; $2.4 billion for antiterrorism activities; $6.8 billion to improve military readiness; and $5.9 billion in additional aid to farmers. Many items among them drew fire from budgetwatchers, including $100 million for a new visitors center for the U.S. Capitol—an idea entertained for years which received a boost following last summer's fatal shootings there—and $100 million for a buyout of fishermen working in the Bering Sea, where pollock stocks have plummeted.

Singled out for particular opprobrium, however, was the $5.9 billion in emergency farm relief. Citizens Against Government Waste (CAGW) President Tom Schatz called it a "bipartisan and cynical attempt to buy the farm vote before this fall's election," pointing to studies showing that actual farm losses because of drought or other disasters were much lower. The group also condemned increased subsidies to sugar, peanuts and mohair producers contained in the agriculture appropriations bill. Such subsidies, said CAGW, represented "a first step toward dismantling the 1996 farm bill"; which made history by beginning to phase out farm price supports that have been in place since the 1930s.

Of course, more pedestrian and parochial kinds of pork projects also were packed into the bill, a random sampling of which includes: $37.5 million for a ferry and docking facilities at King Cove, Alaska; $2 million for the National Center for Cool and Cold Water Aquaculture in West Virginia ("The seafood capital of Appalachia!" one wag said); $1 million for peanut quality research in Georgia; $1.4 million for the Jimmy Carter National Historical Site; a $200,000 grant to Vermont's Center for Rural Studies; $1 million to restore a German submarine at a museum in Chicago (the project received $900,000 last year); $1.2 million for a project called "Building America"; $400,000 for another called "Rebuilding America"; and $67,000 for the New Orleans Jazz Commission.

Christmas came early to the nation's capital this year. The party was a hoot-and-a-half while it lasted, but the inevitable hangover followed as its fuller consequences have become clear.

The 1998 spending spree "has made it almost impossible to stay within the budget caps set in the 1997 [budget] agreement," Senate Budget Committee staff director G. William Hoagland told a gathering just weeks after the bill became law. The committee estimates that when everything is factored in, the extra spending in the omnibus bill will drain $38.2 billion from any future budget surplus. And as the bills for its "forward-funding" mechanisms come due, deep and painful cuts in next year's discretionary spending will be necessary. And that, Hoagland says, is "unlikely unless we can come up with more user fees or some quick gimmicks in the budget."

But even if such a plan fails and the fiscal restraint that took decades to muster caves in on itself like a black hole, sucking the rest of the republic in after it, one thing will be said of the ludicrous budget battle of 1998: At least the duck hunters of Mississippi are happy.

Jonathan Cohn

Roll Out the Barrel: The Case Against the Case Against Pork

On most days, the lobby of the U.S. Chamber of Commerce's Washington, D.C., headquarters has a certain rarefied air. But on this Tuesday morning it is thick with the smell of greasy, grilled bacon. The aroma is appropriate, since the breakfast speaker is Republican Representative Bud Shuster of Pennsylvania, chairman of the House Transportation Committee and, his critics say, one of the most shameless promulgators of pork-barrel spending in all of Congress. The odor seems even more fitting given that the topic of Shuster's address is the Building Efficient Surface Transportation and Equity Act, the six-year, $217 billion highway-spending package about to pass Congress—and, according to these same critics, the single biggest hunk of pork Washington has seen in a decade.

The critics, of course, are absolutely right. The House version of BESTEA, which hit the floor this week, contains at least $18 billion in so-called "demonstration" and "high-priority" projects. Those are the congressional euphemisms for pork—public works programs of dubious merit, specific to one congressional district, designed to curry favor with its voters. And Shuster's record for bringing home the bacon is indeed legendary. BESTEA's predecessor, which

Published in *The New Republic*, April 1998.

passed in 1991, included $287 million for 13 projects in Shuster's central Pennsylvania district. Today, visitors can see these and other shrines to his legislative clout by driving along the newly built Interstate 99, a shimmering stretch of asphalt the state has officially christened the Bud Shuster Highway.

None of this much bothers the suits at the Chamber of Commerce, who savor every line of Shuster's pitch as if it were just so much more fat-soaked sausage from the buffet table. Money for roads—whether in Shuster's district or anybody else's—means more ways to transport goods and more work for construction companies. But, outside the friendly confines of groups like this, a relentless chorus of high-minded watchdog groups and puritanical public officials complains that pork-barrel spending wastes government money. These critics also protest the way pork becomes law in the first place, as last-minute amendments designed to bypass the hearings and debate bills normally require.

To be sure, these arguments are not exactly novel. The very term "pork barrel" is a pre-Civil War term, derived from what was then a readily understandable (but, to modern ears, rather objectionable) analogy between congressmen gobbling up appropriations and slaves grabbing at salt pork distributed from giant barrels. "By the 1870s," William Safire writes in his *Political Dictionary*, "congressmen were regularly referring to 'pork,' and the word became part of the U.S. political lexicon." Criticizing pork, meanwhile, is just as venerable a tradition. Virtually every president from Abraham Lincoln to Ronald Reagan has promised to eliminate pork from the federal budget, and so have most congressmen, much to the satisfaction of muckraking journalists and similarly high-minded voters.

But rarely have the politicians actually meant it, and even more rarely have they succeeded. Until now. Thanks to an endless parade of media exposés on government waste, and a prevailing political consensus in favor of balanced budgets, pork critics have been gaining momentum. In 1994, anti-pork fervor nearly killed President Clinton's crime bill; in 1995, the same sentiment lay behind enactment of the line-item veto, something budget-balancers had sought in vain for more than a decade. A few years ago, a handful of anti-pork legislators took to calling themselves "pork-busters." Thanks to their vigilance, says the nonprofit group Citizens Against Government Waste, the amount of pork in the budget declined by about nine percent in 1998.

The influence of pork-busters reached a new peak in 1997, when they helped defeat a preliminary attempt at BESTEA. They probably won't be able to duplicate the feat this year—Shuster has nearly 400 votes behind his new pork-laden bill, which House Budget Chairman John Kasich has called an "abomination." But pork-busters won a major public relations victory last week when four House Republicans turned on Shuster and accused him of trying to buy them off with pet projects. "I told them my vote was not for sale," said Steve Largent of Oklahoma. "Shuster bought just about everyone," David Hobson of Ohio told *The Washington Post*. Three weeks ago, Republican Senator John McCain of Arizona, Capitol Hill's most determined pork-buster, won passage of an amendment that could cut at least some of the bill's pork. President Clinton joined the chorus, saying he too deplored the parochial waste Shuster and his cronies added to the measure.

In the popular telling, episodes like these represent epic struggles of good versus evil—of principled fiscal discipline versus craven political self-interest—with the nation's economic health and public faith in government at stake. But this narrative, related time and again by purveyors of elite wisdom and then repeated mindlessly by everyday citizens, has it exactly backward. The pork-busters are more anti-government than anti-waste. As for pork-barrel spending, it's good for American citizens and American democracy as well. Instead of criticizing it, we should be celebrating it, in all of its gluttonous glory.

Nearly a week has passed since Shuster made his appearance before the Chamber of Commerce, and now it is the pork-busters' turn to be making headlines. In what has become an annual rite of the budget process, Citizens Against Government Waste is staging a press conference near Capitol Hill to release its compilation of pork in the 1997 federal budget—a 40-page, pink-covered booklet it calls the "Pig Book." (Actually, the pocket-sized, 40-page version is just a summary of the unabridged "Pig Book," which weighs in at a hefty 170 pages, in single-sided, legal-sized computer printouts.)

CAGW has been fighting this fight for more than a decade, and its steady stream of propaganda, reports, and testimony is in no small part responsible for pork-busting's Beltway resonance. Republican Representative Christopher Cox calls CAGW "the premier waste-fighting organization in America"; the 1995–1996 Congress sought CAGW testimony 20 times. The interest in today's press conference—attended by more than 60 reporters and a dozen television crews—is testimony to the group's high esteem among the Washington press corps, although it doesn't hurt that CAGW has also provided the TV crews with a good photo opportunity.

Like many press conferences in this city, this one features several members of Congress, including McCain and Democratic Senator Russell Feingold. Unlike many press conferences in this city, this one also features a man dressed in a bright pink pig's suit, rubber pig masks free for the media to take, plus a live, charcoal-gray potbellied pig named Porky. For the duration of the event, Porky does little except scarf down some vegetable shreds. But the beast's mere presence gets a few laughs, which is more than can be said for the puns that CAGW's president, Tom Schatz, makes as he rattles off the recipients of this year's "Oinker Awards."

Senator Daniel Inouye of Hawaii secured $127,000 in funding for research on edible seaweed; for this and other appropriations, Schatz says, Inouye (who is of Japanese ancestry) wins "The Sushi Slush Fund Award." Senator Ted Stevens of Alaska sponsored $100,000 for a project called Ship Creek, so he gets "The Up Ship's Creek Award." (Stevens is a double winner: for his other pork, totaling some $477 million since 1991, CAGW also presents him with "The Half Baked Alaska Award.") The Pentagon budget included $3 million for an observatory in South America: "It's supposed to peer back millions of years in time," Schatz says, his deadpan poker face now giving way to a smarmy, half-cocked smile. "Maybe they're looking for a balanced budget." This dubious-sounding project Schatz dubs "The Black Hole Award." And on. And on.

You might think cornball humor like this would earn CAGW the disdain of the famously cynical Washington press corps. But, when Schatz is done, and the question-and-answer period begins, the reporters display barely any skepticism. Instead, that evening, and during the following days, they will heap gobs of attention on the group. They don't flatter or endorse the organization per se, but the coverage shares a common assumption that the group's findings are evidence of political malfeasance. CNN, for example, will use the "Pig Book" 's release as a peg for stories bemoaning the persistence of pork in the federal budget. A story out of Knight Ridder's Washington bureau, which will run in nearly a dozen of the chain's newspapers, basically recapitulates the report. And all this comes on the heels of a front-page *Wall Street Journal* feature— sparked by a similar report from the Tax Foundation—highlighting the profligate pork barreling of the Senate majority leader, Trent Lott of Mississippi. Its headline: "MISSISSIPPI'S SENATORS CONTINUE A TRADITION: GETTING FEDERAL MONEY."

This is typical. Normally jaded Washingtonians, journalists especially, tend to view pork-busters not as ideologues but as politically disinterested watchdogs. Television producers, in particular, regularly summon CAGW experts to validate stories for such waste-focused segments as NBC's "The Fleecing of America" and ABC's "Your Money, Your Choice." While this image has a basis in reality—CAGW truly goes after pork-barreling Republicans with the same fervor it pursues Democrats—it is also a product of the organization's concerted attempt to wrap itself in the flag of nonpartisanship. "No matter how you slice it, pork is always on the menu in the halls of Congress," Schatz said at the press conference. "Some members of Congress simply couldn't resist the lure of easy money and putting partisan political interests over the best interest of taxpayers."

But it's not as if the pork-busters have no partisan or ideological agenda of their own. Some, like the Cato Institute, are explicit about their anti-government predisposition. CAGW is a little more cagey, but it remains true to the spirit of its past chairman, perennial right-wing Republican candidate Alan Keyes, as well as its cofounder, J. Peter Grace, who headed President Reagan's 1984 commission on government waste and whose antipathy to government in general was widely known. "The government is the worst bunch of stupid jerks you've ever run into in your life," he said once at a CAGW fund-raising dinner. "These people just want to spend money, money, money all the time."

That is, of course, a forgivable overstatement of a plausible argument. But it is also an overtly ideological one, and it calls into question the group's reliability when it comes to making delicate distinctions about what is truly wasteful. After all, CAGW is not just against pork, but against much of what the mainstream conservative movement considers bad or overly intrusive public policy—which encompasses an awful lot. In 1995, CAGW was not bashful about embracing the Contract With America, whose expansive definition of waste included many regulatory programs Americans deem quite worthwhile. "Taxpayers . . . demonstrated in two consecutive elections of a Republican Congress that the Washington establishment at its peril ignores the taxpayers' voice," the group's annual report boasts. "CAGW stood shoulder to shoulder with the reformers and enjoyed a sense of accomplishment at this burst of energy from revitalized taxpayers." CAGW's contributor list, not surprisingly, reads like a who's who of conservative interests, from Philip Morris Companies Inc. to the Columbia/HCA Healthcare Foundation Inc.

To be sure, CAGW is not the only Beltway organization whose partisan allegiances belie its nonprofit, nonpartisan status. At least a dozen other groups on both the left and the right do the exact same thing. Anyway, the fact that an argument may be ideologically motivated hardly means it's wrong.

But that doesn't mean it's right, either. Listen closely the next time some smug good-government type starts criticizing pork: it's an awful lot of fuss over what is, in fact, a very small amount of money. In the "Pig Book," for example, CAGW claims last year's budget included pork worth about $13.2 billion—or, as a pork-buster would say, "$13.2 billion!" Yes, you could feed quite a few hungry people with that much money, or you could give a bigger tax cut. But it's less than one percent of the federal budget.

And it's not even clear that all of the $13.2 billion of waste is really, well, waste. A good chunk of CAGW's $13.2 billion in pork comes from a few dozen big-ticket items, costing tens of millions of dollars each, scattered through various appropriations measures, particularly the Pentagon's. Among the programs: research of a space-based laser ($90 million), transportation improvements in Utah ($14 million), and military construction in Montana ($32 million).

But it's hardly self-evident that these all constitute waste, as the pork-busters suggest. At least some national security experts believe the space-based laser is a necessary defense against rogue nations that might get their hands on nuclear missiles. A lot of that Utah money is to help Salt Lake City prepare for Olympic traffic. And, if you've ever been to Montana, you know that there are a lot of military bases scattered across that vast state—which means a lot of soldiers who need buildings in which to live, eat, and work. In other words, all of these serve some credible purpose.

The wastefulness of the smaller items is similarly open to interpretation. Remember Senator Inouye's "Sushi Slush Fund Award"—the $127,000 for research on edible seaweed in Hawaii? It turns out that aquaculture is an emerging industry in Hawaii and that edible seaweed—known locally as "limu," "ogo," or "sea sprouts"—is "rich in complex carbohydrates and protein and low in calories," according to the *Honolulu Advertiser.* "It's a good source of vitamin A, calcium, and potassium, too."

Yes, the federal government is paying $3 million for a telescope in South America. But it has to, because the telescope is part of a U.S. effort to explore the southern hemisphere sky—which, of course, is only visible from the southern hemisphere. Although the telescope will be located in Chile, it will be operated remotely from the University of North Carolina at Chapel Hill. "When completed, the telescope will hold tremendous promise for scientists and the federal government," the university chancellor said when Republican Senator Lauch Faircloth of North Carolina announced the appropriation. "We at the university also have high hopes for what the project will mean for the North Carolina economy as well as for students of all ages—on this campus, across our state, and beyond."

And Senator Stevens's "Up Ship's Creek Award"? The Ship Creek water project was part of a bill authorizing studies of environmental cleanup across the country. Some $100,000 went to the U.S. Army Corps of Engineers to assess the impact of development on Ship Creek, which is Anchorage's primary source of freshwater. Ironically, according to the Corps of Engineers, the study is exploring not only what kind of environmental precautions are necessary, but whether the federal government really has to pay for them, and whether local private entities might be convinced to foot part of the bill. In other words, one objective of the Ship Creek appropriation was to reduce government waste.

You could argue, as pork-busters do, that, while projects like these may serve some positive function in society—perhaps even deserving of government money—they should not be on the federal dime. Let the Hawaiians pay for their own calcium-rich dinners! Let Alaskans foot the bill for their own water study! But there's a respectable argument that sometimes parochial needs are in fact a legitimate federal interest, particularly when it involves things like pollution and commerce that cross state lines.

Certainly, that's the way a lot of people outside of Washington understand it. Last month, while the national media was busy flogging unthrifty lawmakers, several local newspapers rose to their defense. "We elect people to Congress not only to see to the nation's defense and keep the currency sound but also to bring home some pork," editorialized *The Fort Worth Star-Telegram*. "Pork can mean local jobs, local beautification, local pride, etc." The *Dayton Daily News* defended one project, a museum on the history of flight, that appeared on CAGW's hit list: "It is at the heart of a community effort that has been painstakingly nurtured for years by all manner of Daytonians. It combines the legitimate national purpose of recognizing the history of flight with the top-priority local purpose of getting Dayton recognized as a center of the history of flight." Other papers were more critical: they wanted to know why their congressmen hadn't brought home *more* bacon. "Alaskans aren't going to sit still for being No. 2 for long," *Anchorage Daily News* columnist Mike Doogan wrote in a spirited defense of pork. "We need the money. And we have our pride."

This is not to say that all or even most of what gets called pork is defensible on its own terms. (Did Bedford County, Pennsylvania, which happens to be smack in the middle of Shuster's rural district, really need a new airport when there were two others nearby?) Nor is it to say that the local interest in getting federal money should always trump the national interest in balancing the budget and distributing the federal largesse fairly. (Couldn't the state of Pennsylvania have paid for the Bedford County airport instead?) Nor is it even to say that local interests defending pork aren't being incredibly hypocritical—no one thinks an appropriation is pork when it's his.

No, the point is simply that you can't call something waste just because it makes a clever pun. "From what we can tell," says John Raffetto, communications director for the Senate Transportation Committee, "CAGW does no research to determine what purpose the project serves other than to flip through the pages of the bill and find projects that sound funny. If it sounds funny, that's pork. I have not heard from any member's office that has told me they've received a call from CAGW to ask what purpose that project has served."

Pork-busters concede they lack the time or resources to investigate items thoroughly. "Some may be worthy of consideration," says CAGW media director Jim Campi. "Our concern is that, if the projects went through the process the way they were supposed to, there would be a [better] opportunity to judge them on their merits."

This is the same argument that most animates McCain, Feingold, and other pork-busting lawmakers. But what constitutes a fair appropriations process? CAGW would have everyone believe that a project is pork if it is "not requested by the president" or if it "greatly exceeds the president's budget request or the previous year's funding." Huh? The whole point of the appropriations process is to give Congress a chance to make independent judgments about spending priorities. Particularly when Republicans control one branch of government and Democrats the other—as is the case today—differences will exist. The Republican Congress used to routinely declare the president's budget "dead on arrival." Did this mean the entire congressional budget was pork?

Two other criteria for defining pork are equally shaky. Invoking the familiar pork-busting wisdom, CAGW says a program is pork if it was "not specifically authorized"—meaning it wasn't in the original budget which contains general spending limits, but rather added on as part of the subsequent appropriations process, in which money is specifically allocated to each item. But the rationale for a separate budget and appropriations process is to allow Congress (and, for that matter, the president) an opportunity to change their minds about smaller items, as long as they stay within the broad guidelines of the budget agreement. CAGW also damns any projects "requested by only one chamber of Congress." But, just as Congress can disagree with the president over a project's merit, so the House can disagree with the Senate—that's the reason the architects of the Constitution created two houses in the first place. (Also, keep in mind that one reason the Senate doesn't propose as much pork is that senators—wary of getting stung in the national press for lacking frugality—will often wait to see how much pork the House passes. That way, they end up with the best of both worlds: they can quietly tell supporters that they backed the measure without ever incurring the wrath of pork-busting watchdogs.)

Make no mistake, though: Many pork-barrellers are trying to evade the scrutiny bills get when they move through the normal appropriations process. They stick in small bits of pork after hearings end because they know that nobody is going to vote against a multibillion-dollar bill just because it has a few million dollars of pork tucked in. And they can do so safe in the knowledge that, because there's very little in the way of a paper trail, they will not suffer any public consequences—unless, of course, a watchdog group or enthusiastic reporter manages to find out.

Pork-busters call this strategy sleazy, and it is. But remember, the whole point of our Constitution is to harness mankind's corrupt tendencies and channel them in constructive directions. In an oft-quoted passage of *The Federalist Number 51,* James Madison wrote, "if men were angels, no government would be necessary," and "the private interest of every individual may be a sentinel over the public rights." The Founders believed that sometimes local interests should trump national interests because they recognized it was a way to keep federal power in check. It's true this process lends itself to a skewed distribution of benefits, with disproportionate shares going to powerful lawmakers. But, again, pork is such a small portion of the budget that "equalizing" its distribution would mean only modest funding changes here and there.

Which brings us to the final defense of pork, one Madison would certainly endorse. Even if every single pork-barrel project really were a complete waste of federal money, pork still represents a very cheap way to keep our sputtering legislative process from grinding to a halt. In effect, pork is like putting oil in your car engine: it lubricates the parts and keeps friction to a minimum. This is particularly true when you are talking about controversial measures. "Buying off potential coalition members with spending programs they favor is exactly what the Founders not only expected, but practiced," political scientist James

Q. Wilson has argued. He has also written: "If you agree with Madison, you believe in pork."

Think of the NAFTA battle in 1993. Contentious to the bitter end, the fate of the agreement ultimately fell on the shoulders of a handful of congressmen, all of whom privately supported it but feared the political backlash if they voted for it. Clinton gave each of them a little pork—for example, a development bank in border states that ostensibly would provide start-up money for entrepreneurs who had lost jobs because of NAFTA. The bank was just another way to pump some federal money into these districts, but that was the whole point. Thanks to that money, NAFTA became politically viable; these lawmakers could tell their constituents, plausibly and truthfully, that there was something in it for their districts.

To take a more current example, just look at BESTEA. U.S. transportation infrastructure is famously inadequate; the Department of Transportation says unsafe roads cause 30 percent of all traffic fatalities. But, when fiscal conservatives questioned the pork in the original BESTEA last year, the measure failed, forcing Congress to pass an emergency extension. This year, a more permanent, six-year version will likely pass, largely because the appearance of a budget surplus has tipped the scales just enough so that the pork seems tolerable. As John W. Ellwood and Eric M. Patashnik wrote in *The Public Interest* several years ago (in what was the best defense of pork in recent memory): "Favoring legislators with small gifts for their districts in order to achieve great things for the nation is an act not of sin but of statesmanship."

Last week, of course, BESTEA's high pork content had fiscal conservatives downright apoplectic. "Frankly, this bill really is a hog," Kasich said. "It is way over the top." But, without the pork, there might be no highway bill at all. As one highway lobbyist told *National Journal* last year, "The projects are the glue that's going to hold the damn thing together." A former transportation official said: "I've always taken the point of view that every business has some overhead. If that's what it costs to get a significant or a good highway bill, it's worth the price." Kasich would surely be aghast at such logic, but someday he and other fiscal conservatives might find it useful for their own purposes. Remember, they are the ones who say that balancing the budget will likely be impossible without severe and politically risky reforms of entitlements like Medicare. When the time comes to make those tough choices—and they need to pry a few extra votes from the opposition—you can bet they will gladly trade a little pork for *their* greater cause. They might feel guilty about it, but they shouldn't. Pork is good. Pork is virtuous. Pork is the American way.

Representative Jeff Flake
Earmarked Men

Back on the F-Bar Ranch, when I was too young to load the chute, de-horn, vaccinate, hold a hot iron, or otherwise make myself useful as my father and older brothers branded calves, I would spend my time collecting "earmarks"— V-shaped pieces of a calf's left ear detached with two swift strokes of a pocketknife. I would stack these earmarks on the fence surrounding the corral as an unofficial tally of our progress.

Well, the more things change, the more they stay the same. Here I am in Congress, again being asked to collect earmarks. Sorry. I've had enough of that.

Earmarking—in which members of Congress secure federal dollars for pork-barrel projects by covertly attaching them to huge spending bills—has become the currency of corruption in Congress. It is not just the rising number of earmarks (more than 15,000 last year—up from around 1,200 a decade ago), or the dollar amount ($27 billion) that is troubling. More disturbing is that earmarks are used as inducements to get members to sign on to large spending measures. (The disgraced lobbyist Jack Abramoff was astute when he referred to the House Appropriations Committee as an "earmark favor factory.")

It is no coincidence that the growth of earmarks has paralleled the monstrous increase in overall federal spending. And President Bush's new $2.77 trillion budget will only set off another frenzy.

When I was first elected, I had visions of participating in the great debates of our time: How can we give the federal government the tools it needs to identify and root out our enemies while maintaining a free society? What tax and trade policies lend themselves to survival and prosperity in a global economy? How do we assert our influence abroad in a manner that enhances our security?

It is not that these policy debates haven't occurred during my time in Congress. They have. But they are diminishing.

In Congress these days, you establish your priorities by getting money for

Published in *The New York Times*, February 2006.

them. When the carefully designed process of authorization, appropriation, and oversight is adhered to, these policies and priorities are given a thorough vetting. But earmarking circumvents that cycle: the Appropriations Committee ensures that earmarks escape scrutiny by inserting them into conference reports, largely written behind closed doors.

By the time appropriation bills reach the House or Senate floor, passage by a lopsided margin is virtually assured because every member who got earmarks is obligated to vote for the entire bill. Further, the scope of debate is substantially narrowed, with even partisan arguments that would otherwise occur hushed as Republicans and Democrats find common cause: protecting their pork.

Earmarks are also making it increasingly difficult for Congress to oversee federal agencies. It's hypocritical for us to criticize the Defense Department for not providing body armor when we earmark growing portions of its budget for items like a genomics research project at the American Museum of Natural History in Manhattan.

Solving the earmark problem will require transparency—a requirement that earmarks be included in the actual text of legislation (where they can be seen and challenged) rather than hidden in committee and conference reports. I've introduced such legislation in the House and my Arizona Republican colleague John McCain has introduced companion legislation in the Senate. Debate on these measures should begin as soon as possible.

During my last few years on the F-Bar we stopped earmarking our calves altogether. We concluded that a brand on the left side was sufficient, and that the earmark simply marred an otherwise healthy critter. Here's hoping we reach the same conclusion in Congress.

Senator Larry Craig and Representative Mike Simpson
Earnest Earmarks

Recent scandals involving lobbyists and members of Congress cast a new spotlight on the functions of Congress and brought about a flurry of proposals to transform the business of legislating in our nation's capital.

Press release from Senator Craig's office, February 2006.

Unfortunately, as you may know, some unscrupulous Members of Congress have used the awarding of appropriations "earmarks" as a means of enriching themselves and their families at the expense of taxpayers. That's wrong, it's against the law, and they will be going to jail for their transgressions.

In order to prevent these abuses from resurfacing, some Members of Congress have called for an end to earmarking or extreme new restrictions on the practice. Earmarking is the simple practice of funding projects or initiatives whose sponsors have petitioned Members of Congress for support. These include projects to renovate hospitals, improve community drinking water systems, create or expand areas of study at colleges and universities, and assist non-profit charitable institutions in their various missions.

As fiscal conservatives, we take our roles on the House and Senate appropriations committees very seriously. We will continue to work to keep federal spending under control, but we acknowledge that not every one of the thousands of Congressional earmarks has been worthy of taxpayer support. However, we believe it is important to consider the consequences of some of these reform proposals and highlight the way in which earmarking has been extremely beneficial to Idahoans.

Some in Congress have proposed eliminating the practice of earmarking completely, saying it encourages corruption and has led to increased federal spending. For several reasons, this is simply not true. Before Congress appropriates one dollar, it passes a Budget Resolution which sets the overall funding amounts for the federal government. Appropriations and earmarking must fit within the overall budget numbers set in the Budget Resolution. A reduction in the amount of federal spending is unlikely without first reducing budget numbers set in the Budget Resolution.

Furthermore, experts disagree whether eliminating earmarks would effectively reduce federal spending. In a recent article on National Review Online, Brian Riedl of the Heritage Foundation says, "Congress could get rid of every pork project tomorrow and it would not cut federal spending directly."

Why not? Because eliminating earmarks would simply give federal agencies authority over how taxpayer dollars are spent.

Earmarking, by its very nature, shifts discretion over federal dollars away from the federal agencies and puts the funds out on the ground in American communities. Earmarked dollars generally go to projects that are short-term in nature and small in scope. Last year, earmarks we sponsored built new wastewater infrastructure in Bonners Ferry, supported jobs at the Idaho National

Laboratory, improved housing for families at Mountain Home Air Force Base, and expanded course offerings at Boise State University. And that is not all.

If federal dollars weren't earmarked for these projects, they would be deposited in the accounts of federal agencies where they would be spent on the growth of the federal government and creation of never-ending programs. When more of their funding is earmarked, the less federal agencies have to grow their bloated bureaucracies.

We have always believed that better decisions are made by local officials. Who would you rather have making decisions about funding for Idaho? Lawmakers who are accountable to you, or some nameless, faceless bureaucrat in Washington, D.C., who has never stepped foot in Idaho? If we abandon the practice of earmarking funding for our home states, those decisions will instead be made, and dollars spent, by tens of thousands of bureaucrats who have no accountability to taxpayers, voters, or anyone else for that matter.

Clearly, eliminating earmarks would shift responsibility for setting federal spending away from Congress to the federal bureaucracies. We believe it would be wrong to do that, but don't take our word for it. Article 1, Section 9, Clause 7 of the Constitution says, "No money shall be drawn from the Treasury but in Consequence of Appropriations made by law." Congress makes the laws.

Put simply, the Framers of the Constitution clearly stated that Congress, not the President or federal bureaucrats, should allocate funding for the various functions of the federal government. Ending the practice of earmarking would transfer massive funding authority to the President and the federal agencies in defiance of the Constitution. That is not the way to keep spending in check.

That being said, we realize that change is needed in the appropriations process. But those changes should be the result of a reasoned, well-informed debate, not a knee-jerk desire to defuse controversy and shift attention. We will work toward responsible reforms to ensure that potential for corruption is minimized and taxpayer dollars are spent responsibly, not wasted.

QUESTIONS

1. *What would you do?* If you were a member of Congress, how would you balance the desire of your constituents to have you deliver benefits to the district and the national needs of fiscal responsibility and the collective good? If you were a leader in Congress would you use pork as a tool of coalition building,

or would you take a principled stand against it? As a constituent, how would you answer Sen. Craig's question about who should decide how money is spent?

2. How would you define pork barrel projects? Are all pork projects contrary to the national interest? How could one distinguish between local projects that are in the national interest and those that are not?

3. Members of Congress face strong incentives to serve constituent needs and claim credit for delivering federal dollars. Pork barrel projects provide the means to do just that. What changes in Congress or the political process might be made to alter legislative behavior, or to change the incentives they face for securing re-election? Do we want members of Congress to be focused primarily on broad national issues rather than local priorities?

4. If pork-barrel spending is problematic, is the central problem the *process* through which spending decisions are made or the *projects* that are funded with these dollars?

13

An Imperial Presidency?

In 1973, historian Arthur Schlesinger Jr. wrote a landmark book arguing that we were in an era of an "imperial presidency," in which presidents were abusing the powers of their office to wield unchecked authority, especially in international affairs. In large part because of the Cold War between the Soviet Union and United States, power had become concentrated in the presidency, to the point the president could do anything—steamroll Congress into adopting an open-ended authorization for military action in Vietnam; carry out a secret unauthorized war in Cambodia; spy on domestic opponents; abuse law enforcement powers—without interference from the other coordinate branches of government.

Thirty years later critics of the Bush Administration—Schlesinger included—made analogous arguments about the president's actions leading up to the Iraq war. The substance of these arguments is that Bush had already decided to invade Iraq and remove Saddam Hussein from power, and misled Congress and the public by arguing that Iraq posed an imminent threat to U.S. security. The implication is that we had returned—or were getting close—to an era of unchecked presidential power reminiscent of the Vietnam War era.

In a June 2003 article, Schlesinger revisited his imperial presidency thesis. He argues that the Bush policy of preventive war, which the president set out in early 2002, gives the president the power to wage war anywhere and anytime he might like. Under the preventive war doctrine, the United States asserted the right to use military force against another country, even if that country did not pose an immediate or imminent threat to the United States. Supporters of the policy argued that September 11, and the possibility that terrorists might use nuclear weapons, showed that we could not wait until we knew that an attack was an immediate threat, but had to be proactive to prevent such threats from even developing. Schlesinger, however, argues that this will have the effect of making the president the sole arbiter of when the country will go to war. To Schlesinger, this is a clear violation of the Constitution, which grants Congress, and *only* Congress, the power to "declare war."

John Isaacs places blame on Congress, which in his view has abdicated its responsibility over war powers. Rather than have a serious debate over the grave issue of war, Isaacs notes that Congress was preoccupied with trivial commemorations and other issues, including tax cuts, abortion, and judicial nominations. And rather than declare war—or prevent it, by refusing to appropriate money for the war—Congress shirked responsibility by passing a law authorizing the use of force and leaving it up to the president to decide how to proceed.

Concerns over the imperial presidency were raised again when the *New York Times* revealed in December 2005 that President Bush had authorized the National Security Agency to monitor some communications between people inside the United States and suspected terrorists abroad. In 1978, Congress enacted a law—the Foreign Intelligence Surveillance Act, or FISA—that required the president to obtain from a judge a special warrant whenever the executive branch wanted to conduct surveillance, even against suspected foreign agents. Bush's critics argued that the NSA program, which did not ask for warrants, was a violation of the law.

Not so, according to Robert Turner's article. He argues that the president has an inherent constitutional power to conduct intelligence surveillance, based on his constitutional grants as commander in chief and chief executive. The president does not need a warrant to spy on foreign governments or agents abroad, and it does not matter whether those agents are in Europe, Asia, or the United States. What the Constitution grants to the president, Congress may not take away. This is clearly what the Framers intended, as has every court that has examined the issue. If FISA limits the president's intelligence gathering power, Turner asserts, it is itself unconstitutional.

Arthur Schlesinger Jr.
The Imperial Presidency Redux

The weapons-of-mass-destruction (WMD) issue—where are they?—will not subside and disappear, as the administration supposes (and hopes).

The issue will build because many Americans do not like to be manipulated and deceived.

It will build because elements in Congress and in the media will wish to regain their honor and demonstrate their liberation from Bush/Cheney/Rumsfeld.

It will build because of growing interest in the parallel British inquiries by committees of the House of Commons. Robin Cook, the former foreign secretary, formulated the charge with precision: "Instead of using intelligence as evidence on which to base a decision about policy, we used intelligence as the basis on which to justify a policy on which we had already settled."

And the WMD issue will build because hyped intelligence produces a credibility gap. The credibility gap is likely to undermine the Bush doctrine and block the radical transformation of U.S. strategy to which the Bush administration is dedicated.

The strategy that won us the Cold War was a combination of containment and deterrence carried out through multilateral agencies. The Bush doctrine reverses all that. The essence of the Bush doctrine is "anticipatory self-defense," a fancy name for preventive war. Our new policy is to strike an enemy, unilaterally if necessary, before it has a chance to strike us.

Whatever legitimacy preventive war may claim derives from intelligence reliable enough to persuade responsible people, including allies, that the supposed enemy is *really* about to strike the United States. If no WMD turn up in Iraq, President Bush will lose a lot of credibility. It seems doubtful that he would be able to lead the American people into wars against Iran or North Korea simply on his presidential say-so. The credibility gap may well nullify the preventive-war policy.

And if a cache of WMD is found buried somewhere in Iraq, that is not sufficient to rescue the president. The bottom-line question is: Why were the WMD not deployed? When Saddam Hussein was fighting for his regime, his

Published in *The Washington Post*, June 2003.

power, and his life, why in the world did he not use his WMD against the U.S. invasion? Heaven knows, he had plenty of warning.

Unearthing buried WMD would not establish Iraq as a clear and present danger to the United States. Deployment of WMD would have come much closer to convincing people that Iraq was a mortal threat.

Retreat from the preventive-war policy is all to the good, because the Bush doctrine transfers excessive power to the president. Abraham Lincoln long ago foresaw the constitutional implications of the preventive-war policy. On Feb. 15, 1848, he denounced the proposition "that if it shall become *necessary to repel invasion*, the President may, without violation of the Constitution, cross the line, and *invade* the territory of another country; and that whether such *necessity* exists in given case, the President is to be the *sole* judge."

Lincoln continued: "Allow the President to invade a neighboring nation, whenever *he* shall deem it necessary to repel an invasion . . . and you allow him to make war at pleasure. . . . If to-day, he should choose to say he thinks it necessary to invade Canada, to prevent the British from invading us, how could you stop him? You may say to him, 'I see no probability of the British invading us' but he will say to you 'be silent; I see it, if you don't.' "

"The Founding Fathers," Lincoln said, "resolved to so frame the Constitution that *no one man* should hold the power of bringing this oppression upon us."

If the Bush doctrine prevails, the imperial presidency will sure be redux.

John Isaacs
Congress Goes AWOL

On March 17, President George W. Bush announced to the nation that the United States was going to war against Iraq. The next day's headline should have read "Congress Declares War on Iraq"—except that Congress did not declare war, despite its constitutionally delegated responsibility. In fact, Congress has not officially acted on the question of war and peace since its October 2002 vote authorizing the president to decide.

Despite U.S. military actions in Korea in the 1950s and in Vietnam in the

Published in the *Bulletin of the Atomic Scientists*, May/June 2003.

1960s and 1970s, and more recent smaller conflicts in Panama, Grenada, Bosnia, Kosovo, and Afghanistan, Congress has failed to declare war since Pearl Harbor.

As the nation moved toward war in March, debates raged in the U.N. Security Council. The British, Canadian, and Turkish parliaments engaged in major debates. Harsh exchanges were traded between Washington, Paris, London, Moscow, Berlin, and other capitals. Dueling opinion pieces appeared in the nation's editorial pages, and worldwide demonstrations against the war were organized, using the Internet as a major channel of communications.

But Congress was silent.

Congress could have used the power of the purse to curtail the drive toward war. Before the fighting started, the administration adamantly refused to provide any estimate of the costs of the impending war. Administration officials argued repeatedly that the costs of the war and its aftermath were unknowable. Some members of Congress—primarily Democrats—complained, but got nowhere. The Bush team preferred to change the subject by crusading for the centerpiece of its domestic agenda—a $1.6 trillion tax cut, including a $726 billion "economic growth package"—despite rising federal budget deficits and the war.

On March 6, Cong. David Obey, a Wisconsin Democrat, asked wryly: "Can you imagine President Teddy Roosevelt or President Woodrow Wilson or FDR or Harry Truman saying we are going to war and your country needs you to accept a tax cut?"

Congress could have used the appropriations or budget process to deal with the question of war. Independent estimates indicated that the cost—to be borne virtually exclusively by U.S. taxpayers—might top $100 billion. The estimated $60 billion price tag for the 1991 Gulf War, in contrast, was mostly paid for by other nations. Eric Shinseki, army chief of staff, estimated that in addition to immediate costs, the United States would need to maintain an occupying force in Iraq of as many as 200,000 soldiers, perhaps for as long as a decade. And the Council on Foreign Relations estimated that it would cost a minimum of $20 billion a year to rebuild the country. (Finally, on March 24, the Bush administration asked Congress for $74.7 billion for fiscal 2003.)

Earlier, even as U.S. and British troops headed for the Iraqi border, Republicans were trying to pass an annual budget resolution without allocating a dime for the war, for rebuilding Iraq, or even for the continued fighting and reconstruction effort in Afghanistan. The House of Representatives approved a budget resolution without any of these funds, but did endorse the Bush administration's entire tax cut.

In the Senate, the verdict was mixed. The Senate rejected 56–43 an amendment offered by Kent Conrad, North Dakota Democrat, prohibiting the tax cut until the president submitted a detailed estimate of the cost of the war. It then turned around and approved 52–47 an amendment offered by Russ Feingold, Wisconsin Democrat, to set aside a reserve fund of $100 billion to pay for the war. The administration's belated submission of its war funds request did help the success of Louisiana Democrat John Breaux's amendment to halve the centerpiece of the Bush tax cut. The fate of both the Feingold and Breaux amendments was to be determined by a House-Senate conference committee completed after this writing.

The Senate spent the week before the president's war announcement consumed with a debate over the controversial procedure called "late-term" or "partial-birth" abortion and the nomination of D.C. Circuit Court nominee Miguel Estrada. It also found time to deal with National Girl Scout Week and Greek Independence Day. The House adopted medical malpractice insurance legislation. Neither body debated the war.

The Senate leadership of the two parties agreed to set aside a few hours for discussion on a sparsely attended Friday session on March 7. As Virginia Republican John Warner put it, the discussion would be on "the international situation . . . relating to the war on terrorism, with emphasis on Iraq and North Korea." Seven senators participated.

There were a few heroes who tried to get Congress to reconsider the war in a serious manner. In the Senate, 85-year-old Robert Byrd, Democrat of West Virginia, has been eloquent and even strident in denouncing the administration's drive to war. In a widely disseminated speech delivered on the Senate floor on February 12, Byrd argued that the United States was "about to embark upon the first test of a revolutionary doctrine applied in an extraordinary way at an unfortunate time. The doctrine of preemption—the idea that the United States or any other nation can legitimately attack a nation that is not imminently threatening but may be threatening in the future—is a radical new twist of the traditional idea of self-defense."

Byrd castigated the Bush administration for "split[ting] traditional alliances, possibly crippling, for all time, international order-keeping entities like the United Nations and NATO." And yet the Senate, he sadly noted, is "ominously, dreadfully silent. There is no debate, no discussion, no attempt to lay out for the nation the pros and cons of this particular war. There is nothing."

Vermont Democrat Patrick Leahy agreed in a March 3 Senate floor speech: "What I hear from people is: Why is there not any discussion about a possible war against Iraq? The British Parliament has had a major debate on it. The Turkish Parliament had a major debate on it. The Canadian Parliament had a major debate on it. . . . The impression of the American people, both Republicans and Democrats, is that the Senate does not want to discuss a war with Iraq."

Massachusetts Democrat Edward Kennedy, a liberal workhorse who in past years had devoted much of his time to health care, education, and other domestic issues, turned his focus toward the impending war in a March 13 Senate speech. "I am concerned," he said, "that as we rush to war with Iraq, we are becoming more divided at home and more isolated in the world community. Instead of persuading the dissenters at home and abroad, the administration by its harsh rhetoric is driving the wedge deeper. Never before, even in the Vietnam War, has America taken such bold military action with so little international support."

Both Byrd and Kennedy—and in the House, Oregon's Peter DeFazio—introduced resolutions to force Congress to vote a second time on whether the country should go to war.

They got nowhere. The Republican Party was adamantly opposed to a new vote; so too were the Democrats. The Republican motivation was easy to understand. Congress had spoken in October, giving the president full authority to proceed as he desired. As House Appropriations Committee Chairman C. W. "Bill" Young told the March 15 *Congressional Quarterly*, "Congress should now be micromanaging a war. Congress should be in a support role."

For the Democrats, a new vote would only have demonstrated the division within the party. When the Senate voted 77–23 for the use-of-force resolution in October, 29 Democrats voted "yea" and 21 voted "nay." House Democrats were also split; in an overall vote of 296–133, 126 opposed the resolution and 81 voted for it. Even war critics acknowledged that a new vote would have produced a similar outcome.

Congress's failure to act is not new. Many in both parties were uneasy with, or opposed to, U.S. military involvement in Kosovo and Bosnia, but refused to force President Bill Clinton to call the troops home. Since World War II,

Congress has willingly ceded the power to make war—letting the president take responsibility for success or failure. And if the war goes badly, as in Somalia in the 1990s, Congress is also willing to let the president take the fall.

As the Vietnam War wound down and President Richard Nixon became increasingly crippled by Watergate, in 1973 Congress adopted the War Powers Act over a presidential veto. That bill would have forced a president to bring U.S. troops home from any overseas engagement within 60 days if Congress has not in the meantime approved the fighting.

It was a bold action, but there has been no follow-through. For 30 years, Congress and presidents have ignored that law just as they have ignored the Constitution. As the war clouds gathered, Congress went AWOL—again. Senators and representatives decided they would rather talk about Iraq than vote, and better yet, change the subject.

Robert F. Turner
FISA vs. the Constitution

In the continuing saga of the surveillance "scandal," with some congressional Democrats denouncing President Bush as a lawbreaker and even suggesting that impeachment hearings may be in order, it is important to step back and put things in historical context. First of all, the Founding Fathers knew from experience that Congress could not keep secrets. In 1776, Benjamin Franklin and his four colleagues on the Committee of Secret Correspondence unanimously concluded that they could not tell the Continental Congress about covert assistance being provided by France to the American Revolution, because "we find by fatal experience that Congress consists of too many members to keep secrets."

When the Constitution was being ratified, John Jay—America's most experienced diplomat and George Washington's first choice to be secretary of state—wrote in *Federalist No. 64* that there would be cases in which "the most useful intelligence" may be obtained if foreign sources could be "relieved from apprehensions of discovery," and noted there were many "who would rely on the secrecy of the president, but who would not confide in that of the Senate."

Published in *The Wall Street Journal Online*, December 2005.

He then praised the new Constitution for so distributing foreign-affairs powers that the president would be able "to manage the business of intelligence in such manner as prudence may suggest."

In 1790, when the first session of the First Congress appropriate money for foreign intercourse, the statute expressly required that the president "account specifically for all such expenditures of the said money as in his judgment may be made public, and also for the amount of such expenditures as he may think it advisable not to specify." They made no demand that President Washington share intelligence secrets with them. And in 1818, when a dispute arose over a reported diplomatic mission to South America, the legendary Henry Clay told his House colleagues that if the mission had been provided for from the president's contingent fund, it would not be "a proper subject for inquiry" by Congress.

For nearly 200 years it was understood by all three branches that intelligence collection—especially in wartime—was an exclusive presidential prerogative vested in the president by Article II, Section 1 of the Constitution. Washington, Madison, Jefferson, Hamilton, John Marshall, and many others recognized that the grant of "executive power" to the president included control over intelligence gathering. It was not by chance that there was no provision for congressional oversight of intelligence matters in the National Security Act of 1947.

Space does not permit a discussion here of the congressional lawbreaking that took place in the wake of the Vietnam War. It is enough to observe that the Constitution is the highest law of the land, and when Congress attempts to usurp powers granted to the president, its members betray their oath of office. In certain cases, such as the War Powers Resolution and the Foreign Intelligence Surveillance Act [FISA], it might well have crossed that line.

Keep in mind that while the Carter administration asked Congress to enact the FISA statute in 1978, Attorney General Griffin Bell emphasized that the law "does not take away the power of the president under the Constitution." And in 1994, when the Clinton administration invited Congress to expand FISA to cover physical as well as electronic searches, the associate attorney general testified: "Our seeking legislation in no way should suggest that we do not believe we have inherent authority" under the Constitution. "We do," she concluded.

I'm not saying that what the president authorized was unquestionably lawful. The Supreme Court in the 1972 "Keith case" held that a warrant was required for national security wiretaps involving purely domestic targets, but expressly distinguished the case from one involving wiretapping "foreign powers" or their agents in this country. In the 1980 *Truong* case, the Fourth U.S. Circuit Court of Appeals upheld the warrantless surveillance of a foreign power, its agent or collaborators (including U.S. citizens) when the "primary purpose" of the intercepts was for "foreign intelligence" rather than law enforcement purposes. Every court of appeals that has considered the issue has upheld an inherent presidential power to conduct warrantless foreign intelligence searches; and in 2002 the U.S. Foreign Intelligence Surveillance Court of Review, created by the FISA statute, accepted that "the president does have that authority" and noted "FISA could not encroach on the president's constitutional power."

For constitutional purposes, the joint resolution passed with but a single dissenting vote by Congress on Sept. 14, 2001, was the equivalent of a formal declaration of war. The Supreme Court held in 1800 (*Bas v. Tingy*), and again in 1801 (*Talbot v. Seamen*), that Congress could formally authorize war by joint resolution without passing a formal declaration of war; and in the post-U.N. Charter era no state has issued a formal declaration of war. Formal declarations were historically only required when a state was initiating an aggressive war, which today is unlawful.

Section 1811 of the FISA statute recognizes that during a period of authorized war the president must have some authority to engage in electronic surveillance "without a court order." The question is whether Congress had the power to limit such authorizations to a 15-day period, which I think highly doubtful. It would be akin to Congress telling the president during wartime that he could attack a particular enemy stronghold for a maximum of 15 days.

America is at war with a dangerous enemy. Since 9/11, the president, our intelligence services and our military forces have done a truly extraordinary job—taking the war to our enemies and keeping them from conducting a single attack within this country (so far). But we are still very much at risk, and those who seek partisan political advantage by portraying efforts to monitor communications between suspected foreign terrorists and (often unknown) Americans as being akin to Nixon's "enemies lists" are serving neither their party nor their country. The leakers of this sensitive national security activity and their Capitol Hill supporters seem determined to guarantee al Qaeda a secure communications channel into this country so long as they remember to include one sympathetic permanent resident alien not previously identified by NSA or the FBI as a foreign agent on their distribution list.

Ultimately, as the courts have noted, the test is whether the legitimate government interest involved—in this instance, discovering and preventing new terrorist attacks that may endanger tens of thousands of American lives—outweighs the privacy interests of individuals who are communicating with al Qaeda terrorists. And just as those of us who fly on airplanes have accepted intrusive government searches of our luggage and person without the slightest showing of probable cause, those of us who communicate (knowingly or otherwise) with foreign terrorists will have to accept the fact that Uncle Sam may be listening.

Our Constitution is the supreme law, and it cannot be amended by a simple statute like the FISA law. Every modern president and every court of appeals that has considered this issue has upheld the independent power of the president to collect foreign intelligence without a warrant. The Supreme Court may ultimately clarify the competing claims; but until then, the president is right to continue monitoring the communications of our nation's declared enemies, even when they elect to communicate with people within our country.

QUESTIONS

1. *What would you do?* Isaacs argues that Congress could have stopped the Iraq war by refusing to appropriate money for that purpose. Is this a realistic position? Granting that Congress *could* have done this, what are the political obstacles to using the power of the purse to stop a war? How do you think the public might respond to such a step? If you were a member of Congress, what would you have done?

2. Are there significant differences between a policy of preemptive war (using military action to stop a surprise attack that is known to be imminent) and a policy of preventive war (using military action to prevent a threat from emerging)?

3. If Turner is right, would the president have the power to do whatever he wants, as long as he declares that it is for intelligence gathering? What limits could be imposed?

14

Evaluating Bureaucratic Performance: Can Government Be Run Like a Business?

Ask most people what they think of when they hear the term *government bureaucracy*, and you'll likely hear "red tape", "waste", "incompetence", or worse. It is telling that perhaps the worst charge made against President Bill Clinton's ill-fated 1994 Health Care Reform Act was that it would result in health care delivered with the courtesy of the Department of Motor Vehicles and the efficiency of the Post Office. It has become a common refrain that government needs to be run more like a business, with attention to the bottom line, "customer" needs, mission specificity, and efficiency. In the public mind a government agency is the antithesis of an efficient, lean organization. Unlike nimble, well-run organizations (think Southwest Airlines or Amazon.com), government agencies plod along, providing poor service at high cost, and choked by inefficient rules that prevent innovation.

Is this a fair picture? Political scientist James Q. Wilson argues that government agencies will *never* operate like a business, nor should they be expected to. His mid-1980s comparison of the Watertown, Massachusetts Registry of Motor Vehicles (representative of any government bureaucracy) with a nearby McDonald's (representative of private, profit-seeking organizations) shows that the former will most likely never be able to service its clientele as well as the latter. The problem, though, is not bureaucratic laziness or bad employees, but rather the very characteristics of the two types of organizations. In order to understand "what government agencies do and why they do it," Wilson argues that we must first recognize that government bureaucracies operate in a political marketplace rather than an economic one. An agency's annual revenues, personnel resources, and management rules are determined by elected officials, not by the agency's ability to meet the demands of its customers in a cost-efficient manner. Agencies are not, as a rule, rewarded if they become more efficient, nor are they penalized for not performing their functions well. Private organizations, in contrast, have much more control over their own goals and structure, and they are rewarded with increased profits if they become more efficient. Perhaps most critically, a government agency's goals are often vague, difficult if not impossible to measure, and often even contradictory. In business, the goals and evaluation processes are much simpler: the goal of any business is to maximize profit, and it is relatively easy to look at performance to see whether this goal is being met.

But, as Jacob Hacker argues, this does not mean that private organizations are always better than public ones. Governments, he asserts, are almost always more efficient than private entities when it comes to health care, disability, or other broad-based insurance programs. What makes insurance a special case is that the entire premise involves the "socialization of risk." That is, insurance works because the cost of a bad outcome—a burned-down or flooded house, accidental death, needing a heart transplant—is spread out over a large enough population that the cost to each person becomes reasonable. Not everyone who purchases insurance will actually need it: some insurance customers will inevitably subsidize others. Government, as it turns out, is much better able to handle these sorts of risk, because they encompass larger populations and can make participation mandatory. Private insurance companies worry about "adverse selection." No company would survive if it sold health insurance to people who are already very sick, or life insurance to ninety-year olds, or flood insurance only to people who live in New Orleans. Insurance companies make money by selling policies to people who will not need benefits. This is one reason health insurance companies screen applications, deny coverage for pre-existing conditions, charge large premiums for people in high-risk categories, or refuse to issue a policy altogether. From the companies' perspective this makes economic sense. From a social perspective, though, it is not the best outcome.

Here is where government does a better job, Hacker asserts. Because government can spread the risk so widely, it is more efficient. Because it can make participation mandatory, it avoids the adverse selection problem. As evidence, Hacker points to the administrative efficiencies of Medicare. Most private health insurance companies spend about 10 percent of their revenue on administrative expenses: processing claims, mediating disputes, screening applicants. Although other analysts would disagree, Hacker contends that Medicare—the government health program for retirees—spends only about 2–3 percent. Social Security spends only about 1 percent on overhead, far less than any financial services company. No private company would have the incentive to provide these sorts of benefits, nor could any company actually offer them at such low cost, he argues.

James Q. Wilson
What Government Agencies Do and Why They Do It

By the time the office opens at 8:45 A.M., the line of people waiting to do business at the Registry of Motor Vehicles in Watertown, Massachusetts, often will be twenty-five deep. By midday, especially if it is near the end of the month, the line may extend clear around the building. Inside, motorists wait in slow-moving rows before poorly marked windows to get a driver's license or to register an automobile. When someone gets to the head of the line, he or she is often told by the clerk that it is the wrong line: "Get an application over there and then come back," or "This is only for people getting a new license; if you want to replace one you lost, you have to go to the next window." The customers grumble impatiently. The clerks act harried and sometimes speak brusquely, even rudely. What seems to be a simple transaction may take 45 minutes or even longer. By the time people are photographed for their driver's licenses, they are often scowling. The photographer valiantly tries to get people to smile, but only occasionally succeeds.

Not far away, people also wait in line at a McDonald's fast-food restaurant. There are several lines; each is short, each moves quickly. The menu is clearly displayed on attractive signs. The workers behind the counter are invariably polite. If someone's order cannot be filled immediately, he or she is asked to step aside for a moment while the food is prepared and then is brought back to the head of the line to receive the order. The atmosphere is friendly and good-natured. The room is immaculately clean.

Many people have noticed the difference between getting a driver's license

Published in *Bureaucracy*, 1989.

and ordering a Big Mac. Most will explain it by saying that bureaucracies are different from businesses. "Bureaucracies" behave as they do because they are run by unqualified "bureaucrats" and are enmeshed in "rules" and "red tape."

But business firms are also bureaucracies, and McDonald's is a bureaucracy that regulates virtually every detail of its employees' behavior by a complex and all-encompassing set of rules. Its operations manual is six hundred pages long and weighs four pounds. In it one learns that french fries are to be nine-thirty-seconds of an inch thick and that grill workers are to place hamburger patties on the grill from left to right, six to a row for six rows. They are then to flip the third row first, followed by the fourth, fifth, and sixth rows, and finally the first and second. The amount of sauce placed on each bun is precisely specified. Every window must be washed every day. Workers must get down on their hands and knees and pick up litter as soon as it appears. These and countless other rules designed to reduce the workers to interchangeable automata were inculcated in franchise managers at Hamburger University located in a $40 million facility. There are plenty of rules governing the Registry, but they are only a small fraction of the rules that govern every detail of every operation at McDonald's. Indeed, if the DMV manager tried to impose on his employees as demanding a set of rules as those that govern the McDonald's staff, they would probably rebel and he would lose his job.

It is just as hard to explain the differences between the two organizations by reference to the quality or compensation of their employees. The Registry workers are all adults, most with at least a high school education; the McDonald's employees are mostly teenagers, many still in school. The Registry staff is well paid compared to the McDonald's workers, most of whom receive only the minimum wage. When labor shortages developed in Massachusetts during the mid-1980s, many McDonald's stores began hiring older people (typically housewives) of the same sort who had long worked for the Registry. They behaved just like the teenagers they replaced.

Not only are the differences between the two organizations not to be explained by reference to "rules" or "red tape" or "incompetent workers," the differences call into question many of the most frequently mentioned complaints about how government agencies are supposed to behave. For example: "Government agencies are big spenders." The Watertown office of the Registry is in a modest building that can barely handle its clientele. The teletype machine used to check information submitted by people requesting a replacement license was antiquated and prone to errors. Three or four clerks often had to wait in line to use equipment described by the office manager as "personally signed by Thomas Edison." No computers or word processors were available to handle the preparation of licenses and registrations; any error made by a clerk while manually typing a form meant starting over again on another form. [This article was written in 1989—*Editors*.]

Or: "Government agencies hire people regardless of whether they are really needed." Despite the fact that the citizens of Massachusetts probably have more contact with the Registry than with any other state agency, and despite the fact that these citizens complain more about Registry service than about that of any other bureau, the Watertown branch, like all Registry offices, was seriously understaffed. In 1981, the agency lost 400 workers—about 25 percent of its work force—despite the fact that its workload was rising.

Or: "Government agencies are imperialistic, always grasping for new functions." But there is no record of the Registry doing much grasping, even though one could imagine a case being made that the state government could usefully create at Registry offices "one-stop" multi-service centers where people could not only get drivers' licenses but also pay taxes and parking fines, obtain information, and transact other official business. The Registry seemed content to provide one service.

In short, many of the popular stereotypes about government agencies and their members are either questionable or incomplete. To explain why government agencies behave as they do, it is not enough to know that they are "bureaucracies"—that is, it is not enough to know that they are big, or complex, or have rules. What is crucial is that they are *government* bureaucracies. . . . [N]ot all government bureaucracies behave the same way or suffer from the same problems. There may even be registries of motor vehicles in other states that do a better job than the one in Massachusetts. But all government agencies have in common certain characteristics that tend to make their management far more difficult than managing a McDonald's. These common characteristics are the constraints of public agencies.

The key constraints are three in number. To a much greater extent than is true of private bureaucracies, government agencies (1) cannot lawfully retain and devote to the private benefit of their members the earnings of the organization, (2) cannot allocate the factors of production in accordance with the preferences of the organization's administrators, and (3) must serve goals not of the organization's own choosing. Control over revenues, productive factors, and agency goals is all vested to an important degree in entities external to the organization—legislatures, courts, politicians, and interest groups. Given this, agency managers must attend to the demands of these external entities. As a result, government management tends to be driven by the *constraints* on the organization, not the *tasks* of the organization. To say the same thing in other words, whereas business management focuses on the "bottom line" (that is, profits), government management focuses on the "top line" (that is, constraints). Because government managers are not as strongly motivated as private ones to define the tasks of their subordinates, these tasks are often shaped by [other] factors.

* * *

Revenues and Incentives

In the days leading up to September 30, the federal government is Cinderella, courted by legions of individuals and organizations eager to get grants and contracts from the unexpended funds still at the disposal of each agency. At midnight on September 30, the government's coach turns into a pumpkin. That is the moment—the end of the fiscal year—at which every agency, with a few exceptions, must return all unexpended funds to the Treasury Department.

Except for certain quasi-independent government corporations, such as the Tennessee Valley Authority, no agency may keep any surplus revenues (that is, the difference between the funds it received from a congressional appropriation and those it needed to operate during the year). By the same token, any agency that runs out of money before the end of the fiscal year may ask Congress for more (a "supplemental appropriation") instead of being forced to deduct the deficit from any accumulated cash reserves. Because of these fiscal rules agencies do not have a material incentive to economize: Why scrimp and save if you cannot keep the results of your frugality?

Nor can individual bureaucrats lawfully capture for their personal use any revenue surpluses. When a private firm has a good year, many of its officers and workers may receive bonuses. Even if no bonus is paid, these employees may buy stock in the firm so that they can profit from any growth in earnings (and, if they sell the stock in a timely manner, profit from a drop in earnings). Should a public bureaucrat be discovered trying to do what private bureaucrats routinely do, he or she would be charged with corruption.

We take it for granted that bureaucrats should not profit from their offices and nod approvingly when a bureaucrat who has so benefited is indicted and put on trial. But why should we take this view? Once a very different view prevailed. In the seventeenth century, a French colonel would buy his commission from the king, take the king's money to run his regiment, and pocket the profit. At one time a European tax collector was paid by keeping a percentage of the taxes he collected. In this country, some prisons were once managed by giving the warden a sum of money based on how many prisoners were under his control and letting him keep the difference between what he received and what it cost him to feed the prisoners. Such behavior today would be grounds for criminal prosecution. Why? What has changed?

Mostly we the citizenry have changed. We are creatures of the Enlightenment: We believe that the nation ought not to be the property of the sovereign; that laws are intended to rationalize society and (if possible) perfect mankind; and that public service ought to be neutral and disinterested. We worry that a prison warden paid in the old way would have a strong incentive to starve his prisoners in order to maximize his income; that a regiment supported by a greedy colonel would not be properly equipped; and that a tax collector paid on a commission basis would extort excessive taxes from us. These changes reflect our desire to eliminate moral hazards—namely, creating incentives for people to act wrongly. But why should this desire rule out more carefully designed compensation plans that would pay government managers for achieving officially approved goals and would allow efficient agencies to keep any unspent part of their budget for use next year?

Part of the answer is obvious. Often we do not know whether a manager or an agency has achieved the goals we want because either the goals are vague or inconsistent, or their attainment cannot be observed, or both. Bureau chiefs in the Department of State would have to go on welfare if their pay depended on their ability to demonstrate convincingly that they had attained their bureaus' objectives.

But many government agencies have reasonably clear goals toward which progress can be measured. The Social Security Administration, the Postal Service, and the General Services Administration all come to mind. Why not let earnings depend importantly on performance? Why not let agencies keep excess revenues?

* * *

But in part it is because we know that even government agencies with clear goals and readily observable behavior only can be evaluated by making political (and thus conflict-ridden) judgments. If the Welfare Department delivers every benefit check within twenty-four hours after the application is received, Senator Smith may be pleased but Senator Jones will be irritated because this speedy delivery almost surely would require that the standards of eligibility be relaxed so that many ineligible clients would get money. There is no objective standard by which the tradeoff between speed and accuracy in the Welfare Department can be evaluated. Thus we have been unwilling to allow welfare employees to earn large bonuses for achieving either speed or accuracy.

The inability of public managers to capture surplus revenues for their own use alters the pattern of incentives at work in government agencies. Beyond a certain point additional effort does not produce additional earnings. (In this country, Congress from time to time has authorized higher salaries for senior bureaucrats but then put a cap on actual payments to them so that the pay increases were never received. This was done to insure that no bureaucrat would earn more than members of Congress at a time when those members were unwilling to accept the political costs of raising their own salaries. As a result, the pay differential between the top bureaucratic rank and those just below it nearly vanished.) If political constraints reduce the marginal effect of money incentives, then the relative importance of other, nonmonetary incentives will increase. * * *

That bureaucratic performance in most government agencies cannot be linked to monetary benefits is not the whole explanation for the difference between public and private management. There are many examples of private organizations whose members cannot appropriate money surpluses for their own benefit. Private schools ordinarily are run on a nonprofit basis. Neither the headmaster nor the teachers share in the profit of these schools; indeed, most such schools earn no profit at all and instead struggle to keep afloat by soliciting contributions from friends and alumni. Nevertheless, the evidence is quite clear that on the average, private schools, both secular and denominational, do a better job than public ones in educating children. Moreover, as political scientists John Chubb and Terry Moe have pointed out, they do a better job while employing fewer managers. Some other factors are at work. One is the freedom an organization has to acquire and use labor and capital.

Acquiring and Using the Factors of Production

A business firm acquires capital by retaining earnings, borrowing money, or selling shares of ownership; a government agency (with some exceptions) acquires capital by persuading a legislature to appropriate it. A business firm hires, promotes, demotes, and fires personnel with considerable though not perfect freedom; a federal government agency is told by Congress how many persons it can hire and at what rate of pay, by the Office of Personnel Management (OPM) what rules it must follow in selecting and assigning personnel, by the Office of Management and Budget (OMB) how many persons of each rank it may employ, by the Merit Systems Protection Board (MSPB) what procedures it must follow in demoting or discharging personnel, and by the courts whether it has faithfully followed the rules of Congress, OPM, OMB, and MSPB. A business firm purchases goods and services by internally defined procedures (including those that allow it to buy from someone other than the lowest bidder if a more expensive vendor seems more reliable), or to skip the bidding procedure altogether in favor of direct negotiations; a government agency must purchase much of what it uses by formally advertising for bids, accepting the lowest, and keeping the vendor at arm's length. When a business firm develops a good working relationship with a contractor, it often uses that vendor repeatedly without looking for a new one; when a government agency has a satisfactory relationship with a contractor, ordinarily it cannot use the vendor again without putting a new project out for a fresh set of bids. When a business firm finds that certain offices or factories are no longer economical it will close or combine them; when a government agency wishes to shut down a local office or military base often it must get the permission of the legislature (even when formal permission is not necessary, informal consultation is). When a business firm draws up its annual budget each expenditure item can be reviewed as a discretionary amount (except for legally mandated payments of taxes to government and interest to banks and bondholders); when a government agency makes up its budget many of the detailed expenditure items are mandated by the legislature.

All these complexities of doing business in or with the government are well-known to citizens and firms. These complexities in hiring, purchasing, contracting, and budgeting often are said to be the result of the "bureaucracy's love of red tape." But few, if any, of the rules producing this complexity would have been generated by the bureaucracy if left to its own devices, and many are as cordially disliked by the bureaucrats as by their clients. These rules have been imposed on the agencies by external actors, chiefly the legislature. They are not bureaucratic rules but *political* ones. In principle the legislature could allow the Social Security Administration, the Defense Department, or the New York City public school system to follow the same rules as IBM, General Electric, or Harvard University. In practice they could not. The reason is politics, or more precisely, democratic politics.

* * *

Public versus Private Management

What distinguishes public from private organizations is neither their size nor their desire to "plan" (that is, control) their environments but rather the rules under which they acquire and use capital and labor. General Motors acquires capital by selling shares, issuing bonds, or retaining earnings; the Department of Defense acquires it from an annual appropriation by Congress. GM opens and closes plants, subject to certain government regulations, at its own discretion; DOD opens and closes military bases under the watchful guidance of Congress. GM pays its managers with salaries it sets and bonuses tied to its earnings; DOD pays its managers with salaries set by Congress and bonuses (if any) that have no connection with organizational performance. The number of workers in GM is determined by its level of production; the number in DOD by legislation and civil-service rules.

What all this means can be seen by returning to the Registry of Motor Vehicles and McDonald's. Suppose you were just appointed head of the Watertown office of the Registry and you wanted to improve service there so that it more nearly approximated the service at McDonald's. Better service might well require spending more money (on clerks, equipment, and buildings). Why should your political superiors give you that money? It is a cost to them if it requires either higher taxes or taking funds from another agency; offsetting these real and immediate costs are dubious and postponed benefits. If lines become shorter and clients become happier, no legislator will benefit. There may be fewer complaints, but complaints are episodic and have little effect on the career of any given legislator. By contrast, shorter lines and faster service at McDonald's means more customers can be served per hour and thus more money can be earned per hour. A McDonald's manager can estimate the marginal product of the last dollar he or she spends on improving service; the Registry manager can generate no tangible return on any expenditure he or she makes and thus cannot easily justify the expenditure.

Improving service at the Registry may require replacing slow or surly workers with quick and pleasant ones. But you, the manager, can neither hire nor fire them at will. You look enviously at the McDonald's manager who regularly and with little notice replaces poor workers with better ones. Alternatively, you may wish to mount an extensive training program (perhaps creating a Registration University to match McDonald's Hamburger University) that would imbue a culture of service in your employees. But unless the Registry were so large an agency that the legislature would neither notice nor care about funds spent for this purpose—and it is not that large—you would have a tough time convincing anybody that this was not a wasteful expenditure on a frill project.

If somehow your efforts succeed in making Registry clients happier, you can take vicarious pleasure in it; in the unlikely event a client seeks you out to thank you for those efforts, you can bask in a moment's worth of glory. Your colleague at McDonald's who manages to make customers happier may also derive some vicarious satisfaction from the improvement but in addition he or she will earn more money owing to an increase in sales.

In time it will dawn on you that if you improve service too much, clients will start coming to the Watertown office instead of going to the Boston office. As a result, the lines you succeeded in shortening will become longer again. If you wish to keep complaints down, you will have to spend even more on the Watertown office. But if it was hard to persuade the legislature to do that in the past, it is impossible now. Why should the taxpayer be asked to spend more on Watertown when the Boston office, fully staffed (naturally, no one was laid off when the clients disappeared), has no lines at all? From the legislature's point of view the correct level of expenditure is not that which makes one office better than another but that which produces an equal amount of discontent in all offices.

Finally, you remember that your clients have no choice: the Registry offers a monopoly service. It and only it supplies drivers' licenses. In the long run all that matters is that there are not "too many" complaints to the legislature about service. Unlike McDonald's, the Registry need not fear that its clients will take their business to Burger King or to Wendy's. Perhaps you should just relax.

If this were all there is to public management it would be an activity that quickly and inevitably produces cynicism among its practitioners. But this is not the whole story. For one thing, public agencies differ in the kinds of problems they face. For another, many public managers try hard to do a good job even though they face these difficult constraints.

Jacob Hacker
Bigger and Better

Remember those bumper stickers during the early 1990s fight over the Clinton health plan? "National Health Care? The Compassion of the IRS! The Efficiency of the Post Office! All at Pentagon Prices!" In American policy debates, it's a fixed article of faith that the federal government is woefully bumbling and expensive in comparison with the well-oiled efficiency of the private sector. Former Congressman Dick Armey even elevated this skepticism into a pithy maxim: "The market is rational; government is dumb."

But when it comes to providing broad-based insurance—health care, retirement pensions, disability coverage—Armey's maxim has it pretty much backward. The federal government isn't less efficient than the private sector. In fact, in these critical areas, it's almost certainly much more efficient.

To grasp this surprising point, it helps to understand how economists think about efficiency. Although politicians throw the word around as if it were a blanket label for everything good and right, economists mean something more specific. Or rather, they usually mean one of two specific things: *allocational* (or Pareto) efficiency, a distribution that cannot be changed without making somebody worse off; or *technical* efficiency, the most productive use of available resources. (There's a third possibility, dynamic efficiency, but we'll take that up in a moment.)

When the issue is health insurance or retirement security, *allocational* efficiency is really not what's under discussion. Nearly everyone agrees that the private market won't distribute vital social goods of this sort in a way that citizens need. Before we had Social Security, a large percentage of the elderly were destitute. Before we had Medicare, millions of the aged (usually the sickest and the poorest) lacked insurance. If we didn't subsidize medical care—through tax breaks, public insurance, and support for charity care—some people would literally die for lack of treatment. Market mechanisms alone simply can't solve

Published in *The American Prospect*, May 2005.

this problem, because private income is inadequate to pay for social needs. This is one of the chief reasons why government intervenes so dramatically in these areas by organizing social insurance to pay for basic retirement and disability, medical, and unemployment coverage, and by extensively subsidizing the cost of these benefits, especially for the most vulnerable.

What's usually at issue, instead, is *technical* efficiency: Are we getting the best bang for our necessarily limited bucks in these areas? The notion that the private market is, by definition, better at delivering such bang for the buck is the main rationale offered for increasing the already extensive role of the private sector in U.S. social policy. Thus, Medicare vouchers or partly privatized Social Security would supposedly engage the discipline of competition and lead to more efficient use of resources.

Liberals usually retort that social policies have other goals besides efficiency, most notably distributive justice. That's true enough, and it's another major reason why we should be profoundly skeptical of unqualified paeans to the private sector. In theory, it might be possible to design social-insurance programs that rely on the private sector but do everything that current programs do. In practice, however, privatized approaches almost invariably change the distribution of who gets the benefits, because they tend to erode common pools and subsidies (indeed, that's what their advocates often want). Yet there's no reason for advocates of social programs to cede the ground on efficiency while raising broader concerns of this sort, because in health and social policy, what is most just is also, in a great many cases, most efficient as well.

Broad-based insurance, after all, is not like widgets. In the fiercely competitive market of economics textbooks, multiple sellers appeal to multiple buyers who have good information about the comparative merits of relatively similar products. Competition squeezes out inefficiencies and yields optimal outcomes. But "markets" for social insurance don't work like this. In particular, information in these markets is both scarce and unequally distributed. This leads, in turn, to all sorts of familiar distortions on both sides of the transaction. Consumers, for example, can saddle private insurers with "adverse selection," which occurs when only high-risk folks buy insurance. The "moral hazard" problem crops up when people are insured against costs that are partially under their control, and then engage in risky behavior. On the producer side, health insurance companies can take steps to avoid costly patients, and purveyors of retirement products can gull unwary retirees in order to enrich insiders. All of this is why insurance aimed at achieving broad and necessarily social objectives has never worked well, or indeed at all, without some government support and regulation. And it's also why it often makes sense for that support to take the form of public insurance.

Notice I say "insurance." The real issue in the big-ticket areas of U.S. social policy isn't public versus private services. It's public versus private insurance. Medicare buys essentially all its services from the private sector, and no one wants that to change. What some want to change is the degree to which Medicare is in the insurance business, and it's here that all the efficiency advantages of the public sector become clear.

Perhaps the most obvious is the advantage that neither side wants to talk about: compulsion. In the realms of public policy under discussion, however, compulsion is often necessary to make the market work. Think about what would happen if younger and healthier senior citizens were allowed to opt out of Medicare for private coverage: The broad risk-pool of the program would collapse.

Broad programs also have another big advantage: They are ridiculously inexpensive to administer. The typical private health insurer spends about 10 percent of its outlays on administrative costs, including lavish salaries, extensive marketing budgets, and the expense of weeding out sick people. Medicare spends about 2 percent to 3 percent. And Social Security spends just 1 percent. Even low-cost mutual funds have operating costs greater than that.

Here is where critics of social insurance usually pull out their trump card—the claim that social insurance is not just inefficient but unaffordable. Maybe social insurance is, in some sense, efficient; but, these critics argue, its inexorable growth will lead the United States to financial ruin. And it is true that the growth of social insurance isn't slowed by the usual market brake of consumer willingness to pay. (If it were, as just emphasized, it wouldn't work.) But that doesn't mean that there are no brakes at all. If it did, the federal government would now be a leviathan, rather than—as is the case—about as large as it was in the early 1970s. Americans don't decide individually how much of their income to devote to social insurance. But, through their elected representatives, they do decide—in a rough way, of course—how much of the *nation's* income to devote. Spending has trade-offs, in the form of higher taxes and foregone priorities, and those trade-offs are visible in people's tax bills and everyday lives, and in public debate. Anyone who has followed recent political fights knows that politicians are not evading the rising costs of social programs.

What's more, the government has another advantage when it comes to holding down costs: It is a powerful negotiator. Medicare pays doctors and hospitals less per service than does the private sector, and its costs have grown more slowly than private health plans over the last 30 years, despite huge technological advances in care for the aged. Medicaid is even more austere (some might say too austere): Its payments are well below private levels, and it negotiates bargain-basement prices on prescription drugs—something Medicare has been barred from doing. The main reason that Medicaid's costs are rising so rapidly is not that it pays exorbitantly for services but that it covers a lot more children and families than it used to, a good thing in an era in which private coverage has plummeted. Lest government's use of its countervailing power to hold down prices seems illegitimate, it's worth remembering that this is exactly what HMOs and other big health plans were supposed to do—but Medicare and Medicaid do it better.

To be sure, public insurance could still dampen what economists call *dynamic* efficiency, that is, innovation and improvements in quality. But in some areas, like sending out retirement checks, it's not clear where the innovation will come from, while in others, like micromanaging providers, it's not clear that the private sector's "innovations" are really worth emulating. Many of the innovations have to do with discriminating against people at risk of getting sick, micromanaging doctors, and shifting out-of-pocket costs onto patients. Profit-motivated entrepreneurs quickly realize that the most effective way to minimize costs is to get rid of the people most likely to need care. This may be efficient from their perspective, but it's obviously not efficient for society.

Plus, when it comes to the most basic and important form of dynamic efficiency—namely, quality control and improvement—the public sector is arguably as capable as the private sector, and probably more so. As Phillip Longman has argued in an important *Washington Monthly* article on veterans' health care, the Department of Veterans Affairs (VA) has used its central power to create a model evidence-based quality-improvement program. Although the Medicare program still has a long way to go to match the VA, no one disputes that it conducts more rigorous reviews of technology and treatments than private health plans do. Indeed, private plans use Medicare's criteria for covering treatments as their standard of medical necessity. Information about quality is a classic public good—everyone benefits from it, but few have strong incentives to supply it. A large insurer with extensive data on its patients and considerable power to reshape market practice is arguably best positioned to provide such a good.

And this is simply to focus on efficiency. As noted already, the public sector runs circles around the private sector in terms of equity, the other major rationale for social insurance. If the current functions of social insurance were just turned over to the private market, vast numbers of people simply wouldn't be able to afford anything as good as Social Security and Medicare. Conservatives like to argue that everything provided in the Social Security package—the annuity, disability, and life-insurance coverage—could just be purchased in the private market. It could, but at far greater cost for most Americans, and many applicants would be deemed "uninsurable." All of which suggests that the claim that social programs are "inefficient" is often just a politically correct way of saying that they don't follow the usual market logic of giving the most to those with the greatest means.

Liberals frequently stress the equity argument but buy into the efficiency critique because they recognize, correctly, that the market is usually tremendously efficient. But they shouldn't accept that premise when it comes to social insurance. Well-functioning markets are indeed efficient for ordinary commerce, but well-designed social insurance is almost always more efficient than its market counterparts when it comes to dealing with the basic social risks that capitalism invariably produces. It's high time for liberals to say what logic, evidence, and the lived experience of citizens all show: The efficiency attack on social insurance, far from a self-evident truth, is usually an attack on the ideal of social insurance itself—the notion that everyone, regardless of income or likelihood of need, should be covered by a common umbrella of protection. And, ultimately, social insurance is good for the efficiency of society as a whole, not just because it provides much-needed protections at a reasonable cost, but also because it allows people to deal with what FDR once called the "hazards or vicissitudes" of modern capitalism without draconian restraints on the free play of the competitive market.

So the next time someone complains to you about the compassion of the IRS, the efficiency of the Post Office, all at Pentagon prices, tell them you'd be happy with the efficiency of Social Security, the compassion of Medicare, all at Medicaid prices.

QUESTIONS

1. *What would you do?* Imagine that you are the head of a small federal agency, and an employee comes up with a plausible plan that would allow your agency to provide the same level of service with half the budget and half the staff that you currently have. What do you do? Do you present the plan to Congress? What sorts of conflicting pressures might you face?

2. Government insurance programs may be more efficient than private programs, but what are their potential disadvantages? Critics claim that by subsidizing insurance, we wind up encouraging risky behavior (building houses in flood plains, giving people a reason not to save for retirement), or encouraging unlimited or unnecessary use of services such as medical care. Others say that if a program like Medicare pays health care providers less, the providers will simply shift more costs onto customers who have private insurance or no insurance. Are these valid criticisms?

3. What incentives do legislators have to make bureaucracies more efficient? One school of thought holds that legislators, in fact, *prefer* that agencies be inefficient, so that legislators can step in and help constituents with problems that arise. This way, legislators get credit for problem solving. Is this reasoning plausible?

15

Judicial Confirmation Hearings: What Role for the Senate?

Politicians, scholars, lawyers, and judges have long debated the role of the federal courts in a democratic system. Whereas Alexander Hamilton viewed the judiciary as the "least dangerous branch" of government, Thomas Jefferson and others worried about the potential for an imperial judiciary unencumbered by any institutional or electoral checks. The debate continues today, not only over the validity of different philosophies of judicial interpretation, but over the role of the Senate in confirming presidential nominations to the federal bench. Since many controversial and polarizing issues are (or are likely to be) fought over in the courts—abortion, affirmative action, gay rights, criminal law, executive power—these nomination battles have become more important.

The recent hearings for Chief Justice John Roberts and Justice Samuel Alito set the stage for this set of readings. Janet Malcolm provides a fascinating account of how the nominees and senators jockey for position and try to score points against each other. She describes the elaborate ritual of senators trying to extract information that the nominees do not want to reveal. Sometimes senators set complicated traps that momentarily ensnare the nominee, but they usually emerge unscathed. Malcolm points out that many of the senators' comments and questions are really directed at the American public rather than the nominees. She concludes that it is difficult to watch the hearings closely without seeing them as "a well-wrought play" (or to use Senator Biden's more colorful description—a "Kabuki dance") and wonders if anything useful comes from them other than a better understanding of the eighteen senators on the Judiciary Committee.

Senator John Cornyn (R-TX) is also upset with the hearings, but for a different reason. Rather than being concerned the Court nominees are able to bob and weave their way through the sessions without really answering substantive questions, Cornyn flatly states that senators should not even be asking those questions. Instead, senators should exercise their role of providing "advice and consent" on Supreme Court nominations by "focusing its attention on judicial qualifications—not personal political beliefs." Cornyn is also concerned about personal partisan attacks that he believes are too common in nomination hearings and the use of the filibuster by Democratic senators to block some of President Bush's nominations.

In direct contrast to Senator Cornyn, Yale Law School professor Robert Post and Reva Siegel argue that the Senate should be *more* aggressive in their questioning of nominees and that nominees should be more forthcoming about their positions on issues of constitutional law and interpretation. They point out that the current position taken by recent nominees to not talk about any issue that may come before the Court "would effectively nullify the capacity of the Senate to acquire useful information about a nominee's constitutional commitments." They go on to address four objections that could be made to their proposal. They conclude, "The best hope of maintaining the democratic legitimacy of our constitutional law may lie in the extension of democratic scrutiny, rather than its diminishment."

Janet Malcolm
The Art of Testifying

On the second day of David Souter's appearance before the Senate Judiciary Committee in September 1990, Gordon Humphrey, a Republican senator from New Hampshire, with something of the manner of a boarding-school headmaster in a satiric novel, asked the nominee, "Do you remember the old television program 'Queen for a Day'?"

Published *The New Yorker*, March 2006.

"Well, it wasn't something that I spent much of my youth watching," Souter said, "but I've heard the term."

Humphrey fussed with papers and went on, "Yes, well, going back to the days of black-and-white TV, let's play 'Senator for a Day.' "

"I still have a black-and-white TV," Souter put in.

"I don't doubt it," Humphrey said, and continued:

I hope you don't watch it much. My theory is that nothing would do more good for this country than for everyone to smash his television set . . . because people would begin—especially parents and children—would begin talking and children would begin doing their homework instead of watching—having their minds filled with rubbish every evening from our wonderful networks."

Humphrey collected himself and went on to propose that Souter put himself in the shoes of a senator interrogating a Supreme Court nominee and asked him what he would be most concerned about. He added that he was asking not so much for his own benefit as for that of "the young people who are tuned in—"

"On television," the voice of a quick-witted Joseph Biden, the chairman of the committee, rang out.

"On television, yes," Humphrey conceded, as Souter smiled puckishly and the audience burst into laughter.

1

During the confirmation hearings for John Roberts last September, old black-and-white movies came to mind unbidden. Watching Roberts on television was like watching one of the radiantly wholesome heroes that Jimmy Stewart, Joel McCrea, and Henry Fonda rendered so incisively in the films of Capra, Lubitsch, and Sturges. They don't make men like that anymore. But Roberts had all their anachronistic attributes: the grace, charm, and humor of a special American sort in which decency and kindness are heavily implicated, and from which sexuality is entirely absent. It was out of the question that such a man be denied a place on the Supreme Court. The plot of the hearing hinged not on whether Roberts would be confirmed but on how the eight Democrats on the committee—Patrick Leahy, of Vermont; Edward Kennedy, of Massachusetts; Joseph Biden, of Delaware; Dianne Feinstein, of California; Russell Feingold, of Wisconsin; Charles Schumer, of New York; Herbert Kohl, of Wisconsin; and Richard Durbin, of Illinois—would perform.

In his opening statement, Roberts offered a baseball analogy to illustrate his notion of judicial seemliness. He likened judges to umpires, who "don't make the rules; they apply them. . . . They make sure everybody plays by the rules, but it is a limited role." He added, "Nobody ever went to a ballgame to see the umpire." At the game of Senate confirmation, however, Roberts was precisely the person everybody had come to see: he was the batter to whom eighteen pitchers would pitch. Eight of them would try to strike him out while ten (Arlen Specter, of Pennsylvania; Orrin Hatch, of Utah; Charles Grassley, of Iowa; Jon Kyl, of Arizona; Mike DeWine, of Ohio; Jeff Sessions, of Alabama; Lindsey Graham, of South Carolina; John Cornyn, of Texas; Sam Brownback, of Kansas; and Tom Coburn, of Oklahoma) would insure that he got on base.

The fastballs that the Democrats hurled were fuelled largely by memorandums that Roberts had written as a young attorney in the Reagan Administration advising his superiors on how best to undermine civil rights, voting rights, affirmative action, and antidiscrimination legislation. The written record of what Kennedy called "a narrow and cramped and, perhaps, even a mean-spirited view of the law" was the focus of the Democrats' pointed questioning. The Democrats invited Roberts to disavow the misguided views of his youth—Surely you don't believe such stuff now? they asked him in not so many words. And in not so many words Roberts indicated that he still did. But words were not decisive in this hearing. Roberts's dazzlingly sympathetic persona soared over the proceedings and enveloped them in its aura. In the third round of questions, Charles Schumer looked over his glasses at Roberts and said, "You did speak at length on many issues and sounded like you were conveying your views to us, but when one went back and read the transcript each evening, there was less than met the ear that afternoon." But in fact it was the eye that created the illusion.

Roberts had a wonderful way of listening to questions. His face was exquisitely responsive. The constant play of expression on his features put one in mind of nineteenth-century primers of acting in which emotions—pleasure, agreement, dismay, uncertainty, hope, fear—are illustrated on the face of a model. When it was his turn to speak, he did so with equal mesmerizing expressiveness. Whenever he said "With all due respect, Senator"—the stock phrase signalling disagreement—he looked so genuinely respectful, almost regretful, that one could easily conclude that he was agreeing with his interlocutor rather than demurring. During the first round of questions, Biden flashed his famous insincere smile and said, "This shouldn't be a game of gotcha." In point of fact, the Democrats—notably Biden himself—"got" Roberts a number of times, but no matter what disagreeable things were said to him he maintained his invincible pleasantness. Biden scored heavily, for example, when he said:

> In 1999 you said in response to a question . . . "You know, we've gotten to a point these days where we think the only way we can show we're serious about a problem is if we pass a federal law, whether it's the Violence Against Women Act or anything else. The fact of the matter is conditions are different in different states, and state laws are more relevant . . . more attuned to different situations in New York as opposed to Minnesota. And that's what the federal system is based upon." Judge, tell me how a guy beating up his wife in Minnesota is any different condition in New York.

What could Roberts say? He could only flounder, but he floundered so prettily that Biden had to laugh and say "Okay." Schumer, too, repeatedly won debating points but never penetrated Roberts's armor of charm. In the second round of questioning, Schumer offered this inspired set piece:

> You agree we should be finding out your philosophy and method of legal reasoning, modesty, stability, but when we try to find out what modesty and stability mean, what your philosophy means, we don't get any answers. It's as if I asked you: What kind of movies do you like? Tell me two or three good movies. And you say, "I like movies with good acting. I like movies with good directing. I like movies with good cinematography." And I ask you, "No, give me an example of a good movie." You don't name one. I say, "Give me an example of a bad movie." You won't name one. Then I ask you if you like "Casablanca," and you respond by saying, "Lots of people like 'Casablanca.'" You tell me it's widely settled that "Casablanca" is one of the great movies.

Arlen Specter, the chairman of the committee, intervened to say that Schumer's time was up, and that there would be a fifteen-minute break. Roberts meekly asked if he could respond before the break, and, when given permission to do so, he said, "First, 'Dr. Zhivago' and 'North by Northwest' "—bringing down the house. Roberts went on to give an unconvincing defense of his evasiveness, but it was too late—there was too much good feeling wafting through the room like lavender air-freshener—for the weakness of his argument to matter.

Roberts's performance gave the word "disarming" new meaning. In the end, three Democrats—who had been no less pointed in their questioning than their fellow Democrats—voted to confirm Roberts. "I will vote my hopes and not my fears," Herbert Kohl said, confessing, "I was troubled by parts of Judge Roberts's record, but I was impressed by the man himself." The two other Democrats who voted for Roberts—Patrick Leahy and Russell Feingold—similarly allowed Roberts's persona to lull them into unguarded optimism. Even Democrats who voted against Roberts acknowledged his spectacular winningness.

But no performance can be entirely without flaw, and there was one extraordinary moment when Roberts was taken by surprise and propelled into uncharacteristic, unattractive at-a-lossness. Dianne Feinstein—a thirties movie character in her own right, with her Mary Astor loveliness and air of just having arrived with a lot of suitcases—was questioning him. As she later recalled, "When I couldn't get a sense of his judicial philosophy, I attempted to get a sense of his temperament and values, and I asked him about the end-of-life decisions, clearly decisions that are gut-wrenching, difficult, and extremely personal." Feinstein looked at Roberts and said:

> I have been through two end-of-life situations, one with my husband, one with my father, both suffering terrible cancers, a lot of pain, enormous debilitation. Let me ask you this question this way: If you were in that situation with someone you deeply love and saw the suffering, who would you want to listen to, your doctor or the government telling you what to do?

Roberts, his brow furrowed with concern and empathy, replied:

> Well, Senator, in that situation, obviously, you want to talk and take into account the views and heartfelt concerns of the loved one that you're trying to help in that situation, because you know how they are viewing this. You know what they mean when they're saying things like what their wishes are and their concerns are and, of course, consulting with their physicians.

Huh? For once, the ear trumped the eye. What was Roberts saying? What had happened to his syntax? Why all those "you"s and "they"s when the answer clearly called for an "I"? As Roberts went on speaking in this unsettling language of avoidance, Feinstein coldly interrupted, "That wasn't my question."

"I'm sorry," Roberts said demurely. "I'm trying to see your feelings as a man," Feinstein said. But she wasn't able to sustain the moment. She fell into the trap of rephrasing her question in a way that allowed Roberts to say, "Well, that's getting into a legal question." Feinstein quickly backed off. "O.K. I won't go there," she said, as the split screen showed Roberts smiling with relief and perhaps a bit of triumph.

The Republican bridesmaids performed their ceremonial function with varying degrees of perfunctoriness. Specter, who had the role of chairman to play as well, played it as a courtly old man. A recent battle with cancer had left him thin and almost without hair. It was hard to see in this diminished figure the dark-haired man who fifteen years earlier had interrogated Anita Hill with such arrogant ruthlessness. No one who watched the Clarence Thomas hearings will forget the look of hatred that Hill directed toward Specter as she parried his assault on her credibility with her weapon of steely truthfulness. Specter no longer inspires hatred, of course, but he remains an obscurely sour figure. Some fundamental unlovableness adheres. It doesn't help that he speaks with excruciating slowness, as if he were a Southerner.

Lindsey Graham, who is a Southerner, speaks at Northern speed, and to highly entertaining effect. When it was his turn to question Roberts, he didn't just stroke him. He cut to the chase:

> You were picked by a conservative president because you have associated yourself with the conservative administrations in the past, advising conservative presidents about conservative policies. And there's another selection to be made, and you're going to get the same type person. And you can— I'm not even talking to you now—to expect anything else is just not fair. I don't expect—I didn't expect President Clinton to pick you.

I'm not even talking to you now. Graham brought to the surface what is always lying just below it at televised Supreme Court confirmation hearings: namely, that the Judiciary Committee members are never merely talking to the nominee; they are always talking to their constituents as well.

The confirmation hearing as we know it today evolved over the past century. In his excellent book *The Selling of Supreme Court Nominees* (1995), John Anthony Maltese lays stress on the inescapably political character of the nomination process. Since the early days of the Republic—starting with the

Borking of George Washington's appointee for chief justice, John Rutledge—Supreme Court nominations have been fiercely fought over by rival senatorial factions. However, only in the twentieth century did these fights become public spectacles. A pivotal event, in Maltese's account, was the passage of the Seventeenth Amendment, in 1913, which changed the method by which senators come into office—from appointment by the state legislature to direct election—and intensified their activity as jumpy instruments of public will. The first public confirmation hearing took place in 1916, for Louis Brandeis (the first Jew to be named to the high court). Dozens of witnesses, pro and con, flocked to the hearing, but Brandeis himself did not choose to come. His advisers felt, Maltese writes, that "to do so would give the appearance that Brandeis was on trial." Not until 1925 did a nominee—Harlan Fiske Stone—testify before the Judiciary Committee, and thirty more years went by before it became customary, if not obligatory, for the nominee to testify. Between 1930 and 1955, four nominees testified and fifteen didn't. Since 1955, when the second John Marshall Harlan was nominated, every nominee has testified.

Brandeis's advisers were right: the Supreme Court nominee, sitting alone at a table facing a tribunal of legislators seated above him on a dais, is on trial. But so, of course, are the legislators. Each one knows that when he is up for reëlection voters will remember (or someone will remind them of) his words and his demeanor. Graham presently abandoned all pretense of examining Roberts. "Let's talk about righting wrongs here," he said to the folks back home, and went on:

> I think it stinks that somebody can burn the flag and that's called speech. What do you think about that? ROBERTS: Well [laughter]. We had the Flag Protection Act after the Supreme Court concluded that it was protected speech. GRAHAM: Show me where their term "symbolic speech" is in the Constitution. ROBERTS: Well, it's not. GRAHAM: It's not. They just made it up, didn't they? And I think it stinks that a kid can't go to school and say a prayer if he wants to voluntarily. What do you think about that? ROBERTS: That's something that's probably inappropriate for me to comment on. GRAHAM: What do you think Ronald Reagan thought about that? ROBERTS: His view was that voluntary school prayer was appropriate. GRAHAM: I think it's not right for elected officials to be unable to talk about or protect the unborn. What do you think about that? ROBERTS: Well, again, Senator . . .

The fifty-year-old Graham has a gift for comedy—he delivers his lines as if he were working a night-club crowd—and exudes an air of cynicism that right-wing politicians do not usually permit themselves, and that is very refreshing. The right-wing politician Sam Brownback has a more conventional style. During his questioning of Roberts, he paused to say that because of *Roe v. Wade* "we now have forty million fewer children in this country to bless us with" and that "eighty per cent to ninety per cent of children prenatally diagnosed with Down's Syndrome never get here—never get here." Roberts as gracefully declined to engage with the anti-abortion Republicans as he had declined to engage with the pro-choice Democrats. He was like the host of a successful and elegant party. Everybody could go home feeling good and good about himself. No one had spilled his champagne or been rude. When, four months later, Roberts joined Scalia and Thomas in their dissent to the majority opinion in *Gonzalez v. Oregon*, which upheld the state's law permitting assisted suicide, no one even seemed to feel betrayed. Good parties cast lovely long shadows.

2

The Democrats came home from the hearing for Samuel Alito as if they had been beaten up by a rival gang in a bar. At the Roberts hearing, they had been vigorous and assured, sometimes even magnificent, in their defense of liberal values. At the Alito hearing, they were erratic and disoriented, as if suffering from a malaise they had fallen into between the two proceedings. In fact, what they were suffering from was the nominee. In his opening statement, Alito told this story:

> During the previous weeks, an old story about a lawyer who argued a case before the Supreme Court has come to my mind, and I thought I might begin this afternoon by sharing that story. The story goes as follows. This was a lawyer who had never argued a case before the court before. And when the argument began, one of the justices said, How did you get here? Meaning how had his case worked its way up through the court system. But the lawyer was rather nervous and he took the question literally and he said—and this was some years ago—he said, "I came here on the Baltimore and Ohio Railroad."

Throughout the hearing, in answer to almost every question, Alito said, in effect, that he had come here on the Baltimore and Ohio Railroad—and thus defeated every attempt to engage him in a dialogue. Each answer ended the matter then and there. He was like a chauffeur who speaks only when spoken to, and doesn't presume to converse. While Alito listened to questions, his face was expressionless. When giving answers, he spoke in a mild, uninflected voice. His language was ordinary and wooden. His manner was sober and quiet. He was a negligible, neutral presence.

It seemed scarcely believable that, in his fifteen years on the federal bench, this innocuous man had consistently ruled against other harmless individuals in favor of powerful institutions, and that these rulings were sometimes so far out of the mainstream consensus that other conservatives on the court were moved to protest their extremity. Or that in 1985, on an application for a job in the Reagan Justice Department, he had written, "I am particularly proud of my contributions in recent cases in which the government has argued in the Supreme Court that . . . the Constitution does not protect a right to an abortion." And, further, that "in college I developed a deep interest in constitutional law, motivated in large part by disagreement with Warren Court decisions, particularly in the areas of criminal procedure, the Establishment Clause, and reapportionment."

If Roberts was a pill the Democrats could agree to swallow even before tasting its delicious sugar coating, and Harriet Miers was a pig in a poke that some Democrats were prepared to buy, Alito was a nominee no Democrat could accept. But no Democrat could touch him. The impassive Alito paralyzed the Democrats. Their hopes of blocking the nomination by bringing forward two stains on his character—his membership in a notorious organization called Concerned Alumni of Princeton, which opposed the admission of women and minorities; and his failure to recuse himself in a case involving the Vanguard company, in which he had a financial stake—were decisively dashed. The stains proved too small—the garment remained presentable.

Twenty years ago, William Rehnquist, at the hearing for his elevation to Chief Justice, offered a model for how to parry embarrassing questions about your past. When asked about reports that as a young poll watcher he had harassed minority voters, Rehnquist shook his head sadly and said, "No, I don't think that's correct," and when asked about a restrictive clause in the lease to his country house barring "members of the Hebrew race" he said, "I certainly don't recall it." Alito, similarly, didn't recall joining the Concerned Alumni. "I have racked my memory," he said each time he was asked why he had joined. Nor could he explain why he hadn't recused himself in the Vanguard case. The

Democrats realized too late that their pursuit of the Concerned Alumni and Vanguard matters was a trap. This time, the Republican bridesmaids didn't merely simper. They hastened to close ranks and attack the Democrats for their cruel badgering of Alito.

Lindsey Graham rose joyfully to the occasion. Rules of seniority placed him late on the program (he was elected to the Senate in 2002) and gave him the material for great shtick. He did a little preliminary routine with Vanguard ("Why would Judge Alito sit down in the corner of a room and say, I think I've got a conflict, but I'm just going to let it go and hear the case anyway?") and moved on to the Concerned Alumni:

> GRAHAM: Now this organization that was mentioned very prominently earlier in the day, did you ever write an article for this organization? ALITO: No, I did not GRAHAM: O.K. And some quotes were shown, from people who did write for this organization, that you disavowed. Do you remember that exchange? ALITO: I disavow them. I deplore them. They represent things that I have always stood against and I can't express too strongly . . . GRAHAM: If you don't mind the suspicious nature that I have is that you may be saying that because you want to get on the Supreme Court; that you're disavowing this now because it doesn't look good. And really what I would look at to believe you're not—and I'm going to be very honest with you—is: how have you lived your life? Are you really a closet bigot?

Is Lindsey Graham really a closet liberal? The sense of double-entendre that always faintly hovers over Graham's speech is almost palpable in this passage. "I'm not any kind of a bigot, I'm not," Alito said. Graham assured Alito that he believed him, not because of his good reputation but because of "the way you have lived your life and the way you and your wife are raising your children." Then Graham had the audacity to cite—not by name—the Abramoff scandal as an instance of the kind of guilt by association that Alito was being subjected to:

> We're going to go through a bit of this ourselves as congressmen and senators. People are going to take a fact that we got a campaign donation from somebody who's found to be a little different than we thought they were— and our political opponent's going to say, "Aha, I gotcha!" And we're going

to say, "Wait a minute. I didn't know that. I didn't take the money for that reason." . . . We have photos taken with people—and sometimes you wish you didn't have your photo taken. But that doesn't mean that you're a bad person because of that association. Judge Alito, I am sorry that you've had to go through this. I am sorry that your family has had to sit here and listen to this.

It was at this moment that Mrs. Alito got up and left the hearing room to have her famous cry. The TV camera barely caught the image of her figure brushing past two seats, and the TV watcher would have attached no significance to the sight. Unlike the forbiddingly beautiful and elegant Mrs. Roberts—who sat motionless during her husband's hearing, with a look of intense, almost anxious concentration on her face—the buxom Mrs. Alito fidgeted and looked around and never seemed to be fully engaged by the proceedings. As it was later reported (around the globe), Mrs. Alito had been so upset by the bad things the Democrats had said about her husband, and so moved by Graham's defense, that she had to leave in tears. But to anyone who had observed Mrs. Alito's demeanor in the days before the incident, Charles Isherwood's comment in the Times—"Surely grinding boredom may also have played a part in her scene-stealing eruption and flight from the Senate chamber"—had the ring of truth.

The Alito hearings were indeed grindingly boring. Although subjects of the highest interest were introduced—spying on citizens, torture, abortion, the right to privacy, civil rights, discrimination, executive power—the talk was never interesting, since Alito could never be drawn. Like Roberts, he eluded the Democrats' attempts to pry his judicial philosophy out of him, but, unlike Roberts, he offered no compensatory repartee. He was always just a guy answering questions very carefully. Over and over, the Democrats quizzed Alito on his pro-police, pro-prosecution, and pro-employer opinions. (The legal scholar Cass Sunstein analyzed forty-five of Alito's dissents in cases where individual rights and institutions were in conflict and found that in thirty-eight of them Alito took the side of the institution.) And over and over—like an accountant patiently explaining why the figures on a tax return are correct—Alito spared no dry detail in justifying his reasoning.

As the hearings wore on, and the fight between the Democratic and Republican committee members took on heat, Alito became an almost peripheral figure. The charge that the Democrats were cruelly badgering Alito was in fact unfounded. They had been a lot tougher on Roberts. At one point in the Roberts hearing, Joe Biden pushed Roberts so hard—indeed, was so fresh to him—that Specter had to intervene and say, "Let him finish his answer, Joe." But, when questioning Alito, Joe practically tugged his forelock. "Presumptuous of me to say this," "You'd know better than I, Judge," "I don't mean to suggest I'm correcting you," "I'm not presuming to be as knowledgeable about this as you," "All I'm suggesting is," "You've been very gracious" are among the examples of Biden's nervous servility. (In the second round of questioning, in a gesture of propitiation that can only be called deranged, Biden put on a Princeton cap.) But the very idea of questioning Alito's probity left the Democrats open to charges of bullying. Where the fair Roberts had been fair game, the mousy Alito was out of bounds. Why don't you pick on someone your own size? By the time the Democrats realized their tactical error, it was too late to correct it. That the judge who consistently rules against little guys should become the confirmation hearing's own little guy was one of the proceedings' more delicious (and, for the Democrats, bitterest) ironies.

* * *

3

Another memorable passage in the David Souter confirmation hearings occurred while he was being questioned by the Democratic senator from Ohio, Howard Metzenbaum. Metzenbaum asked Souter, as fifteen years later Feinstein asked Roberts, to give a personal rather than a legal response to a question about a controversial issue—abortion, in this case. Metzenbaum described in gruesome detail cases of illegal abortion from the pre-*Roe* era, and then said, "My real question to you isn't how you will rule on *Roe v. Wade* . . . but what does a woman face, when she has an unwanted pregnancy, a pregnancy that may be the result of rape or incest or failed contraceptives or ignorance of basic health information? And I would just like to get your own view and your own thoughts of that woman's position under those circumstances."

Souter paused before replying. Then he said, "Senator, your question comes as a surprise to me. I wasn't expecting that kind of question, and you have made me think of something that I have not thought of for twenty-four years." Souter went on to tell a story from his days at Harvard Law School. He had an appointment as a resident proctor (a student adviser) in a Harvard College freshman dormitory, and one day a student came to him for counsel. "He was in pretty rough emotional shape," Souter recalled,

> and we shut the door and sat down, and he told me that his girlfriend was pregnant and he said, "She's about to try to have a self-abortion and she doesn't know how to do it." He said, "She's afraid to tell her parents what has happened and she's afraid to go to the health services," and he said "Will you talk to her?" and I did. . . . I will not try to say what I told her. But I spent two hours in a small dormitory bedroom that afternoon, in that room because that was the most private place we could get . . . listening to her and trying to counsel her to approach her problem in a way different from what she was doing, and your question has brought that back to me, and I think the only thing I can add to that is I know what you were trying to tell me, because I remember that afternoon.

As Souter spoke—gravely and slowly (but not too slowly), with his strong New England accent (he said "lore" for "law" and "sore" for "saw" and "floor" for "flaw")—one had the feeling of lights dimming on a set. One of the characters would soon get up to draw the curtains and turn on a lamp. This was not the only time in the Souter hearing that one felt as if one were seeing a well-wrought play rather than witnessing a piece of left-to-chance reality. In his opening statement, Souter told the senators that he was looking forward to "our dialogue," and dialogue did indeed take place—often very gripping dialogue. As Alito had unnerved, you could almost say unmanned, his questioners, so Souter gave his interlocutors to know that this was a play in which all the roles had good lines. If Souter—a slight man (his thinness had a mildly ascetic cast) of enormous, subtle intelligence and a moving absence of self-regard—was the star turn, he permitted the supporting cast of senators to perform no less brilliantly. Watching tapes of the Souter hearings makes one feel how things have deteriorated.

* * *

After the debacle of the Alito hearing, Joseph Biden said that confirmation hearings should be abolished. (During the Roberts hearing, he had already remarked, "These hearings have become sort of a Kabuki dance" and "I am moving to the view that I'm not sure these hearings are the proper way to determine how to vote for a judge.") Biden is not the first to make such a proposal. In 1988, in response to the noisy Bork hearings, a Twentieth Century Fund Task Force on Judicial Selection recommended that the confirmation process be restored to a quieter former mode, whereby the nominee was judged solely on his written record and on the testimony of legal experts. These recommendations were ignored, as we know. As John Anthony Maltese points out, they were posited on the dubious idea of

> a golden age when Supreme Court nominees were not required to testify, when the factious whims of public opinion were ignored by senators, when the legal qualifications of nominees were considered without the taint of political motivation, and when senators deliberated behind closed doors rather than posturing in the glare of television lights. The problem is that the apolitical nature of that golden age is largely fictitious.

Maltese's book is devoted to the political fights by which Supreme Court nominations are by their very nature dogged. Another book could be written about Supreme Court nominations since television lights first glared at them, in 1981, when Sandra Day O'Connor appeared before the Judiciary Committee. The televised hearings have not been uniformly edifying—the Alito hearing may be the least instructive of the lot—but each has its atmosphere and, so to speak, plot. The hearing for the nomination of Ruth Bader Ginsburg had the atmosphere of a garden party held to fête a beloved aunt about to embark on a wonderful journey. Ted Kennedy, who usually sits at confirmation hearings looking as if he had a toothache, was charming and funny. The Republicans were polite and deferential. During the recent hearings, the Republicans repeatedly boasted of their gracious acceptance of Ginsburg in contrast to the Democrats' sulky resistance to Roberts and Alito. Lindsey Graham was particularly mordant in his description of Ginsburg as an A.C.L.U. Commie whom, nevertheless, the Republicans manfully swallowed because Clinton had won the election. So why don't the Democrats manfully swallow Bush's appointees? Why are they being such poor sports? "Elections matter," Graham said. As the Democrats might have retorted—but didn't think or know to do until Senate debate on Alito was under way—Ginsburg had not been thrust on the Republicans the way Roberts and Alito had been thrust on the Democrats. She had been pre-approved by Orrin Hatch. Hatch recalls the circumstances in his book *Square Peg: Confessions of a Citizen Senator*. He writes that when Byron White resigned from the

Court, Bill Clinton called him to ask how his Secretary of the Interior, Bruce Babbitt, would go over as a nominee. Hatch, then chairman of the Judiciary Committee, told Clinton that Babbitt was too liberal and would be hard to confirm, and gave him two names as alternatives: Ginsburg and Stephen Breyer. (In a footnote, Hatch writes that Ginsburg's record as a federal-appeals-court judge was "very similar to that of another subsequent Supreme Court Justice, Antonin Scalia.")

The Thomas hearings, in contrast, with their incredible final act, had a dark character—though it wasn't until Jane Mayer and Jill Abramson published their tour de force of reporting, *Strange Justice: The Selling of Clarence Thomas*, that we understood just how dark. Thomas's "high-tech lynching" speech, in which he denied Anita Hill's accusations with moving vehemence, was one of the great performances of its time. But Mayer and Abramson's research—their interviews with confidants of Hill who corroborated her account and with schoolmates of Thomas who recalled his crude sexual humor and regular attendance at pornographic movies—makes it all but impossible to believe that the zealot who sits in Thurgood Marshall's place on the high court didn't say those crassly dirty things to Anita Hill. Even more disturbing is the book's account of how the far right, the lesson of Bork fresh in its memory, stopped at nothing to get this nominee on the Court.

Since Bork, nominees have played their cards close to their chests. Bork could conceivably have saved his nomination by not constantly showing his losing hand, but more likely the combination of powerful organized opposition on the left and the Democratic majority in the Senate was always enough to defeat it. By the time of Thomas, the right had mobilized, and has never again failed a stricken nominee. The so-I-lied convention, established by Thomas (who told the senators that he believed in a constitutional right to privacy and when safely on the Court said that, well, actually, he didn't), along with the mantra of "If I talk about recent Supreme Court cases, the sky will fall," has been firmly in place since the Thomas hearing. Biden's misgivings about the hearings are justified: when they are over we know no more about the nominee's judicial philosophy than we did before they started. But they yield another kind of knowledge: a portrait of the nominee emerges from them that may be as telling as any articulation of his judicial philosophy. When Alan Simpson asked David Souter whether he would be able to remove his personal feelings from his judgments, Souter said, "We always ask, we constantly ask ourselves,

Senator, whether we can do that. We have no guarantee of success, but we know that the best chance of success comes from being conscious of the fact that we will be tempted to do otherwise." Neither Alito nor Roberts showed himself capable of such fineness of mind. In the light of Souter's testimony before the Judiciary Committee, his opinions on the high court should not have been surprising. And, in the light of theirs, Roberts's and Alito's probably will not be, either.

Biden also left out what may be the most compelling reason of all for the continued life of confirmation hearings: the intimate glimpse they give us of eighteen of our legislators. Which ones we love and which ones we hate is determined by our partisanship, of course. But as we watch them playing their big-league game we may sometimes forget to root, and just sit transfixed by their remarkable athleticism.

Senator John Cornyn
R-E-S-P-E-C-T

It wouldn't be summertime in Washington if speculation weren't running rampant about the possibility of a retirement announcement from the Supreme Court. But whatever the time frame for a Supreme Court vacancy, the process for selecting the next associate or chief justice should reflect the best of the American judiciary—not the worst of American politics. We deserve a Supreme Court nominee who reveres the law—and a confirmation process that is civil, respectful, and keeps politics out of the judiciary.

History affords us some important benchmarks for determining whether the Senate has undertaken a confirmation process worthy of the Court and of the American people. There is a right way and a wrong way to debate the merits of a Supreme Court nominee. The Senate's past record, unfortunately, has been mixed.

Whoever the nominee is, the Senate should focus its attention on judicial qualifications—not personal political beliefs. Whoever the nominee is, the Senate should engage in respectful and honest inquiry, not partisan personal at-

Published in *National Review Online*, June 2005.

tacks. And whoever the nominee is, the Senate should apply the same fair process that has existed for over two centuries: confirmation or rejection by majority vote.

Whoever the nominee is, the Senate should focus its attention on judicial qualifications—not personal political beliefs. We should not be surprised if a person of the stature and legal ability to be considered for appointment to the Supreme Court has spent at least some time thinking, and perhaps speaking and writing, about the important and sensitive issues of the day. But a nominee should not be punished simply for exercising his talents. After all, judges swear an oath to obey and to apply the law—not their own personal, political views.

When President Clinton nominated Ruth Bader Ginsburg to the Court in 1993, senators knew that she was a brilliant jurist with a strong record of service in the law. Senators also knew she served as general counsel of the American Civil Liberties Union—a liberal organization that has championed the abolition of traditional marriage laws and attacked the Pledge of Allegiance. And they knew she had previously written that traditional marriage laws are unconstitutional; that the Constitution guarantees a right to prostitution; that the Boy Scouts, Girl Scouts, Mother's Day, and Father's Day are all discriminatory institutions; that courts should force taxpayers to pay for abortions against their will; and that the age of consent for sexual activity should be lowered to age 12. The Senate nevertheless confirmed her by a 96-3 vote.

Similarly, Stephen Breyer (nominated in 1994 by President Clinton) and Antonin Scalia (nominated in 1986 by President Reagan) are brilliant jurists with strong records of service. Breyer had previously served as chief counsel to Senator Ted Kennedy on the Senate Judiciary Committee, and his nomination to the Court was opposed by many conservatives because of his alleged hostility to religious liberty and private religious education, while Scalia was known to hold strongly conservative views on a number of topics. The Senate nevertheless confirmed them by votes of 87-9 and 98-0, respectively.

The confirmation proceedings of Ginsburg, Breyer, and Scalia provide a helpful model for future behavior. Each of those nominees enjoyed exceptional legal credentials. Each possessed strongly held personal political views. And each commanded the support of a broad bipartisan majority of senators.

Whoever the nominee is, the Senate should engage in respectful and honest inquiry, not partisan personal attacks. Any debate over the next nominee to the Supreme Court must be conducted with respect and honesty. At a minimum, senators can disagree without being disagreeable. At a minimum, senators can debate the issues honestly, and refrain from distorting and misrepresenting records and rulings.

Unfortunately, respect for nominees has not always been the standard.

Lewis Powell was accused of demonstrating "continued hostility to the law" and waging a "continual war on the Constitution," and Senate witnesses warned that his confirmation would mean that "justice for women will be ignored." John Paul Stevens was charged with "blatant insensitivity to discrimination against women." Anthony Kennedy was scrutinized for his "history of pro bono work for the Catholic Church" and found to be "a deeply disturbing candidate for the United States Supreme Court." And David Souter was described as "almost Neanderthal," "biased," and "inflammatory." One senator said Souter's civil rights record was "particularly troubling" and "raised troubling questions about the depth of his commitment to the role of the Supreme Court and Congress in protecting individual rights and liberties under the Constitution." That same senator condemned Souter for making "reactionary arguments" and for being "willing to defend the indefensible," and predicted that if confirmed, Souter would "turn back the clock on the historic progress of recent decades." At Senate hearings, witnesses cried that "I tremble for this country if you confirm David Souter," warning that "women's lives are at stake" and even predicting that "women will die."

The best apology for these ruthless and reckless attacks is for them never to be repeated again. Unfortunately, the record is not promising. Even before President Bush took office in January 2001, the now-Senate Democrat Leader told Fox News Sunday that "we have a right to look at John Ashcroft's religion," to determine whether there is "anything with his religious beliefs that would cause us to vote against him." And over the last four years, this president's judicial nominees have been labeled "kooks," "Neanderthals," and "turkeys." Respected public servants and brilliant jurists have been called "scary" and "despicable."

Unfortunately, honest debate about a nominee's record has not always been the standard, either.

Records and reputations have been distorted beyond recognition. Rulings that stated one thing have been characterized to say precisely the opposite. For example, during the debate over the nomination of my former Texas Supreme Court colleague, Justice Priscilla Owen, I chronicled numerous examples of her previous rulings that were blatantly misrepresented by partisan opponents of her nomination.

Moreover, in recent weeks, we've begun to see a particularly odd tactic take form. Some lower-court nominees have been attacked for belonging to a movement that, to my knowledge, does not even exist—the so-called "Constitution in Exile." What's more, opponents of this fictional movement seem to talk out of both sides of their mouth. Senate Democrats excoriated Justice Owen in part for her refusal to adhere to an allegedly central tenet of the Constitution in Exile—the nondelegation doctrine. And it was four Ninth Circuit judges appointed by Presidents Clinton and Carter who recently used another alleged doctrine of the Constitution in Exile—the Commerce Clause—to strike down federal laws prohibiting the use of marijuana and the possession of child pornography. If a "Constitution in Exile" movement really exists, its membership seems to include Senate Democrats and Democrat-appointed federal judges.

Reasonable lawyers can and do often disagree with one another in good faith. They do so respectfully and honestly—without distortions and false charges of being "out of the mainstream." We should likewise demand that the Senate restore respectful and honest standards of debate to the confirmation process.

And whoever the nominee is, the Senate should apply the same fair process that has existed for over two centuries—and that is confirmation or rejection by majority vote. The rules governing the judicial confirmation process should be the same regardless of which party controls the White House or the Senate. Since our nation's founding over two centuries ago, the consistent Senate tradition and constitutional rule for confirming judicial nominees—including nominees to the Supreme Court—has been majority vote. (In the case of Abe Fortas, his nomination to be chief justice was withdrawn, after a procedural vote revealed that his nomination did not command the support of a majority of senators.)

Indeed, throughout history the Senate has consistently confirmed judges who enjoyed majority but not 60-vote support—including Clinton appointees Richard Paez, William Fletcher, and Susan Oki Mollway, and Carter appointees Abner Mikva and L. T. Senter. Yet for the past two years, a partisan minority of senators tried to impose a 60-vote standard on the confirmation of President Bush's judicial nominees. Thankfully, that effort was recently repudiated, when the Senate restored Senate tradition by confirming a number of this president's nominees by majority vote.

The effort to change our 200-year custom and tradition by imposing a new

and unprecedented supermajority requirement for confirming judges is dangerous to the rule of law, because it politicizes our judiciary and gives too much
power to special interest groups. As law professor Michael Gerhardt, a top Democrat adviser on the confirmation process, has written, "the Constitution also
establishes a presumption of confirmation that works to the advantage of the
president and his nominees." According to Professor Gerhardt, a supermajority
rule for confirming judges "is problematic because it creates a presumption
against confirmation, shifts the balance of power to the Senate, and enhances
the power of the special interests."

Senate Democrats have recently asked to be consulted about any future
Supreme Court nomination—even though the Constitution provides for the advice and consent of the Senate, not individual senators, and only with respect to
the appointment, not the nomination, of any federal judge. If senators want
such a special role in the Supreme Court nomination process, the president
should first insist on their commitment to the three principles described above.

After years of unprecedented obstruction, and destructive politics, we must
restore dignity, honesty, respect, and fairness to our Senate confirmation
process. That is the only way to keep politics out of the judiciary.

Robert Post and Reva Siegel
Questioning Justice: Law and Politics in Judicial Confirmation Hearings

I.

Like all constitutional democracies, the United States is committed to both self-
government and the rule of law. Our Constitution embraces each of these two
distinct aspirations, and it carefully negotiates the complex tension between
them.

The Constitution awards federal judges life tenure, with removal only by
impeachment. In freeing judges from forms of democratic accountability that
constrain the representative branches of government, the Constitution structures courts in ways that enable judicial independence and help establish the

Published in *The Pocket Part: A Companion to The Yale Law Journal,* January 2006.

autonomy of law from politics. But because in a democracy the legitimacy of law ultimately depends upon the acknowledgment of the people, the Constitution also creates a variety of devices for ensuring that judges endowed for life with Article III power remain connected to the democratically accountable branches of government. The Constitution allocates primary responsibility for organizing the judiciary and enforcing court orders in Congress and the executive branch. The Constitution structures relations between the judiciary and the representative branches of government to accord with a fundamental insight: The rule of law requires legal institutions that have democratic legitimacy.

This insight informs the constitutional appointment process for Supreme Court Justices. Article II provides that the President "shall nominate, and by and with the Advice and Consent of the Senate, shall appoint . . . Judges of the [S]upreme Court." By requiring Justices to be nominated by a democratically accountable President and confirmed by a democratically accountable Senate, Article II establishes a selection process that underwrites the democratic accountability of constitutional law. Article II creates a process for selecting judges that makes it possible for the people to accept the judgments of those charged with interpreting "the fundamental and paramount law of the nation."

Soon after the Constitution was amended to require the direct election of Senators in 1913, the Senate began voting on nominees in open session, and since 1939 it has called upon nominees to testify in public confirmation hearings. In recent times, these hearings have come to play a significant role in building the public confidence that is necessary to sustain judicial independence in a constitutional democracy. There are many reasons for the contemporary prominence of confirmation hearings, including a growing public appreciation of the interpretive discretion of Justices and an escalating expectation of governmental transparency. Confirmation hearings are now the central forum in which Senators engage the public in the question of whether nominees possess the vision and qualifications necessary to justify investing them with the interpretive autonomy and discretion that judges exercise in our constitutional democracy.

II.

A President nominates a candidate to become a Justice because the President believes that the constitutional vision of the nominee is good for the country.

There is now general consensus across the political spectrum, from commentators as distinct as Charles Black and William H. Rehnquist, that the Senate, "which is just as responsible to the electorate, and just as close to the electorate, as is the President," is independently obliged to determine whether it agrees with the President, or whether in its opinion "the nominee's views on the large issues of the day will make it harmful to the country for him to sit and vote on the Court."

During the controversial 1987 nomination of Robert H. Bork, it was argued that the Senate ought to pass judgment only on the professional competence of nominees and ought not to consider the substance of their constitutional vision. Conservative commentators defended this position as recently as 2001. But in objecting to President Bush's selection of Harriet Miers, conservatives made clear that they also now believe that Senators should consider a nominee's constitutional vision in deciding whether to vote for confirmation. Conservatives urged senators "to ask—and to require Miers to answer, as a condition of confirmation—direct questions about her judicial philosophy and its application to concrete constitutional issues." Liberals had made an analogous demand in the context of John Roberts's nomination.

Direct and probing questions about constitutional philosophy are potentially controversial, however, because Americans believe that law ought to be separate from politics. Requiring nominees to explain in detail their constitutional commitments can seem "embarrassing" or "inappropriate" if senatorial questioning appears to threaten the independent prerogative of the Court to interpret the law. Although senators have interrogated nominees about their substantive views whenever they have perceived that the consequences for important constitutional doctrine were sufficiently serious, such questioning has also been tentative and controversial. Ambiguity about the appropriate constitutional reach of senatorial questioning has undermined its force and authority.

The uncertainty of the practice was well illustrated when, during the bitter controversy over the school desegregation decisions, Senator John McClellan pressed Potter Stewart on whether he agreed "with the view, the reasoning and logic applied, . . . and the philosophy expressed by the Supreme Court in arriving at its decision in the case of *Brown v. Board of Education*." Senator Thomas Hennings intervened at that juncture to object that "I do not think it proper to inquire of a nominee for this court or any other his opinion as to any of the decisions or the reasoning upon decision which have heretofore be handed down. . . . [I]t does violence to my sense, to my concept of what the judiciary is." Senator Sam Ervin rose to the defense of McClellan, arguing that if he could not ask questions designed to elicit Stewart's "attitude . . . towards the Constitution, or what his philosophy is," then "I don't see why the Constitution was so foolish as to suggest that the nominee for the Supreme Court ought to be confirmed by the Senate. . . . I intend to ask questions of that kind. I don't think I would be faithful to my country if I didn't do it."

As Stewart's dilemma makes clear, it is often to the strategic interest of nominees to avoid explicit statements that will entangle them in controversial Supreme Court decisions. By appealing to the autonomy of law as a reason to refuse to answer direct and detailed questions about the content of their constitutional commitments, nominees have exacerbated senatorial discomfort. During her confirmation hearing, Sandra Day O'Connor articulated this appeal in a particularly forceful and successful way:

> There is . . . a limitation on my responses which I am compelled to recognize. I do not believe that as a nominee I can tell you how I might vote on a particular issue which may come before the Court, or endorse or criticize specific Supreme Court decisions presenting issues which may well come before the Court again. To do so would mean that I have prejudged the matter or have morally committed myself to a certain position. Such a statement by me as to how I might resolve a particular issue or what I might do in a future Court action might make it necessary for me to disqualify myself on the matter.

Because almost any constitutional issue "may come before the Court," O'Connor drew a line that would effectively nullify the capacity of the Senate to acquire useful information about a nominee's constitutional commitments. O'Connor's reservations would deny the Senate material of central importance to its constitutional deliberations, undermining the democratic design and function of confirmation hearings. The refusal of nominees to discuss their constitutional views is especially disturbing in the context of "stealth" candidates, who have been nominated because their constitutional commitments are literally unknown to the Senate and the American people.

III.

In the balance of this Article we propose and defend a method of questioning that will enable the Senate to evaluate the constitutional commitments of nominees while preserving the independent integrity of the law. We argue, in brief, that senators can with confidence and authority ask nominees to explain the grounds on which they would have voted in past decisions of the Supreme Court. Such questions serve the democratic design of the confirmation process by revealing the operational content of nominees' constitutional commitments. Asking nominees to disclose how they would have decided well-known Supreme Court cases prevents nominees from explaining their constitutional commitments in terms of abstract principles like "liberty" or "equality," whose practical significance in particular cases and contested areas of constitutional law is unknown. The goal would be to sustain a colloquy capable of adequately informing a senatorial vote on whether to invest a nominee with the independent authority to interpret the Constitution.

We emphasize at the outset that the purpose of such questions is not to bind future interpretive judgments of nominees. To the contrary, it is precisely because the Senate must decide whether to vest nominees with the discretion and authority to interpret the Constitution that the Senate may need nominees to explain their constitutional philosophies. The Senate should expressly affirm that its questions are solely for the purpose of clarifying a nominee's constitutional philosophy, and that a nominee's answers would not be construed as any kind of promise or guarantee of how the nominee would vote in future cases. When undertaken in this spirit and subject to this express understanding, the colloquy we propose should not compromise the independence of the Court, but instead should contribute to the democratic legitimacy that is its necessary precondition. In the remainder of this Article, we answer four prominent "rule of law" objections that have been raised against the kinds of questions that we advocate.

1. The Separation of Powers Objection

The idea that it would be inconsistent with "what the judiciary is" for nominees to be asked and to answer questions about their views of the law ultimately rests on a view of separation of powers. All agree that judges must be free to exercise independent judgment. It would be inconsistent with the rule of law for Congress to dictate to courts how individual cases should be decided or how they should interpret the Constitution. But it is Article II itself that requires Supreme Court Justices to pass through the gateway of nomination and confirmation. It is therefore no violation of separation of powers for President Eisenhower in his appointments to have "clearly and undeniably attempted to influence the Supreme Court in the direction of entrenching *Brown v. Board of Education* and enforcing its terms." And it would have been no violation of separation of powers if the Senate had refused to confirm any nominee who did not wish to uphold *Brown*. To the contrary, this is precisely how the structure of Article II was designed to work.

2. The Due Process Objection

In her confirmation hearings, Justice O'Connor refused to answer questions about "specific Supreme Court decisions presenting issues which may well come before the Court again" because she believed that it would be unfair to future litigants if she were forced to prejudge questions of law that might arise. This objection ultimately sounds in the values of due process of law, because everyone agrees that judges must consider cases without prejudgment and in an open-minded way. These values, however, are not impaired by the kinds of questions we propose.

In refusing to answer Senate questions, O'Connor necessarily assumed that judges could not be "open-minded" if they had previously expressed views about the substance of the law relevant to deciding a case. But this assumption is hard to reconcile with ordinary judicial practice. Once O'Connor had co-authored an opinion about the nature of the constitutional right to an abortion in *Planned Parenthood of Southeastern Pennsylvania. v. Casey*, she was not thereafter disqualified from participating in future cases involving abortion because she has "prejudged" the relevant law.

From the perspective of a litigant seeking vindication of a right to an abortion, and who is concerned about the prejudgment of her case, there is no pertinent difference between being judged by Justice O'Connor, who has expressed in an authoritative opinion her view of the merits of Casey, and by a new Justice who has in a confirmation hearing recounted how he would have voted in Casey had he been on the Court at the time. Nominees who explain the grounds on which they would have voted in an already decided case do not prejudge future cases any more than do judges who write or join opinions in actual cases.

3. The Appearance of Impropriety Objection

In preparing O'Connor for her confirmation hearings, (now) Chief Justice John Roberts strongly urged that the

> proposition that the only way Senators can ascertain a nominee's views is through questions on specific cases should be rejected. The suggestion that a simple understanding that no promise is intended when a nominee answers a specific question will completely remove the disqualification problem is absurd. The appearance of impropriety remains.

The idea of an "appearance of impropriety" is inherently vague, so it is important to offer some precise account of the exact impropriety that is feared. Apparently the impropriety is that for a nominee

> to express any but the most general observation about the law would suggest that, in order to obtain favorable consideration of his nomination, he deliberately was announcing in advance, without benefit of judicial oath, briefs, or argument, how he would decide a particular question that might come before him as a judge.

Questions about past Supreme Court decisions do not ask nominees to represent how they will decide future cases, but rather to disclose their present understanding of the law. It is ultimately circular to argue that answering such questions might nevertheless create the "appearance of impropriety" by inviting a promise to decide future cases in a certain way. The issue turns on the social meaning that should be attributed to a colloquy of this kind. We believe that the structure of Article II suggests that such a colloquy, whether regarded from the point of view of nominees, or the Senate, should not be understood to implicate any such promise.

From the perspective of nominees, confirmation hearings are like job interviews. Nominees may wish to trim their views to avoid antagonizing Senators, but this is ultimately a matter of the honor and integrity of particular candidates. They can misrepresent their substantive constitutional views just as they can misrepresent other aspects of their record. But the questions we propose probe only the present constitutional convictions of nominees, and seek to ascertain their practical significance with respect to particular patterns of facts (whose constitutional significance has already been closely analyzed). Nominees are not asked to explain how they would respond to different hypothetical fact patterns, nor to pledge to adhere to their present views when responding to new arguments or changing circumstances.

From the perspective of the Senate, questions about specific Supreme Court decisions should be designed to learn the present constitutional commitments of nominees, not to bind their future judgments. All agree that the judiciary should be independent and that, if confirmed, a nominee should be free to make legal judgments in ways that escape congressional control. The questions we propose help create the democratic support necessary to sustain this freedom, and thereby underwrite, rather than compromise, judicial independence. The only pledge about future conduct that the country exacts from nominees is to uphold the Constitution as they understand it.

It is also relevant to note that the Court itself has explicitly held that the appearance of impropriety could not justify a Minnesota canon of judicial ethics "prohibiting candidates for judicial election from announcing their views on disputed legal and political issues," in part because statements of such views by candidates could not plausibly be understood as equivalent to "promises" about future decisions.

4. The Politicization of the Judiciary Objection

A final objection to our proposal is that it would blur the ideological separation between law and politics. After her own confirmation as a circuit court judge, Ruth Bader Ginsburg articulated this objection to a proposed line of senatorial inquiry that would require nominees to reveal their beliefs on "important issues of social policy." She argued that such questions would constitute improper "attempts to politicize the judiciary." In essence, Ginsburg claimed that the "high esteem" of Article III judges should depend upon the apolitical values of professional competence and craft. She cited with approval a 1980 resolution of the House of Delegates of the American Bar Association responding to a plank in the Republican Party's platform advocating "the appointment of judges . . . who respect traditional family values and the sanctity of innocent human life." The ABA condemned the Republican Party's deviation "from the selection of judges on the basis of merit by superimposing a test of the candidate's 'particular political or ideological philosophies.' "

The values of professional competence and craft no doubt are and should remain significant dimensions of a nominee's qualifications. Their importance was evident during Roberts's confirmation hearings. The question, however, is whether these values alone are sufficient for Senate confirmation. Ginsburg apparently believed that democratic approval of nominees ought to depend upon whether nominees demonstrate "integrity, experience, and temperament," rather than upon the specific content of their constitutional vision. But few now believe that differences over matters of controversial constitutional law, such as abortion or affirmative action, are due primarily to differences of professional competence. Interested members of the public understand full well that such differences flow from deep divisions in constitutional philosophy.

Conservatives and liberals have developed distinct frameworks for expressing these divisions. During the Miers nomination, conservatives demanded a candidate they believed would interpret the Constitution based on its original intent. Although conservatives denounced the living Constitution and judges who legislated from the bench, they nevertheless employed the language of constitutional restoration to demand change in the prevailing interpretation of the Constitution. They used the language of originalism and constitutional fidelity to sketch the profile of a judge who knew how to construe the Constitution in ways that accorded with contemporary conservative sensibilities in questions concerning religion, the family, race, and the scope of federal power.

In recent years liberals have been more uncertain about how to speak of judicial nominations in politics. Twenty-two liberals voted against Roberts' confirmation, reasoning that they would not entrust Roberts with Article III power because in too many important questions he did not share the constitutional vision of the nation. But many liberals seek to defend the Warren Court by appealing to the independent professional expertise of judges, and this has made them genuinely ambivalent about requiring nominees to disclose their constitutional vision or making the Senate's confirmation vote openly depend on judgments about whether a nominee's constitutional philosophy is "harmful to the country." In a time of conservative dominance, many liberals seem to believe that disinterested professional expertise may be the best they can hope for.

We recognize that the questions we propose will force substantive constitutional differences into the open, and that they thus carry the potential to deepen national divisions about the meaning of the Constitution. Ginsburg's objection ultimately rests on the hope that these divisions can be ameliorated if public debate is restricted to a relatively anodyne discussion about norms of professional competence. But if intense divisions already exist, and if they already influence all aspects of the confirmation process, deflecting the focus of confirmation hearings away from the substantive constitutional views of nominees may allow Justices to be appointed who will move the Court in contentious ways that have not received democratic warrant and review. If these new directions are controversial enough, the nation will come to regret the Senate's failure to exercise its Article II authority to protect the Constitution from Justices who will estrange the people from their Court.

In such circumstances, the best hope of maintaining the democratic legitimacy of our constitutional law may lie in the extension of democratic scrutiny, rather than in its diminishment. The potential politicization of the judiciary feared by Ginsburg must be weighed against the possibility that nondemocratically sanctioned appointments may alienate the people from their own constitutional law. It must also be weighed against the possibility that vigorous Senate confirmation hearings that directly address and debate contested issues of substantive constitutional law may stimulate popular engagement with the meaning of our Constitution, which we hope all agree would be a positive democratic good. The Constitution balances competing commitments to self-government and to the rule of law in its design for appointing tenured Article III judges; this balance between self-governance and the rule of law is well served by a confirmation process that encourages popular debate about the Constitution in circumstances that maintain respect for the independence of the judicial branch.

QUESTIONS

1. *What would you do?* If you were a senator who opposed the president's nominee to the Supreme Court, how would you try to get him or her to answer your questions? How could the nomination process be changed to make them more informative?

2. What types of questions should judicial nominees have to answer and which questions can they legitimately avoid?

3. During the first five years of George W. Bush's presidency, Democratic senators used the filibuster to block several of his lower court nominees whom
they viewed as extreme. With the Supreme Court nominations looming, Republican leaders vowed to change the rules of the Senate to prevent fili-
busters of judicial nominees. Democrats threatened a revolt before a
compromise was reached that protected the right of a filibuster, but only in
the most extreme cases. Should senators be permitted to filibuster judicial
nominees? What are the arguments for and against the practice?

4. To what extent would problems concerning judicial nomination hearings go
away if the live testimony was abolished and all questions and answers were
submitted in writing? That is, to what extent are the problems caused by the
theatrics of the televised hearings, and to what extent is there a more fundamental problem with how senators ask questions and how nominees answer
them?

16

Economic Policy: Should Government Reduce Income Inequality?

Should government concern itself with income inequality? Or is income inequality a natural outcome of the economic system that should be left alone by government? Is income inequality in fact a serious problem?

Although the measurement problems are significant and analysts debate the size of the changes, there is little doubt that income inequality has been on the rise in recent decades. At times, income growth toward the bottom of the income ladder has lagged; at other times, people at the middle income levels have seen the least growth: the overall net result has been an income decline at the bottom while the middle has held steady or gained slightly. One constant across the past few decades is a rising share of income going to the people at the top of the income ladder. The share of national income going to the top 20 percent has increased sharply since 1980; the percentage going to the top 1 percent has doubled (to 16 percent), to the top one-tenth of a percent has tripled (to 7 percent), and to the top one-hundredth of a percent has quadrupled (to 2.8 percent). Compared to previous generations, however, the income at the top is much more the product of work rather than inheritance, dividends, or interest: ninety years ago, only one-fifth of the income going to the top 1 percent of the population was compensation for work; today it is three-fifths.

Several reasons have been offered for these trends, including the new skills demanded by a new technological and information age, greed, immigration, international trade, globalization, the decline of labor unions, the absorption of vast new groups into the workplace, more single-parent families at lower income levels, increased divorce rates, and more. But to what degree is income inequality an important problem justifying government intervention in the economy? Americans generally do not place reducing income inequality high on a list of goals for government, and they still fervently believe that the United States generates enough economic opportunity for all to thrive. And Americans at virtually all income levels today take for granted as necessities what would have been considered luxuries mere decades ago, including an array of household appliances; air conditioning; multiple cars in one family; vacations by airplane; cable or satellite television, and so on.

Anna Bernasek believes that the "alarming" growth in income inequality is a significant economic problem. She cites studies that find inequality producing undesirable effects on health, corruption, and work effort, all of which have damaging implications for the economy. Equally troubling, these effects mean that inequality begets further inequality, making the damage even more severe. Although she does not indicate specific policies she would change, she implies that policy change is necessary because "current policies appear to be worsening the situation."

Not so fast, replies Donald Luskin. Yes, income inequality may be on the rise, but this has always been true in periods of high prosperity at the outset of economic revolutions. The income gains of the rich have not come at anyone else's expense, as income has increased among all segments of the population. Inequality is a result of choices that for the most part are freely made by individuals. And the complaints about inequality really have little to do with inequality's effect on the economy. Rather, he argues, income inequality is useful to liberals for political purposes, as justification for policies they would support even if inequality were decreasing, and as a way to bash conservative policies they would similarly oppose regardless of income trends in the economy.

The editors at *The Economist* stake out a middle ground in the debate. Inequality is not inherently wrong, they argue, so long as society is getting richer, there is support for the poorest, and meritocracy—where rewards depend on one's skills and talent—is vibrant. It is here, with meritocracy, where the editors see the most help to be provided by government. Government should allow the economy to remain vibrant and reward risk takers, but health care and the retirement system should be repaired to make sure that rapid economic change and job displacement does not leave individuals without vital coverage in these areas. Most important, they write, rather than try to manipulate the economy to produce less income inequality, or artificially hold back the income of high earners, government must redouble its efforts to improve the education system to boost up those in the lower and middle portions of the income ladder.

Anna Bernasek
Income Inequality, And Its Cost

Inequality has always been part of the American economy, but the gap between the rich and the poor has recently been widening at an alarming rate. Today, more than 40 percent of total income is going to the wealthiest 10 percent, their biggest share of the nation's pie in at least 65 years. The social and political repercussions of this disparity have been widely debated, but what about the effects on the economy?

Oddly, despite its position in the political debate, the question has received little attention from economists. Mostly, they have focused on measuring income inequality and establishing its causes. Some research has been done, however, and the results, including insights from related disciplines like psychology and political science, are disturbing.

Start with recent findings in the field of public health. Some scientists believe that growing inequality leads to more health problems in the overall population—a situation that can reduce workers' efficiency and increase national spending on health, diverting resources away from productive endeavors like saving and investment.

Sir Michael Marmot, a professor of epidemiology and public health at University College London and director of its International Institute for Society and Health, has spent most of his career studying the link between inequality and health around the world. In a much-publicized paper published in May in *The Journal of the American Medical Association*, Sir Michael and three colleagues studied health in the United States and in Britain. They found that at various points throughout the social hierarchy, there was more illness in the United States than in Britain.

Published in *The New York Times*, June 2006.

Sir Michael theorizes that a reason for the disparity was the greater inequalities in the United States and heavier stresses resulting from them.

Other researchers have focused on how income inequality can breed corruption. That may be especially true in democracies, where wealth and political power can be more easily exchanged, according to a study of 129 countries by Jong-Sung You, a graduate student at the Kennedy School of Government at Harvard, and Sanjeev Khagram, a professor of public affairs at the University of Washington in Seattle.

Corruption, of course, can hurt growth by reducing the efficient allocation of public and private resources and by distorting investment. That may end up creating asset price bubbles.

Unchecked inequality may also tend to create still more inequality. Edward L. Glaeser, a professor of economics at Harvard, argues that as the rich become richer and acquire greater political influence, they may support policies that make themselves even wealthier at the expense of others. In a paper published last July, he said, "If the rich can influence political outcomes through lobbying activities or membership in special interest groups, then more inequality could lead to less redistribution rather than more."

In the United States, there is plenty of evidence that this has been occurring. Bush administration policies that have already reduced the estate tax and cut the top income and capital gains tax rates benefit the well-to-do. It seems hardly an accident that the gap between rich and poor has widened.

There may be other ways in which growing inequality hurts the economy. Steven Pressman, professor of economics at Monmouth University in West Long Branch, N.J., has identified a psychological effect that may lower productivity and reduce efficiency. Professor Pressman draws on the work of Daniel Kahneman, a Nobel laureate in economics, and his experiments on fairness. One experiment, called the ultimatum game, involves two people with a fixed sum of money that must be divided between them. One person is to propose any division he likes; the other can only accept or reject it. If the division is accepted, each person receives the proposed amount; if it is rejected, neither gets anything.

It might be expected that a rational individual in the role of divider would take a large part of the money and that rational receivers would accept a small portion rather than walk away with nothing. But it turned out that when faced with an offer they considered unfair, most people rejected it outright. Perhaps in anticipation of this, many dividers made substantial offers.

Professor Pressman relates those results to economic behavior in corporate America. "If a CEO's salary is going through the roof and workers are getting pay cuts, what will happen?" he said. "Workers can't outright reject the offer—they need to work—but they can reject it by working less hard and not caring about the quality of what they are producing. Then the whole efficiency of the firm is affected."

The effects of income inequality aren't entirely negative. Without some inequality, there would be little economic incentive to earn more. And some researchers, particularly advocates of supply-side theories, predict that as the rich get richer, their increased wealth will be used for greater savings and investment, thereby bolstering growth. The latest data on the American economy, though, do not seem to support this prediction.

Savings among top-income earners have actually declined. According to the Federal Reserve's latest Survey of Consumer Finance, the percentage of families in the top 10 percent by income that saved anything at all dropped to 80.6 percent in 2004 from 84.3 percent in 2001. And this was during a period when President Bush cut top marginal income tax rates and taxes on capital gains and dividends.

The trend of growing income inequality may eventually be reversed, but at the moment, current policies appear to be worsening the situation. If more researchers turned their attention to the subject, they would find plenty to explore.

Donald Luskin
Still Movin' On Up
The Death of Income Mobility Has Been Greatly Exaggerated

Starting on May 13 [2005], the *Wall Street Journal* ran a series of four front-page stories—totaling almost 10,000 words—about what it manifestly considered a major threat to the Republic. Two days later, the *New York Times* launched a series of a dozen stories about the same threat, most of the articles splashed on page one, above the fold: a total of nearly 50,000 words. *Business Week*, the *Christian Science Monitor*, and the *Los Angeles Times* have taken up

Published in *National Review*, July 2005.

the story, too; Michael Kinsley, writing in the *L.A. Times*, even suggested that the *Washington Post* get into the act.

Was the furor about al-Qaeda? Iran? North Korean nukes? Nope. The sword of Damocles hanging over our national future—and discovered, coincidentally, by *all* of these mainstream liberal media outlets at once—is . . . income inequality. But a concerned citizen who wades through these tens of thousands of words, and pores over the studies they solemnly cite as authoritative, will find a simple, but highly reassuring, truth: *There's no story here.*

The *Journal* and the *Times* are exercised by reports that, over the last three decades, a new class of what the *Times* calls the "hyper-rich" has arisen in the United States, resulting in a disparity in incomes between rich and poor not seen since the 1920s: the most severe income inequality in the developed world today. How did this happen? As the *Times* explains it, "The hyper-rich have emerged . . . as the biggest winners in a remarkable transformation of the American economy characterized by, among other things, the creation of a more global marketplace, new technology and investment spurred partly by tax cuts."

Fair enough. We have indeed seen a transformative era of economic growth. That era has indeed produced a whole new class of extremely wealthy individuals—or, more accurately, a whole new class of individuals became extremely wealthy as their reward for taking the risks that made that growth happen. And indeed tax cuts were at the root of it—supply-side tax cuts that increased the incentives for risk-taking in the first place.

But none of this is exactly man-bites-dog material. What the *Times* reports as news is a pattern that should be familiar to economic historians: Times of great prosperity have been associated with greater income inequality (for example, the 1920s), and conversely times of economic decline have been associated with greater equality (the 1930s). The lines of causality here are complex, and no doubt run in both directions: Prosperity is both the cause and the effect of inequality, and decline is both the cause and the effect of equality. So ideological advocates of income equality for its own sake ought to be careful what they wish for.

The great prosperity of the last three decades has been dominated by American technological and commercial prowess. So no one should be surprised that the emergence of the new hyper-rich has been preeminently an American phenomenon. Today 341 of the world's 691 billionaires—including five of the top ten—are Americans. These aren't old-money names, either. You have to get all the way down to number 243 before you find a Rockefeller. At the top of the chart are Gates, Buffett, Ellison, Allen, Walton—precisely the people whose innovations and risk-taking made our current prosperity possible. Much of the rise in American income inequality could probably be erased in one fell swoop just by getting these 341 people to move to another country.

We need to focus, then, on the question: What *harm* has it done to have this new class of the hyper-rich on the American scene? The *Times* and the *Journal* both go on at length about how Americans who used to consider themselves very rich—one thinks inevitably of the Sulzbergers of the *Times*, and the Bancrofts of Dow Jones—are rather annoyed to have to compete socially with the new hyper-rich; old money has never liked new money. But in truth, the incomes of the hyper-rich have not come at the expense of anyone else. The poverty rate, for example, hasn't risen over the last 30 years; it has actually fallen slightly. Average after-tax, inflation-adjusted income has risen for every income quintile in the population. Yes, it has risen the most for the highest quintile, and risen the least for the lowest—but this can be explained to some extent by the great wave of immigration over the same period. The fact remains that income has risen for all: The rising tide has lifted all boats.

Three Cheers For Diversity

Before the present era of transformative growth and its concomitant income inequality, many economists had expected the mid-twentieth-century trend toward greater equality to persist forever. According to the influential hypothesis of Simon Kuznets, nearly a half-century of steadily rising equality of income following the technology revolution that peaked in the 1920s was explained by the fact that more and more workers were joining the high-productivity sectors of the economy. Now it appears that what Kuznets described may be, in fact, a cyclical phenomenon that restarted at some point about 25 years ago. Economists Emmanuel Saez and Thomas Piketty have written that "a new industrial revolution has taken place, thereby leading to increasing inequality, and inequality will decline again at some point, as more and more workers benefit from the innovations."

In other words, at the beginning of each cycle a small band of risk-takers get extremely wealthy in the vanguard of economic transformation, but that's only a one-time effect. For years afterward, everyone else in the economy adapts to the new, higher productivity potential that the new rich have made possible, and incomes gradually gravitate toward greater equality. Happily, then, those who hope for greater income equality need not wish for slower growth, or for the mass deportation of our billionaires. All that is required is patience—and hard work.

But income inequality will never go away entirely—and it's not at all clear that we should want it to. Even if a socialist-minded fairy godmother were to wave her magic wand and set all incomes to perfect equality, in a free economy they would immediately drift toward inequality owing entirely to voluntary choices made by each individual. Each of us would choose freely whether to work hard or take it easy; to marry a working spouse or a stay-at-home; to educate ourselves for a better job, or settle for less; to invest in income-producing securities or just spend our money. All these things would determine our unequal incomes, just as they do today. To be sure, in the real world we don't make those choices from an initial position of equality. Some of us are born rich, others poor, most in between. Nevertheless it's choices like these that determine whether we will rise or fall within the class in which we are born, or move upward or downward to another class. So we shouldn't fear income inequality: We should celebrate it as "income diversity."

Changing our incomes by making choices different from those of our parents is called "income mobility." Both the *Wall Street Journal* and the *New York Times* correctly acknowledge this practice as fundamental to American life (and both happen to discuss Benjamin Franklin as its exemplar). Yet the papers argue that income mobility is on the decline just as income inequality is on the rise. You'd think that the emergence of a whole new class of the hyper-rich would prove that income mobility is alive and well (they had to come from somewhere, after all). But no.

The *Times* and the *Journal* cite many authoritative-sounding studies on declining income mobility. But to get an accurate picture, you'd have to track hundreds of millions of individuals through time, monitoring changes across generations in such factors as income, tax rates, wealth, lifestyle, and education. Looking back further than a couple of decades, robust statistics are hard to find in standard databases; you can't ask all the individuals concerned, because many of them are deceased. So researchers end up relying on surveys of small samples of people, containing what they can recollect about their parents' and grandparents' economic circumstances. As a result, hard facts about economic mobility are elusive, and studies about it are approximate and subjective at best.

Yet for all that, the *Times* and *Journal* stories are peppered with definitive-sounding statements, like this one from the *Times*: "One study, by the Federal Reserve Bank of Boston, found that fewer families moved from one quintile, or fifth, of the income ladder to another during the 1980s than during the 1970s and that still fewer moved in the 90s than in the 80s." If you follow the *Times*'s link to this study, it turns out actually to be about women in the workforce and what happens to families when a spouse dies; the more general findings cited by the *Times* are buried in an appendix. Yes, that appendix shows that about 4 percent more households stayed in their income quintile during the 1990s than in the 1970s. But it also shows—though the *Times* doesn't mention this—that in the 1990s more households than ever jumped from the poorest quintile to the richest. But none of this is reliable anyway: A footnote reveals that the statistics are derived from the Panel Study of Income Dynamics database, an ongoing survey that tracks only 8,000 families out of a U.S. population of 295 million individuals.

The other studies cited are based on evidence equally unreliable, and come to conclusions even less interesting. At most, these surveys suggest that—maybe—income mobility has stopped improving over the last 30 years.

Perhaps the best research method for getting our arms around the slippery topic of income mobility is simply to take a poll, and ask people how they feel about it. The *New York Times* itself took such a poll, and its optimistic results are strikingly at odds with the paper's gloomy conclusions. Eighty percent of respondents said "it's still possible to start out poor in this country, work hard, and become rich"—up from 57 percent in 1983. Twenty-five percent said they believed their children's standard of living would be "much better" than their own—up from 18 percent in 1994. Forty-six percent said hard work is "essential" for getting ahead in life—up from 36 percent in 1987.

Resenting Prosperity

So where's the beef? Everyone's gotten richer—and a few have gotten hyper-rich. And there's no real reason to think that income mobility isn't alive and well. So why this full-court press by the liberal mainstream media to create the impression that America is becoming a feudal society? Maybe it's a media thing; there's no other industry more obsessed with pigeonholing people by class. Here, for example, is how the *New York Times* sees its readers: They're "nearly three times as likely as the average U.S. adult to have a college or postgraduate degree, more than twice as likely to be a professional/managerial and more than twice as likely to have a household income exceeding $100,000."

Or maybe it's a liberal thing. You're more likely to vote Democratic if you're convinced that "the rich" are keeping you from getting your fair share—you know, "Two Americas" and all that. And you're more likely to support liberal initiatives like affirmative action if you think that the American dream based on income mobility is falling apart. So liberal media outlets such as the *Times* go through periodic frenzies about income inequality, regardless of who's in the White House. (Two typical *Times* headlines, from 1998: "In Booming Economy, Poor Still Struggle to Pay the Rent" and "Benefits Dwindle for the Unskilled Along with Wages.")

And, of course, the putative problem of income inequality is yet another opportunity for the liberal media to excoriate the Bush tax cuts. Whatever the problem—Social Security solvency, economic growth, outsourcing to China, budget deficits—repealing those tax cuts is always the liberal answer. In this case, the *Times* claims they "stand to widen the gap between the hyper-rich and the rest of America." This year Congress will vote on the extension of President Bush's tax cuts on income from dividends and capital gains, and on making permanent the repeal of the estate tax. For the liberal media, demonizing the rich is a powerful way to fight against those conservative initiatives. There's good reason, though, to think it won't work. That *Times* poll that showed how much faith Americans have in their income mobility also produced a striking result about taxes on "the rich": Seventy-six percent of respondents said they opposed the estate tax.

The Economist
Inequality and the American Dream

More than any other country, America defines itself by a collective dream: the dream of economic opportunity and upward mobility. Its proudest boast is that it offers a chance of the good life to everybody who is willing to work hard and play by the rules. This ideal has made the United States the world's strongest magnet for immigrants; it has also reconciled ordinary Americans to the rough

Published in June 2006.

side of a dynamic economy, with all its inequalities and insecurities. Who cares if the boss earns 300 times more than the average working stiff, if the stiff knows he can become the boss?

Look around the world and the supremacy of "the American model" might seem assured. No other rich country has so successfully harnessed the modern juggernauts of technology and globalisation. The hallmarks of American capitalism—a willingness to take risks, a light regulatory touch and sharp competition—have spawned enormous wealth. "This economy is powerful, productive and prosperous," George Bush boasted recently, and by many yardsticks he is right. Growth is fast, unemployment is low and profits are fat. It is hardly surprising that so many other governments are trying to "Americanise" their economies—whether through the European Union's Lisbon Agenda or Japan's Koizumi reforms.

Yet many people feel unhappy about the American model—not least in the United States. Only one in four Americans believes the economy is in good shape. While firms' profits have soared, wages for the typical worker have barely budged. The middle class—admittedly a vague term in America—feels squeezed. A college degree is no longer a passport to ever-higher pay. Now politicians are playing on these fears. From the left, populists complain about Mr. Bush's plutocratic friends exporting jobs abroad; from the right, nativists howl about immigrants wrecking the system.

A Global Argument

The debate about the American model echoes far beyond the nation's shores. Europeans have long held that America does not look after its poor—a prejudice reinforced by the ghastly scenes after Hurricane Katrina. The sharp decline in America's image abroad has much to do with foreign policy, but Americanisation has also become synonymous with globalisation. Across the rich world, global competition is forcing economies to become more flexible, often increasing inequality; Japan is one example. The logic of many non-Americans is that if globalisation makes their economy more like America's, and the American model is defective, then free trade and open markets must be bad.

This debate mixes up three arguments—about inequality, meritocracy, and immigration. The word that America should worry about most is the one you hear least—meritocracy.

Begin with inequality. The flip-side of America's economic dynamism is that it has become more unequal—but in a more complex way than first appears. America's rich have been pulling away from the rest of the population, as the returns for talent and capital in a global market have increased. Even if American business stopped at the water's edge, Bill Gates and the partners of Goldman Sachs would still be wealthy people; but since software and investment banking are global industries, Mr Gates is worth $50 billion and the average pay-and-benefits package for Goldman's 22,400 employees is above $500,000.

On the other hand, the current wave of globalisation may not be widening the gap between the poor and the rest. Indeed, the headwinds of the global economy are being felt less by Americans at the bottom than by those in the middle. The jobs threatened by outsourcing—data-processing, accounting and so on—are white-collar jobs; the jobs done by the poor—cleaning and table-waiting, for example—could never be done from Bangalore.

Those at the bottom have different fears, immigration high among them. Their jobs cannot be exported to rival countries perhaps, but rival workers can and are being imported to America. Yet there is surprisingly little evidence that the arrival of low-skilled workers has pulled poor Americans' wages down. And it has certainly provided a far better life for new arrivals than the one they left behind.

A Long Ladder Is Fine, but It Must Have Rungs

To many who would discredit American capitalism, this sort of cold-hearted number-crunching is beside the point. Any system in which the spoils are distributed so unevenly is morally wrong, they say. This newspaper disagrees. Inequality is not inherently wrong—as long as three conditions are met: first, society as a whole is getting richer; second, there is a safety net for the very poor; and third, everybody, regardless of class, race, creed or sex, has an opportunity to climb up through the system. A dynamic, fast-growing economy may sometimes look ugly, but it offers far more hope than a stagnant one for everybody in the United States.

This is not to let the American system off the hook when it comes to social mobility. Although the United States is seen as a world of opportunity, the reality may be different. Some studies have shown that it is easier for poorer children to rise through society in many European countries than in America. There is a particular fear about the engine of American meritocracy, its education system. Only 3% of students at top colleges come from the poorest quarter of the population. Poor children are trapped in dismal schools, while richer parents spend ever more cash on tutoring their offspring.

What, if anything, needs to be done? A meritocracy works only if it is seen to be fair. There are some unfair ways in which rich Americans have rewarded themselves, from backdated share options to reserved places at universities for the offspring of alumni. And a few of Mr. Bush's fiscal choices are not helping. Why make the tax system less progressive at a time when the most affluent are doing best?

That said, government should not be looking for ways to haul the rich down. Rather, it should help others, especially the extremely poor, to climb up—and that must mean education. Parts of the American system are still magnificent, such as its community colleges. But as countless international league tables show, its schools are not. Education is a political football, tossed about between Republicans who refuse to reform a locally based funding system that starves schools in poor districts, and Democrats who will never dare offend their paymasters in the teachers' unions.

The other challenge is to create a social-welfare system that matches a global business world of fast-changing careers. No country has done this well. But the answer has to be broader than just "trade-adjustment" assistance or tax breaks for hard-hit areas. Health care, for instance, needs reform. America's traditional way of providing it through companies is crumbling. The public pension system, too, needs an overhaul.

These are mightily complicated areas, but the United States has always had a genius for translating the highfalutin' talk of the American Dream into practical policies, such as the GI Bill, a scholarship scheme for returning troops after the Second World War. The country needs another burst of practical idealism. It is still the model the rest of the world is following.

QUESTIONS

1. *What would you do?* You are a candidate for public office and you have just been asked by a potential voter what you think about flat versus progressive income taxes. Flat taxes take the same percentage of income from every taxpayer, after deductions for children, charitable contributions, and the like. Progressive income taxes take a higher percentage of your income as you earn more. On one hand, a progressive income tax, perhaps from jealousy, pena-

lizes those individuals who have worked hard and been financially successful by requiring them to pay more than their fair share. Only a flat tax is fair, because everyone contributes the same percentage of their taxable income. On the other hand, a progressive income tax is justified because it takes a greater percentage of income from precisely those individuals who have disproportionately benefited from the opportunities in the American economic system. A flat tax is not fair, say those who support a progressive tax, because 15 percent (for example) of one's income matters more to the person making $40,000 than the person making $140,000. What would your position be and why?

2. The articles present three different perspectives on how serious a problem inequality is for the economy. Which argument do you find most convincing? Are there possible effects on the economy, or on society more generally, that you think the authors miss? In your view, would these effects justify government action? If so, what kinds of policies would you favor?

3. Before government acts to reduce income inequality, it should have an idea of how much inequality is "too much." How should it decide? What factors should it consider in deciding whether there is too much inequality?

17

Social Policy: Who Wins and Who Loses If Social Security Is Privatized?

Social Security affects tens of millions of Americans; according to the Social Security Administration, nearly 50 million Americans received some sort of support from the program in 2006. There is wide agreement that the program requires major reform if it is to continue to provide economic security to future retirees and their survivors. Even so, there is much less agreement about what, specifically, should be done. At the heart of the debate are two contrasting perspectives on what the Social Security system is designed to do, both deeply rooted in U.S. political culture. One perspective is that Social Security is a national guarantee of basic income for all individuals in retirement; it is the ultimate "safety net" for the elderly. The other holds that Social Security should be an individualistic program that allows people to make choices about their own retirement. To put it another way, is Social Security a social welfare program, or a social investment program?

For several decades, the libertarian Cato Institute has been arguing that the Social Security system be privatized—that individuals should control their own retirement accounts, and be permitted to make specific decisions about how the account should be invested. In return for foregoing future claims, individuals would be permitted to keep control over their own contributions, which they could then invest in the stock market. Andrew Biggs sets out this case and argues that the market's recent performance should not affect its feasibility. There is, in his view, no alternative, because the entire system is currently structured as an unsustainable pyramid scheme, in which each generation's retirees are funded through the next generation of workers. When the baby boomers begin retiring in 2008, there simply won't be enough people contributing to pay for all the benefits. Allowing people to take responsibility for their own accounts—in effect, eliminating the current "pay as you go" funding—would lower costs, spur savings, and give individuals a much higher rate of return on their contributions. Even with the recent period of poor market performance, workers would still be better off handling their own investments. "The stock market," argues Biggs, "has never lost money over any twenty-year period." Private accounts would save the system, which otherwise will require huge tax increases or harsh benefit cuts.

But others argue that privatizing Social Security would destroy the program's core, by eliminating a sense of shared sacrifice and collective responsibility. These critics point out that privatization will make Social Security's revenue-benefits imbalance worse, by reducing current contributions without doing anything about current benefits. Brooke Harrington has a slightly different spin on this issue. She points out that most people lack the skills and knowledge necessary to make good investment decisions. The central problem, she says, is one of "information asymmetries," in which sellers have more information than buyers. Furthermore, some groups of potential investors, such as women or minorities, are more likely to make conservative investment decisions that will hurt their long term returns, and reduce their economic security under a privatized system. Rather than serving the redistributive and social insurance purposes of the current Social Security system, privatization would exacerbate existing income and wealth inequalities.

Andrew G. Biggs
Stock Market Declines' Effect on the Social Security Reform Debate

Imagine the following deal: You could invest part or all of your Social Security taxes in a personal retirement account. However, your account could hold nothing but stocks, and you would retire during the biggest bear market since

Published in *USA Today Magazine*, May 2003.

the Great Depression. Would you accept such a deal? I would, because even to-day, personal accounts would increase retirement benefits while giving workers greater ownership and control over their savings.

Slumping stock markets have opponents of personal accounts claiming vin-dication. The situation shows, they argue, that only a traditional government-run, defined-benefit Social Security program can provide adequate retirement security. As then-Senate Majority Leader Tom Daschle put it on July 12, 2002, "After what's happened in the stock market the last few weeks, we think it's a terrible idea. . . . Imagine if you were retiring this week, with most major stock indexes hitting five-year lows." Indeed, many Americans are sure to be con-cerned after hearing such comments.

Yet, in judging the risks of long-term market investment based on just a few months or years of returns, these opponents of personal accounts are victims of the so-called law of small numbers—the propensity to believe that a small sam-ple is representative of the larger universe of outcomes. Like those who took a few years of double-digit stock returns in the 1990s and predicted that they sig-nified a future of limitless investment riches, personal account opponents have failed to take an in-depth look at the historical facts regarding stock and bond returns over the long term.

These facts show that, even now, personal accounts would increase benefits and help strengthen Social Security for the future. However had the market's recent performance, a worker retiring today would have begun investing in the late 1950s. The stock market has never lost money over any twenty-year pe-riod. Even without diversification, a worker retiring today would have forty years of investment behind him or her to make up for recent losses. A worker just entering the market would have forty years to regain lost ground. There is simply no way recent events can credibly justify a disastrous scenario for per-sonal accounts. Even a worker retiring in the Great Depression would have re-ceived a four percent annual return after inflation, and one retiring today would do substantially better.

Personal accounts give workers the opportunity to diversify their invest-ments across hundreds or even thousands of stocks and bonds, reducing the risk that declines in a single company or asset class would severely impact re-tirement income. Moreover, longtime horizons provide "time diversification" that smoothes out the short-term volatility of investments in the stock market.

Historically, in almost all cases, workers with diversified market invest-ments would have received substantially higher benefits if allowed to invest part or all of their payroll taxes in personal retirement accounts. Looking forward to Social Security reform proposals already on the table, practically all workers could expect to increase their total retirement incomes by opting to participate in personal accounts, even if they had to give up part of their traditional benefits to do so.

Asset diversification: mixing stocks and bonds

Stocks are risky investments over the short run, varying greatly from year to year. Bonds and other fixed-income investments, while producing lower returns over the long term, provide the year-to-year stability that many investors demand.

For this reason, most financial advisors recommend that investors move from a predominantly stock-based portfolio when they are young to fixed-income investments such as bonds as they near retirement. Younger workers have more time to make up for market losses, as well as more future labor income with which to supplement their savings. A common rule of thumb is that the percentage of stocks in a worker's portfolio should equal "100 minus your age," so that a twenty-year-old would begin his or her working life with 80 percent of savings going into stocks and retire at sixty-five with just 35 percent in equities.

Statistics from 401(k) plans show that most workers stick reasonably close to these guidelines. The average worker aged 60–65 keeps about 40 percent of 401(k) assets invested in stocks and 60 percent put in fixed-income assets such as bonds. A younger worker, by contrast, reverses the mix to 60–40 percent in favor of stocks.

To illustrate the impact of life cycle investing, imagine a sixty-five-year-old average-wage worker retiring today. One year ago, he or she had $100,000 in a personal account and allocated 40 percent to the S&P 500 stock index and 60 percent to the Lehman Brothers aggregate bond index. What would that account be worth today, assuming no additional contributions were made in the last year?

Believe it or not, despite truly awful stock market returns in the past year, the account balance would be virtually unchanged. The loss of 21.6 percent on the stock portion of the portfolio would be almost matched by the 9.9 percent gain on the larger bond portion, for a total year-end loss of just 3.25 percent. In other words, if that worker had started the year with $100,000 in the account, he or she would have ended with $97,288. This loss would reduce monthly retirement income by merely around $15. Moreover, a typical low-income worker aged 60–65 has just 23 percent of his or her 401(k) invested in equities. This low-income worker would have made money over the last year, earning a return of 2.6 percent as gains from the bonds in the portfolio outweighed losses in the stock market.

Any investor would rather make money than lose it, but these results show that even the poor stock market results of the past year would have had just a small impact on a typical worker holding a personal retirement account. As Dallas Salisbury of the Employee Benefit Research Institute remarks, "There is no retirement crisis because of the stock market decline." Workers' retirement accounts are sufficiently diversified that they lost only 5–10 percent on average over the last year, according to the *Los Angeles Times*, with those nearing retirement presumably suffering even smaller declines.

Time diversification: stocks for the long run

While the relatively small declines despite recent stock market losses may reassure the nervous, what really matters for personal accounts isn't how they would have performed over the last year, or over any single year. For retirement investment, what matters is where you start and where you wind up. What happens in between is much less important. Retirement investing is about the long run, and over the long run, stocks have been remarkably safe investments.

As noted above, most workers diversify their investments between stocks and bonds, moving out of equities as they approach retirement. Personal account opponents, however, often assume that workers have their entire account invested in stocks, maximizing their risk in the event of a market decline.

If that is what account opponents insist on, let's see what it would mean. To illustrate, take a male worker earning the average wage each year, currently around $35,000, and retiring in 2002. Assume that he deposited 3 percent of his wages into a personal account investing exclusively in the S&P 500 stock index. The account balance will be compared to the notional "wealth" he would have accumulated from putting the same amount of money into the current system.

The annual return from Social Security for a single male retiring today is 1.74 percent above inflation, according to the Social Security Administration. This estimate includes all retirement, survivors, and disability benefits. Married couples, particularly those with a single earner, could expect somewhat higher returns. Future retirees can generally expect lower returns than those retiring now.

Even with the recent stock market decline, a single male investing solely in stocks would receive benefits 2.8 times higher than had he "invested" the same amount of money in the current program. Put another way, the recent decline in stock prices means the worker's personal account would be worth the same today as it was worth in 1997. Nevertheless, that worker's Social Security "savings" would be worth today only what the personal account was worth in the late 1980s. It would take a much-larger decline than the one we have seen for a personal account to be a worse "deal" than the current program.

Simulating personal account returns through history

The Congressional Research Service took a more wide-ranging look at the issue of market risk and personal retirement accounts, utilizing stock and bond returns dating back to 1927 to simulate how individuals with personal accounts would have fared had accounts been introduced in the past. It is true, as the CRS finds, that stock returns vary greatly from year to year, but this variation takes place at a level *higher* than that provided by Social Security. That is, while a worker could not be sure from historical returns of receiving higher benefits than a person retiring last year or next year, that individual could be reasonably sure of receiving more than if he or she had invested the same amount of money in the traditional pay-as-you-go program. Over the thirty-five different forty-one-year periods the CRS studied, there is not one in which a worker who had invested payroll taxes in stocks would have been better off remaining in the current system. On average, a personal account invested solely in stocks would produce benefits two and one-half times higher than had those same funds been devoted to the traditional pay-as-you-go program.

A mixed portfolio of stocks and bonds was not always better than Social Security, but it nearly always was so. Of the thirty-five different forty-one-year periods studied, in seven of them a worker would have been better off investing payroll taxes in Social Security than in a 60–40 stock-bond portfolio, although the difference is small—an average of just 6 percent.

The relative weakness of a mixed portfolio during the 1970s is attributable to two factors. First, investment returns were low by historical standards, with a slow economy reducing stock returns and high inflation making real bond returns negative from 1970 to 1979. Second, Social Security paid substantially higher returns during that period than it does today or will in the future. Workers retiring in the 1970s received real annual returns from Social Security averaging around 10 percent. Future retirees can expect to receive returns of approximately two percent, depending on their income and marital status. While low market returns are possible in the future, the current Social Security program can never again pay returns similar to those received during the 1970s and before.

Overall, however, a 60–40 stock-bond portfolio would have paid an average of 39 percent more than Social Security, even compared to the higher rates of return the current program has paid in the past. From the late 1970s onward, no individual—including one retiring today—would have been worse off with a personal account than by remaining in the current system. All workers would have received higher benefits by investing in personal accounts, even if their account contained a high proportion of bonds, and many workers would have received much higher benefits.

These results may understate somewhat the returns from personal account plans such as those from the President's Commission, since the CRS assumes administrative costs of one percent of assets managed, vs. an estimate of 0.3 percent of assets managed by Social Security's independent actuaries for the Commission's account structure. Over a forty-one-year working lifetime, a 0.7 percent increase in the net investment return would raise the final asset accumulation by slightly over 20 percent, further increasing the advantage of personal accounts over pay-as-you-go financing.

Long-run market risk

Another way to consider stock market risk is to compare the variations in returns over various holding periods. The influential book *Stocks for the Long Run*, by Wharton School finance professor Jeremy Siegel, shows the standard deviation of returns for stocks, bonds, and Treasury bills held for different periods of time. The standard deviation measures the dispersion of statistical data, showing how much individual instances tend to vary from the average for the group.

In the short run, the standard deviation of stock returns is very high, so the return in one year could be very different from that of another. Fixed income investments, by contrast, have lower standard deviations and thus lower risk. Over the long term, though, the standard deviation of stock returns has fallen. The return from holding stock for, say, twenty years does not vary so much, regardless of which twenty-year period of American history you choose. For thirty-year periods, the standard deviation of returns is lower still.

Moreover, for long holding periods, the standard deviation of stock returns is actually lower than for bonds or Treasury bills. That is to say, in a certain sense at least, stocks were *less* risky over the long term than bonds. It is this reduction of the variance of returns over the long run that forms the basis for time diversification and the common advice given younger individuals to hold riskier investments.

Worst-Case Scenarios

Personal-account opponents are quick to point that that, while stocks have high *average* returns, the promise of guaranteed protection against poverty cannot be "averaged out" if some people feast on the rewards of a rich stock account while others cannot afford to eat. Social Security is supposed to be there for everyone, regardless of whether they have good luck or know how to manage investments. Hence, reform opponents are justified in demanding we look not just at the average returns available from personal accounts, but how people would fare if they experienced low returns over their lifetimes.

Another way to look at stock investment for personal accounts, then, is to examine the extremes. If you had a personal account and received below-average returns on your investments, how badly would you have fared?

As expected, stocks have often produced large losses in the short term. For instance, over single-year holding periods, the worst performance from stocks in American history was a loss of 38.6 percent; for bonds in a single year, a loss of 21.9 percent; and for Treasury bills, a loss of 15.6 percent.

Over the long term, however, annual gains and losses offset each other. When stocks are held for ten years, the largest average annual loss was 4.2 percent after inflation. Over twenty years or more, though, stocks have never failed to produce positive returns, with the worst annual return being one percent. Over thirty years, the worst annual return from stocks was a gain of 2.6 percent after inflation.

Bonds actually produced lower worst-case returns over the long run than stocks. The worst thirty-year return from bonds was an annual loss of two percent; for Treasury bills, a loss of 1.8 percent. In other words, the true worst-case scenarios would not have involved stock investment, but holding supposedly "safe" government bonds.

These figures assume that workers hold a diversified portfolio replicating the performance of the stock market as a whole. A worker could lose his or her savings simply by investing the entire portfolio in one of the approximately two hundred public corporations that declare bankruptcy in any given year. It is precisely for this reason that all major personal account-based reform legislation mandates that workers could not invest in single stocks or even in single corporate sectors. Workers with accounts could purchase only highly diversified mutual funds holding dozens, hundreds, or even thousands of stocks and bonds. Some reform plans base their account administration on the Federal Thrift Plan, which gives workers the option to invest in one or more of five stock or bond index funds, coupling simplicity and extremely low administrative costs with high levels of diversification. Hence, while personal account opponents cite the amount a worker might have lost by investing in the NASDAQ index, there is no existing reform legislation that would allow such an investment to take place.

In practice, it would be next to impossible for an individual to lose money. To illustrate, imagine a worker who could invest in either the S&P 500 stock index or in a fund of AAA-rated corporate bonds. Each year, he or she moved his entire portfolio to the investment that would reap the lowest returns for that year. Even after making the worst investment choices possible, if retiring today, the worker still would have had positive net returns on his or her portfolio as a whole.

Short-term investors are right to be concerned about short-term stock market volatility. Long-term investors, such as those saving for retirement, should focus more on long-term returns and long-term volatility. Additionally, over the time frames in which individuals would utilize personal accounts for Society Security, diversified investments in stocks and bonds remain perfectly adequate means to prepare for retirement.

Indeed, review of the evidence shows the hysterical reactions of personal account opponents to recent stock market declines to be wholly overblown. Most workers nearing retirement would have relatively little exposure to stock market risk and thus would have merely experienced small declines in their account values. Most workers who did have large proportions of their accounts invested in stocks would be young, with many years to make up for today's losses. Even workers invested entirely in stocks and retiring precisely when the market had fallen would still have received higher returns than the current Social Security program can produce. Historical evidence shows that even a worker retiring in 1933, when the Great Depression dragged the stock market to its lowest, would have still received a 4 percent average annual return, over twice what today's average worker can expect from Social Security.

Moreover, experience shows that workers can invest their assets wisely to account for stock market risk. In the 1980s and 1990s, millions of new investors entered the market as employers shifted from traditional defined-benefit pensions to employee-controlled defined-contribution accounts. Many of these new investors had little experience with stocks or bonds, but data shows that generally they have made reasonable decisions on how to allocate their assets as they aged. Personal accounts would be designed with new investors in mind, ensuring low costs and adequate diversification so that inexperienced investors would not find themselves losing money due to high administrative fees or inappropriate reliance on merely a few stocks.

Just as importantly, personal accounts give workers the opportunity to stay out of the stock market entirely if they so choose. They could invest solely in corporate or government bonds and still receive higher benefits than by staying in the current program. This stands in contrast to plans in which the government itself would invest the Social Security trust fund in the stock market. Not only would that plan open the fund to political manipulation, it would make workers and retirees subject to stock market risk, whether they desired it or not.

Personal accounts are voluntary, and no worker would be forced to choose one or to invest even a penny in the stock market. Given the relative safety of long-run diversified market investment, there is little reason why individual workers should not be allowed to choose.

Yes, the stock market is risky, and individuals should bear this risk in mind when making investment decisions. Nevertheless, while opponents of personal accounts trumpet the amount that accounts might have lost in the past four years, they decline to discuss how much workers would have gained over the last forty—not just in dollars, but in the security and dignity that comes from ownership and control over one's own retirement wealth.

Brooke Harrington
Can Small Investors Survive Social Security Privatization?

It has become nearly axiomatic in this country to argue that everything would be better if it were run like a business. In response, government has shifted its mission: If it used to operate like Super Glue, bonding Americans to one another, it is now working more like WD-40, minimizing friction in the pursuit of individual (and corporate) profit.

Social Security is not only the largest government program but the embodiment of the Super Glue approach to politics: the ultimate test case for privatization. The Bush administration proposes to allow contributors to invest a portion of their public Social Security pensions in the stock market. What a coup that would be for the WD-40 contingent.

Privatization proponents rest their proposal on three claims: Social Security funds are comparable to private investments, like IRAs; since most Americans manage their own IRAs, there is no reason they shouldn't manage their public pensions as well; and given the average returns on American stocks, we'd all have much more money at retirement if we could take some of our Social Security fund out of government bonds and put it into the stock market. This shift could be interpreted as the financial equivalent of "bowling alone," Robert Putnam's much-quoted phrase about the decline of community life in the United States. Or you could think of it as the 401(k)-ification of America: The defined-contribution plan has shifted our view of retirement into something that is purely an individual matter, rather than a collective one.

A *New York Times* poll conducted earlier this year indicates that many Americans are increasingly persuaded by these ideas. Despite the market downturn, there has been a marked increase in the percentage of Americans who expect to rely only on their own savings—rather than private pension plans or Social Security—in retirement. Only 15 percent now believe that Social Security will be a primary source of their retirement funds. As one survey participant put it, "These decades to come are going to be more about what you do for yourself, as opposed to what you allow other people to do for you. It's not pro-government, not anti-government, just me myself and I." But while Americans

Published in *The American Prospect*, September 2001.

may think they are well prepared to give up a piece of their social safety net, the evidence from recent economic studies suggests otherwise.

The prospect of higher returns is the main attraction of privatization, despite the seemingly insurmountable problems of logistics, costs, and implementation it poses. Belief in this claim seems to be curiously robust, even in the face of the recent stock-market decline and attempts to explain the costs, risks, and problems associated with privatization. People have dollar signs in their eyes, and nothing seems able to dislodge them.

In part, this can be attributed to the increasing displacement of belief in the public good by belief in the marketplace. The movements to bring market forces to the management of public schools, Medicare, and electrical-power transmission are among the most visible recent examples.

The central problem facing these hybrid public-private organizations is "information asymmetry": Market forces can't bring efficiency if there are large information differences among sellers and buyers. The classic example is the purchase of a used car. The seller has more information than the buyer and has no incentive to tell the buyer the truth. Therefore, the buyer may end up (1) buying a lemon or (2) spending a lot of time and money on research, both of which offset the savings from getting a "bargain" on the price.

When you introduce market forces into a formerly public service, you run into all of these problems of information asymmetry and opportunism. Thus, the key question for success in any hybrid is: Are citizens prepared to act as informed consumers?

In the case of Social Security, support for a privatized system rests entirely (and often implicitly) on assumptions about public knowledge and competency with regard to stock investing. But recent studies by economists and finance scholars suggest that Americans really don't understand the risks associated with stock investments and stand a good chance of doing worse financially under a hybrid system than under the current one.

Risk, Return, and Transaction Costs

In the language of finance, the benefits of a privatized Social Security system depend upon the "equity premium." This is the increased return that investors can get for investing in risky securities such as stocks as opposed to risk-free securities such as Treasury bonds. Investors are compensated for assuming risk; the higher the risk, the greater the compensation.

During the century that just ended, the return on U.S. stock investments has averaged about 11 percent per year. The U.S. Treasury bonds in which Social Security funds are invested returned much less—averaging more like 5 percent per year. Offered a choice between the two investments, the answer seems obvious: Take the higher return.

But of course there is a catch—two catches, in fact. The equity premium is not guaranteed (if it were, there would be no risk). It is just an average return, and some individual investors will actually lose money on stock investments. Not only are the risks of any individual stock unpredictable, but the historical-average return of U.S. stocks may not apply in a given time period. A grinding bear market or high inflation around the time you retire could mean that you have to cash out your portfolio when it's under water. In any case, the historical-average returns involve periods much longer than the relevant individual time frame, which is basically the forty-odd years between the start of one's working life and retirement. That means many of us will not be able to capitalize on long-range returns; as Keynes put it, "in the long run, we are all dead."

A second, related catch is that once investors capture the equity premium, they have to be careful not to give it away to their brokers. Trading stocks incurs transaction costs: Each buy or sell order means paying a commission. These costs can easily eat up all the gains from a profitable investment. Unless the government wants to become the world's first no-commission broker, transaction costs are going to be a serious issue in a privatized Social Security system.

The entire proposition that Social Security participants will come out ahead financially in a privatized system depends on their knowledge of and ability to manage investment risk and transaction costs. The evidence on this subject is not encouraging.

For example, polls conducted to examine Americans' attitudes toward Social Security privatization have shown that it is alarmingly easy to reverse support for the proposal by simply mentioning risk. When questions about privatization are phrased so that they don't mention risk, about 58 percent of Americans support the proposal. But if the questions are rephrased so that they mention risk in any way, the results are reversed: 59 percent of respondents *oppose* privatization.

Studies of actual investor behavior support the polls. Ordinary individuals seem to have a polarized response to risk; they become either very conservative or very risk-seeking. Unfortunately, neither strategy is profitable. Though *on average* risk is compensated by return in the stock market, some risks don't pay off. Rather than being a linear relationship, in which more risk always pays off with higher returns, the risk-return relationship is more like an inverted U-shaped curve: Risks pay off up to a certain point, after which they become a waste of money. As with gambling, most of the fun in investing consists of locating that fine line between risks that pay off and those that don't.

Unfortunately, the vast majority of people guess wrong. Finance professor Terrance Odean has found that the portfolios of average American households and of investment clubs underperform the stock market by about 4 percent annually. In addition, Odean found that Americans trade their accounts excessively, creating high transaction costs. Apparently unaware that they were giving away their profits in the form of commissions, American households turned over their portfolios—that is, sold existing stocks and bought new ones—at the astronomical rate of 75 percent per year. Investment clubs weren't far behind, with a 65 percent annual turnover rate. At the end of the day, they mostly made money for their brokers. There is no reason to expect that Americans would fare any better or trade any less in a privatized system.

Of course, an ultraconservative approach to investing doesn't provide much of an alternative. Several economic studies indicate that the populations most likely to need Social Security in old age—people of color and women—are also the least likely to benefit from a privatized system. For example, a study by economists Nancy Jianokoplos and Alexander Bernasek indicates that women invest too conservatively, putting only 40 percent of their investment dollars into stocks, compared with 46 percent for men. This conservatism doesn't pay off: If a man and a woman start with equal amounts of investment capital (which is of course a highly stylized assumption in itself) and invest it according to the averages over a twenty-year period, that 6 percent difference in allocation results in the woman having 47 percent less money in her retirement fund than the man has. Thus, conservative behavior in a privatized system may not result in more retirement dollars for everyone. For the people who need a nest egg most, privatization may be no better, and perhaps worse, than the current public system.

This difference doesn't have anything to do with innate characteristics of men and women—or of blacks and whites—but rather with lack of exposure to investment opportunities, such as working the kind of job where you get a 401 (k) plan that forces you to learn something about investing. That's how

most Americans got into investing in the first place. But the investing band-
wagon that swept the country during the 1990s left behind large numbers of
women, people of color, and the poor. To correct this problem, the government
would have to create a national investor-education program—an undertaking
so costly that the Social Security trustees warned against it in 1999, saying that
the expenses incurred would almost certainly outweigh the gains from
privatization.

Privatization: Ready or Not?

Historically, Social Security has served multiple purposes, providing savings, insurance, and income redistribution in a single program. Privatization would
shift the program away from redistribution and toward individual savings. This
is part of the larger trend toward distrust of government and detachment from
notions of the common good. In this sense, after years of erosion of public-
sector institutions and faith in their mission, Americans *are* well prepared for a
hybridized Social Security. More than twenty years of retreat from the notion
of entitlement has changed our expectations and led many of us to accept the
notion that we should individually bear most of the risk and responsibility for
funding our retirements.

But all of us are vulnerable to the possibility of bad luck. Privatization
would introduce a lottery-like element into the system that undercuts security
for everyone. There is no guaranteed profit in the stock market: neither risk
seeking nor conservatism reliably pays off, and neither investment professionals
nor ordinary Americans have been successful at guessing where stock prices
would go. Americans may think that they know something about investing—
remember when everyone agreed that you couldn't go wrong in dot-com
stocks?—but their confidence, and the confidence of policy makers, is not supported by the evidence.

The evidence suggests that the people who would be most likely to see financial benefit from privatization in the Social Security system are white, male,
affluent, and young. Unfortunately, recent polls indicate that these are also the
people most likely to say they don't need Social Security and would like to drop
out of the program entirely.

The end of Social Security in its purely public form would mean losses for
Americans that are not just economic but social. In abandoning the largest and
most popular public program that binds us together through its benefits, we

would lose an institutional and economic linchpin of our political community. When stacked up against the uncertain financial gains from privatization, the benefits of a public Social Security system look increasingly priceless.

QUESTIONS

1. *What would you do?* If you had the choice of opting out of the Social Security system, foregoing any future guaranteed benefits in return for being able to invest your contributions, would you do it? What are the advantages and disadvantages of giving individuals the power to control their own accounts?

2. Social Security is not, at present, means tested: retirees are eligible for benefits no matter how wealthy they are. In 2006, over 2 million retirees received benefits even though their household income was over $100,000. What would happen if benefits were means tested? Would this jeopardize the broad public support for the program?

3. Do you think most people are able to make their own investment decisions? Under a privatized system, should the government guarantee any of these investments? How might such a guarantee affect the decisions that individuals made about where to put their money?

4. One important point that neither Briggs nor Harrington address is the issue of "transition costs." That is, because Social Security is a pay-as-you-go system, in which today's workers pay for today's Social Security benefits, by allowing people to put a portion of their payroll taxes into private accounts it would divert funds that go to current beneficiaries. If private accounts were adopted, what would be the best way to fund the transition costs?

18

Foreign Policy: Can Nation Building Succeed?

When terrorists crashed airplanes into the World Trade Center in New York City and the Pentagon in Washington, Americans were stunned and disbelieving. How could this happen? Who was responsible? When President Bush indicated that he was prepared to fight a war on terrorism to ensure that the guilty parties were punished and to prevent any similar incident in the future, he rode a wave of public opinion demanding action. Dislodging the Taliban in Afghanistan was the first leg of this strategy. Changes in domestic security procedures, such as safety and inspection procedures at airports, constituted the second leg. The third leg was a plan to remove Saddam Hussein from power in Iraq. Although his interpretation and analysis were disputed by some observers, the president declared that Iraq not only was a haven for terrorists in general, but also perhaps provided support for the terrorists involved in the events of September 11. The president also declared that, even if not involved in September 11, Iraq was an identifiable risk for supporting future terrorism and creating international turmoil through weapons programs and aggressive stances toward its neighbors. On these stated grounds, the president ordered the United States into battle against Iraq. In short order, American troops and their allies had taken control of Baghdad and chased Hussein from power. The question then became: what next?

In the 2000 presidential campaign, candidate Bush expressed skepticism about the concept of "nation building," suggesting that it stretched the military thin and often got the United States bogged down in situations that were unlikely to be resolved by outside forces. After September 11, 2001, however, the president found himself directing nation-building efforts in Afghanistan and Iraq. Although there is some dispute over precisely what nation building entails, at the minimum most analysts would agree that it means constructing a functioning government that can govern even in a society composed of disparate ethnic, linguistic, religious, and geographical groupings. It also involves building an economic infrastructure and system that will reduce the likelihood of social and political instability. Today, these tasks typically involve the efforts of individuals and governments outside the targeted country as well as individuals and groups within the country. The United States itself has gone through its own nation-building experiences, particularly in the period following the Revolutionary War, the time of the writing of the Constitution, and also in the aftermath of the Civil War. To state the obvious, nation building is difficult. By mid-2006, the United States had been in Iraq for over three years, and though Hussein had been removed from power, violence against American troops continued daily as a political system slowly took root. Public opinion in the United States turned less supportive of the war, and this unsettled opinion contributed to increasing disapproval of President Bush's job performance.

Marina Ottaway offers a set of principles by which to evaluate and understand nation building. She suggests that we have to have realistic expectations about these efforts at reconstruction. We may hope democracy will result, but it quite possibly will not. We might wish to see nation building accomplished without military force. This, too, she argues, is unlikely. Ottaway also contends that hoping a truly integrated "nation" will emerge is often wishful thinking—the best that might be achievable is a country in which rival forces are not shooting at one another. Nation building need not become an endless quagmire, though. In her view, clear goals and sufficient resources can prevent nation building from becoming an endless exercise.

That is unlikely, say Justin Logan and Christopher Preble. They lament the Bush Administration's support for nation building, noting that the State Department now has what is in effect a nation-building office and the Defense Department has labeled "stability operations"—in their view a euphemism for nation building—a "core U.S. military mission." Logan and Preble argue the United States should only be involved where national security is seriously at risk, and in their view security is rarely at risk in "failed states" where internal conflict is no longer controllable and authority has severely eroded. Moreover, they state, there is no model for nation building that can be easily applied in country after country. To Logan and Preble, nation building has a long history of failure, has vague goals, is extremely expensive and time consuming, and is a distraction from combating terrorism.

Marina Ottaway
Nation Building

Once, nations were forged through "blood and iron." Today, the world seeks to build them through conflict resolution, multilateral aid, and free elections. But this more civilized approach has not yielded many successes. For nation building to work, some harsh compromises are necessary—including military coercion and the recognition that democracy is not always a realistic goal.

"Nation Building Is a Quagmire"

Not necessarily

Nation building is difficult, but it need not become a quagmire as long as the effort has clear goals and sufficient resources. Compare Somalia and East Timor: The United States and the United Nations stumbled into Somalia without a plan. As a result, what began as a humanitarian mission to feed people starved by rival warlords became a misguided attempt at ad hoc nation building as U.S. troops sought to capture Somali warlord Mohammed Farah Aidid. The United States extricated itself from that quagmire by leaving Somalia to its fate in 1994, and the United Nations later did the same.

In East Timor, by contrast, the international community followed a plan and was not dragged into a situation it could not control. Right from the start, the United Nations sought consensus for nation building by organizing an unprecedented plebiscite on independence from Indonesia. Learning from the mistakes of the Balkans and elsewhere, peacekeepers (led by Australia) were authorized to use deadly force against pro-Indonesia militias who sought to disrupt East Timor's bid for autonomy through a campaign of violence, looting, and arson. At the time of this writing [October 2002], the East Timorese have

Published in *Foreign Policy*, September/October 2002.

democratically elected a new government, which has hired more than 11,000 civil servants and retrained former guerrillas as soldiers for the country's nascent defense force. East Timor is still a construction site, but it is not a quagmire.

"Nation Building Is About Building a Nation"

No

Nationhood, or a sense of common identity, by itself does not guarantee the viability of a state. In Haiti, for example, citizens already share a common identity, but the state has collapsed nevertheless. Other states are so deeply divided along ethnic (Bosnia), religious (Northern Ireland), or clan (Somalia) lines that forging a common identity is currently out of the question. The international community cannot hope to make Muslims, Croats, and Serbs in Bosnia forget their differences, nor can it compel Catholics and Protestants in Northern Ireland to bridge the religious gulf.

Even successful states are less homogenous than they claim. Many European countries, such as France and Spain, grudgingly have recognized the existence of regional cultures. In the United States, the notion of the melting pot has been debunked, particularly as a new wave of immigrants from the developing world has shunned outright assimilation by forming a mosaic of hyphenated Americans. And contrary to the mythology inherited from nineteenth-century Europe, historical evidence reveals that the common identity, or sense of nationhood, that exists in many countries did not precede the state but was forged by it through the imposition of a common language and culture in schools. The Gauls were not France's ancestors until history textbooks decided so.

Thus, the goal of nation building should not be to impose common identities on deeply divided peoples but to organize states that can administer their territories and allow people to live together despite differences. And if organizing such a state within the old internationally recognized borders does not seem possible, the international community should admit that nation building may require the disintegration of old states and the formation of new ones.

"Nation Building Is a Recent Idea"

Absolutely not

Take a look at how the political map of the world has changed in every century since the collapse of the Roman Empire—that should be proof enough that nation building has been around for quite a while. Casting a glance at the nineteenth and twentieth centuries will reveal that the types of nation building with the most lasting impact on the modern world are nationalism, colonialism, and post-World War II reconstruction.

Nationalism gave rise to most European countries that exist today. The theory was that each nation, embodying a shared community of culture and blood, was entitled to its own state. (In reality, though, few beyond the intellectual and political elite shared a common identity.) This brand of nationalism led to the reunification of Italy in 1861 and Germany in 1871 and to the breakup of Austria-Hungary in 1918. This process of nation building was successful where governments were relatively capable, where powerful states decided to make room for new entrants, and where the population of new states was not deeply divided. Germany had a capable government and succeeded so well in forging a common identity that the entire world eventually paid for it. Yugoslavia, by contrast, failed in its efforts, and the international community is still sorting out the mess.

Colonial powers formed dozens of new states as they conquered vast swaths of territory, tinkered with old political and leadership structures, and eventually replaced them with new countries and governments. Most of today's collapsed states, such as Somalia or Afghanistan, are a product of colonial nation building. The greater the difference between the precolonial political entities and what the colonial powers tried to impose, the higher the rate of failure.

The transformation of West Germany and Japan into democratic states following World War II is the most successful nation-building exercise ever undertaken from the outside. Unfortunately, this process took place under circumstances unlikely to be repeated elsewhere. Although defeated and destroyed, these countries had strong state traditions and competent government personnel. West Germany and Japan were nation-states in the literal sense of the term—they were ethnic and cultural communities as well as political states. And they were occupied by the U.S. military, a situation that precluded choices other than the democratic state.

"Only War Builds Nations"

Not quite

The most successful nations, including the United States and the countries of Europe, were built by war. These countries achieved statehood because they developed the administrative capacity to mobilize resources and to extract the revenue they needed to fight wars.

Some countries have been created not by their own efforts but by decisions made by the international community. The Balkans offer unfortunate examples of states cobbled together from pieces of defunct empires. Many African countries exist because colonial powers chose to grant them independence. The British Empire created most modern states in the Middle East by carving up the territory of the defeated Ottoman Empire. The Palestinian state, if it becomes a reality, will be another example of a state that owes its existence to an international decision.

Such countries have been called quasi states—entities that exist legally because they are recognized internationally but that hardly function as states in practice because they do not have governments capable of controlling their territory. Some quasi states succeed in retrofitting a functioning country into the legalistic shell. The state of Israel, for example, was formed because of an international decision, and Israel immediately demonstrated its staying power by waging a successful war to defend its existence. But many quasi states fail and then become collapsed states.

Today, war is not an acceptable means of state building. Instead, nation building must be a consensual, democratic process. But such a process is not effective against adversaries who are not democratic, who have weapons, and who are determined to use them. The world should not be fooled into thinking that it is possible to build states without coercion. If the international community is unwilling to allow states to be rebuilt by wars, it must provide the military muscle in the form of a sufficiently strong peacekeeping force. Like it or not, military might is a necessary component of state building.

"Nation Building is Not a Task for the 82nd Airborne"

Maybe not, but it's certainly a task for a strong military force with U.S. participation. Current White House National Security Advisor Condoleezza Rice [now Secretary of State] had a point when she quipped during the 2000 presidential campaign that the 82nd Airborne has more important tasks than "escorting kids to kindergarten." But no one ever said that the primary task of U.S. troops should be babysitting. If the international community does not want to give war a chance by allowing adversaries to fight until someone prevails, then it has to establish control through a military presence willing to use deadly force. And if nation building is in the interests of the United States (as the Bush administration has reluctantly concluded), then the United States must participate in imposing that control.

It is not enough just to participate in the initial effort (in the war fought from the sky), because what counts is what happens on the ground afterward. Newly formed states need long-term plans that go beyond the recent mission statement outlined by one U.S. diplomat: "We go in, we hunt down terrorists, and we go out as if we'd never been there." Even if the United States succeeds in eliminating the last pockets of the Taliban and al-Qaeda in Afghanistan, Americans could face another threat in a few years. And although warring armies are no longer active in Bosnia, the country would splinter apart if international troops went home.

The United States does not have to take the central role in peacekpeeing [sic] operations, but U.S. participation is important because the country is the most powerful member of the international community. Otherwise, the United States sends the message that it doesn't care what happens next—and in doing so, it undermines fragile new governments and encourages the emergence of feuding factions and warlords.

"The International Community Knows How to Build Nations But Lacks Political Will"

It has neither the will nor the way. Many of the nation-building methods used in the past are inconceivable today, but the international community has yet to find effective substitutes. For instance, the first step colonial powers took when engaging in nation building was "pacification," invariably a bloody undertaking described by the British writer Rudyard Kipling as "the savage wars of peace." In today's gentler world of nation building, such violent agreements are fortunately unacceptable. Instead, peacemakers usually try to mediate among rival factions, demobilize combatants, and then reintegrate them in civilian life—a theoretically good idea that rarely works in practice.

Political will for state reconstruction is also in short supply nowadays. That's hardly surprising, given that countries expected to help rebuild nations are the same ones that until recently were accused of neoimperialism. Sierra Leoneans today welcome the British peacekeeping force with open arms and even wax nostalgic about the old days of British rule. But they revolted against British colonialism in the 1950s, and not so long ago, they condemned it as the root cause of all their problems. Should we be surprised that the British are, at best, ambivalent about their role?

And even when the international community demonstrates the will to undertake nation building, it's not always able to figure out who should shoulder the burden. The international community is an unwieldy entity with no single center and lots of contradictions. It comprises the major world powers, with the United States as the dominant agent in some situations and as a reluctant participant in others. In Afghanistan, for instance, the United States wants to have complete control over war operations but refuses to have anything to do with peacekeeping. Meanwhile, the multilateral organization that by its mandate should play the dominant role in peacekeeping and state reconstruction—the United Nations—is the weakest and most divided of all.

* * *

"Nation Building Should Be Limited to Strategically Important States"

Only if anyone can determine which ones they are. "No sane person opposes nation building in places that count," writes conservative columnist Charles Krauthammer. "The debate is about nation building in places that don't." But this type of reasoning eventually forced the United States to fight a war in Afghanistan, a country deemed so unimportant after the Soviets departed that it was left to become a battleground for warlords and a safe haven for al-Qaeda. In 1994, the United States abandoned strategically insignificant Somalia, too, only to start worrying after September 11, 2001, whether that country had also been infiltrated by terrorist networks.

For most countries, strategic significance is a variable, not a constant. Certainly, some countries, such as China, are always significant. But even countries that appear of marginal or no importance can suddenly become crucial. Afghanistan is not the only example. In the days of the Cold War, countries or regions suddenly became prominent when they were befriended by the Soviet

Union. "SALT," then National Security Advisor Zbigniew Brzezinski declared in 1980, "was buried in the sands of the Ogaden"—referring to the cooling of U.S.-Soviet relations when the countries were dragged in to support opposite sides in a war between Ethiopia and Somalia. A few years later, the Reagan administration sent people scrambling for small-scale maps of Lebanon by declaring that Souk el-Gharb, an obscure crossroads town, was vital to U.S. security.

The lesson by now should be clear: No country is so insignificant that it can never become important. So, by all means, let us focus our efforts only on strategically important countries, as long as we can predict which ones they are. (Good luck.)

"The Goal of Nation Building is a Democratic State"

Let us not indulge in fantasy

It is politically correct to equate state reconstruction with democracy building. Indeed, the international community has a one-size-fits-all model for democratic reconstruction, so that plans devised for Afghanistan bear a disturbing resemblance to those designed for the Democratic Republic of the Congo (DRC). This model usually envisages a negotiated settlement to the conflict and the holding of a national conference of major domestic groups (the *loya jirga* in Afghanistan and the Inter-Congolese Dialogue in the DRC) to reach an agreement on the structure of the political system, followed by elections. In addition to these core activities, the model calls for subsidiary but crucial undertakings, beginning with the demobilization of former combatants and the development of a new national army, then extending to reforming the judiciary, restructuring the civil service, and establishing a central bank—thus creating all the institutions deemed necessary to run a modern state.

This model is enormously expensive, requiring major commitments of money and personnel on the part of the international community. As a result, this approach has only been implemented seriously in the case of Bosnia, the only country where the international community has made an open-ended commitment of money and power to see the job through to the end. Six years into the process, progress is excruciatingly slow and not even a glimmer of light is waiting at the end of the tunnel. But elsewhere in the world, including Afghanistan, the international community prescribes this model without providing the resources. The most obvious missing resource in Afghanistan is a robust international peacekeeping force.

Justin Logan and Christopher Preble
Are Failed States a Threat to America?

Throughout the 1990s, conservatives castigated the Clinton administration for conducting foreign policy like social work, taking on vague, ill-defined missions in remote locales from Haiti to Bosnia. Although the editors of *The Weekly Standard* enthusiastically supported the Clinton administration's interventions in the Balkans, most on the right were encouraged when George W. Bush and his senior foreign policy adviser, Condoleezza Rice, came out strongly against such missions during the 2000 presidential campaign. In 2000 Rice famously declared that "we don't need to have the 82nd Airborne escorting kids to kindergarten." Bush was equally blunt. During one of his debates with Al Gore, he said: "I don't think our troops ought to be used for what's called nation building. . . . I mean, we're going to have some kind of nation-building corps from America? Absolutely not."

We agree. That's why we're alarmed that the Bush administration has created a nation-building corps from America: the State Department's new Office of the Coordinator for Reconstruction and Stabilization, which was established by Congress in July 2004. The office's mandate is to "help stabilize and reconstruct societies in transition from conflict or civil strife, so they can reach a sustainable path toward peace, democracy, and a market economy." Meanwhile, a November 2005 Defense Department directive makes stability operations a "core U.S. military mission." Such operations would involve on-the-ground assistance, not unlike the provisional reconstruction teams in Iraq; Secretary of State Condoleezza Rice says the office is presently looking at action in Haiti, Liberia, and Sudan. Beyond that, the details are unclear.

Bush and Rice's change of heart regarding nation building is usually attributed to 9/11. But while the terrorist attacks on the World Trade Center and the Pentagon certainly underscored the dangers that nontraditional threats can pose, they did not transform every poorly governed nation into a pressing national security concern. Nor did 9/11 change the dismal track record of past nation-building efforts. This debate has obvious relevance in Iraq, where the absence of a functioning state following the U.S. invasion is the most widely

Published in *Reason*, July 2006.

accepted argument against withdrawing American forces. But it has much wider implications for America's post—Cold War, post–9/11 foreign policy, pitting nation builders who want to protect the United States by fixing failed states against skeptics who believe such a strategy is unnecessary, impractical, and dangerous.

Depending on how you count, the United States is currently involved in as many as ten nation-building missions—arguably more. Most of these—from Djibouti to Liberia to Kosovo—are far removed from America's national security interests, just as they were in the '90s. Taking on such missions in conflicted environments is even more worrisome today because it would threaten to embroil Americans in an array of foreign conflicts for indefinite periods of time with vague or ambiguous public mandates and little likelihood of success at a time when we should be focused on defeating Al Qaeda and other Islamic terrorist groups that intend to attack the United States. This approach to security policy squanders American power, American money, and American lives. Unless events in a failed state are genuinely likely to dramatically affect the lives of Americans, we should have normal diplomatic relations with their governments, assess potential threats discretely, and otherwise leave them alone.

Getting in on the Coming Anarchy

The idea that state failure is inherently threatening to the United States has been circulating for some time. In an influential 1994 article, *The Atlantic Monthly*'s Robert Kaplan sounded the alarm about "the coming anarchy," urging Western strategists to start worrying about "what is occurring . . . throughout West Africa and much of the underdeveloped world: the withering away of central governments, the rise of tribal and regional domains, the unchecked spread of disease, and the growing pervasiveness of war." He warned that "the coming upheaval, in which foreign embassies are shut down, states collapse, and contact with the outside world takes place through dangerous, disease-ridden coastal trading posts, will loom large in the century we are entering." He argued that insecurity and instability in remote regions should be high on the list of post–Cold War foreign policy concerns because the damage and depredations of the Third World would not always be contained, and would inevitably—though he doesn't really explain how—touch the lives of those in America and Western Europe. Although humanitarianism was the most frequently heard justification for the Clinton administration's attempts at nation building, the president's defenders in and out of government also offered a Kaplanesque rationale that fixing failed states would make the United States safer.

Despite his initial skepticism toward Clinton-era nation building, President Bush changed course dramatically after September 11, 2001. The *United States National Security Strategy*, released in September 2002, made "expand[ing] the circle of development by opening societies and building the infrastructure of democracy" a central plank of America's response to the 9/11 attacks. Part of the administration's new security policy would be to "help build police forces, court systems, and legal codes, local and provincial government institutions, and electoral systems." The overarching goal was to "make the world not just safer but better."

According to the administration's October 2005 *National Intelligence Strategy*, "the lack of freedom in one state endangers the peace and freedom of others, and . . . failed states are a refuge and breeding ground of extremism." The strategy therefore asks our overworked intelligence services not just to gather information on America's enemies but to "bolster the growth of democracy and sustain peaceful democratic states." The premise is, as the former Cato foreign policy analyst Gary Dempsey put it, that "if only we could populate the planet with 'good' states, we could eradicate international conflict and terrorism."

Many foreign policy pundits agree with the Bush administration's goal of making the world safe through democracy. Lawrence J. Korb and Robert O. Boorstin of the Center for American Progress, for example, warn in a 2005 report that "weak and failing states pose as great a danger to the American people and international stability as do potential conflicts among the great powers." A 2003 report from the Center for Strategic and International Studies agrees that "as a superpower with a global presence and global interests, the United States does have a stake in remedying failed states." In the course of commenting on a report from the Center for Global Development, Francis Fukuyama, a professor at the Johns Hopkins School of Advanced International Studies, argued that "it should be abundantly clear that state weakness and failure [are] the single most critical threat to U.S. national security."

Even foreign policy specialists known for their hard-nosed realism have succumbed to the idea that nation building is a matter of self-defense. A 2005 Council on Foreign Relations task force co-chaired by Brent Scowcroft, national security adviser in the first Bush administration and a critic of the current war in Iraq, produced a report that insists "action to stabilize and rebuild states marked by conflict is not 'foreign policy as social work,' a favorite quip of the 1990s. It is equally a humanitarian concern and a national security priority." The report says stability operations should be "a strategic priority for the armed forces" and the national security adviser should produce an "overarching policy associated with stabilization and reconstruction activities."

Those arguments suffer not so much from inaccuracy as from analytical sloppiness. It would be absurd to claim that the ongoing state failure in Haiti poses a national security threat of the same order as would state failure in Indonesia, with its population of 240 million, or in nuclear-armed Pakistan. In fact, the overwhelming majority of failed states have posed no security threat to the United States. Take, for example, the list of countries identified as failed or failing by *Foreign Policy* magazine and the Fund for Peace in 2005. Using 12 different indicators of state failure, the researchers derived state failure scores, and then listed 60 countries whose cumulative scores marked them as "critical," "in danger," or "borderline," ranked in order. If state failure is itself threatening, then we should get very concerned about the Democratic Republic of the Congo, Sierra Leone, Chad, Bangladesh, and on and on.

In short, state failure ranks rather low as an accurate metric for measuring threats. Likewise, while the lists of "failed states" and "security threats" will no doubt overlap, correlation does not equal causation. The obvious nonthreats that appear on all lists of failed states undermine the claim that there is something particular about failed states that is necessarily threatening.

The dangers that can arise from failed states are not the product of state failure itself. They are the result of other factors, such as the presence of terrorist cells or other malign actors. Afghanistan in the late 1990s met anyone's definition of a failed state, and the chaos in Afghanistan clearly contributed to Osama bin Laden's decision to relocate his operations there from Sudan in 1996. But the security threat to America arose from cooperation between Al Qaeda and the Taliban government, which tolerated the organization's training camps. Afghanistan under the Taliban was both a failed state and a threat, but in that respect it was a rarity. More common are failed states, from the Ivory Coast to Burma, that pose no threat to us at all.

It's true that Al Qaeda and other terrorist organizations can operate in failed states. But they also can (and do) operate in Germany, Canada, and other countries that are not failed states by any stretch of the imagination. Rather than making categorical statements about failed states, we should assess the extent to which any given state or nonstate actors within it intend and have the means to attack America. Afghanistan is a stark reminder that we must not overlook failed states, but it does not justify making them our top security concern.

That Fixer-Upper Isn't As Cheap As It Looks

If state failure does not in itself pose a threat to U.S. security, an ambitious program of nation building would, in turn, be a cure worse than the disease. One particularly troubling prospect is the erosion of internationally recognized sovereignty. As Winston Churchill said of democracy, sovereignty may be the worst system around, except for all the others. A system of sovereignty grants a kernel of legitimacy to regimes that rule barbarically; it values as equals countries that clearly are not; and it frequently enforces borders that were capriciously drawn by imperial powers. But it's far from clear that any available alternative is better.

Yet in his previous life as an academic, Stephen Krasner, the director of policy planning at the U.S. State Department, flatly declared that the "rules of conventional sovereignty no longer work." A stroll through the work of scholars who support nation building reveals such alternative concepts as "shared sovereignty," "trusteeships," even "postmodern imperialism." (The latter is supposed to mean an attempt to manipulate domestic politics in foreign countries without all that old-fashioned imperial messiness.)

If the United States proceeds on a course of nation building, based largely on the premise that sovereignty should be de-emphasized, where will that logic stop? Who gets to decide which states retain their sovereignty and which states forfeit it? Will other powers use our own rhetoric against us to justify expansionist foreign policies? It's not hard to envision potential flashpoints in eastern Europe and East Asia.

An American exceptionalist might reply that the *United States* gets to decide, because we're different. But such an argument is unlikely to prevent other countries from using our own logic against us. If we tug at the thread of sovereignty, the whole sweater may quickly unravel.

An aggressive nation-building strategy would also detract from the struggle against terrorism, by diverting attention and resources, puncturing the mystique of American power, and provoking anger through promiscuous foreign intervention. A prerequisite for nation building is establishing security in the target country, which requires the presence of foreign troops, something that often inspires terrorism. In a survey of suicide terrorism between 1980 and 2003, University of Chicago political scientist Robert A. Pape concluded that almost all suicide attacks "have in common . . . a specific secular and strategic goal: to compel modern democracies to withdraw military forces from territory that the terrorists consider to be their homeland."

Such risks might be justified if the chances of success were high. But history suggests they're not. In the most thorough survey of American nation-building missions, the RAND Corporation in 2003 evaluated seven cases: Japan and West Germany after World War II, Somalia in 1992–94, Haiti in 1994–96, Bosnia from 1995 to the present, Kosovo from 1999 to the present, and Afghanistan from 2001 to the present. Assessing the cases individually, the authors count Japan and West Germany as successes but all the others as failures to various degrees. They then try to determine what made the Japanese and West German operations succeed when all the nation-building efforts since have failed.

Their answer is complex and not entirely satisfying. To the extent that any clear conclusion can be drawn from this research, the report says, it is that "nation building . . . is a time- and resource-consuming effort." Indeed, "among controllable factors, the most important determinant is the level of effort—measured in time, manpower, and money."

In its 2004 *Summer Study on Transition to and From Hostilities*, the Defense Science Board, a panel that advises the Defense Department on strategy, reached a similar conclusion. Although "post-conflict success often depends on significant political changes," it said, the "barriers to transformation of [an] opponent's society [are] immense." And in the absence of a decisive outcome between warring parties (such as happened in World War II), there is always a danger that violence will continue.

Not surprisingly, successful nation building is highly contingent on security within the target country. The non-war-fighting roles a nation-building military has to play would be tremendously taxing for both the armed services and the U.S. treasury.

By the Defense Science Board's calculations, achieving "ambitious goals" in a failed state requires 20 foreign soldiers per 1,000 inhabitants. Applying this ratio to a few top-ranked failed states yields sobering results. Nation building in the Ivory Coast would require 345,000 foreign troops. Sudan would take

800,000. Iraq, where the U.S. and its allies currently have 153,000 troops, would need 520,000. And if history is any guide, effective execution would require deployments of 10 years or longer.

All this means that nation-building missions are extremely expensive, regardless of whether they succeed or fail. Zalmay Khalilzad, former U.S. ambassador to Afghanistan and current ambassador to Iraq, believes that in the case of Afghanistan, "it will take annual assistance [of $4.5 billion] or higher for five to seven years to achieve our goals." Operation Uphold Democracy in Haiti, which restored a government and installed 8,000 peacekeepers but left that country in its perpetual state of chaos, cost more than $2 billion. Operations Provide Relief and Restore Hope in Somalia, which provided tons of food as humanitarian relief (which were in turn looted by warlords) and eventually got dozens of Americans killed and injured, leading to a hasty and disastrous American retreat, ended up costing $2.2 billion. As of 2002 the United States had spent more than $23 billion intervening in the Balkans since the early '90s. In Iraq, we have already crested the $300 billion mark, having decided that the vagaries of Iraqi sectarian politics should decide our future mission in that country.

Even Francis Fukuyama, a staunch advocate of nation building, admits such efforts have "an extremely troubled record of success." As Fukuyama wrote in his 2005 book *State Building: Governance and World Order in the 21st Century*, "It is not simply that nation building hasn't worked; in cases like sub-Saharan Africa, many of these efforts have actually eroded institutional capacity over time." Put simply, there is no "model" for nation building. The few broad lessons we can draw indicate that success depends on a relentless determination to impose a nation's will, manifested in many years of occupation and billions of dollars in spending.

In this light, the position of the more extreme neo-imperialists is more realistic than that of nation builders who think we can fix failed states on the cheap. The Harvard historian Niall Ferguson argues that a proper approach to Iraq would put up to 1 million foreign troops on the ground there for up to 70 years. If resources were unlimited, or if the American people were prepared to shoulder such a burden, that might be a realistic suggestion. But the notion that such enterprises can be carried out quickly and inexpensively is badly mistaken.

A Really Distant Mirror

People who believe that failed states pose a threat to U.S. security and that nation building is the answer see the world as both simpler and more threatening than it is. Failed states generally do not represent security threats. At the same time, nation building in failed states is very difficult and usually unsuccessful.

There is certainly a point at which Robert Kaplan's "coming anarchy," if it were to materialize, would threaten American interests. Here's how Ferguson, in *Foreign Policy* magazine, describes a world in which America steps back from its role as a global policeman: "Waning empires. Religious revivals. Incipient anarchy. A coming retreat into fortified cities. These are the Dark Age experiences that a world without a hyperpower might quickly find itself reliving."

It's telling that to find a historical precedent on which to base his argument, Ferguson has to reach back to the ninth century. His prediction of a "Dark Age" hinges on a belief that America will collapse (because of excessive consumption, an inadequate army, and an imperial "attention deficit"), the European Union will collapse (because of an inflexible welfare state and shifting demographics), and China will collapse (because of a currency or banking crisis). There is little reason to believe that if America refuses to administer foreign countries, the world will go down this path. The fact that advocates of fixing failed states have to rely on such outlandish scenarios to build their case tells us a good deal about the merit of their arguments.

QUESTIONS

1. *What would you do?* As president, you ask your advisors to assess the advantages and disadvantages of a nation-building effort. One set of advisors favors a large-scale effort in which the United States would be a leader, commit substantial financial resources and personnel, and be prepared to stay involved for up to ten years. In the long term, they suggest, this will enhance the image of the United States. Another set of advisors argues that the U.S. effort should be limited in scope and designed to extract the United States from the country in a short amount of time, perhaps a year. Rather than a lead role, the United States should let the United Nations lead the effort and pay most of the costs. A long-term effort led by the United States, they contend, would

produce resentment toward the United States. A third set of advisors argues that the United States should not get involved in nation building at all, that such efforts need to be entirely internal to a country for them to have legitimacy and credibility. Unless the people of a country are allowed to work out their problems like Americans were after the Civil War, they will always feel that their government and system are puppets of the United States. As president, what questions do you ask these advisors to help you make a decision? Under what conditions would you choose the first, second, and third options respectively? What are the risks associated with each option?

2. If Ottaway's analysis is right, what should we expect from nation-building efforts? From what you have heard, read, or seen about nation building in Iraq, does Ottaway's analysis appear to be accurate?

3. Logan and Preble are skeptical about the effectiveness of nation building and recommend that the United States not be involved in such efforts unless the lives of Americans are strongly and directly affected by the situation in a foreign country. Do you agree? Are there times when the United States should become involved in nation building for humanitarian reasons? How would you determine when this is an appropriate use of U.S. military power?

Endnotes

Chapter 2

1. *Plessy*, 163 U.S. 537 (1896) (racial segregation of public railway passengers is constitutional); *Brown*, 347 U.S. 483 (1954) (racial segregation of public education facilities is unconstitutional).
2. *Bowers*, 478 U.S. 186 (1986) (upholding a state law criminalizing sodomy); *Lawrence*, 539 U.S. 558 (2003) (striking down state anti-sodomy laws as unconstitutional).

Chapter 3

1. Charles Neider, ed. The complete short stories of Mark Twain. New York: Hanover House, 1957:1–6.
2. 39th District Agricultural Association. Animal welfare policy (Calaveras County Fair and Jumping Frog Jubilee). April 2003. (Accessed November 3, 2005, at http://www.frogtown.org.)
3. U.S. v. Lopez, 514 U.S. 549 (1995).
4. NLRB v. Jones & Laughlin Steel Corp., 301 U.S. 1 (1937).
5. Wickard v. Filburn, 317 U.S. 111 (1942).
6. U.S. v. Morrison, 529 U.S. 598 (2000).
7. Gonzales v. Raich, 125 S.Ct. 2195 (2005).
8. Raich v. Ashcroft, 3352 F.3d 1222 (9th Cir. 2003).

9. Annas GJ, Glantz LH, Mariner WK. The right of privacy protects the doctor-patient relationship. JAMA 1900;263:858–61.

10. Annas GJ. Reefer madness—the federal response to California's medical-marijuana law. N Engl J Med 1997;337:435–9.

11. Oregon v. Ashcroft, 368 F.3d 1118 (2004).

12. Annas GJ. The bell tolls for a constitutional right to physician-assisted suicide. N Engl J Med 1997;337:1098–103.

13. GDF Realty v. Norton, 326 F.3d 622 (5th Cir. 2003).

14. Rancho Viejo v. Norton 323 F.3d 1062 (D.C. Cir. 2003).

15. Rancho Viejo v. Norton 357 F.3d 1158 (D.C. Cir. 2003).

16. Cummings J. Environmentalists uncertain on Roberts. Wall Street Journal. August 15, 2005:A3.

Chapter 5

1. Legal citations and references for quotes are omitted. For the sources of internal quotations see the original document at clrn.law.cuny.edu/clea/clea%20grutter.pdf.

Chapter 6

1. The political disposition of most radio talk-show hosts is explained by William G. Mayer in "Why Talk Radio Is Conservative," *Public Interest*, Summer 2004.

2. True, the "elite effect" may not be felt across the board. With most of the issues Zaller investigated, even well-informed citizens would have had little firsthand experience, and so their minds were of necessity open to the influence of their "betters." Results might have been different had he measured their views on matters about which most Americans believe themselves to be personally well-informed: crime, inflation, drug abuse, or their local schools.

Permissions Acknowledgments

Annas, George. "Jumping Frogs, Endangered Toads, and California's Medical-Marijuana Law," in *The New England Journal of Medicine*, vol. 353, no. 21 (November 24, 2005). Copyright © 2005 Massachusetts Medical Society. All rights reserved.

Bernasek, Anna. "Income Inequality, And Its Cost." © 2006 by The New York Times Co. Reprinted with permission.

Biggs, Andrew. "Stock Market Declines' Effect on the Social Security Reform Debate," in *USA Today Magazine* (May). © 2003 by the Society for the Advancement of Education.

Brooks, David. "Don't Worry, Be Happy." © 2006 by The New York Times Co. Reprinted with permission. Originally published in *The New York Times*, May 11, 2006.

Cohn, Jonathan. "Roll Out the Barrel," in *The New Republic* (April 20, 1998). Reprinted by permission of *The New Republic*, © 1998 The New Republic, LLC.

Cornyn, John. "R-E-S-P-E-C-T," in *National Review Online* (June 27, 2005). © 2005 by *National Review Online*. Reprinted by permission.

The Economist [editors]. "Inequality and the American Dream." © 2006 The Economist Newspaper Ltd. All rights reserved. Reprinted with permission. Further reproduction prohibited.

Fiorina, Morris P. "Letter to the Editor," in *Commentary* (May 2006). Reprinted by permission of the author.

———. "What Culture Wars?" in *The Wall Street Journal* (July 14, 2004). Reprinted by permission of the author.

Flake, Jeff. "Earmarked Men." © 2006 by The New York Times Co. Reprinted with permission. Originally published in *The New York Times*, February 9, 2006.

Glassman, James. "Reform the Electoral College, Don't Toss It," in *The American Enterprise*, vol. 12, no. 2 (March 2001). Reprinted with permission of *The American Enterprise*.

Graglia, Lino. "Revitalizing Democracy," in *Harvard Journal of Law and Public Policy* (Fall 2000). Reprinted with permission.

Hacker, Jacob. "Bigger and Better," in *The American Prospect*, vol. 16, no. 5 (May 6, 2005). Reprinted with permission from Jacob Hacker. All rights reserved.

Harrington, Brooke. "Can Small Investors Survive Social Security Privatization?" in *The American Prospect*, vol. 12, no. 16 (September 10, 2001). Reprinted with permission from Brooke Harrington. All rights reserved.

Huntington, Samuel P. Excerpted and adapted from *Who Are We? The Challenges to America's National Identity*. Copyright © 2004 by Samuel P. Huntington. Excerpted and adapted by permission of Simon and Schuster Adult Publishing Group.

Isaacs, John. "Congress Goes AWOL" in *Bulletin of the Atomic Scientists*, vol. 59, no. 3 (May/June 2003), pp. 20–21, 72. Reprinted with the permission of the *Bulletin of the Atomic Scientists*.

Latham, Earl. "The Group Basis of Politics: Notes for a Theory," in *American Political Science Review*, vol. 46, no. 2 (1952). Reprinted with the permission of Cambridge University Press.

Lizza, Ryan. "But Is a Third Party Possible?" in *New York Magazine* (April 24, 2006). Reprinted by permission of the publisher.

Logan, Justin, and Christopher Preble. "Are Failed States a Threat to America?" from reason.com (July 2006). Reprinted by permission of the Reason Foundation.

Lund, Nelson. "Putting Federalism to Sleep," in *The Weekly Standard*, vol. 11, no. 7 (October 31, 2005). Reprinted with permission.

Luskin, Donald. "Still Movin' On Up," in *National Review* (July 4, 2005), pp. 31–33. © 2005 by *National Review Online*. Reprinted by permission.

Malcolm, Janet. "The Art of Testifying," in *The New Yorker* (March 13, 2006). Reprinted by permission of the author.

McCarthy, Andrew C. "How to 'Connect the Dots,' " in *National Review* (January 30, 2006), pp. 37–39. © 2006 by National Review, Inc. Reprinted by permission.

Menand, Louis. "Patriot Games." First Published in *The New Yorker* (May 17, 2004). © 2004 by Louis Menand, permission of The Wylie Agency.

Noonan, Peggy. "Third Time," in *The Wall Street Journal Online* (June 1, 2006). Copyright © 2006 by Dow Jones and Company, Inc. Reproduced with permission of Dow Jones and Company, Inc.

Ottaway, Marina. Excerpts from "Nation Building," in *Foreign Policy* (September/October 2002), pp. 16–18, 20, 22. Reprinted with permission.

Paige, Sean. "Rolling Out the Pork Barrel," in *Insight on the News* (January 4, 1999), pp. 32–33. Reprinted with permission of *Insight*. Copyright © 1999 News World Communications, Inc. All rights reserved.

Perlmutter, Daniel. "The Ascent of Blogging," in *Nieman Reports* (Fall 2005). Reprinted by permission.

Post, Robert, and Reva Siegel. "Questioning Justice: Law and Politics in Judicial Confirmation Hearings," in *The Pocket Part*: *A Companion to The Yale Law Journal* (January 2006). Reprinted by permission.

The Progressive [editors]. "Casualties of War," in *The Progressive*, vol. 67, no. 1 (January 2003). Reprinted with permission from *The Progressive*.

Rauch, Jonathan. "The Hyperpluralism Trap." © 1994 Jonathan Rauch. First published in *The New Republic*.

Sarasohn, David. "Taking (Back) the Initiative," in *The Nation* (June 18, 2001). Reprinted by permission of *The Nation*.

Schlesinger, Arthur M., Jr. "The Imperial Presidency Redux," in *The Washington Post* (June 28, 2003), p. A25. Reprinted with permission of the author.

———. "Not the People's Choice," in *The American Prospect*, vol. 13, no. 6 (March 25, 2002). Reprinted with permission from Arthur M. Schlesinger, Jr., all rights reserved.

Sullivan, Kathleen M. "What's Wrong with Constitutional Amendments?" in *New Federalist Papers: Essays in Defense of the Constitution,* by Alan Brinkley, Nelson W. Polsby, and Kathleen M. Sullivan. Copyright © 1997 by The Twentieth Century Fund, Inc. Used by permission of W. W. Norton and Company, Inc.

Sunstein, Cass. "Democracy and Filtering," in *Communications of the ACM,* vol. 47, no. 12 (December 2004), pp. 57–59. © 2004 by Association for Computing Machinery, Inc. Reprinted by permission.

Tabin, John. "Supreme Substance," in *The American Spectator Online* (January 18, 2006). Reprinted by permission of *The American Spectator*.

Turner, Robert. "FISA vs. the Constitution," in *The Wall Street Journal Online* (December 28, 2005). Copyright © 2005 by Dow Jones and Company, Inc. Reproduced with permission of Dow Jones and Company, Inc.

Vaden, Ted. "Blogs Challenge Newspaper Standards," in *The News and Observer* (October 16, 2005). Reprinted by permission of *The News and Observer* of Raleigh, North Carolina.

Vermeule, Adrian. Excerpted from "Constitutional Amendments and the Constitutional Common Law," in *The Least Examined Branch,* ed. Bauman and Kahana. Reprinted with the permission of Cambridge University Press.

Wilson, James Q. "How Divided Are We?" © James Q. Wilson. Reprinted from *Commentary*, February 2006, by permission; all rights reserved.

———. "What Government Agencies Do and Why They Do It," in *Bureaucracy*. Copyright © 1989 by Basic Books. Reprinted by permission of Basic Books, a member of Perseus Books, L.L.C.